MERIDIAN

Crossing Aesthetics

Werner Hamacher

Editor

Edited, Translated,
and with an Introduction
by Peggy Kamuf

Stanford
University
Press

Stanford
California
2002

WITHOUT ALIBI

———————

Jacques Derrida

"Psychoanalysis Searches the States of Its Soul" was originally
published in French in 2000 under the title *Etats d'âme de la
psychanalyse* by Editions Galilée. © 2000 by Editions Galilée.

Stanford University Press
Stanford, California

© 2002 by the Board of Trustees of the
Leland Stanford Junior University

Printed in the United States of America,
on acid-free, archival-quality paper

ISBN 0-8047-4410-6 (alk. paper) —
ISBN 0-8047-4411-4 (pbk. : alk. paper)

Original Printing 2002
Last figure below indicates year of this printing:
11 10 09 08 07 06 05 04 03 02

Typeset by BookMatters in 11/13 Adobe Garamond

Acknowledgments

Earlier versions of "History of the Lie" appeared in *Graduate Faculty Philosophy Journal*, New School for Social Research, vol. 19, 2–vol. 20, 1, and *Futures of Jacques Derrida*, ed. Richard Rand (Stanford: Stanford University Press, 2001). "Typewriter Ribbon" appeared initially in *Material Events: Paul de Man and the Afterlife of Theory*, ed. Barbara Cohen et al. (Minneapolis: University of Minnesota Press, 2001), and appears here with the permission of the publisher. "Psychoanalysis Searches the States of Its Soul" is a translation of *Etats d'âme de la psychanalyse* (Paris: Galilée, 2000).

Contents

Preface: Toward the Event

PEGGY KAMUF

The idea for this volume arose as I was working on the translation of "'Le Parjure,' *Perhaps*," which Jacques Derrida originally wrote for a collection of essays honoring his dear friend J. Hillis Miller. Having had the good fortune to translate numerous essays by Derrida for occasions of one kind or another in recent years, I was keenly aware of strong continuities among several of them. Indeed, many connections are so plainly in view that a reader certainly would not need, like a translator, to keep her attention pressed close to the language of the essays in order to see the carryover from one to the other. I therefore suggested to their author that four of them be published together, even though the resulting collection would constitute a book in English translation for which there was no corresponding French original. Jacques Derrida immediately assented and proposed that a fifth, as yet untranslated essay be included as well. This is the text of a keynote lecture that had just been delivered to the States General of Psychoanalysis, held at the Sorbonne in the summer of 2000 and translated here as "Psychoanalysis Searches the States of Its Soul."

These five essays, then, were never intended to share space between the covers of a same book. True, many books get written that way, although usually not first of all in translation. It is also not unusual for such collections to be made up of what are called occasional pieces, although a common practice in such circumstances is to erase as far as possible marks of the original occasion, the thought being that these limit or detract from the general import of what is being said. Such editing was simply out of the question here, for reasons closely bound up with Derrida's practice of thinking *toward* the event, by which I mean: letting thought unfold in response to occasions, invitations, demands, contexts, situations, but also, always, in or as friendship. It is this practice toward the event that is being remarked here each time, and each time differently.

Four of the essays were written for initial presentation as lectures, and these were, of course, for specific occasions at specific locations. "History of the Lie: Prolegomena" was initially delivered at the New School for Social Research, in a lecture series dedicated to the memory of Hannah Arendt's association with that institution. That year, the series was also dedicated to Reiner Schürmann, the brilliant young German philosopher who, like Arendt, emigrated to the New School and, also like Arendt, was a strong reader of Heidegger. The lecture was given on this first occasion within a year after Reiner Schürmann's death from AIDS in 1993 at age fifty-six.

The occasion for "Typewriter Ribbon" was a conference held in 1998 at the Humanities Center of the University of California, Davis, organized by a host of friends and colleagues (Hillis Miller, Thomas Cohen, Andrzej Warminski, Barbara Cohen, Georges Van Den Abbeele). The improbable title of this conference—which Derrida analyzes at some length and to comic effect—includes reference to Paul de Man's late work, collected posthumously (by Andrzej Warminski) under the title *Aesthetic Ideology*.

"The University Without Condition" was initially written in response to an invitation from the Presidential Lecture Series, hosted by President Gerhard Casper of Stanford University and organized by Hans Ulrich Gumbrecht in 1999. Professor Gumbrecht having generously invited me, along with Samuel Weber, to attend this lecture, we heard Richard Rorty issue his warm and wry welcome to Derrida on this occasion, which was the first time the latter had spoken at this great university. There is no specific mark of this context in the lecture—although it was addressed directly in some prefatory remarks Derrida read out—but its outline appears, to me at least, never to be far in the background as I reread the essay now. Which is not to say that one had to be there. The argument of the essay is or ought to be clear as a bell for whoever continues to profess belief in the teaching of the Humanities.

"Psychoanalysis Searches the States of Its Soul" is not merely the sole essay of the five that bears mention of its date (July 16, 2000); it is also a long, dramatized response to its context and occasion, about which, therefore, no more need be added here. As for "'Le Parjure,' *Perhaps*," the only essay destined originally for a publication and not for delivery at a specific place and time, its context will have been, as already mentioned, a volume celebrating the work of Hillis Miller. It was written in the context of this friendship, therefore, for the friend and the friend's work, but also for a work signed by another, the novel *Le Parjure* (1964), by Henri Thomas. Because that work has not yet been translated into English, I can point to this part of the context only in French. The long passages Derrida cites from Thomas's text suffer no doubt from this lack of a full translation of the novel. Perhaps someday I'll finish the job, so for now I ask that it be seen as still work in progress, a draft.

Friendship has been no less the context or accompaniment for this book. That is why I have tried to name so many friends in so few lines. Foremost there has been the friendship of Jacques Derrida, shown most recently by his ready assent to this project. Since 1974, when I had (I will never know how) the foolhardy temerity to speak up in his seminar, Derrida has responded never less steadily with friendship. Werner Hamacher and Helen Tartar have given help and encouragement since the beginning, and have even made it possible for all of us to proceed quickly. Michael Naas showed exemplary friendship for the work in a reader's report that I was tempted to take over as introduction to this book, since it outlined so well what is perhaps the book's essential trait, common to all its chapters: the trait of sovereignty. If I ended up having to take my own responsibilities in an introduction, it was not without the wish to respond to all these exigent readers.

Provocation: Forewords

JACQUES DERRIDA

I

Is it not a little as if, without obligating me but by inviting me, someone had one day defied me to do it? Provocation: would you dare, for *this* book, right here, right now, without alibi, a foreword?

A foreword is not necessarily provoked or provocative, to be sure. But a provocation will always resemble a foreword. What do we call a provocation? Before all other senses of the word,[1] a pro*vocation* proffers; it is the act of a speaking. A speech act, so to speak. Perhaps every speech act acts *like* a provocation. To provoke, is that not to cause (in French, *causer* means "to speak with the other," but also "to produce effects," "to give rise" to what takes place, to what is called, in a word, the event)? Is to pro*voke* not to let resonate a vocal appeal, a vocative, a "vocable," as we say in French, in other words, a word? Is it not to turn the initiative over to the word, which, like a foreword and in a thousand ways, *goes out ahead, to the front of the stage*: to expose itself or to dare, to face up to, here and now, right away, without delay and *without alibi*? A pro*vocation* is always somewhat "vocal," as one might say in English, resolved to make itself heard, sonorous and noisy. The most inventive provocations should not be vocal, but this is difficult to avoid.

Well, whence would come the provocation here, right here, here and now, without alibi? Right here, at the multiple entry point, on the several steps [*marches*] making up the threshold of a very "American" book. American in an unusual sense. For this book is originally American; it is a "native" of America even if it appears to be "translated," in a likewise unusual and plural sense of translation, by an American. It is as if it went from American English to American English, in the course of a trajectory where, from one detour to another, a certain "question of America," no less, suddenly finds itself lit up, otherwise, and harshly laid bare by Peggy Kamuf. This *here-now* is also therefore the already multiple one of an American book whose author will always remain to be determined (this is my hypothesis). In other words, it will be forever undecidable in the figure of the proper name, Jacques Derrida, Peggy Kamuf, etc. The law, civil status, publication contracts are here so many fables. "Legal fictions." Hardly useful. One may therefore ask, at every level and every stage of this book, between the "who" and the "what": Who provokes whom? Who provokes what? Who provokes whom to what? I will remain for a long time at great pains to say.

To provoke, we were saying, is to go out ahead, put oneself forward: to expose oneself or to defy/dare/challenge, to face up to or confront, here and now, *without delay* [sans attendre] and *without alibi*. Let us be attentive to this: although "alibi" means literally an *alleged* "elsewhere" in space, it extends beyond either topology or geography. "Without alibi" can mean *without delay*, without waiting [*attendre*]. As an *allegation*, an alibi can *defer/differ* in time. *Referring back* in this way, which an allegation always does, it can save itself by invoking another time ("I wasn't *there at the moment* of the crime" or "I was *already no longer there*" or "I was intending to go *there at another moment, later*," "I wasn't thinking of it *at that moment*").

Calling back or referring, *rappel ou renvoi*, reminder or send-off: There have been so many who hurried to confuse *differance* and *alibi*. But in this haste, the impatience of their "without waiting" can also play, on their side, the role of a paradoxical alibi: one hurries to hurry up, one pretends to lose patience and to go straight at the target so as to disavow that one is doing everything just to avoid, at that moment, the thing itself, meaning here differance "itself," which precisely will never be a thing or some "thing itself." Yes, they are many who, suffering from what I would call premature conclusion, couldn't resist the temptation to interpret differance as an alibi, above all as a political alibi, an allegation destined to delay the deadline, to do everything it takes to do nothing right away. Well, there is one thing I think I know, but it is a perilous knowledge: What remains no doubt to be thought *without alibi* is precisely a differance *without alibi*, right there where, it's true, this same differance goes on endlessly producing irreducible effects of alibi through traces that refer to some other, to another place and another moment, to something else, to the absolute other, to the other to come, the event, and so forth. One has to go elsewhere to find oneself here. The here-now does not appear as such, in experience, except by differing from itself. And one trace always refers to another trace. It thus secretes, it produces, it cannot not produce some alibi. Ubiquity of the alibi.

But if every *allegation* in some way sends one off or back to another instance, toward another place, for another moment (*lego, legare* means also to send, send back, or even delegate, but also to leave a legacy or inheritance), not every sending, referral, or trace comes down to or can be reduced to what seeks refuge and disculpation in an *allegation*. We would thus have to sharpen our sense of this word and concept. And refine it beyond the difference between (1) *lego, legare* and (2) *lego, legere*.[2]

II

I believe I also know that what I just called a perilous knowledge (the knowledge of what *remains* always to be thought and thus still *resists* thinking: a trace without alibi, a differance without alibi) can always be paralyzing, to be sure, but it also offers the only chance not to give in to paralysis.

I would be tempted to say that paralysis is the negative symptom of aporia. Paralysis arrests, whereas aporia, at least as I interpret it (the possibility of the impossible, the "play" of a certain excess in relation to any mechanical movement, oriented process, path traced in advance, or teleological program), would be the very condition of the *step* [pas], or even of the experience of pathbreaking, route (*via rupta*), march [*marche*], decision, event: the coming of the other, in sum, of writing and desire.

How to overcome paralysis before the challenge or provocation of such an impossible task? How to write, on the subject of texts whose legal author I am supposed to be, a kind of foreword, between the translator's preface and the editor's introduction?

To transform the paralysis into aporia, to break a path for myself, I tried, gropingly, to find my voice in the following way.

"This is her oeuvre, Peggy Kamuf's. I ask her to leave this word in French. She knows why and explains it very well in 'Toward the Event' and 'Event of

Resistance.' She, Peggy Kamuf, reads me better, down to the unconscious, than I will have ever read myself. This is an incalculable debt that I must first of all name and recognize here and now, without alibi.

"It is by reading me in this way that she writes me, me, to me, in her language, and first of all from her country, I mean the United States of America. Moreover, concerning the United States and what is so difficult to think today in that name, she describes and deduces intractably its site, its singular and current situation in the history of the world. Her book is also, and this is perhaps its greatest audacity, the book of an American thinker about the United States of America.

"Well, as impossible as it may seem—and this is the event to which she was able to give rise, beyond any assurance and any performative authority—for once I like feeling myself interpreted beyond what I wrote. Interpreted, that is, at once exposed and given to be read *(*legere: *to select and configure, elect and gather, discern and put together, discriminate and compose, etc.). I am glad that this is the way it is and I would like to pose no resistance to it. As if I were surrendering [me rendais], for once, receiving it with gratitude, to an incredible gift, a gift come from a place where, despite certain appearances, I will never have been capable of going [me rendre] myself.*

"There could be some violence, even some cruelty, in going beyond, as Peggy Kamuf has done, what their presumed author (me, therefore) will have been able to decipher of his own texts, his compulsions, his phantasms, and his alibis, so as to question them, problematize them, suspend them in the tension of their own incompletion, articulate in this way their diachronic multiplicity as a genealogy or even as a synchronic composition. Well, for this one and only time, I felt no violation in this gesture. On the contrary.

"I know it will be hard to read, *to appropriate, above all to translate these first words in italics. But I venture that no reader will understand them or even countersign them without having first sized up, if not the whole book, then at least the sovereign operation, in truth the* position of the *mise en oeuvre, the putting to work and putting into perspective, the selective interpretation and the configuring reading that Peggy Kamuf signs in 'Toward the Event' and 'Event of Resistance.' For one could then remark after the fact that I have just used—as if it were no big deal, like some contraband—each of the words that* remain to be thought *and that she gives to be rethought, for the future:* 'oeuvre,' 'event,' 'United States,' 'as if,' 'performative,' 'resistance,' 'cruelty.' *But also* 'phantasm,' 'contraband,' *and* 'alibi.' *And above all, above all,* 'sovereignty.'

"Why 'sovereignty'? Kamuf underscores a trait, the trait that seems to her, for good reason, 'the essential trait of this book, common to all its chapters: the trait of sovereignty.' The first and last question, if not the only one, could then become: What happens when this trait divides? When it must, when it cannot not divide? When its division follows from the necessity of a law that is undecidably that of a duty or a fate? Divisibility of this trait of sovereignty (divided sovereignty, sovereignty legitimately deconstructed here, but claimed there, necessity of a strategy that, without relativism, does battle here against sovereignty so as to support it elsewhere, etc.), this would be the proper place of the ultimate questions introduced by this book. Such would be the place, therefore, where it gets decided, where it chooses, gathers, collects itself, or where it gets read. Through Peggy Kamuf's introduction, as throughout this book, there is recognition, to be sure, that it is necessary to deconstruct sovereignty, more precisely, the phantasm—thus a certain fable and a certain 'as if'—of the political onto-theology of sovereignty. But without simply losing the horizon of its unity, sovereignty divides two or three times. Its concept has constantly been displacing itself throughout its history.

"*1.* On the one hand, the sovereignty of the nation-state (which is not just any one and which today gives to the political *dimension of sovereignty its primary, if not its sole figure*): one can deconstruct it and combat it on one level, while continuing, for the same reasons, to support it on another. The sovereignty of the nation-state can become, under certain conditions and as long as it does not ally itself with the adversary, a force of resistance and regulation when faced with the cruel savagery of international capital and of a certain mondialisation or 'globalization.'

"*2.* On the other hand, one can deconstruct and combat the sovereignty of the nation-state, the figure of the sovereign in general, even while recognizing that all the fundamental axiomatics of responsibility or decision (ethical, juridical, political) are grounded on the sovereignty of the subject, that is, the intentional auto-determination of the conscious self (which is free, autonomous, active, etc.). One cannot therefore, in a responsible manner, threaten the whole logic of the principle of sovereignty without compromising, by the same token, what are today the most stable foundations of morality, law, and politics, and the only requirements said to be universalizable. In particular, of human rights.[3]

"*3.* Hence the necessity of another problematic, in truth, an aporetic, of divisible sovereignty. For a long time now, at least since the end of the nineteenth century, people have spoken of nation-states with 'limited' or 'shared' sover-

eignty. But is not the very essence of the principle of sovereignty, everywhere and in every case, precisely its exceptional indivisibility, its illimitation, its integral integrity? Sovereignty is undivided, unshared, or it is not. The division of the indivisible, the sharing of what cannot be shared: that is the possibility of the impossible, that is the question taken up again by Kamuf when she retraces so strongly the 'trait of sovereignty.' And when she recognizes in it 'perhaps the essential trait of this book,' namely, its most proper place. Well, this proper place, this 'trait of sovereignty' divides like any frontier. Kamuf also speaks of 'the always divisible border, and not least . . . the frontiers dividing the world's map into nation-states, or even . . . the natural borders of its continents' (2), 'every sovereign border divides' (16). A frontier limit divides only by partitioning, sharing itself [se partageant*], it is shared only by dividing itself.*

*"Well, if this proper place divides itself like the proper itself, reading has the effect of distancing, delegating (*legare*) as much as it does of gathering, collecting, giving to read (*legere*). Even as it ties together and articulates an ensemble, it inevitably gives rise, out of fidelity, to dispersion, allegation, referral and send-off, displacement, and all sorts of other figures, in short, to what risks once again proliferating alibis. Kamuf's unique and inaugural gesture, in the book that she thereby makes come into existence, would consist in linking-unlinking two essential forces of reading, a force and a counter-force: a resistance of the same to itself, which is likewise a resistance to appropriation by the other, in other words, the expropriation of the proper. That is perhaps what gives tension to the writing: dispersing, dividing, decentering, delegating (*legare*) and simultaneously gathering, collecting but also choosing, electing, selecting, thus again dividing, privileging (*legere*).*

*"Where is the good division [*partage*] here, the good divisibility? The good and the bad alibi? What of the frontier inside this book? And if it divides itself, what about the frontier's thresholds, in French, the* marches? *And the margins?"*

III

Then I had to give it up. In this first attempt at a foreword, I still suspected the alibi: not only the inevitable alibi, but, precisely, the bad alibi. So I made a second attempt. Will I pull it off by multiplying the attempts? Since a foreword is impossible, will my chances be better with more than one foreword, one coming to supplement or second the other?

As if one had to keep repeating the rehearsals before a "premiere" or before a "dress rehearsal" [*une générale*] in the theater, the second foreword would have followed, to begin again thus:

~

"For such a procession of *my* texts, would it not be vain, more vain than ever, to precede them with a foreword, or what is called in French an *avertissement*?

"*Vain*, in fact: Would it not be at once superfluous, superficial, and self-satisfied to the point of vanity to persist in presenting these five texts, so I can pretend to reappropriate them? Texts I signed, legally, but that come back to me less than ever? For they do not properly return to me, they come back only transformed, put into another perspective, reinscribed in another configuration, written and interpreted otherwise; *countersigned* in the most unstable and contradictory sense of this word, which implies, to be sure, confirmation of an agreement, but also a wholly other signature and, especially, a counterforce—in short, the resistance that, as Peggy Kamuf tells us quite rightly at the opening of the volume, remains to be thought?

"Why take the risk of vanity, why plunge headlong toward these reproaches? To attempt to justify myself again and to allege, without alibi, two good reasons. First, I will not speak of the texts gathered here, at least not directly. Peggy Kamuf will have analyzed, interpreted, x-rayed, if I may say that, replaced and displaced them better than ever I could have done myself. She has done it in a powerful, dazzling, and even intimidating fashion. Second, I believe I have the right here to salute, before anyone else and with immense gratitude, what is owed to Peggy Kamuf's sole initiative: nothing less than the existence of this book, in truth. I myself would never have thought of such a book, neither of its unity nor its title, which is but one of the reasons we are entitled to consider it as more and other than a translation. For, as a book, it has neither equivalent nor precedent in French or another language. What I believe I must salute, and be the first able to do so, is an *invention*, the event that consists in *finding*, in an altogether inaugural fashion, in *discovering* what no doubt *appeared already to be found there*, seeming to await analysis, explicitation, unveiling (the task is not easy and it is not nothing, anything but, it is almost everything), but also in *making exist*, like a singular *oeuvre*, what undeniably, this time, *was not yet there* and what comes about as public and readable existence only at the instant an irreplaceable signature comes to interrupt the continuity of an unveiling discovery, to mark a leap into explicitation and displace the whole apparatus. Kamuf will have discovered *and* produced, deciphered, formalized, *and* posed a law that had never yet appeared. This law, therefore, in a certain way did not as such have any phenomenal or recognizable existence. This law will have presided at the configuration of these texts, over the last several years, and well beyond what their supposed author ('me') could perceive of it himself.

"In its irruptive invention, this law offers the most resistant of singularities. Despite its character as *law*, namely, its generality, its typical form, its universal intelligibility, it concerns a *unique* linking, a historical concatenation without example: that which, under the arbitrary and 'supple' (essentially and by vocation not very rigid[4]) name 'deconstruction,' will have linked adventures, events of thought, or 'oeuvres' in the United States of America of the last half century. Not only, as Kamuf says, in the sense of 'deconstruction in America'—that feeble prejudice or obscurantist disavowal according to which deconstruction found *its only or its best* welcome in the United States, or even more narrowly, in certain departments of American universities. No, at stake is a prudent and contrasted deconstruction of the sovereignty that touches a *unique* place in the world—today, here now—and that nothing designates better or in a more condensed, undeniable, but also enigmatic fashion than the name 'United States of America.' Peggy Kamuf's argument analyzes this in a luminous and convincing way. At the point at which she specifies the link between 'response' and 'resistance,' then (and I should come back to this later) situates, at the same time as 'my' response, the obscure placement of 'my' resistance, and in truth of a 'resistance' whose meaning or concept remain themselves obscure, she justifies her *choice*, her *legere*, the writing of a reading that sifts while keeping an ensemble assembled. Such a choice consists in privileging the motif of 'resistance,' even as, we read it just a moment ago, 'the essential trait of this book, common to all its chapters' is 'the trait of sovereignty.'

"Everything is knotted up, then, between 'resistance' and 'sovereignty.' Since the knot is unique, since it has no other place in the world, it also has the form of the 'without alibi.' What has to be endured 'without alibi,' that *to* which and *for* which one must answer, would be the absolutely singular knot, the irreplaceable entwining of this conjunction: a historical conjunction, others might say a historial liaison between the *de-*

construction underway, *resistance, sovereignty,* and the *United States of America.*

"Kamuf has just quoted my quotation of Thoreau's phrase 'civil disobedience.' She continues right away by placing quotation marks around a proper name, the 'United States.' In order to summon to appear what is called the 'United States,' these quotation marks signal a 'mention' rather than an ordinary 'use.' They confer on this whole argument the sort of anxious gravity required by such an act of nomination: thinking, prudent, reflective, solemn, suspended in the *ēpokhē* of the epoch, it is a fabulous act of nomination that, as always, passes by way of speech, in other words, *fabula.* Like *provocation, fabula* recounts, but also deciphers a *history,* in other words, the phantasm of an accredited myth, a myth by force of law, an 'enforced' myth:

This mention of Thoreau's great phrase, attributed here to the country in which it was forged, will remind us not to lose sight of what we said at the beginning, namely, that we wanted to try to discern some movement of response, gestures that could have left traces on the text of what was destined first for a U.S. readership, to be heard or read in translation. In choosing the path of "resistance," we seem to have specified or qualified things, since resistance is often, as we say, a *negative* response, thus one kind of response among others. But this is to suppose that there has ever been a response that does not somewhere pose resistance, or it is to speak *as if,* once again, we knew what we meant by resistance. Yet, what else could it be that responds in a response, if not some resistance, something that resists there where it responds, *as this one and no other* [?—JD]. There can be response, what we call response, only where some "this one and no other" responds, that is, resists. Are we saying, then, that the movement of response we've discerned would be that of Derrida's resistance to something that is specifically being named, today, the United States?

Yes, but on the condition that we also recognize today that "United States" is the effective or practical name for the theologico-political myth we call sovereignty: it names the conjunction of forces sufficient, for the moment, to enforce the myth of its own absolute, if theologically buttressed, sovereignty. (13–14)[5]

"What would be the "decisive" moment for those who, like me, will have admired, among other things, the way in which Peggy Kamuf rearticulates the question of the 'name' of the United States? Well, here's my hypothesis: it would be the moment of 'decision,' precisely, a decision to come, thus still undecidable. What the 'United States' means *remains to come.* The decision also supposes passage through the undecidable of a *crisis*, *krinein*, or *krisis* (that is, a choice or election, a selection, a triage, returning us to the semantics of *legere* and of *lecture/*reading, with which we have been concerned for awhile). At the point at which she has just recalled 'that the "United States" is the effective or practical name for the theologico-political myth we call sovereignty,' and after allusion to the 'convulsive crisis that this country is undergoing with regard to the death penalty,' Kamuf makes an audacious, but necessary gesture: she metonymizes and generalizes, she goes so far as to make 'United States' the name of the most general *crisis*, the condensation or displacement, the localization of a worldwide crisis that greatly exceeds the frontiers of a nation-state. Kamuf's formulations are at once daring and careful, provocative and confident, but also suspicious as regards confidence itself:

That it has or makes for itself a sovereign name, however, also makes the United States the name of a crisis within the myth, within the effective enforcement or imposition of its sovereignty, both domestically and in diplomatic or military theaters abroad. But, internally and externally, this is the same crisis; that is, if there is a crisis and a crisis of *sovereignty*, then it is because the distinction can no longer be made with the same confidence between domestic and foreign, national and international, internal and external, or other oppositions of the kind that suppose the very frontier at which state sovereignty can be or has been or may yet be breached. This *double crisis* [emphasis added] is brought into focus here and elsewhere through the lens of the death penalty "debate," which is not a debate but a struggle for the abolition of this sovereign state violence against the lives of its citizens. (14)

"According to the configuration that is thus privileged and gathered up, the stake in this 'double crisis' would concern, basically, what the name 'United States' will have meant, in the future or in the future anterior. And thus as well in some other possible phrases (for example, those that have currency, like 'deconstruction *in* America,' 'deconstruction *is* America,' deconstruction *as* deconstruction *of* America, and so on), what will be meant one day or what will have meant from then on the name 'deconstruction.' These two stakes are, in any case, indissociable. Isn't that what Kamuf suggests? For she proposes nothing less than a powerful and dense historial interpretation of this strange liaison between the United States and deconstruction. Because response always supposes, Kamuf warned us, some resistance, or even, I would add, some disadjustment, in-adequation, and anachrony, that is, a certain dissociative disorder in the correspondence of the reading (Respond to what or to whom? Before whom does one make the appeal of the *provocatio*? How to distinguish this disadjoinment from a fault or pathology?), there will have been over the past decades, between the United States and deconstructions an intense flow of responses and thus of correspondences, alliances, disjunctions, ruptures, sometimes turbulent, dramatic, comic, between war and peace, but incessant and undeniable.

"(Out of modesty, Peggy Kamuf says nothing, in the history she thus deciphers, of the major role she herself continues to play there. From almost the beginning. Discreetly, in a phrase, she recalls merely the year 1974 and our encounter in a Parisian seminar—on Nietzsche's *Zarathustra*, if memory serves. But everyone can attest to what is very well known, quite beyond the chance and privilege that I believe I can claim here: on an easy-to-read map, which would be not only bibliographical, the trajectories crossing through something like "deconstructions" *and* the "United States" have almost always crossed with the work of Peggy Kamuf. They have largely depended on that work, in the places of their greatest critical intensity. One could cite her many titles, her books, articles, translations, her teaching and participation in so many conferences. But may I be permitted at least once to say publicly, in a word, what many know: my immeasurable indebtedness. Besides numerous and admirable translations, which were always more than translations between two languages, I have always received from Peggy Kamuf, from her trust, her friendly vigilance, her advice, her rigorous collaboration, a force without which my work, I am sure, would never have been possible.)"

∼

Close the quotation. This second attempt at a foreword leaves me once again dissatisfied. It risks being read as yet another series of alibis, as just so many pretexts to avoid speaking of the thing itself of this book: the alibi, the "without alibi." I am thus going to try another maneuver, at the risk of delaying once again the beginning of reading.

IV

For reasons explained in the book, the word "alibi" will thus have been chosen as the title. By Peggy Kamuf. It remains as enigmatic as the "without" that precedes it. On this subject—the relation between the "alibi" and the "without alibi"—I would like to take the risk of a few *parentheses*. When I say "risk," I should confess rather that, in the face of too many risks, I am once again going to take refuge elsewhere, in those more secure places I call parentheses. After italics and quotation marks, parentheses. My rule here will be that all three parentheses refer to what will not have been said, not yet explicitly marked in the book, regarding the terrible logic of the alibi. Unless they remain still to be deciphered in the book, as its invisible elsewhere.

A. *(The supplement: too much alibi, too little alibi.* The rhetoric of parentheses is not limited to what typographic signs ((. . .)) indicate. There are parentheses everywhere. Well, parentheses are also alibis in a way. In the contortion of a disavowal and not altogether politely, as if they were interrupting a current contract and leaving you in the lurch, they attest: "I am elsewhere, and moreover I have something else to say, I tell you this in passing, very quickly, within parentheses, you can skip this ellipsis or this anacoluthon, what is more, what is more [*d'ailleurs, d'ailleurs*], are not all tropes alibis? And are not alibis allegories, words come from elsewhere, in the place of the other? I say more than one thing at a time, I will develop this in another place, when the time comes, this is neither the right place nor the best occasion, wait, you lose nothing by waiting, but I seize on the pretext to say it to you, etc." What hypocrisy all this is. The alibi always tells a story of lying. And thus of perjury, every lie being first of all a perjury. But a perjurer will always be able to claim that he neither lied nor perjured: he was simply elsewhere, his mind was elsewhere, and his attention disjointed. His distraction or amnesia, thus his finitude, serve him as an alibi. As the perjurer says in *Le Parjure*, by Henri Thomas: "Just imagine, I was not thinking about it." What is more, one must also recall something obvious concerning the ordinary *usage* of the word "alibi," its *pragmatic* meaning, therefore, which is always more forceful and determining than the neutral semantics of the lexicon. According to this lexicon, in the slumber of dictionaries, "alibi" means simply "elsewhere," "in another place [*alius ibi*]." But no one ever uses the adverb, and it is never translated into a substantive—"the alibi," "an alibi"—except in situations where the alibi is, in good or bad faith, veraciously or mendaciously, alleged in order to disculpate (oneself), justify (oneself) in the course of an investigation, an accusation, or a trial. The allegation of an alibi always has the form of a plea for the defense. It acquires meaning only in an experience that puts into play an incrimination, accusation, guilt, and thus responsibility (judicial or penal, but first of all ethical or political). Hence the most general question: Can one speak of an alibi, of an experience of referral to an *elsewhere*, to *another* (another place, another moment, another "who" or "what") *before* this scene of culpa-responsi-bility, of duty or debt (*Schuld, Schuldigsein*)? If one thinks, as I was suggesting above, that every trace secretes some alibi, will it be possible to think the trace, and thus the alibi, in a neutral fashion, before the proceedings of culpa-responsi-bility? Or is the injunction to answer (to answer to, to answer for, and so forth) inscribed right on the trace? In the hypothesis according to which a kind of originary alibi would precede the juridico-ethico-political alibi, does one then hold it to be a sort of transcendental and ontological neutrality? No, for it happens that the thinking of the trace (one of the oldest premises of this book) also passes by way of a prudent, complicated, but determined deconstruction of transcendental and ontological instances. Nevertheless, will one say that the discourse of law, morality, or politics determines through and through this thinking of the trace and thus of the alibi? Once again, no, which explains one of the difficulties marking, right away in the title, the concerns of the book Peggy Kamuf has *mis en oeuvre*. It is necessary to distinguish an alibi (or the allegation of an "alibi) that, albeit more "originary" and universal than any "trial" and any "culpa-responsi-bility" (juridical, ethical, or political), all the same would not be reducible to an ontologico-transcendental neutrality. And how is one then to reaffirm the "it is necessary" of the "without alibi"? How is one to credit psychoanalysis, as I have done, with having in principle heard and understood this "it is necessary"? In trying to pull this off, one risks avoiding one pitfall only to be cast into another. For it would be necessary to assume the "it is necessary" of the "without alibi" on at least three conditions: (1) without, on the one hand, yielding to the old axiomatics of the sovereign subject and *autonomous* responsibility ("I who am free, here I am present *without alibi*" and so forth); (2) without, on the other hand, returning to a predeconstructive thinking of pure and untouched presence of every trace, thus of every referral to the elsewhere of the other (place, moment, who, or what), which would come down to saying, "This presents itself, or I, myself, conscious subject, I present myself intentionally *without alibi*"; (3) without, all the same, finally, making of the alibi an invincibly transcendental or ontological structure.

If we suppose that the condition of these three "withouts" can ever be fulfilled, whence would come, still, the imperative urgency of an "it is necessary"? It must necessarily proceed from some alterity exceeding the circle of the same or the self, the sovereignty of *autonomy*, but without, all the same, taking the form of a duty or a debt that would have to be discharged so as to reclose the economic circle of exchange. This then is what, remaining to be thought, would still resist what is called "thinking."

I repeat: I would have liked more than once to promise myself (in vain, for it's impossible) to say nothing here that repeated anything whatsoever of the book. Here, then, is what I would be given to think, at the moment and among other things, in the margin but in the first place, by the way Kamuf will have linked, according to numerous modalities, the "question of the alibi" and the "question of the United States." As for national places or the places of nation-states, as for national sovereignties, I will have spent my life undergoing alibis: metropolitan France was a first alibi for the young French Jew from colonial Algeria that I was. Then Algeria became in turn the alibi for the French intellectual that I remain. I began to explain myself on this subject in *Monolingualism of the Other*, where language itself becomes, through and through, structurally, the very element of the alibi: nonbelonging, impossible appropriation. Then, since 1956 and especially since 1966, the United States and France, or even Europe, have become for "me" (for my life but also my work of writing and teaching) multiple alibis, between which I endlessly move, always alleging that I am to be found elsewhere, always invoking other evaluations, appealing (I recall that to make an appeal is the *provocatio*) to other perspectives, other hierarchies, and so forth. Would this book have been possible otherwise? No, as Peggy Kamuf magisterially shows. People have sometimes taken advantage of this situation (especially in France, in what remains "anti-American" there) to claim that I am "elsewhere," better received "elsewhere," only received elsewhere, especially in the United States. This is the alibi manipulated by those who would like to make believe that all of this goes on only in the U.S., not in France or in other "elsewheres" of the world, and so forth. These French allegations are also comical denegations (and every alibi has the form of a denegation or disavowal, a negative allegation, let us say an *alledenegation*). To this always domestic maneuver frequently corresponds, in inverse but perfectly symmetrical fashion, the no less comic, no less domestic gesticulation coming from abroad. For example, from America. It seeks to reassure itself by all manner of means: "Deconstruction? Oh, come on! It passed out of fashion a long time ago elsewhere, even in France, which is where the invasion is supposed to have originated!"

B. (*The advocate's plea: the alibi of the prosecutor and Peggy Kamuf's provocation.* There are several roles that could be attributed to me on the stage of this book: reader, spectator, or actor. As for the character of the observer, he would be fascinated by the distribution of places, in other words, by the dramaturgy invented or *mis en oeuvre* by Peggy Kamuf. Look at "Event of Resistance," the subtitle of what is called, with so much irony, "Introduction" but orchestrates in truth an impressive interpretive strategy. Several times, and always in a rigorous way, Kamuf points to the difficulties, hindrances, enigmas, knots, and so on that accumulate on the road of the texts she has *chosen to collect*. (To choose to collect, thus choosing *and* collecting: these are, moreover, the two meanings of *legere* that we have had in view and that, in truth, have had us under surveillance since the beginning). Crowding on the road, traffic jam, risks of collision at every turn. Difficulties, hindrances, enigmas, knots constitute as many forms of resistance in the course of the analysis, the formalization, the theorization, in short, in what is philosophical about these attempts. Well, the traffic jam of these resistances intensifies particularly around the concept, precisely, of resistance. In all of these texts, and for a long time now, this concept plays an indispensable role, an eminent role that seems at times to condition all the others (even if an "unconditional resistance" is part of a chain, for example, "the three-word conjunction, *sovereignty-cruelty-resistance*" [15]), an operative role and a thematic role—perhaps more operative than thematic. It may be because of the difference between these two roles that Kamuf is right to worry: "It means resistance (whatever that means)," she writes at one point (ibid.).

What is she worried about, exactly? She begins by recalling the principle of ruin that threatens the concept of resistance and makes it resemble anything but a concept, almost a word without concept. She asks: *What is it*, resistance? "So, then, what is 'resistance,' not only in or for psychoanalysis, but in general? Can we have a general concept of resistance that does not include a resistance to itself, which would ruin it as a concept?" (8). You will read the analysis that prepares and follows this question. It demonstrates and justifies the whole conceptual concatenation that links this "resistance," and the very resistance of this chain, both strengthened and weakened in its links, to the numerous motifs of *response* and *responsibility*, of *sovereignty, cruelty, oeuvre* (both literary and not), *fiction*, the *as if, perjury, phantasm, event, machine*, and so forth. It also does not neglect to specify that, among all these paradoxes, resistance is not necessarily active or actual; it can be "passive," "infinite or abyssal" (12).

Yet, by the same token, where everything seems suspended from resistance, it suffices that this resistance, this "word," which is far too equivocal and of doubtful suppleness, no longer corresponds to any rigorous sense or any certain concept for everything to appear to be mere words, idle talk, *dit "en l'air,"* as we say in French. Without foundation. It suffices that said "resistance" remain, likewise, suspended, instead of firmly upholding the whole chain that depends on it, like a strong nail driven into a solid and resistant wall, for everything to appear to hang on a breath, on almost nothing.

I think this is true: the foundation is lacking, the ultimate justification is missing, there precisely where I would no doubt have to respond, without alibi, to what might look like some irresponsibility.

But first I must draw the reader's attention to the serious and laughing provocation that I think I detect in this courtroom scene. I began by noting that every *provocatio* is played out, like the alibi itself, before the law. Well, what does Kamuf do here? Visibly, she more readily takes sides *for* the texts ("mine") of which she is proposing a *reading*, in the strong sense of the term (choice, gathering, interpretation, response, etc.). As an advocate for the defense, she pleads for them, she foresees and forestalls the adversary's resistances, according to a rhetoric whose law she herself exhibits, with impeccable lucidity, precisely on the subject of resistance and response: "But why anticipate, why call up resistance? It's a familiar tactic, we've all used it many times—to respond in advance to imagined or anticipated objections, as if one could conquer the other's resistance before it has even had a chance to manifest itself" (7).

Yet, in truth, on the other side of the same gesture, with one and the same turn of the hand, contraband, or prestidigitation, what does the advocate for the defense do? Doesn't she turn herself into a prosecutor? Even as she argues the case for the defense, doesn't she produce damning evidence against the virtual defendant, the one who stands accused, indicted? Doesn't everything happen as if, addressing herself to the court, she demonstrated that her client has nothing but alibis to stand on? As if he always sent you off, referred you elsewhere ("va voir ailleurs si j'y suis [go look elsewhere and see if I'm there]," a rude expression in French for getting rid of someone). And if he has only alibis, if he goes from alibi to alibi, from allegation to allegation, not knowing at bottom where he is going nor where he is, well, then finally he has no alibi. No alibi that holds up. He is without alibi, but there is no reason to be proud of this "without alibi": it does not prove innocence; it does not correspond to an assumed responsibility, here now, but rather to an unjustifiable fault or lack. Almost to a blatant offense, *flagrante delicto*. In the best of cases, to a flagrant offense of irresponsibility. Having reconstituted, through many motifs, the displacements, contexts, modalities of usage, and so forth of the concept and name "resistance," Kamuf in fact recalls that they have perhaps no general, stable, unifiable, and thus reliable meaning. No more than do "insistence" or "response," which seem inseparable from "resistance." At most, there would be simulacra, phantasms, or some "as if's." And therefore questions whose answer would be endless, indefinitely deferred:

We were supposed to be following a link between *oeuvre* and resistance. Although the term itself does not occur in these passages . . . there is . . . an insistence: that the *oeuvre*'s phenomenal appearance does not or cannot show, that it resists showing the truth of its operation. If we want to trace the link further, however, we should not give up too easily the noun or the name "resistance," as if we were certain enough of its meaning to know how to recognize it in other names or descriptions. For the problem is precisely to know what we mean by resistance, as if we had a general concept of the response or the force of response we still call resistance. But whose resistance? To what? The resistance of what to what? Questions for which there would always be no end of response. (11–12)

And further down: "The *oeuvre* would always somewhere be opposing a resistance to the movement of appropriation whereby the subject sustains and is sustained by its legal fiction. But resistance, we also understand, does not mean cancellation, annulment, destruction, or negation of the subject. It means resistance (whatever that means)" (15).

Whether or not this is how she meant things to go, whether she played it out in the most serious or the most ironic way, Kamuf will have exposed before the court, as if she were denouncing them, firmly and without mercy, all the conceptual alibis of the texts that she supports and that she is supposed to be defending against virtual objections. She objects (to) herself with these conceptual alibis, what I could almost call alibis *of the* concept, the other or the elsewhere, the "always further and later," the "always elsewhere" of the finished and simply determinable concept. She knots and unknots before the members of the jury all the "conceptual" intertwinings of these alibis around the major alibi: resistance.

And I, far from complaining about such a dangerous strategy, I, who could find myself in the position of the accused denounced by his advocate, I, the cornered defendant, back against the wall, really without alibi this time, what do I do? I thank her; on the contrary, I applaud, I'm in complete agreement. Trying to get myself out of this tight spot, and at the risk of making my case worse, I confirm: "Yes, that is indeed what I wanted to show; there is precisely the difficulty, the source of all that I have trouble thinking and that nevertheless I cannot not think, there where it resists thinking, yes, those are indeed the aporias that not only I never sought to dissimulate but that I hold to be the most urgent path for thought. I have no alibi. *D'ailleurs*, moreover, one could find many signs of this in earlier texts or ones that are contemporary with these. One would find, in particular, what brings the concept without concept of *resistance* into line, although through many twists and turns, with that of *desistance* and especially that of *restance* [remaining]. Concerning *restance*, already in *Glas* I tried to think how it is that, being "nothing," no being, thus not at all reducible to the substantial or essential permanence of what remains, *restance* undid the ontological question "What is it?" and appeared to be older than the distinction between "who" and "what." It seems to me that my advocate does not give absolute credence to this question or this distinction, even if she does recall their indispensable necessity and interminable longevity, even if she does ask "So, then, what is 'resistance,' not only in or for psychoanalysis, but in general?" or "But whose resistance? To what? The resistance of what to what?" (12).

C. ((*What*) res(is)ts: *what remains resists thought*. Kamuf will have thus shown the way toward what remains for us to think beyond these signs, those of yesterday or today. What remains to be thought: the very thing that resists thought. It resists *in advance*, it gets out ahead. The rest gets there ahead of thought; it remains *in advance* of what is called thought.

For we do not know what thought is. We do not know what this word means before or outside of this resistance. It can only be determined from, in the wake of, what resists and remains thus to be thought. Thought remains to be thought.

The future-to-come, whose grammar is necessary here and imposes the very injunction of its "it is necessary," has precisely the impossible-to-anticipate figure of that which comes, which is coming, which remains to come. Irreducible to calculation, program, project, subject, object, and anticipation, what is coming can receive indifferently the names "event" or "other." What remains to be thought remains to come and thus resists thinking. The word "thinking" thus takes in, without being able to house or contain it, this inappropriable resistance of the other. To take in without being able to lodge the other *chez soi* [at home in the self] is one of the formulas, among others, for the possibility of the impossible that provokes all these provocations, these calls to an instance that does not yet exist, being presently neither constituted nor even instituted. From this instance to come, but only in return, will be legitimated *perhaps*, in any case in an always unequal and unfinished way, all these provocations.

For example (I will pull only this one thread), what remains to be thought about this unthinkable *passivity* that Kamuf recalls so profoundly to its abyssal depth ("A certain passive resistance, then, which will go on working as resistance, 'infinite or abyssal'"; 12). What is this passivity? The passivity of resistance resists thought because it is what *does* the most, *makes* the most happen, more than the most, the impossible itself, at the heart of the possible. In fact, one may say of the impossible that it marks the limit of a possible or a power, more precisely, of an "I can" or a "we can." Such passivity remains at work in the work [*à l'oeuvre dans l'oeuvre*]. For one of the enigmas of *l'oeuvre* is that its event does not totally depend on an action carried out by my sovereign initiative.[6] The same passivity marks the experience of all unconditional and pure events as such (gift, forgiveness, hospitality, death). It marks and thus doubly limits the most active and productive performativity: on the one hand, a performative depends passively in itself on conventions that are prior and external to the act, which supposes them and does not control them; on the other hand, by virtue of an "I can," "I am authorized, competent to," "I have the right and the power to," whereby the performative tries to master the event it is supposed to produce, it neutralizes and annuls that event in the same stroke. Precisely because it has the power and the possibility. A performative remains, therefore, passively exposed to what is coming, to the other who comes and carries the day against any performativity, which is exceeded by the event worthy of the name.

What remains to be thought and presently resists thinking thus passively exposed, in its very passivity, is not only *l'oeuvre*. What indeed can an *oeuvre* be as singular event, irreplaceable but iterable and constituted by the "if" of a fiction that is heterogeneous, as I try to show, to so many other "as if's" of tradition?

What remains to be thought and presently resists thinking thus passively exposed, in its very passivity, is not only the *phantasm*, the phantasm that operates, *fait oeuvre*, makes the work (at the crossing of the unconscious, the phenomenological *phainesthai*, the noema as an intentional but not real component of consciousness, and of spectrality [*phantasma*] of phantoms). How is one to think the durable hardness, the until now invincible, although always threatened, effectivity of an onto-theo-logico-political phantasm—sovereignty, for example?

What remains to be thought and presently resists thinking thus passively exposed, in its very passivity, is not only the *fictionality*, phantasmatic or not, of an "as if" that exceeds all the "as if's" of tradition.

No, to remain with the figure of the alibi, what remains to be thought and presently resists thinking thus passively exposed, in its very passivity, is another experience of the "without alibi." It goes to the heart of what we would still like to call a "response" or a "responsibility," be it ethical, juridical, or political. This responsibility—here's another *provocatio*—will never be able to avoid appealing to someone who would dare to say, "Here I am, without alibi, and here is the first decision that I sign." Well, it would be necessary that this "Here I am, I sign" designate neither the presence of a sole, unified subject, present and present to itself, identifiable, sovereign, without difference, nor a decision that is already a decision, nor yet the predicate of this subject, its possible or its "I can."

That is why, as I too well know, when I speak so often of heteronomy or of a *passive* decision that, as decision of the other in me, does not all the same exonerate me from any responsibility, I provoke common sense by appealing, with another *provocatio*, to the other to come who/that resists common sense.

The question, the demand then becomes: How can one continue to say, "Here I am"? How can one reaffirm the ineffaceable passivity of a heteronomy and a decision of the other in me? How can one do it without giving in to the alibi? Without the other—the Other, any other or God, the law itself or duty—becoming the first and last alibi of my irresponsibility? Nor even an ultimate creditor whose debt would still remain mine to discharge?

End of the last parenthesis.)

You will never discharge, never acquit yourself, said I, somewhere between assertion and decision, between "you cannot" and "you must not, it is necessary that you not do that, especially not that." The impossibility of acquitting oneself, the duty not to want to acquit oneself: that is what I would have liked to attest to here, at the moment of signing, without "mercy" and without alibi.

It would remain for me still to think, perhaps, among other things, something I dared to say one day, something that happened or in truth arrived to me when, on a certain date, a common expression—"without alibi"—revealed and then imposed itself on me all of a sudden, at once unforeseeable and irresistible, in the middle of a lecture collected in this book. The lecture began by declaring, others might say by confessing, a merciless, thankless suffering, and it entrusted the provocation to the keeping of an "as if," another "if":

If I say right now, speaking in your direction but without identifiable addressee: "Yes, I am suffering cruelly," or again, "You are being *made* or *allowed* to suffer cruelly," or yet again, "You are making *her* or you are letting *him* suffer cruelly," or even: "I am *making* myself or *letting* myself suffer cruelly," well . . . (238)

AUGUST 2001

WITHOUT ALIBI

Introduction: Event of Resistance

PEGGY KAMUF

In 1966, as part of a soon to be famous conference at Johns Hopkins University, Jacques Derrida for the first time gave a public lecture in the United States. Delivered in French, this lecture undertook a deconstruction of the concept of structure as deployed by the structuralism of Claude Lévi-Strauss. "Structure, Sign, and Play in the Discourse of the Human Sciences," perhaps the most frequently anthologized essay by Derrida, has now become a classic of "poststructuralism." Indeed, it is difficult not to see some connection between the regular reprinting of this essay and the extraordinary sticking power of the poststructuralist label to so many other critical discourses that, in the years since, have not needed to situate themselves by any reference whatsoever to structuralism. It is as if, by taking aim at the center of the structuralist enterprise in his 1966 intervention, Derrida had legitimated once and for all this otherwise usually inapt designation.

I recall these events because I wish to see the occasion of the present collection in light of the more than thirty-five years since that first lecture to a U.S. audience. Derrida has now given hundreds of lectures at U.S. universities and other public institutions. He has also taught at several of them: Johns Hopkins, Yale, the City University of New York, the University of California at Irvine, New York University, the New School for Social Research. The influence of his writing on the course of critical reflection in humanities disciplines in particular has been enormous and undeniable, in the U.S. but of course not only there. All of this is well known or obvious, and I am not proposing yet another review of Derridean "deconstruction in America," its fortunes or misfortunes. Instead, an almost contrary gesture has been called up for me as I reread and revised the translations of these essays, all but one of which, the last in the collection, were written for an occasion in or of the U.S. university. I have been led to reflect on how certain figures of Derrida's thought might have taken the shape they did in part (but only in part) in response to conditions encountered, not at all exclusively but perhaps more manifestly, in the U.S. Certainly this is not to suggest that one could identify in those conditions a source of his thought. Derrida is quite patently a thinker without borders, or rather a thinker of the always divisible border, not least the frontiers dividing the world's map into nation-states, or even the natural borders of its continents.[1] His writings have been able to touch chords or nerves everywhere they circulate precisely because they keep open the gap articulating thought in general to particular languages, traditions, and histories. The articulation of particularity and generality is always at issue whatever specific questions he addresses, which is also why his work is pulled or driven into translation.

What I want to try to discern, however, is a movement of response whereby this thinking engages with a U.S. context. That it has been so engaged, for more than thirty-five years, is not a question or in question; it is a fact, and a massive one. But this fact does not interest us as such. What would be of interest, rather, is the event of this engagement and response: the engagement by and with Derrida's work, the response to that work but also by that work. It is this work of engagement and response that will have been the event, perhaps, in which the last thirty-five years have unfolded for a significant portion of the U.S. university—and beyond.

Work and event: these two notions are brought together explicitly, as you will see, in the essays collected here. This conjunction is the central idea being worked out in both "The University Without Condition," where Derrida engages most directly with the institution of the university, and "Typewriter Ribbon," which takes up the challenge to think together "event" and "machine." This latter essay begins by asking:

Will we be able to think, what is called thinking, at one and the same time, *both* what is happening (we call that an event) *and* the calculable programming of an automatic repetition (we call that a machine)?

For that, it would be necessary in the future (but there will be no future except on this condition) to think *both* the event *and* the machine as two compatible or even indissociable concepts. Today they appear to us to be antinomic. (72)

Derrida wants to call this possible/impossible conjunction of event and machine *work*—or rather, since he insists on keeping the French name, *oeuvre*. (Possible reasons for this insistence are the even harsher antinomy between machine and *oeuvre*—whereas mechanical *work* is routine in English—as well as the occurrence within *oeuvre* of *ouvre*, thus keeping in view the opening of the work to the event of the future. But there is also the difference in French between *oeuvre/oeuvrer* and *travail/travailler*.)[2] As we will be able to verify in a moment, Derrida has been asking questions about event-ness for at least thirty-five years. And machines of repetition have also been principal engines in the deconstruction of self-presence. What seems to be new here, in other words, is the attention to *oeuvre*, the care with which Derrida's thought approaches the term that it is taking as the name of this unheard-of thing: an event-machine. Moreover, this innovation, renovation, or reinvention of the term occurs, at least on this initial occasion, through an engagement with the particular *oeuvre* of Paul de Man, which Derrida was again addressing in response to a demand (once again, at a conference in a U.S. university). It engages that work at what has become, in the course of events, one of its most sensitive points: de Man's reading of Rousseau's excuse for an inexcusable lie. Skewered there, on this sensitive point, lies de Man's version of *oeuvre*, what he calls the text-machine, in an oft-quoted line from his essay "Excuses," on Rousseau: "There can never be enough guilt around to match the text-machine's infinite power to excuse."[3] Without pretending to limit its resonance to this initial occasion, one might still discern how the thinking that is being newly gathered around *oeuvre* also responds to what *will have been* the *oeuvre*-event of Paul de Man, still taking place and not only, of course, in the U.S. academy. The *oeuvre*-event, however, always bears more than one signature; it is not a *chef-d'oeuvre* because the one and only head (*chef*), is absent, as is the center, therefore, just as Derrida said thirty-five years ago with regard to the center of structures.

We have begun to follow what I called above the movement of response and engagement. But we have begun with the latest and with what has come later, the essays in this volume. Written between 1994 and 2000, these five texts join what is now a very long list of works in English by Derrida. In the still-unfolding *oeuvre*-event of deconstruction, these essays would be part of its wave. We are going to consider in a moment some implications of the figure of *oeuvre* that is being worked out in these pages. First, however, I want to return to the beginning, a certain begin-

ning, the beginning of a text, which was also, perhaps, the beginning of
an event.

At the Hopkins conference in 1966 (where, as it happens, Derrida and
de Man first met), Derrida began his intervention with questions about an
"event": "Perhaps something has occurred in the history of the concept of
structure that could be called an 'event,' if this loaded word did not entail
a meaning which it is precisely the function of structural—or structuralist—thought to reduce or to suspect. Let us speak of an 'event' nevertheless, and let us use quotation marks to serve as a precaution. What would
this event be then?"[4] The question will be given a provisional answer in the
next and last sentence of this opening paragraph: "Its exterior form would
be that of a *rupture* and a redoubling." As the rest of the essay will argue,
this event of rupture happens at the center or to the center; it would be,
then, the event of a decentering.[5] But just as he does at the beginning,
Derrida later shows some ambivalence or caution about using the term
"event" to speak of this decentering, at least where the rupture of the center is redoubled in or as thought. For if we ask how or where this decentering *as* thinking occurs, then, he suggests, it "would be somewhat naïve
to refer to an event, a doctrine, or an author in order to designate this occurrence" (280). Let us retain this warning against naïveté, for we also need
to take precautions as we reread this very text *as if* it were an event of in-
auguration. It is this *as if* that is naïve from the moment we forget to interrogate it. But we should also notice how, in the same passage, Derrida
emphasizes that this occurrence, without author or original event, has
begun *to work*. "[The decentering] is no doubt part of the totality of an
era, our own, but still it has always already begun to proclaim itself and
begun to *work* [travailler]" (ibid.). Between *travailler* or *travail* and *oeuvre*
there is semantic overlap, but there is also an important distinction, which
Derrida will examine, in one of the essays collected here, in the course of
arguing that the university must be not only a place of *travail*, of work, but
also of *oeuvres*, works. We'll return later to this distinction.

Before leaving "Structure, Sign, and Play," we can repeat the question
it asks: "What would this event be then?" Now, at the risk of appearing
somewhat naïve, let us hear the question turned back on itself, *as if* it were
asking about the event inaugurated by Derrida's first lecture in the U.S.
The *as if* poses a fictional condition on our ability to speak of this event
as punctually beginning in this or that occurrence in the past. To be more
precise, the condition of fiction allows us to speak *as if* this were a narra-

tive event, and thus subject to the laws whereby one tells a story from its ending, *as if* the end had already been present at the beginning. As you will see, all of the essays here interrogate this structuring possibility or condition of the *as if*, and three of them ("The University Without Condition," "Typewriter Ribbon," and "Psychoanalysis Searches the State of Its Soul") do so explicitly and by that name: the "as if." As in the 1966 lecture, the concern here is still with the event, but it is even more insistent, although still posed in terms that are consonant and consistent with those at the beginning of that first lecture. What is new, I venture to say,[6] is the inclusion of theories of the performative and performativity among modes of thought that, like structuralism, function to reduce, if not suspect, events. Derrida has long been engaged, of course, in a constructive (i.e., deconstructive) critique of speech act theory, but here there would be a more explicit response, as I hear it, to a generalized tendency (perhaps especially, but not only, in the U.S.) toward theories of "empowerment" insofar as they draw, sometimes only very vaguely, on notions of the performative.[7] This response can even be quite direct in the text, as when we read, in "The University Without Condition," an articulated disengagement with something that is "too often said": "It is too often said that the performative produces the event of which it speaks. To be sure. One must also realize that, inversely, where there is the performative, an event worthy of the name cannot arrive" (234).

"What would this event be then?": let us attempt to repeat the question now in the space not of narrative, but of *oeuvre*, the *oeuvre*-event. We might then say that this question *opens* the work as an event of response, but to open here would not mean to begin, initiate, inaugurate, originate, etc. A response does not have a beginning in itself. The question "What would this event be then?" opens an engagement to speak about events, but it will also have been opened by or to events, for example, the event of a now much-discussed conference in 1966 when "French Theory" was invited to speak *en masse* at a U.S. venue. The question was and still is the event of an "engagement" in many senses of the term at once, in English and in French, where it can also mean something like beginning.[8] But as we saw, the engagement begins by disengaging the term "event" from a prevalent or even dominant use, a use that is an abuse. What has been abused is the thing being called thus, the very sense or experience of event that centered thought has precisely the function "to reduce and to suspect," as we read at the beginning of the lecture.

At one point, in the impromptu discussion transcribed from that afternoon in 1966, this attempt to disengage event from the abuse of reduction or suspicion is quite explicitly articulated by Derrida, in response to what someone has just said. An interlocutor, Charles Morazé, has intervened to make a prediction: we are on the verge, he announces, of discovering or inventing the "grammar of the event." He claims, not too modestly, that "in the coming years" we will learn how to constitute such a grammar. Well, after Morazé has said this:

I would like to point out that there is also a grammar of the event—that one can make a grammar of the event. It is more difficult to establish. I think that in the coming months, in the coming years, we will begin to learn how this grammar or rather this set of grammars of events can be constituted. And [this grammar] leads to results, may I say, anyway with regard to my personal experience, which are a little less pessimistic than those you have indicated[9]

Derrida responds merely: "Concerning Mr. Morazé's allusion to the grammar of the event, there I must return his question, because I don't know what a grammar of the event can be."[10] This disengaging response appears also disingenuous, but its disingenuousness here seems to be strategic, of strategic necessity: knowing what someone might mean to say by "grammar of event," Derrida can respond that he does not know what such a thing can be—except a reduction, a cancellation of the very thing being called "event." It is a response that, by returning the question, implicitly asks whether the other speaker himself can know such a thing. And indeed, we notice in announcing this event, which would be the reduction of events to their appropriate grammars, Morazé hesitates between claiming a knowledge in the present ("there is also a grammar of the event . . . one can make a grammar of the event") and a knowledge that will only become possible "in the coming months, in the coming years." Thus, although the present confidence is only the confidence, or the belief, that such knowledge is coming, it is *as if* we could already say "there is a grammar of the event." Not really, of course. (More than thirty-five years later, the same claim is perhaps still being made by generative grammarians or cognitive scientists.)

It is time now to look closer at this notion of *oeuvre*, since that is the space, we said, in which we have to hear this question of the event. Derrida, as we've already observed, begins in these essays to write *oeuvre-event*, thus invoking *oeuvre* as also the name of something that takes place or happens. So what is it that is being called *oeuvre*? Why the need for this new term or this displacement of an old term? We may notice that the *oeuvres* discussed here are written works or even works of literature, that is, works of fiction. Does this suggest that, despite its reinvention in this discourse, the term *oeuvre* remains essentially tied to art, if not to the art of writing? In other words, is the *oeuvre* still essentially an *oeuvre d'art*? And if so, should we welcome this as an invention or see above all a recycled concept, if not of the *chef d'oeuvre*, then of the formal, romantic concept of the work of art?

The short answer to all these questions is: no, although the elaboration of *oeuvre* here cites, as one would expect, Kant's distinction of the *oeuvre d'art* or *Kunstwerk* from other kinds of working or products of work.[11] But Derrida is also very consistent in affirming, reaffirming the value of the legacy we call *oeuvres d'art*, literature, and even many of the traditions and institutions that have carried them down to us. *Oeuvre* inherits from *oeuvre d'art* according to a structure he has described elsewhere as affirmative inheriting, which is critical and selective.[12] So, the longer answer to all these questions would be, as always in Derrida's thought, affirmative: yes, between *oeuvre* and *oeuvre d'art*, there is an affirmative relation. The questions we've asked or pretended to ask intimate, however, that one ought not to affirm this relation, as if one had to resist all inheritance from the work of art as thing of the past. This kind of question arises no doubt as an effect of introducing these essays to an English-speaking audience. It anticipates a certain form of resistance there.

But why anticipate, why call up resistance? It's a familiar tactic; we've all used it many times—to respond in advance to imagined or anticipated objections, as if one could conquer the other's resistance before it has even had a chance to manifest itself. Many books are written almost entirely in this mode of preconquered resistance, which usually makes them quite unreadable. But that would hardly be a propitious mode for the present introduction, which should aim to attract rather than drive away readers. Perhaps, then, we had to call up a figure of resistance to address it as such, *as resistance*. And this so that resistance can be invited to engage the work of these essays by reading them. If so, then the invitation is not to abandon resistance—what would life be without it?—but rather to sharpen it, test it, focus it, learn to know what it is that must be resisted.

In another text, Derrida has declared openly that he loves the word "resistance" because of its resonance in French ever since the Second World

War, when "Resistance" became the name of the just cause.[13] This remark occurs in a long essay entitled "Resistances" within a collection whose title also repeats the loved word: *Resistances of Psychoanalysis*. He shows there that no homogeneity stabilizes Freud's concept of resistance because in fact several different concepts are being stashed by him under the same term. So, then, what is "resistance," not only in or for psychoanalysis, but in general? Can we have a general concept of resistance that does not include a resistance to itself, which would ruin it as a concept? In our collection, Derrida takes up these questions again particularly in "Psychoanalysis Searches the State of Its Soul," where "resistance" is one of the three problematic words, along with "cruelty" and "sovereignty," that the essay searches into.

We've been led to speak of a resistance in the vicinity of *oeuvre*, as if that very term's own resistance to translation had called it up. Perhaps, however, this is not a coincidence; perhaps there is a connection between *oeuvre* and resistance, and the one never comes without the other. *Oeuvre* as work of resistance? Let us see.

The essay that engages with this notion of *oeuvre* in the most detailed way, "Typewriter Ribbon," makes the connection to resistance we are suggesting. As we mentioned, the principal undertaking of the essay is to think together machine and event, the antinomy that would be bridged by the *oeuvre*. Derrida does this in large part by following closely what de Man has to say about the "text-machine." But he is also, I believe, posing some questions about possible limits placed on this text-machine in de Man's thinking, limits that cannot obtain for *oeuvre* as Derrida wants to conceive of it. In one pertinent passage, these questions can be seen to focus on de Man's intimations about a certain force of resistance in what he calls "the materiality of the letter":

Without any doubt, many passages would demonstrate, in their very letter, that Rousseau's text, however singular it may be, serves here as exemplary index. Of what? Of the text *in general*, or more rigorously (and this makes a difference that counts here) of "what we call *text*," as de Man says, playing with the italics and with the "definition" that he gives by putting the word "definition" in quotation marks. These are literal artifices that mark . . . that one must be attentive to every detail of the letter, the literality of the letter defining here the place of what de Man will call materiality. The literality of the letter situates this materiality not so much because it would be a physical or sensible (aesthetic) substance, or even matter, but because it is the place of prosaic resistance . . . to any organic and aesthetic totalization, to any aesthetic form. And first of all, I would say for my part, a resistance to every possible reappropriation. . . . The materiality in question—and one must gauge the importance of this irony or paradox—is not a thing, it is not *something* sensible or intelligible; it is not even the matter of a body. As it is not something, as it is nothing and yet it works, *cela oeuvre*, this nothing therefore operates, it forces, but as a force of resistance. . . . At work here is a force of resistance without material substance. This force derives from the dissociative, dismembering, fracturing, disarticulating, and even disseminal power that de Man attributes to the letter. To a letter whose dissociative and inorganic, disorganizing, disarticulating force affects not only nature but the body itself—as organic and organized totality. . . . The textual event is inseparable from this formal materiality of the letter. (150–51)

Delineating the link de Man maintains between the material resistance of the letter and the machinelike event, these lines set up the question about a literal limit on the force of resistance that can be thought to be at work, there where, as Derrida writes, switching the syntax of our word: *cela oeuvre*. Although dictionaries now see this intransitive verb as restricted to *literary* usage (its sense conveyed in everyday language by *travailler*),[14] and thus to a certain practice of writing, Derrida would appear to adopt it here precisely to signal beyond the "formal materiality of the letter" toward an *oeuvre* or *oeuvrer* that could never be solely or essentially a literal or literary work. But de Man, we're told, attributes this force of resistance to the literality of the letter and sees the disruptive force of what he calls "textual events" as inseparable from the letter's materiality. Earlier in the essay, however, Derrida has reminded us that we cannot take the textual in "textual events" too literally if we want to use it synonymously with *oeuvre*: "An *oeuvre* is an event, to be sure; there is no *oeuvre* without singular event, without textual event, if one can agree to enlarge this notion beyond its verbal or discursive limits" (133). This is far from the first time Derrida will have been prompted to issue a warning that he uses words like "text," "trace," and "writing" in a general sense not restricted to their verbal, linguistic, or, as we say, *literal* reference. But here the reminder is also issued in the direction of a certain de Manian tendency to literalize the text, the text-machine, or the textual event. Even though for de Man this literalization would be both a grammatization and a rhetoricization, therefore not in the least a simple affair (i.e., there is resistance), this complexity or contradiction within literality is not yet, it would seem, sufficient to take account of what has to be at work, *à l'oeuvre*, beyond the letter of any text, but also beyond any truth as posed by the letter. Which is why, when Derrida goes back over de Man's reading of the textual event that will have been Rousseau's confession and attempt at excuse, a few features emerge that would have to be left out of consideration by a too-literal reading.

Of these features, one in particular should interest us as the site of a certain resistance.[15] It is possible, Derrida remarks, that the whole story of the ribbon is Rousseau's invention, a literary device, a fiction within the now-literary genre of confession inaugurated by Augustine.[16] After having pointed out some striking narrative coincidences between Augustine's and Rousseau's confessions—both confess a theft of fruit at the same age and at the same place in their books—Derrida conditionally advances the hypothesis of a "supplement of fiction." "As if," he writes,

> through a supplement of fiction in what remains a possible fiction, Rousseau had played at practicing an artifice of composition: he would have invented an intrigue, a narrative knot, as if to knot a ribbon around a basket of pears. This fabulous intrigue would have been but a stratagem, the *mēkhanē* of a dramaturgy destined to inscribe itself in the archive of a new, quasi literary genre, the history of confessions entitled *Confessions*, autobiographical stories inaugurated by a theft. And each time it is the paradigmatic and paradisiacal theft of forbidden fruit or a forbidden pleasure. (82)

This long sentence traces out what one may call a certain operation of fiction. Under the dispensation of the "as if," it poses an initial gesture that would have set in motion a whole chain of events or *oeuvre*-events. The gesture is outlined at the juncture of writing and desire, where desire would have given the impulse to writing (along with everything else). But we should notice that there are two different stories being told here, or rather two different modes being traced, one of which would not be narrative or in the space of narrative. Also being traced is the movement of *oeuvre*, in a space exceeding that of narrative. This is the excess over any desire, any one desire or anyone's desire, however it manifests itself, in whatever impulse of performative repetition, for example, the impulse to confess, to do or to make what is called a confession. By *oeuvre*, then, we should understand an operation in excess of the enabling, performative condition under which some "I" says, desires to say: "I can" or "I may," for example, I can confess the truth, without lying, without perjury.

Not, however, without fiction, because the "supplement of fiction" remains irreducible in the operation of truth-telling. This remainder or remains of fiction allies the *oeuvre* to a machine and to a mechanical repetition. There would thus have to be a kind of truth-telling machine, which is a contradiction in terms, or, as we were saying above, an antinomy. What if instead we had to say that truth is not *told* (as if it were narrative), but made (*fictio-*, *fictionis*, from *fingere*, to fashion, make)? Derrida is fond of a phrase in Augustine and alludes to it more than once in this collection, for example, in "History of the Lie": "For better and for worse, this performative dimension *makes the truth*, as Augustine says" (51). In "Typewriter Ribbon," Derrida is calling *oeuvre* that which unfolds not merely performatively, but, as we will see when we continue the quotation, virtually subterraneously, through the ligneous fibers of a materiality without substance, the material repetitions of thought by means of an *oeuvre* that is also a machine. The passage continues a little further on and with the help, we notice, of another "as if":

As if it were a matter for Jean-Jacques of inscribing himself into this great genealogical history of confessions entitled *Confessions*. The genealogical tree of a more or less literary lineage that would begin with the theft, from some tree, in the literal or the figural sense, of some forbidden fruit. A tree with leaves or a tree without leaves that produced so many leaves of paper, manuscript paper and typing paper. Rousseau would have inscribed his name in the archival economy of a palimpsest, by means of quasi-quotations drawn from the palimpsestuous and ligneous thickness of a quasi-literary memory: a clandestine or encrypted lineage, a testamentary cryptography of confessional narration, the secret of an autobiography between Augustine and Rousseau, the simulacrum of a fiction right there where *both* Augustine *and* Rousseau claim truth, a veracity of testimony that never makes any concessions to the lies of literature. (83)

We were supposed to be following a link between *oeuvre* and resistance. Although the term itself does not occur in these passages, nor with any frequency in the rest of this essay, a certain concept, work, or force of resistance is figured in the lines we've just cited, for example, in the secrecy of the secret, the "clandestine or encrypted lineage," in the "testamentary cryptography" or the "simulacrum of a fiction." There is, in other words, an insistence: that the *oeuvre*'s phenomenal appearance does not or cannot show, that it resists showing the truth of its operation. If we want to trace the link further, however, we should not give up too easily the noun or the name "resistance," as if we were certain enough of its meaning to know how to recognize it in other names or descriptions. For the problem is precisely to know what we mean by resistance, as if we had a general concept of the response or the force of response we still call resistance. But whose resistance? To what? The resistance of what to what? Questions for which there would always be no end of response.

Although "Typewriter Ribbon" makes no more sustained use of the term, two of the other essays here invoke the name "resistance" with some insistence, while the remaining two texts each use the term only once or twice. In "'Le Parjure,' *Perhaps*," the essay that takes its own principal title from that of a narrative fiction, the novel by Henri Thomas, the only mention of resistance concerns narrative: "Like the 'reality' it fictionalizes, *Le Parjure* opposes an infinite or abyssal resistance to any meta-narrative" (177). Derrida affirms this right before he undertakes, or pretends to undertake, to furnish just such a meta-narrative (a "plot") of the novel, as needed for his exposition. "Infinite or abyssal resistance" says that this resistance posed or opposed by the work can only be respected (for its power of resistance is infinite), and yet this power to resist ties no one's hands, indeed it is altogether indifferent to what anyone's hands may be doing. A certain passive resistance, then, will go on working as resistance, "infinite or abyssal," no matter how little respect it is shown. We're reminded again of the phrase Derrida interjected above, as he was following out the implications of what de Man calls "text." For de Man, the literality of the letter "is the place of prosaic resistance . . . to any organic and aesthetic totalization, to any aesthetic form. *And first of all, I would say for my part, a resistance to every possible reappropriation.*" The work opposes an "infinite or abyssal resistance" to reappropriation, no matter how many meta-narratives have or will have been issued with regard to it. Given the "subject" of Thomas's novel, that is, given the real event it fictionalizes—an act of perjury by the young Paul de Man in the U.S. in the 1950s—there will have been many such meta-narratives produced in the vicinity of this resistance, which, as Derrida remarks, is no less that of the work than of the "'reality' it fictionalizes." Abyssal, infinite resistance, then, is not the property of the narrative's fictionality; or, to put it another way, "reality" depends no less on fictionality to make the truth, to impose and institute it as legal truth. The charge of perjury can be proved only against the fiction of the legal subject, the subject who has promised and sworn to speak *as if* such a subject were not a fiction but the seat of truth.

This "as if" constitutive of the legal subject, but also of the legal state, is under constant examination in all of the essays here, especially in "'Le Parjure,' *Perhaps*" and "History of the Lie." The latter text mentions resistance by name only twice, and both times the reference is specifically political or ethical: it is resistance to a state or to reasons of state. In one of these passages, Derrida has just picked up the thread of the Marrano, a name he takes here and elsewhere as a figure for absolute secrecy.[17] Or in the terms we've just been using, we could say that the Marrano is a figure of resistance to or within the fiction of the legal subject. This thread is pursued in terms that recall our earlier remark about the *oeuvre's* resistance to its own appearance or phenomenalism:

If one were to insist on an unconditional right to the secret against this phenomenalism and this integral politicism and if such an absolute secret had to remain inaccessible and invulnerable, then it would concern less the political secret than, in the metonymic and generalized figure of the Marrano, the right to secrecy as right to resistance against and beyond the order of the political, or even of the theologico-political in general. In the political order, this principle of resistance could inspire, as one of its figures, the right to what the United States names with that very fine phrase for the most respectable of traditions, in the case of *force majeure*, where the *raison d'état* does not dispense the last word in ethics: "civil disobedience." (63–64)

This mention of Thoreau's great phrase, attributed here to the country in which it was forged, will remind us not to lose sight of what we said at the beginning, namely, that we wanted to try to discern some movement of response, gestures that could have left traces on the text of what was destined first for a U.S. readership, to be heard or read in translation. In choosing the path of "resistance," we seem to have specified or qualified things, since resistance is often, as we say, a *negative* response, thus one kind of response among others. But this is to suppose that there has ever been a response that does not somewhere pose resistance, or it is to speak *as if*, once again, we knew what we meant by resistance. Yet, what else could it be that responds in a response, if not some resistance, something that resists there where it responds, *as this one and no other*. There can be response, what we call response, only where some "this one and no other" responds, that is, resists. Are we saying, then, that the movement of response we've discerned would be that of Derrida's resistance to something that is specifically being named, today, the United States?

Yes, but on the condition that we also recognize today that "United States" is the effective or practical name for the theologico-political myth we call sovereignty: it names the conjunction of forces sufficient, for the moment, to enforce the myth of its own absolute, if theologically buttressed, sovereignty. Here is how "Psychoanalysis Searches the States of Its Soul" glosses the name for us today:

I allude to America so as to indicate virtually what should be a more insistent return to what this country name designates for us here, today, whether it is a matter of the so-called globalization or worldwide-ization under way, in which American hegemony is at once obvious and more and more critical, I mean vulnerable, whether it is a matter of the Anglo-American language about to become, irresistibly, the only effectively universal language, whether it is a matter of the market in general, of teletechnics, of the principle of nation-state sovereignty, which the United States protects in an inflexible manner when it's a question of their own and limits when it's a question of others, of less powerful countries (see Arendt), whether it is a matter of the fate of Freudian psychoanalysis, more and more ostracized in the U.S., or again (and I take this to be one of the most significant signs), whether it is a matter of the convulsive crisis that this country is undergoing with regard to the death penalty. (261–62)

That it has or makes for itself a sovereign name, however, also makes the United States the name of a crisis within the myth, within the effective enforcement or imposition of its sovereignty, both domestically and in diplomatic or military theaters abroad. But, internally and externally, this is the same crisis; that is, if there is a crisis and a crisis of *sovereignty*, then it is because the distinction can no longer be made with the same confidence between domestic and foreign, national and international, internal and external, or other oppositions of the kind that suppose the very frontier at which state sovereignty can be or has been or may yet be breached. This double crisis is brought into focus here and elsewhere through the lens of the death penalty "debate,"[18] which is not a debate but a struggle for the abolition of this sovereign state violence against the lives of its citizens. As you will see, Derrida poses questions about the possibility of resistance to the sovereign myth or, as he more precisely calls it, phantasm. This does not mean and I do not mean that he questions whether one must resist, in an effective, organized way, certain sovereign impositions of the state. There is no doubting here the necessity to organize resistance against capital punishment.[19] In question, rather, is the concomitant necessity of having somehow to conceive of this resistance beyond the level of the subject or subjects, beyond performative effectivity in the world.

We have up until now seen resistance identified as the operation, the force, or the force of operation of *oeuvre*, which is not reappropriable by any subject. That is, the *oeuvre* would always somewhere be opposing a resistance to the movement of appropriation whereby the subject sustains and is sustained by its legal fiction. But resistance, we also understand, does not mean cancellation, annulment, destruction, or negation of the subject. It means resistance (whatever that means).

In the two concluding essays, Derrida also asks about the possibility of resisting the phantasm of sovereignty, sovereign mastery, and the cruelty it authorizes. This is the three-word conjunction, *sovereignty-cruelty-resistance*, put under examination in "Psychoanalysis Searches the States of Its Soul." However, before cruelty and the "cruel and unusual punishment" of the death penalty is placed at the center of this three-way soul-searching, "The University Without Condition" strongly affirms one site of possible resistance to sovereignty. This site is the university or, rather, the idea that Derrida calls the "unconditional university" or the "university without condition." In the modern, post-Enlightenment, secularized university, the research or scientific university—still essentially ours—this unconditionality operates like a principle of sovereignty, since the idea commits the university to seek autonomy or independence from any other power. But any resemblance between the university's principle of autonomy (or academic freedom) and the principle of sovereignty must also be resisted, which here it explicitly is, several times."[20] Indeed, it is this very resistance that should be unconditional in the university without condition. That is, the university in principle should be the site of unconditional resistance to every other sovereignty but that of the principle of truth. Thus it would also be a place in which the truth of sovereignty or sovereign mastery is declared a "phantasm," in Derrida's designation, for example, in this passage, which draws a first consequence of the thesis posing the university as unconditional resistance: "such an unconditional resistance could oppose the university to a great number of powers, for example, to state powers (and thus to the power of the nation-state and to its phantasm of indivisible sovereignty, which indicates how the university might be in advance not just cosmopolitan, but universal, extending beyond worldwide citizenship and the nation-state in general"; 204). Twice more in this essay sovereignty will be called a phantasm, and each time the university is appealed to as the place where that phantasm meets or should meet the unconditional resistance of the truth that is professed there. It is necessary, it will always have been necessary to distinguish and dissociate the work of the university from the operation, however powerfully it appears, of the phantasm ("it would be necessary to dissociate a certain unconditional independence of thought, of deconstruction, of justice, of the Humanities, of the University, and so forth from any phantasm of sovereign mastery"). And it would be a matter not only of a resistance in principle, but of an organized site and force of resistance at the border where indivisible sovereignty divides when it meets, not another sovereign claim, but as we should prefer to say with Derrida: its own deconstruction.

In the strongly worded next-to-last paragraph, which I am going to cite in part, the phantasm of sovereignty is one last time, I want to say denounced, but the mode here is not denunciatory. Nor is it celebratory; it is declarative, that is, affirmative. It affirms that every border between inside and outside, every sovereign border, divides. To think this deconstruction of the border affirmatively, while still saying yes to truth, this is the profession of the university of resistance, of dissidence: the university deconstructs, resists, resists by deconstructing the phantasm of the indivisible border—of the subject, the state, the nation, or any other sovereign institution. As site of resistance, the university is less a place, however, than a *doubling* or *thinking* of place, and not a geographical place, but a world, the world that the university is in *and* that it is attempting to think, at its divisible, unsovereign borders:

It is there that the university is in the world that it is attempting to think. On this border, it must therefore negotiate and organize its resistance. And take its responsibilities. Not in order to enclose itself and reconstitute the abstract phantasm of sovereignty, whose theological or humanist heritage it will perhaps have begun to deconstruct, if at least it has begun to do so. But in order to resist effectively, by allying itself with extra-academic forces, in order to organize an inventive resistance, through its *oeuvres*, its works, to all attempts at reappropriation (political, juridical, economic, and so forth), to all the other figures of sovereignty. (236)

These imperative lines come very near the end of an essay that declared, openly and at the beginning, that it was no doubt going to be like a profession of faith ("This will no doubt be *like* a profession of faith" are the first words) and that it would be presenting less a thesis than a "declarative engagement" (202). We should not neglect this performative force that the lecture engages, wants to engage, professes and declares it will engage. For this performativity will be brought forward as the mark of those *oeuvres* that the university without condition must recognize as an integral part of its professed work in the sole name of truth. But, as we said earlier, *oeuvre* or *oeuvre*-event is also in excess of the performative, in excess therefore of any instituted subject's power to make certain things happen ("I can," "I may"), within the rules of a particular performance. Performatives are not yet sufficient to produce *oeuvres*, which exceed the performative's purview. To recall the put-down line we already cited from this essay: "It is too often said that the performative produces the event of which it speaks. One must also realize that, inversely, where there is the performative, an event worthy of the name cannot arrive."

As long as the event that happens is produced or happens according to the instituted rules of a performative gesture, then the "event" they produce can never arrive as what we call an event, a *singular* event. An event is something that happens for the first time, and as a singular occurrence. An *oeuvre*-event is a work of some sort, which means it bears the mark of singularity. *Oeuvres* are signed, and this is why they are not classically included within the work of the professor, the one who professes a truth that cannot bear any one signature—unless it were the signature of God. But in the nontheological, postenlightenment university, the scientific university, truth, we profess to believe, must bear no signature, not even, especially not that of God. We cite a long paragraph from "The University Without Condition":

Certain products of this working activity are held to be objectivizable use or exchange values without deserving, it is believed, the title of *oeuvres* (I can say this word only in French). To other works, it is believed, one can attribute the name *oeuvres*. Their appropriation, their relation to liberal or salaried work, to the signature or the authority of the author, and to the market are of a great structural and historical complexity, which I will not analyze here. The first examples of *oeuvres* that come to mind are *oeuvres d'art* (visual, musical, or discursive, a painting, a concerto, a poem, a novel). But since we are interrogating the enigma of the concept of *oeuvre*, we would have to extend this field as soon as we tried to discern the type of work proper to the university and especially to the Humanities. In the Humanities, one no doubt treats in particular *oeuvres* (*oeuvres d'art*, either works of discursive art or not, literary or not, canonical or not). But in principle the treatment of works, in the academic tradition, depends on *a knowledge that itself does not consist* in *oeuvres*. To profess or to be a professor, in this tradition, which is, precisely, undergoing mutation, was no doubt to produce and to teach a knowledge even while professing, that is, even while promising to take a responsibility that is not exhausted in the act of knowing or teaching. But, in the classical-modern tradition that we are interrogating, to know how to profess or to profess a knowledge or even how to produce a knowledge is not to produce *oeuvres*. A professor, as such, does not sign an *oeuvre*. His or her authority as professor is not that of the author of an *oeuvre*, a work. It is perhaps this that has been changing over the last few decades, encountering the frequently indignant resistance and protestations of those who believe they can distinguish, in writing and in the language, between criticism and creation, reading and writing, the professor and the author, and so forth. The deconstruction under way is no doubt not unrelated to this mutation. It is even its essential phenomenon, a more complex signal than its detractors admit, one we must take into account. (217)

The argument, then, is that the idea of the professor, the professor as such, is undergoing mutation. A professor may now often be someone who signs *oeuvres*. But so what? This does not appear to be particularly new, at least not in the U.S., where long before anyone pronounced the name "deconstruction," poets and writers were working at universities, that is, they were professors of "creative writing," as it came to be called. And there have long been university departments of music, studio art, architecture, drama, and, more recently, cinema, television, media production, and now even departments of performance art. Professors in these departments are often expected not only to give instruction in the doctrine of their arts but also to practice them and to sign works. So the mutation Derrida is talking about seems to have happened some time ago, at least in the U.S., and to have already entered later "phases." These would be later at least by comparison with other university models, sponsored by or in other states. In France, as Derrida well knows, there has been strong resistance to the integration of artistic practice into the university institution. The reasons for this are complex, but the fact is that the French university, even in its most renovated parts, including the institution where Derrida has taught since 1983, the Ecole des Hautes Etudes en Sciences Sociales, continues to exclude artist-professors from its faculties.

Ever since he helped found the Group for Research on the Teaching of Philosophy in 1974, Derrida has been engaged with the French university and the politics of national education in France. He has been challenging it, like a Socratic gadfly, to lift even more conditions, not just on what can be professed, but how, and when—Greph fought hard against curtailing the number of hours of philosophy taught in high schools—where, and by whom. When he wrote the report that would become the founding document for the Collège International de Philosophie, he helped envision an institution that could lift almost every condition and still have standing as a college. In that document as well, he called for an institution that would welcome artists, performers, poets—in other words, those who can sign an *oeuvre*.[21] The point is, then, that Derrida's thinking commitment, his "declarative engagement" to and with the university without conditions, comes not just a little out of his experience there, at the deconstructing border that has just been described as where "the university is in the world that it is attempting to think." In Derrida's "world," the university will first of all have been the French one that he and others have worked to change.[22] But we cannot think the unconditional university under these conditions, that is, the conditions of a specific state or national university. And Derrida doesn't, of course; on the contrary, he emphasizes the necessary deconstruction of the concept of sovereignty, which also underwrites the idea of a national university, French, U.S., or whatever. The U.S. university, it is true, seems largely to have dealt with the question of *oeuvres* signed by professors, thus the urgency expressed here seems to have passed and to have passed without incident. So what?

Derrida's analyses appeal to be heard where once again "the university is in the world that it is attempting to think." The question then is how to hear, from within or at the dividing border of the U.S. university, the six tasks set here or the predictions made for the "new Humanities," and in particular this one:

These new Humanities would treat, in the same style, the history of profession, the profession of faith, professionalization, and the professoriat. The guiding thread could be, today, what is happening when the profession of faith, the profession of faith of the professor, gives rise not only to the competent exercise of some knowledge in which one has faith, not only . . . to the classical alliance of the constative and the performative, but to singular *oeuvres*. (233)

It may be that, given a certain institutional history, we have a particular responsibility in the U.S. to ask about this history and the place of the *oeuvre*-signing professor, to see what can become of things when, for example, poet-professors sign works of literary criticism or theory. If New Criticism instituted its effects as doctrine only because it was received as the work of knowledge, as critical knowledge about poetry or fiction, then *The Well-Wrought Urn* had to become a textbook, a book of knowledge, and even a how-to book. This could suggest at the very least that the reception of *oeuvre* in the U.S. university has not been entirely untroubled, or that it has met with resistance. The example of New Criticism is notorious and has been admirably studied, although not yet perhaps from the angle of *oeuvre* or *event* called for here.[23] I suspect, however, there are many other examples within our brief history of an *oeuvre*-signing professoriat that would confirm this tendency to appropriate *oeuvres* in the name of knowledge, and that these would be found across the disciplines, the operation of *oeuvre* having as one of its effects the lifting or suspension of the pertinence of disciplinary distinctions.

Because the reduction of *oeuvre* can take different forms (e.g., appropriation to the domain of knowledge or exclusion from it), instruments for its analysis and deconstruction must be supple. I think we have been saying, in effect, that this "enigmatic concept of *oeuvre*" is extraordinarily supple. It can in principle take account of many forms of resistance, that unclosed category, without essence or essential trait, around which this supple concept or enigma unfurls.

Let us not drop the overworked example of New Criticism, however, without acknowledging the argument made by some and repeated by many that deconstruction, at least as it has played out in North America, inherited all the faults of that American invention, to begin with, its antihistorical formalism. This "charge" has been replied to many times, but it's worth pointing out again what still seems to be at stake there. I'll take the risk of saying that what is at stake is the notion of singularity, as implied by *oeuvre* (but also event, resistance, response, etc.), which, for some reason, had to be buried under the same headstone with New Criticism. Mistaking, misrecognizing, or misreading this notion, with all its implications, historians of literary studies in the U.S. over the last five or six decades chose to take it as pointing to the formal self-identity of the work, its solipsism, and thus to the same division that, according to New Critical doctrine, *cuts* every well-wrought urn *off* from the world, in splendid, solipsistic isolation. For those who have had the task of inheriting from and in this institution, it is this solipsistic illusion that, after the New Criticism, must be undone, not repeated in a new vocabulary.

If we've insisted above on the long-standing engagement that has carried Derrida's thought to affirm, over and over, the condition of being in the world with that which one is attempting to think, it is to emphasize the importance of the misprision or the error of this translation. It is of a size to make one wonder which other-than-rational process could have produced it, somewhat the way Freud, for example, could wonder about the motives or impulses behind errors of translation, writing, or reading in *The Psychopathology of Everyday Life*. (We mention Freud, and thus psychoanalysis, for another reason that will become clear in a moment.)

It is, we've suggested, this separation or *cutting-off* that our new historians of the U.S. literary professoriat do not want to see repeated or wish not to inherit. To put it more affirmatively, they wish to preserve the link or connection between their work and the world, but also, since their work is with literary texts, between such works and the world. Theirs is the work, then, of making the connection, of *making* it happen through or in the work they do. (Derrida would remind us of the irreducible performative gesture here.) I say "theirs" and "they," but I would, of course, include myself in the category of those who at least desire to make the connection, through the work they undertake (and sign), to a world not just as it has been or as it is, but also as it appears to be becoming, as it is not yet, but as it *could be* tomorrow—to echo the third part of Derrida's original title to this lecture: "Thanks to the 'Humanities,' What *Could Take Place* Tomorrow." This modality of "could be" or "could take place," like the modality of the "perhaps" frequently invoked in these pages, ties this work to its political responsibilities in the world it is attempting to think, a world whose horizon can only be justice.[24] I would even say that the notion of *oeuvre* being elaborated here must be understood as this work of making connections to a world that *could* still be more just, that is thereby being urged or called to more justice, more justice for all, for all the living and all the dead, past and still to come.[25]

To put it still more boldly or baldly: the work of the *oeuvre* is justice and resistance to injustice.

But can one think justice, its *oeuvre*, as if there had never been a cut that incised its figure on the living and the dead, on all mortals, all who were, are, and will be mortal? The singularity of the *oeuvre* would be the way it carries or bears the mark of this mortal cut. If so, then perhaps there is a very understandable "reason" (albeit not a reason that reason could or should accept) to want to mistake this mark of mortal singular-

ity for the solipsistic illusion. In so doing, one could pretend to dispose of
this singular mode of thinking that repeats the mark of a singularity by repeating the cut. This reason could be described as, in fact, the wish to give
oneself an *alibi* for not surrendering belief, *contra* all reason, that the cut
has not already *incised* the world, given it to us with a cut-off. Among the
many relevant passages from "Typewriter Ribbon," there is one that we
should have cited earlier, since it declares clearly the engagement with
oeuvre. We saved it for here near the end, however, because it speaks so in-
cisively of a certain cut:

> We are seeking in this way to advance our research on the subject of that which
> . . . as event, requires not only an operation, an act, a performance, a *praxis*, but
> an *oeuvre*, that is, at the same time the result and the trace left by a supposed op-
> eration, an *oeuvre* that survives its supposed operation and its supposed operator.
> Surviving it, being destined to this sur-vival, to this excess over present life, the
> *oeuvre* as trace implies from the outset the structure of this sur-vival, that is, what
> *cuts* the *oeuvre* off from the operation. This *cut* assures it a sort of archival inde-
> pendence or autonomy that is quasi-machinelike (not machinelike but *quasi*-ma-
> chinelike), a power of repetition, repeatability, iterability, serial and prosthetic
> substitution of self for self. This cut is not so much effected by the machine (even
> though the machine can in fact cut and repeat the cut in its turn) as it is the con-
> dition of production for a machine. The machine is *cut* as well as *cutting* with re-
> gard to the living present of life or of the living body: it is an *effect of the cut* as
> much as it is a *cause of the cut*. (133)

That is, the *oeuvre* is the effect of the cut producing it by cutting it off
from any producer or act of production. But it is not less a *cause* of the
cut, a cause of cutting. It cuts both ways, but it *cuts*. It is the *oeuvre*'s intransitive activity of cutting (an "activity" that is more than passive, an
"infinite and abyssal resistance") that one might wish to avoid behind the
cover of an alibi. But this would have to be, in effect, an alibi *for* singularity, in the sense of *another place* which can be appealed to that puts the
accused "somewhere else" than a committed crime and its consequence,
guilt. In French, which is closer to Latin here, to be guilty is to be
coupable: literally, cut-able. Singularity is *coupable*, cuttable, because it
will always have been the trace of a mortal, singular life, with (usually) an
unknown cut-off date written into the "program."

Everybody knows this; that is, everybody knows that there is no alibi
for one's life, which remains cuttable.[26] But there would also be and has

been in that very knowledge—the knowledge of the singular cut-ability that one is or that one lives—motive enough to forget what one knows. And even to forget one has forgotten it, or forgotten it again, forgotten— but can we speak here simply of forgetting when a life of forgetting can be lived up until the very end? Does not such "forgetting" (or "not think- ing about it," as Stéphane Chalier says in *Le Parjure*) resemble what we elsewhere, in the codes, for example, of ethics, law, scientific knowledge, or philosophy, call by the names "lying," "perjury," "error," or "untruth"? Although we have just named the fields of many disciplines that might well examine this mode of "forgetting," and although these disciplines of law, philosophy, and science have had long university careers of study and research, they have not really raised the question we're asking about this resemblance. Perhaps that is because one can pose a resemblance between this "forgetting" and the other objects of science, law, ethics, politics, or philosophy only on the condition of a cut. The very notion of singularity ruins in advance whatever resemblance is held up to it, which is also how it cuts. A singularity cannot even be said to resemble itself, since it can- not be in two places at once and remain the singularity it is. It remains, in other words, always "without alibi." This troubling phrase, which seems to pose already the guilt that it will always be unable to disprove, itself says the ruin, the ruin of resemblance, but also speaks of the threat of ruin posed everywhere to the sense of resemblance, that is, all the sense that can be made by presuming resemblance.

If indeed these disciplines of law, philosophy, and the sciences have largely ignored questions that can be raised about this presumption, if they have not seen fit to interrogate this "as if," is that because they have "forgotten" it, in this odd sense of "not thinking about it," or do they have a good reason, a reason that is not an alibi, as we say when we don't fully believe the excuse? Is this not a valid question, and if not, why not? If it is valid, then it has a place in the university, where it can be asked with impunity and without alibi.

Derrida will certainly be heard as saying that the place where this question of the "as if" can be asked is, in the university, its Humanities division, and especially literary studies. He says this quite explicitly many times in the course of this lecture. But there might be some in- terference on the line if one also heard these affirmations as identifying a privilege other than the one that he has always acknowledged for lit- erature or fiction: the right to say anything or to say nothing, with impunity, without guilt.[27] This privilege is always identified with the very concept of democracy ("democracy-to-come"), and as such it is conferred by that concept and not by some inherent or immanent value-in-itself, which is the status that has been reserved elsewhere for the *oeuvre d'art.*

"The university without conditions does not, in fact, exist, as we know only too well" (204). That is, we know only too well that conditions remain to be lifted from the university, at least if it is to continue to deconstruct the phantasm of sovereignty. And this will indeed be the task of the university today, the task of resisting and surviving all the threats of takeover by so-called sovereign entities. But if the survival of this institution has mattered up until now, that is because it has also meant the surviving or the *sur-vivance* of the work of justice, democracy, and the principle of unconditional truth. In that context, we would be heard asking other urgent questions about the conditions that remain to be lifted from the kind of truth professors may profess to believe, perhaps especially in the U.S. university.

We *would* be heard asking these questions, I said—a tense of the conditional that, in English, has more uses than just posing conditions. It may also serve, for example, to speak in a mode of wish or command or desire for this or that to *be* true: we can thus say "I would that," for instance, "I would that he would come back," or even "I would that he comes back," as if the very force of the wish or command could make something *be* the case, in the present indicative, where another language—French, for example—might need a subjunctive: *Je veux qu'il revienne.*

I am going to take advantage of just this ambiguous mode, modality, or modification to bring to a close this already overlong introduction. What *would* it allow us to say, in conclusion?

A few final words, perhaps, concerning the movement of response, in Derrida's work, in particular the trace of its engagement with U.S. universities.

As you will notice, there is a relative silence regarding psychoanalysis in "The University Without Condition." It is mentioned by name only twice, and once that name is enclosed in parentheses. In the first instance, Derrida is spelling out how the principial right to say everything, the unconditional principle of truth, "distinguishes the university institution from other institutions founded on the right or the duty to say everything, for example religious confession and even psychoanalytic 'free association'" (205). In the second occurrence, however, Derrida speaks of psychoanalysis in general and not just one of its truth techniques. But it is also mentioned this time only within parentheses, and as subsumed into a formation, also called an "original articulation": "This new concept of the Humanities, even as it remains faithful to its tradition, should include law, 'legal studies,' as well as what is called in this country, where this formation originated, 'theory' (an original articulation of literary theory, philosophy, linguistics, psychoanalysis, and so forth)." (208).

Now, this formation in parentheses appears to do nothing more than reflect back onto itself "what is called" theory and to do so right there "in this country where this formation originated." But at the same time it has to reflect the place where psychoanalysis has been, in effect, smuggled back into the U.S. university. "Smuggled," because, as we know very well, psychoanalysis has always been contraband in the university, and not just in the U.S. The truths it considers, including famously that of a singular "forgetting," are banned there by scientific truth, which would be or would promise to be general.

After this parenthetical reflection, there is no more mention of psychoanalysis by that name. However, the multiple references we've already noted to "phantasm" and specifically to the phantasm of sovereign mastery indicate clearly enough that, for Derrida, psychoanalytic categories are still very much in force. A "phantasm" is not the same thing as what we call either "lie," "perjury," "error," or "mistake," although it is, like these, a form of untruth or falsity. Nor can we fill in this conceptual gap with the philosophically incoherent figure that Hannah Arendt, like many others, wants to call "lying to oneself." One cannot admit such a concept into philosophy, Derrida insists, without ruining the very seat of the true lie, the subject—that which cannot lie to itself, but only to another and in order to deceive another.[28]

No doubt Derrida could have been more direct if he had wanted to point out how the absence of or the limited play given to psychoanalysis conditions the work of the university as a negative capability—if, in other words, he had wanted to make apparent how this absence conditions and limits the university as the place in which this thing called phantasm *cannot* be properly examined. Or else as the place where it can be examined only as the contraband or with the alibi of literature. Having said this, however, let us not be heard taking anyone to task for not speaking more directly of this resistance to psychoanalysis in the university. Certainly not Derrida, who probably couldn't even dream of speaking or writing, about the university or anything else, without admitting the pertinence of psychoanalysis for what he is saying. But this means, precisely, that one cannot easily suppose that he has forgotten to mention it, not just because he *does* mention it in very precise locations or formations, as we've just seen, but also because this would be an unaccountable omission for someone who manifestly believes—has believed—that psychoanalysis *as such*, in its own formation, belongs to the university without conditions.

In 1968–69, when, along with Hélène Cixous and others, Derrida helped to write and institute the charter of a new French university, Paris-Vincennes, this belief could put in place that university's famous department of psychoanalysis. Likewise, after that experiment failed or was forced to close down, Derrida made sure that Lacan and other professors of psychoanalysis could continue to profess from within the precincts of the university. The point of recalling such facts is not just to remark, once again, Derrida's ongoing engagement with the university at its borders. They also highlight why it is that the very measured or muted mentions of psychoanalysis in "The University Without Condition" sound like a silence and not just a "forgetting," not even the forgetting called repression. Yet, and here's the thing, it's a silence or a muting that can also be heard *responding* to a repression imposed by the other, first of all by the other on itself.

I admit that this configuration is very difficult to discern in its negative form, where, as in a photographic negative, figures are manifested only in silhouette and reversed. In the subsequent lecture, and with the direct address to the state or the States of psychoanalysis in the world, this picture is, as it were, developed. But I find it is possible to wonder whether this very development did not have to await the change of address that "Psychoanalysis Searches the States of Its Soul" introduces into our volume. Consider, for example, how the strange statement "Freud is dead in America" is cited here in this address to psychoanalysts, in France and in French. It is a strange statement or assertion because it is, as I said, cited, repeated: Derrida is citing and repeating Elisabeth Roudinesco, the well-known historian of psychoanalysis in France, who has said and written that "Freud is dead in America." In this, however, she only repeats what she had found and heard and been told in America—where "Freud is dead" (not *l'homme*, of course, but *l'oeuvre*). This repetition and citation makes any address of the statement *indirect* at any and every destination including the first one, the States General of Psychoanalysis, or now, in translation in the States. Yet, even if such indirection has been generalized or made irreducible by this repetition,[29] would there not remain a particular call to responsibility and response "in America," which would be a call, in effect, to question the statement's "truth"?

Suspending just this question, let us leave this anticipated scene to the responsibility of its future readers. They will judge for themselves whether and how taking up the "truth" of the statement "Freud is dead in America" requires engagement with the phantasmatic "truth" of the sovereignty that underwrites or alibis the death penalty, also still in America—where "Freud is dead." For them, for you, then, to determine whether this engagement and resistance would have to follow if one follows Derrida when he writes:

The only discourse that can today claim the thing of psychical suffering as its own affair would indeed be what has been called, for about a century, psychoanalysis. Psychoanalysis would perhaps not be the only possible language or even the only possible treatment regarding this cruelty that has no contrary term or no end. But "psychoanalysis" would be the name of that which, without theological or other alibi, would be turned toward what is most *proper* to psychical cruelty. Psychoanalysis, for me, if I may be permitted yet another confidential remark, would be another name for the "without alibi." (240)

What would it mean to be able to pronounce a work, an *oeuvre*, dead? And one whose name, "Freud" or "psychoanalysis," can be synonymous, if only in a single idiom, with the "without alibi"? More questions that I will leave suspended for you.

Will we, then, have traced a movement of response? Or have we done nothing but inventory terms that acquire a certain force through these essays, which engage them into a powerfully resistant discourse? Event, *oeuvre*, text-machine, the "as if," resistance, profession, deconstruction, as well as truth and unconditionality—without alibi and without conditions.[30] Are we saying that these are all words of *response*? Yes, no doubt. But whose?

Well, I would that the answer finds you and, when it does, that your resistance is awake.

LOS ANGELES
JUNE, 2001

§ 1
History of the Lie: Prolegomena

Before even a preface or an epigraph, allow me to make two confessions. Which I must therefore ask you, without waiting, to believe.

Two confessions, also two concessions that, although they are sincere, will nonetheless say something about the fabulous and the phantasmatic, more precisely, about what we understand by fable and phantasm, namely, the return of some specter. As we know, *phantasma* also named for the Greeks the apparition of the specter, the vision of the phantom, or the phenomenon of the revenant. The fabulous and the phantasmatic have a feature in common: *stricto sensu*, in the classical and prevalent sense of these terms, they do not pertain to either the true or the false, the veracious or the mendacious. They are related, rather, to an irreducible species of the simulacrum or even of simulation, in the penumbral light of a virtuality that is neither being nor nothingness, nor even an order of the possible that an ontology or a mimetology could account for or subdue with reason. No more than myth, fable and phantasm are doubtless not truths or true statements as such, but neither are they errors or deceptions, false witnesses or perjuries.

The first conceded confession touches on the proposed title: "History of the Lie." By a slight displacement, by slipping one word in beneath another, it seems to mimic the famous title of a text that some years ago very much interested me. In *The Twilight of the Idols*, Nietzsche gives the title "History of an Error" ("Geschichte eines Irrtum") to a sort of narrative in six episodes that, on a single page, recounts, in effect, and no less, the true world, the history of the "true world" (*die wahre Welt*). The title of this fictive narrative announces the narration of a fabrication: "How the 'true world' finally becomes a fable" ("Wie die 'wahre Welt' endlich zur Fabel wurde"). It is not, then, a fable that is going to be told, but rather the story of how a fable fabricated itself, so to speak. The teller is going to proceed *as if* a true story were possible on the subject of the history of this fabrication, a fabrication that produces, precisely, nothing other than the idea of a true world—which risks hijacking the supposed truth of the narration: "How the 'true world' finally becomes a fable." "History of an error" is only a subtitle. This fabulous narration about a fabulation, about the truth as fabrication, is a *coup de théâtre*. It puts on stage some characters who will remain more or less present, like specters, in the wings: first Plato, who says, according to Nietzsche, "I Plato, I *am* the truth," then the Christian promise in the form of a woman, then the Kantian imperative, "the pale Koenigsbergian idea," then the positivistic cock's crow, and finally the Zarathustrian midday. We will call upon all these specters again, but we will also call on another, whom Nietzsche does not name: Saint Augustine. It is true that the latter, in his two great treatises on lying (*De mendacio* and *Contra mendacium*), is always in dialogue with Saint Paul, Nietzsche's most intimate enemy and the privileged adversary of his ferocity.

Although the memory of this fabulous text will remain with us, the history of the lie cannot be the history of an error, not even an error in the constitution of the true, in the very history of the truth as such. In Nietzsche's polemical and ironic text, in the vein of this fable about a fabrication, the truth, the idea of a "true world," would be an "error." Even in his "Theoretical Introduction to Truth and Lie in an Extramoral Sense," a text to which we will return later, Nietzsche continues to pose or to suppose some continuity between the error and the lie, thus between the true and the veracious, which allows him to treat the lie in the neutrality of an extramoral sense, as a theoretical and epistemological problem. This gesture is neither illegitimate nor without interest, but we will come back to it only after having taken account of the irreducibly ethical dimension of the lie, where the *phenomenon* of the lie as such is intrinsically foreign to the problem of knowledge, truth, the true, and the false. This evening, I would like to take a few steps toward the abyss that opens between this ethical dimension and a certain political history of the lie.

In principle and in its classical determination, a lie is not an error. One can be in error or mistaken without trying to deceive and therefore without lying. It is true, however, that lying, deceiving, and being mistaken are all three included in the category of the pseudological. In Greek, *pseudos* can mean lie as well as falsehood, cunning, or mistake, and deception or fraud as well as poetic invention, which increases the possible misunderstanding about what a misunderstanding may mean—and does not simplify the interpretation of a "refutative" dialogue as dense and sharp as the *Hippias Minor* (*ē peri tou pseudous, anatreptikos*). The common translation of the subtitle, *ē peri tou pseudous*, by "On the Lie" is, to be sure, neither a lie nor an error but already a reductive decision, and thus it falsifies. *Pseudos* does not mean merely "lie," and, what is more, this extraordinary dialogue complicates rather a lot the question of the relation between lying and the doubles, analogues, or false friends that it might hide in its folds, at least virtually, everything that I am getting ready to say this evening, including all that refers to the most modern political history. Distinguishing between several senses of the word *pseudos*, at least three of them (in things, *pragma*; in the utterance, *logos*; and in man, *anthrōpos*— and this is the lie), Aristotle already contested, in the *Metaphysics* (Δ, 29) many of the theses of the *Hippias Minor*, including the one according to which the liar (*pseudēs*) is the one who has the faculty to lie. Aristotle specifies, and this is the essential thing as far as we are concerned, that the liar is not only whoever can lie but the one who prefers to lie and, being so inclined, does it by choice, intentionally (*ho eukherēs kai proairetikos*), for which reason—and this is another objection to Plato—he is worse than the involuntary liar, if such a thing exists.

To this kind of Aristotelian pseudography, and under the title "The Aristotelian Determination of the *Logos*," Heidegger devotes a few pages in a Marburg seminar from 1923–24. Perhaps I will return to it, but I note in the meantime that if the theme of the lie as such was not subsequently given a major place, for example, in the analytic of *Dasein* in *Being and Time*—for reasons that it would be interesting and necessary to analyze— well, in 1923–24, no doubt already beyond a simple anthropology, a theory of the *ego* or of consciousness, a psychology or a morality, Heidegger says of *Dasein* that it "bears within itself the possibilities for deceit and lying [*Das Dasein trägt in sich selbst dies Möglichkeiten der Täuschung und der Lüge*]." Before that he had written: "The *Dasein* of speech—of speaking [*das Dasein des Sprechens*] bears within it the possibility of deceit."

It is also true that Nietzsche seems to suspect Platonism or Christianity, Kantianism and positivism of having *lied* when they tried to get us to believe in a "true world." But the fact remains that, if we limit ourselves, as we must do to start, to what ordinary language as well as philosophy *mean to say*, if we rely on this *meaning-to-say*, to lie *does not mean to say* in general to be mistaken or to make an error. One can be mistaken, one can be in error without lying; one can communicate to another some false information without lying. If I believe what I say, even if it is false, even if I am wrong, and if I am not trying to mislead someone by communicating this error, then I am not lying. One does not lie simply by saying what is false, so long as one believes in good faith in the truth of what one believes or assents to in one's opinions. It is the question of faith and of good faith that we must treat this evening. Saint Augustine recalls this at the opening of *De menda-cio*.[1] He proposes there, moreover, a distinction between belief and opinion that could still have great pertinence for us today, in a new way. To lie is *to want* to deceive the other, sometimes even by saying what is true. One can speak falsely without lying, but one can also say what is true with the aim of deceiving someone, in other words, while lying. But one does not lie if one believes what one says even if it is false. By declaring that "the person who utters a falsehood does not lie if he believes or, at least, is of the opin-ion that what he says is true," Saint Augustine seems to exclude the lie to oneself, the "being-mistaken" as "lie to oneself." Here is a question that will stay with us from now on out and that later we will have to evaluate for its properly political sense: Is it possible to lie to oneself, and does every kind of self-deception, every ruse with oneself, deserve to be called a lie? In a word, how is one to understand the expression *se tromper*, whose idiom is so rich and equivocal in French? Lie to oneself or error?

It is difficult to believe that the lie has a history. Who would dare to tell the history of the lie? And who could promise to tell it as a true story? Even supposing, *concesso non dato*, that the lie has a history, one would still have to be able to tell it without lying. And without giving in too quickly, too easily, to a conventionally dialectical schema whereby the his-tory of error, as history and work of the negative, would be made to con-tribute to the process of truth, to the *verification* of the truth in view of absolute knowledge. If there is a history of the lie, that is, of false witness and of perjury (for every lie is a perjury), and if this history touches on some radicality of evil named "lie" or "perjury," then, on the one hand, it cannot let itself be reappropriated by a history of error or of the truth in the "extramoral" sense. On the other hand, although the lie supposes, or so it seems, the deliberate invention of a fiction, nevertheless not all fiction or fable amounts to lying—and neither does literature.

In the "Fourth Reverie" of *The Reveries of the Solitary Walker*, which is another great "pseudology," another abyssal treatise on lying and fiction that we should consider with infinite patience, Rousseau proposes a whole taxonomy of lies (imposture, fraud, calumny, which remains the worst), and he recalls that a lie that hurts neither oneself nor another, an innocent lie, does not deserve to be called a lie; it is, he says, a "fiction."[2] Such a "fiction" would no more be a lie, according to him, than the dissimulation of a truth that one is not obligated to divulge. This dissimulation, which includes a simulation, poses other problems for Rousseau. If instead of being satisfied with not divulging, with silencing a truth that is not owed, someone also said the contrary, "Is he then lying or not?" Rousseau asks this before replying: "According to the definition, we could not say that he lies; for if he gives counterfeit money to a man to whom he owes nothing, he undoubtedly deceives this man, but he does not rob him." Which means that the definition that would exempt him from lying is no good. If he deceives, even if he does not steal, he lies, Kant would say, for according to him truth is always owed as soon as one addresses others. We will get to this is a moment, but we should extend this fiduciary association, if I can put it that way, between lying and money or even counterfeit money. I am not speaking only of all the discourses on counterfeit money that are *ipso facto* discourses on lying, but of the counterfeit money that often arises in definitions of the lie. This association is significant and constant, from Montaigne to Rousseau and even to Freud, who eroticizes it in a striking way in a little text from 1913 titled "Zwei Kinderlügen": one of his patients identifies, not by chance, with the figure of Judas, who betrayed for money.

After having proliferated distinctions that are as subtle as they are necessary, after having insisted on the fact that, in his profession of "veracity," "forthrightness," and "fairness," he had followed the "moral directions" of his "conscience" more than "abstract notions of true and false," Rousseau nevertheless does not consider his account closed. He still confesses, he admits that these conceptual distinctions unfold their theoretical subtlety only to exonerate him from a more inadmissible lie, as if the theoretical discourse on lying was yet one more lying strategy, an unavowable technique of disculpation, an unforgivable ruse by which theoretical reason deceives practical reason and silences the heart: "I do not, however, feel my heart to be sufficiently satisfied with these distinctions as to believe myself entirely irreprehensible."[3] But this last, this next-to-last remorse does not concern only the inexhaustible duty to be truthful with others; it also turns in the direction of a duty to oneself. Rousseau as well seems sensitive to this possibility of lying to oneself, which will define today both the magnetic field and the line of division of our problematic. Is there a lie to oneself? Is it possible to lie to oneself, that is, at the same time to tell oneself intentionally something other than what one knows one thinks in truth—which seems absurd and impracticable—and to do so in order to hurt oneself, to damage oneself by acting thus at one's own expense, which supposes a duty to oneself as to another? Rousseau does not exclude this madness because at the point at which he says he is not satisfied, in his "heart," with these "distinctions," he adds: "In weighing so carefully what I owed others, have I sufficiently examined what I owed myself? If it is necessary to be just to others, it is necessary to be true to oneself: that is an homage an honest man should render to his own dignity." Rousseau goes even further in the confession of the inexcusable. He does not end up merely confessing this or that lie, or even this or that fiction, invented, he says, to "supplement" the sterility of his "conversation"; he judges himself "inexcusable" by reason of the very motto that he had chosen, a motto that is so inflexible that it should have excluded not only lying but also fable and fiction. And this, no matter what the cost to him, for this ethics of veracity is always a sacral ethics of sacrifice.[4] Rousseau speaks of it, in fact, in a code of consecration and a sacrificial lexicon.

But one can already imagine countless fictive histories of the lie, countless inventive discourses devoted to simulacrum, to fable, and to the production of new forms on the subject of the lie, which nevertheless would not be deceitful histories, that is, if we may rely on the *classical and dominant* concept of the lie, untrue histories or stories, but innocent, inoffensive ones, simulacra unsullied by perjury and false witness. Why not tell histories of the lie that, without being true, do no harm? Fabulous histories of the lie that, doing harm to no one, might give pleasure here or there, or even do some people some good?

You might ask me why I invoke here, with so much insistence, a *classical and dominant* concept of the lie. And why, as I do so, I orient reflection as much toward what "classical and dominant" may mean, in their concept, as toward the stakes, singularly the political stakes, today, of what we continue to call by this old name, the "lie." Is there, practically and theoretically, a prevalent concept of the lie in our culture? Why recall right away the features of this concept? I am going to formalize these features, in my own fashion, which I hope is true, correct, and adequate—for the thing is not so simple, and if I am wrong, it would not be a lie unless I did it on purpose, unless I said deliberately something other than what I think I think, and especially unless it hurt someone in some way, myself or another. It will be difficult, I will even venture to say *impossible* to prove that I did it on purpose. I underscore this merely to announce right away a hypothesis, namely: for structural reasons, it will always be impossible to *prove*, in the strict sense, that someone has lied even if one can prove that he or she did not tell the truth. One will never be able to prove anything against the person who says, "What I said is not true; I was wrong, to be sure, but I did not mean to deceive; I am in good faith," or, alleging the always possible difference between the said, the saying, and the meaning-to-say, the effects of language, rhetoric, and context: "I said that, but that is not what I meant to say; in good faith, in my heart of hearts, that was not my intention; there has been a misunderstanding." One will never be able to prove anything that overturns such an allegation, and we must draw the consequences of this. They are formidable and without limit.

Here, then, is a definition of the traditional definition of the lie, as I believe I must formulate it here. In its prevalent form, recognized by everyone, the lie is not a fact or a state; it is an *intentional* act, a lying. There is not *the* lie, but rather this saying or this meaning-to-say that is called lying. We should not ask ourselves "What is a lie?" but rather "What does a lying do, and, first of all, what does it want?" To lie would be to address oneself to another (for one lies only to the other; one cannot lie to oneself, unless it is to oneself as another), in order to direct his way a statement or more than one statement, a series of statements (constative or performative) that the liar knows, consciously, in explicit, thematic, current consciousness, form assertions that are totally or partially false. This knowledge, science, and consciousness [*conscience*] are indispensable to the act of lying, and the presence-to-itself of this knowledge must concern not only the content of what is *said* but the content of what is *owed* to the other, in such a way that the lying appears fully to the liar as a betrayal, a wrong, a falling short in a debt or a duty. The liar must know what he is doing and means to do by lying; otherwise he does not lie. One must insist right away on this plurality and on this complexity, even on this heterogeneity. These *intentional* acts are destined to the other, an other or others, with the aim of deceiving them, harming them, misleading them, before any other consequence, by the simple fact of *making* them *believe* what the liar knows to be false. This dimension of making believe, of belief, credit, faith, is irreducible, even if it remains obscure. The bad faith of the liar, his betrayal of an at least implicit sworn faith, consists in surprising the good faith of his addressee by *making* him *believe* what is said, where this making believe harms the other, damages him, or operates at his expense, where the liar, for his part, is supposed, by an explicit commitment, an oath, or an at least implicit promise, to tell the whole truth and only the truth. What matters here, in the first and last place, is thus the intention. Saint Augustine also underscored this point: there is no lie, whatever one may say, without the intention, the desire, or the explicit will to deceive (*fallendi cupiditas, voluntas fallendi*).[5] This intention, which defines veracity and lying in the order of *saying* or the act of saying, remains independent of the truth or falsity of the content, of what is *said*. The lie pertains to the saying, and to the meaning-to-say, not to the said: "He who does not know that what he says is false does not lie if he thinks it is true, but he does lie who tells the truth when he thinks it is false, because persons must be judged according to their deliberate intention [*ex anima sui*]."[6]

This definition seems at once clear and distinct, obvious, a platitude even—and yet overdetermined to infinity. It is a labyrinth where one can take a wrong turn at every step. We will need each of its elements for our analysis. It would demand of us—but for obvious reasons we will fall short of this demand—that we treat directly the essence of the will, intentionality, intentional consciousness and its presence to itself. The question of the lie should also be a guiding thread for a reflection on the essence and the history of intentionality, the will, consciousness, self-presence, and so forth. We will of course keep this in reserve. This reserve is imposed on us not only by the limited time at our disposal. It is also because, however difficult this may be, we must preserve a concept of the lie that has about it something unrefined, square, rigid, unpretentiously solid, if we do not wish to dissolve it, that is, to liquidate it in the torrential flux of undecidable half-tints that makes up our experience: half-lies, quarter-lies, lies that are not altogether lies because they slide very quickly into the shadow zone between the voluntary and the involuntary, the intentional and the unintentional, the conscious, subconscious, and unconscious, presence and absence to oneself, ignorance and knowledge, good faith and its twilight of bad faith, between what is useful and harmful to the other, the "who knows whether this lie will not be useful to the development of the truth, or even to a veracity that is hierarchically more important and in whose name I must bend it?" If, albeit for reasons of conceptual finesse and rigor, I engaged the concept of the lie in all the mobile and fluid folds of this complication, this theoretical or phenomenological demand would risk—and we will return to this risk—losing sight of a classical defining edge of the lie, which is no doubt difficult to delimit, but without which no ethics, no right or law, and no politics would survive. For these need, in their fundamental axiomatics, references that are as perfunctory but also as decidable as the oppositions between mendacity and veracity, good and bad faith, and so forth. I propose calling this square, decidable, indispensable but also unrefined and brutal concept of the lie the *frank concept* of the lie, the frontal and cutting frankness (even if, at the moment of its enfranchisement from every other consideration, its phenomenon remains, in all purity, unlocatable, unprovable, inaccessible to a theoretical and determinant judgment). Among the immense difficulties that would still disturb this frank definition, we must recall at least two, which both have to do with a certain silence. This is, first, that of a certain keeping silent, a dissimulation, or even a silent simulation, which we have already mentioned and about which it is difficult to know if a finite language can ever be done with it in order to acquit itself of a "tell-the-whole-truth-and-nothing-but-the-truth." Our beloved Montaigne already said it all concerning this impossibility to say it all, this indefiniteness of the lie: "If a lie, like truth, had only one face we could be on better terms, for certainty would be the reverse of what the liar said. But the reverse side of truth has a hundred thousand shapes and no defined limits."[7]

But there is above all the question of whether, as I rather quickly asserted a moment ago, the lie, even the frank lie, always consists in a declarative utterance. Without even opening the immense, problematic vein of simulation or dissimulation among "animals," whose language does not pass by way of what we call words, what is the relation to the discourse (implicit or explicit) of silent manifestations destined to deceive the other, sometimes with the worst, sometimes with the best intentions? Can one recognize a lie in the politeness of an affected smile, the ellipsis of a look, or a gesture of the hand? Is the whole literature on faked orgasm, which today would fill several libraries, a literature on the

lie, even the serviceable, generous, officious lie (*mendacium officiosum*), if
this feint of orgiastic ecstasy can remain silent or at least not articulated
in words? Not to mention that this feint can fictionalize only in a performative register that is at once *at the heart of* and *exterior to* any concept of the lie. Inside and outside, and here is the whole difficulty with
this topology of the lie, within which I have nevertheless, with temerity
and naively, decided to try to remain this evening. The lie includes a
manifestation of the performative type, since it implies a promise of
truth where it betrays it, and since it also aims to create an event, to produce an effect of belief where there is nothing to state or at least where
nothing is exhausted in a statement. But, simultaneously, this performativity implies reference to values of reality, truth, and falsity that are presumed not to depend on performative decision. This jurisdiction of the
lie *versus* veracity, namely of an experience that is itself a performative
one, including constative claims, thus excludes all performative experi-
ences regarding which the true/false distinction has no pertinence, for
example, to limit ourselves to just this indication, prayer (*eukhē*), which
Aristotle already said is neither true nor false. Whether or not prayer or
imprecation has a delimitable space within language, which I don't believe, one sees the enormous and impracticable exclusion that would
have to be practiced in order to isolate rigorously a frank zone of the lie,
a zone in which the frank concept of the lie would come to find decidable frontiers.

If I have insisted on a massive fact, namely, that this unrefined, square,
solid, decidable, in a word *frank* definition of the lie delimits a *prevalent*
concept in our culture, it is first of all because no ethics, no law or right,
no politics could long withstand, precisely in our culture, its pure and
simple disappearance. We must recall this, know it, and, beyond knowledge, think it. I also insist on it so as to improve the chances of the hypothesis that such a concept—prescribed by a culture, by a religious or
moral tradition, perhaps by more than one legacy, a multiplicity of languages and so forth—that such a concept, then, itself had a history, one
that is not only ethico-philosophical but also juridical and political.

Here, then, are a first and then a second complication: if what is apparently the most common concept of the lie, if good sense concerning
the frank lie has a history, then it is caught up in a becoming that risks always relativizing its authority and value. But, second complication, we
also have to distinguish between the history of the concept of the lie and

a history of the lie itself, a history and a culture that affect the practice of the lie, the manners, motivations, techniques, means, and effects of the lie. Within a single culture, where a self-identical and identifiable concept of the lie would reign without division, the social experience, the interpretation, the operation of lying can change. Lying can give rise to another historicity, an internal historicity of the lie. Assuming that we have at our disposal, in our so-called Western tradition (Jewish, Greek, Christian, Roman, Islamic), a unified, stabilized, and therefore reliable concept of the lie, it would not be enough to grant it an intrinsically theoretical historicity, namely, that which would distinguish it from other concepts in other histories and other cultures; one would also have to examine the hypothesis of a practical, social, political, juridical, technical historicity, which would have transformed it, or even marked it with ruptures within our tradition.

It is to this latter hypothesis that I would like to grant some provisional privilege here. But will it ever be possible to distinguish among the following *three things*, namely: (1) a history (*Historie*) of the concept of the lie, (2) a history (*Geschichte*) of the lie, made up of all the events that have happened *to the* lie or *by way of* the lie and, finally, (3) a true history that orders the narrative (*Historie, historia rerum gestarum*) of these lies or of the lie in general? How is one to dissociate or alternate these three tasks? We must not ever overlook this difficulty.

Still, before getting to the epigraphs, before even beginning to begin, I must make a second confession. You would have every right to distrust it, as you would with any confession. By reason of all sorts of limits, in particular the strictly assigned limits of time, I will not say everything, not even the essential part of what I may think about a history of the lie. That I do not say the whole truth about a history of the lie, this will not surprise anyone. But I will not say even the whole truth of what I myself, today, am able to think or to testify to concerning a history of the lie and the manner, altogether different, in which, according to me, it would be necessary to listen to or to tell this history. I will not say, therefore, the whole truth of what I think. My testimony will be lacunary. Am I guilty of this? Does this mean that I will have lied to you? I leave this question suspended, I turn it over to you, at least until the discussion period and doubtless beyond that.

By way of epigraph, two fragmentary quotations will now have to watch over these prolegomena. We will first hear from two thinkers whose memory we must honor here. Their memory inhabits this institution. The first epigraph concerns a certain historicity of the lie, the other the sacredness or sanctity of the truth, outside of which it is impossible to condemn or even to determine that there is a lie. The lie has no sense and the interdiction that institutes its concept would be unthinkable outside of this sacral horizon, without this "sacred name of truth," as Rousseau says in the same *Reverie*, which also celebrates "holy truth."[8] Far from being content to tell a certain history, each of these two fragments reflects in its glow a paradoxical and strange *historicity*.

Historicity of the lie, to begin with. That politics is a privileged space of lying is well known, as Hannah Arendt recalls more than once:

> Lies have always been regarded as necessary and justifiable tools not only of the politician's or the demagogue's but also of the statesman's trade. Why is that so? And what does it mean for the nature and the dignity of the political realm, on one side, and the dignity of truth and truthfulness, on the other?[9]

This is how "Truth and Politics" begins; its first English version appeared in 1967 in the *New Yorker* magazine and was a response to a journalistic polemic that had followed the publication of *Eichmann in Jerusalem*. As we all know, Hannah Arendt, in her own way, had taken on the mission of journalist at the Eichmann trial. She then denounced numerous lies and falsifications concerning her of which the press, in particular, had been guilty. She recalls this context in the first note to "Truth and Politics." She thereby points to an effect of the media, and she does so in a highly regarded magazine, the *New Yorker*. I underscore without delay the dimension of the media, the places of publication, and the magazine titles, both New York and international publications, for reasons that will continue, I hope, to become clear. It is in the *New York Review of Books* of the period (for this magazine also has a history and Hannah Arendt wrote frequently for it) that she published some years later, in 1971, "Lying in Politics: Reflections on the Pentagon Papers." As for the "Pentagon Papers," the secret documents that then Secretary of Defense Robert McNamara commissioned on American policy in Vietnam from the Second World War to 1968, they themselves had been published by another newspaper, the *New York Times*, which is also both a New York paper and an international paper. Speaking of what was "in the minds of those who compiled *The Pentagon Papers* for the New York *Times*," Hannah Arendt specifies:

The famous credibility gap, which has been with us for six long years, has suddenly opened up into an abyss. The quicksand of lying statements of all sorts, deceptions as well as *self-deceptions* [I emphasize "self-deceptions," which will be
one of our problems later on: Is "self-deception" possible? Is it a rigorous and pertinent concept for what interests us here, that is, the history of the lie? In strictest
terms, does one ever lie to oneself?], is apt to engulf any reader who wishes to
probe this material, which, unhappily, he must recognize as the infrastructure of
nearly a decade of United States foreign and domestic policy.[10]

If history, especially political history, is full of lies, as everyone knows,
how could the lie *itself* have a history? How could the lie—which is such
a common experience, whose structure is apparently so simple, whose
possibility is as universal as it is timeless—have a history that is intrinsic
and essential to it? How could this lie, the experience of which seems so
common, whose structure seems apparently so obvious, and whose possibility seems as universal as it is atemporal, have a history? Yet Hannah
Arendt, once again in "Truth and Politics," draws our attention to a *mutation* in the history of the lie. This mutation would be at work in the history of both the *concept* and the *practice* of lying. Only in our modernity,
according to Arendt, has the lie attained its absolute limit and become
complete and final. Ascension and triumph of the lie. Oscar Wilde had
complained, in days gone by, of what he called—and this was the title of
a famous text—"the decay of lying" in the arts and letters, a decay that he
diagnoses among politicians, lawyers, and even journalists, who know less
and less how to lie, who no longer cultivate the art of lying, for lying is an
art whose salvation should be entrusted to artists and first of all to the art
of discourse, literature, which is likewise threatened by this decadence.
Well, where Wilde deplores an agony of the lie, Hannah Arendt, on the
contrary, diagnoses in the political arena a hyperbolic growth of the lie, its
hypertrophy, its passage to the extreme, in short, the absolute lie: not absolute knowledge as the end of history, but history as conversion to the
absolute lie.

How are we to understand this?

Such completeness and potential finality, which were unknown to former times,
are the dangers that arise out of the modern manipulation of facts. Even in the
free world, where the government has not monopolized the power to decide and
tell what factually is or is not, gigantic interest organizations have generalized a
kind of *raison d'état* frame of mind such as was formerly restricted to the han-

dling of foreign affairs and, in its worst excesses, to situations of clear and present danger. And national propaganda on the government level has learned more
than a few tricks from business practices and Madison avenue methods. (TP, 255)

It would be tempting but somewhat facile to oppose, like two ends of
history, the negative concept of this evil, the absolute lie, to the positivity
of absolute knowledge, whether in the major mode (Hegel) or the minor
mode (Fukuyama). One could doubtless be suspicious about this notion
of the absolute lie given what it still supposes of absolute knowledge, in
an element that remains that of reflexive self-consciousness. By definition,
the liar knows the truth, if not the whole truth, at least the truth of what
he thinks, he knows what he *means to say*, he knows the difference between what he thinks and what he says: he knows that he is lying. This essential link between knowing, knowledge, self-consciousness, and lying
was already professed and played with by Socrates in the other major text
in our tradition on the subject of lying, the *Hippias Minor* (*ē peri tou
pseudous*). If it must operate in consciousness and in its concept, then the
absolute lie of which Arendt speaks risks being once again the other face
of absolute knowledge.

Elsewhere in the same article, two examples taken from European politics restage "lies" of the modern type. The actors in this restaging are de
Gaulle and Adenauer. The former claimed, and almost succeeded in making people believe, that "France belongs among the victors of the last
war"; the latter "that the barbarism of National Socialism had affected
only a relatively small percentage of the country" (TP, 252). These examples are framed by formulas that oppose once again the *traditional* political lie to the *modern* rewriting of history. They suppose a new status of
the image:

We must now turn our attention to the relatively recent phenomenon of mass manipulation of fact and opinion as it has become evident in the rewriting of history,
in image-making, and in actual government policy. The traditional political lie, so
prominent in the history of diplomacy and statecraft, used to concern either true
secrets—data that had never been made public—or intentions, which anyhow do
not possess the same degree of reliability as accomplished facts. . . . In contrast, the
modern political lies deal efficiently with things that are not secrets at all but are
known to practically everybody. This is obvious in the case of rewriting contemporary history under the eyes of those who witnessed it, but it is equally true in
image-making of all sorts . . . for an image, unlike an old-fashioned portrait, is

supposed not to flatter reality but to offer a full-fledged substitute for it. And this substitute, because of modern techniques and the mass media, is, of course, much more in the public eye than the original ever was. (TP, 252)

Because the image-substitute no longer refers to an original, not even to a flattering representation of an original, but replaces it advantageously, thereby trading its status of representative for that of replacement, the process of the modern lie is no longer a dissimulation that comes along to veil the truth; rather, it is the destruction of reality or of the original archive: "In other words, the difference between the traditional lie and the modern lie will more often than not amount to the difference between hiding and destroying" (TP, 253).

We will have occasion to return at length to the logic of these propositions. Are the word and the concept "lie" still appropriate, given their conceptual history, to designate the phenomena of our political, techno-mediatic, testimonial modernity, to which Hannah Arendt will have so early and so lucidly drawn our attention—often because she had herself experienced it most painfully, in particular when she was a reporter during the Eichmann trial?

Here now is the other epigraph. The historicity that it also names would be that of a certain *sacredness* or *sanctity*. This sacrosanctity (*Heiligkeit*) is constitutive—in Kant's view, for example, as well as in an Augustinian tradition that Kant does not explicitly claim—of the duty or the unconditional imperative not to lie. The duty one has to tell the truth is a sacred imperative. Reiner Schürmann (a friend and colleague to whose memory I wish to pay tribute here) notes in *Heidegger on Being and Acting: From Principles to Anarchy*, in the course of a reading of Heidegger, that:

Since the notion of the *sacred* belongs in the context of the original, it keeps historical connotations: the sacred is "the trace of the fugitive gods," leading toward their possible return (says Heidegger in *Holzwege*, pp. 250ff.). On the other hand, *awe* and *piety*, since they accompany the phenomenon of the originary, direct thinking toward that event, presencing, which is not at all historical.[11]

I

I will now try to begin—and without lying, believe me—by telling a few stories. In an apparently narrative mode, that of a classical historian or chronicler, I will propose a few specific examples on the basis of which we will try to progress in a reflective fashion, by analogy with what Kant calls "reflective judgment." We would thus proceed from the particular to the general, so as to *reflect* rather than *determine*, and to reflect in view of a principle that experience cannot provide. If I refer already, at least by analogy, to the great and canonical Kantian distinction between determinant judgment and reflective judgment, it is for three reasons: *first*, this distinction gives rise, in the *Critique of Judgment*, to antinomies and to a dialectic that are doubtless not foreign to those in which we will soon find ourselves entangled; *second*, Hannah Arendt, once again in "Truth and Politics," recalls at length the virtue Kant accords to the example, and she quotes, moreover, the *Critique of Judgment*; *finally and especially*, Kant is also the author of a brief (about six pages), dense, difficult essay on the lie. Written in polemical response to Benjamin Constant, here called *Der französische Philosoph*, while Constant had incriminated *un philosophe allemand*, as if this debate about lying were also a conflict between philosophical nationalities, these few pages constitute, in my view, one of the most radical attempts to think the lie in the history of the West, after the two great signatories of *Confessions*, Augustine and Rousseau, and also one of the most powerful attempts to determine, reflect, proscribe, or prohibit any lie. Unconditionally. I am referring to the short text, more celebrated than it is in general analyzed, entitled "On a Supposed Right to Lie Because of Philanthropic Concerns" ("Uber ein vermeintes Recht aus Menschensliebe zu lügen"; 1797).

Hannah Arendt frequently cites Kant in the article to which I have just referred and elsewhere, but she never mentions this essay even though it is so necessary and at the same time formidable, even irreducible to the profound logic of what she wants to demonstrate. Without going this evening as far as would be necessary in the reading of this text, one can already take account of the manner in which Kant defines the lie and the imperative of *veracity* or *veridicity* (for the contrary of the lie is neither truth nor reality but veracity or veridicity, truth saying, the true-meaning-to-say, *Wahrhaftigkeit*). The Kantian definition of the lie or the duty of veracity seems so formal, imperative, and unconditional that it appears to exclude any historical consideration. One must tell the truth; one must be truthful on every occasion, in every hypothesis, at all costs, whatever the historical circumstances. There is no useful lie, obliging, serviceable lies (no *mensonge officieux*, as Rousseau says, translating the classical expression *mendacium officiosum*). Without any casuistical concern for all the difficult and troubling cases that Augustine analyzes, most often based on Biblical examples, Kant seems to exclude any historical content when he defines veracity (*Wahrhaftigkeit; veracitas*) as an absolute formal duty: "Veracity in statements [*Wahrhaftigkeit in Aussagen*] that cannot be avoided," he says, "is the formal duty [*formale Pflicht*] of man to everyone, however great the disadvantage that may arise therefrom for him or for any other."[12]

Although his text is expressly juridical and not ethical, although it deals, as its title indicates, with the "right to lie [*Recht . . . zu lügen*]," although he speaks of *duty of right* (*Rechtspflicht*) and not of *ethical duty*, which could appear at first more propitious for or less incompatible with a historical viewpoint, Kant seems all the same to exclude in his definition of the lie all the historicity that, by contrast, Hannah Arendt introduces into the very essence, into the event and the performance of the lie. This is because Kant's viewpoint, if it is in fact that of right, remains purely and formally juridical or meta-juridical; it corresponds to the concern with the formal conditions of right, the social contract, and the pure source of right. He writes:

> Hence a lie defined merely as an intentionally untruthful declaration [*unwahre Declaration*] to another man does not require the additional condition that it must do harm to another, as jurists require in their definition (*mendacium est falsiloquium in praejudicium alterius*). For a lie always harms another; if not some other human being, then it necessarily does harm to humanity in general, inasmuch as it vitiates the source of right [it makes it useless: *die Rechtsquelle unbrauchbar macht*]. (64–65)

Kant no doubt means to define in the lie what is a priori bad in itself, in its immanence, whatever may be its motivations or its consequences. Without any doubt, he would have denounced faked orgasm as a lie insofar as it is intentionally meant to deceive the other, even if it is for the good, for the other's supposed good. (And there is more than one lecture that could be devoted to what links the history of the lie to the history of sexual difference, to its erotics and its interpretations, without ever excluding, quite on the contrary, that the paradigm of the lie has an essential link to the experience of sexual pleasure). Kant is concerned above all with the very source of human law and of sociality in general, namely, an immanent necessity to tell the truth, whatever may be the expected effects or the external and historical contexts. If the lie is not unconditionally banned, then humanity's social bond is ruined in its very principle. Sociality is made impossible. Montaigne said so in his own way.[13] Thus, Kant goes precisely counter to Benjamin Constant, who reproached the rigor of the "German philosopher" for making "all society impossible."[14] According to Kant, on the contrary, society would become impossible if one justified the least lie, that is, an action whose maxim could not be universalized without itself destroying its own law. What can be said of the lie can also be said of the false promise, and Kant associates the two in *Fundamental Principles of the Metaphysics of Morals*.[15] I can address myself to someone only by promising him at least implicitly the truth, my truth, that is, my veracity. And what looks like a hyperbolic and untenable prescription on Kant's part (never lie, never make a false promise, not in any case or under any pretext, even if it is for what seem to be the best reasons in the world) can also be described as a modest and tenacious description, a simple, constative analysis of the essence of language: "Of course, you can always lie and lie while promising, who hasn't done that," Kant himself might say, "but in that case, you cease speaking, you no longer address another, another as a human being; you have renounced language because all language is structured by this promise of veracity." A very strong proposition, difficult to refute, unless one thinks otherwise the specter of the possible, of the possible lie that must continue to haunt veracity. We will allow it to return later. In any case, the *sacredness* or *sanctity* of the rational commandment to tell the truth, to mean to say what is true, would reside in this pure immanence of the promise of veracity in language. A moment ago, Reiner Schürmann was saying that sacredness was historical. In another sense, it seems that, in this case, for Kant it is not, at least not in the common sense. But the hypothesis remains that it is historical in another sense: as origin and condition of a history and of a human sociality in general. Everything must be sacrificed to this sacredness of the commandment. Kant writes: "To be truthful [*wahrhaft*; loyal, sincere, honest, in good faith: *ehrlich*] in all declarations is, therefore, a sacred [*heiliges*] and unconditional [*unbedingt gebietendes*] commanding law of reason [*Vernunftgebot*] that admits of no expediency whatsoever."[16]

I come finally to the promised examples and to my European chronicle of two worlds. I select them, in fact, from the closest proximity to the two continents that can be considered European, Europe and North America, the United States (between Paris and New York), and from our newspapers, the *New York Times* and the Paris edition of the *International Herald Tribune*. Soon after his election, when he had already announced his irrevocable decision that France would resume its nuclear tests in the Pacific, President Jacques Chirac, you recall, solemnly recognized, on the anniversary of the infamous Vel d'Hiv raid, the responsibility, which is to say, the culpability of the French State under the Occupation in the deportation of tens of thousands of Jews, in the institution of a *statut des Juifs*, and in numerous initiatives that were not undertaken only at the order of the Nazi occupier. This culpability, this active participation in what is today judged to be a "crime against humanity," has now been recognized. Irreversibly. It is now admitted by a state as such. The admission is signed and sealed by a head of state elected by universal suffrage. It is publicly declared, in the name of the French State, before the world, in the face of international law, in a theatrical act widely publicized by the written press, by radio and television (I am underscoring once again this relation between the *res publica* and the media because it, along with this mutation of the status of the image, is one of our themes.) The truth proclaimed by President Chirac has from now on the status, that is, both the stability and the authority, of a public, national, and international truth.

Yet this truth concerning a certain history has itself a history. It will have been legitimated, accredited, established as such more than fifty years after the facts in question. Six presidents of the French Republic (Auriol, Coty, de Gaulle, Pompidou, Giscard d'Estaing, Mitterrand) until now deemed it neither *possible* nor *opportune* nor *necessary*, nor even *correct* or *just* to stabilize it as a truth of this type. Not one of them believed he was obliged to commit France, the French nation, the French state, the French Republic with a kind of signature that would have come to assume responsibility for this truth: France guilty of a crime against humanity. One could cite numerous such examples and such situations today, in Japan, the United States, or Israel, which concern past violence or acts of repression, notorious war crimes, whether they are recently discovered or have worried the conscience of the world for a long time. Thus we know that, despite the testimony of numerous historians, President Clinton continued to hold that the use of atomic bombs in Hiroshima and Nagasaki was a justifiable decision and refused to reconsider this state doctrine. One could also speak of what may still happen regarding the politics of Japan in Asia during the war, the Algerian War, the Gulf War, ex-Yugoslavia, Rwanda, Chechnya, and so forth.

Given that I have just mentioned Japan, Prime Minister Murayama initiated a gesture several years ago when he made a declaration whose every word and whole pragmatic structure would have to be evaluated. Without committing the Japanese State at its head and in the permanence of its imperial identity, in the person of the emperor, a prime minister confesses, he tells the truth in the form of a confession. Before what he calls significantly "these irrefutable facts of history" and an "error in our history," Murayama expresses in his own name (a name that says more than his own name but in no way commits the name of the emperor) his "heartfelt apology." He confesses the suffering of a remorse, a grief that is at once personal and vaguely, very confusedly, that of the nation and the state. What is a state grief, when it grieves for the deaths of those who are neither heads of state nor even fellow citizens? How can a state from now on ask for forgiveness or excuse? And what does this imply about an international political conscience? In what way does it depend on a transformation of international law, for example, in the creation of an absolutely new concept, crime against humanity, and the new judicial agencies, the new tribunals it calls for? This is a swarm of questions that could not have been posed in these terms some fifty years ago. I quote Murayama's letter of declaration: "I regard, in a spirit of humility, these irrefutable facts of history, and express here once again my feelings of deep remorse and state my heartfelt apology." And then, having evoked "colonial" repression—which ought to give other former empires some ideas—the Japanese prime minister adds: "Allow me also to express my feelings of profound mourning for all victims, both at home and abroad, of that history." This confession seeks not only to be truthful; it is put forward as a promise and declares also the responsibility of a task; it makes a commitment for the future: "Our task is to convey to the younger generation the horrors of war, so that we never repeat the errors in our history." The language of fault and confession are allied, so as to attenuate the effect, with the heterogeneous language of error; here, then, and probably for the first time in history, someone dares dissociate the concept of the state or nation from what had always characterized it, in a constitutive and structural fashion, namely, good conscience.

However confused this event may be, and however impure its motivation remains, however calculated and conjunctural the strategy, there is here a progress in the history of humanity and its international law, of its science and its conscience. Kant perhaps would have seen in it one of those events that are a "sign" toward a perfectibility, toward the possibility of a progress of humanity, a sign that, like the French Revolution, for example, and despite the failure or the limitation, reminds, demonstrates, heralds (*signum rememorativum, demonstrativum, prognosticum*), thereby attesting to a "tendency" and the possibility of a "progress" of humanity. All of this remains incomplete, for Japan, France, or Germany, but it is better than nothing. Whereas the Soviet Union or Yugoslavia, which no longer exist, are protected from any guilty conscience and any public recognition of past crimes, the United States—and France—have a whole future before them. Let us return to them.

That for more than a half century no head of the French State deemed it possible, opportune, necessary, correct, or just to constitute as truth an immense French guilt, to recognize it as truth, all of this can cause thought, disturbance, or trembling. Would it signify that the value of truth in this case—that is, veracity, the value of a statement concerning real facts (for truth is not reality), but above all a statement in conformity with what one thinks—might depend on a political interpretation concerning values, which are, moreover, heterogeneous (possibility, opportunity, necessity, correctness, or justice)? Would truth or veracity therefore in principle be subordinate to these values? This is an enormous problem, as you know, doubtless a classical one, but it is a problem for which we must try today to find some historical, political, techno-mediatic specificity. Among former presidents, de Gaulle himself, to whom Chirac nevertheless says he owes his whole political inspiration, never dreamed of declaring the culpability of the French state under the Occupation, even though or perhaps because the culpability of the "French State" (this was moreover the official name of France under Vichy, the Republic having been abolished and renamed *Etat français*) was in his eyes that of a nonlegitimate if not illegal state. We can also think of the case of Vincent Auriol, that other president of the Republic who did not deem it possible, necessary, opportune, correct, or just to recognize what Chirac has just recognized—and to recognize it for conjunctural reasons and hypothetical imperatives that are no doubt more complex than the simple, unconditional obedience to the sacred commandment of which Kant speaks. Out of eighty French parliamentary representatives, Vincent Auriol was one of the very few who refused to vote full powers [*les pleins pouvoirs*] to Pétain on July 10, 1940. He therefore knew, alas, that the interruption of the Republic and the transition to this *Etat français* guilty of the "status of Jews" and of the deportation of Jews was a legal act committing the responsibility of a government of France. The discontinuity of the interruption was itself inscribed in the legal continuity of the Republic in the *Etat français*. The French Republic, by way of its legally elected representatives, resigned its own status. Such, at least, is the truth in its formal and juridical legality. But where is the truth of the thing itself here, if there is one? Can one speak of lie, that is, of nonveracity where the truth cannot be stabilized?

François Mitterrand, on several occasions and until the end of his last term, also refused to recognize the official culpability of the *Etat français*. He explicitly alleged that the *Etat français* had been installed through usurpation by interrupting the history of the French Republic, the only political or moral person that could account for its actions, which, at the time, found itself either gagged or in illegal resistance. The French Republic, today, had nothing, according to him, to "confess"; it did not have to assume the memory and culpability of a period in which it had been put out of action. The French nation, as such and in its continuity, had no obligation to accuse itself of crimes against humanity committed unjustly in its name. François Mitterrand refused to grant such a recognition even as he inaugurated the public and solemn commemorations of the Vel d'Hiv raid, and even when there were many who, over the course of many years, through letters and official petitions—with which I am very familiar for having signed them—urged him to do what President Chirac has no longer delayed doing.

One could cite yet another typical position on this problem, that of Jean-Pierre Chevènement, former cabinet minister under Mitterrand, a very independent Socialist, opposed to the model of Europe now being constituted, worried about national sovereignty and honor, who resigned his post as Minister of Defense during the Gulf War. For Chevènement, although Chirac did well to recognize the incontestable culpability of the *Etat français*, the consequences of this "veracity" and the terms in which it was elaborated raise grave risks, for example, that of legitimating Pétainism in return and encouraging all the forces that today seek to accredit the idea according to which "Pétain is France."[17] This was also, most likely, the viewpoint of General de Gaulle himself and perhaps, in a less determined fashion, that of the presidents who succeeded him. In a word, from this point of view, truth and veracity are certainly necessary, but they must not be put into operation in just any fashion, at just any price, unconditionally. "Toute vérité n'est pas bonne à dire," as the French proverb puts it; that is, it is not always good to tell the truth, which means the imperative is not as sacred and unconditional as Kant wished. One would have to take into account hypothetical imperatives, pragmatic opportunity, possible consequences, the moment and the forms of the statement, rhetoric, the addressee to be harmed or indemnified, and so forth. To distinguish between the legality of the Vichy government and the popular will that resigned in the face of it, moreover, Chevènement has to go back much further in time, at least five years, in order to determine real responsibilities. By right, the properly historical analysis would be infinite, and with such an analysis the distinction between lie and veracity risks losing the strict outline of its borders.

Here then is a first series of questions: By not declaring officially what is now a historical truth of state, were former presidents, from de Gaulle to Mitterrand, lying or dissimulating? Does one have the right to say that? Could they, in their turn, accuse Chirac of "lying"? Are any of them lying? Who lied and who told the truth?[18] Can one speak here of lie? Is that a pertinent concept? And if it is pertinent, what would be the criterion of the lie? What would be the history of this lie? And especially, a still different question, what would be the history of the *concept of the lie* that would support such questions? If there were some lie here and if it were pertinent to determine this or that to be a lie, who would be its subject and who the addressee or the victim? We will have to come back to the formation and formulation of this first series of questions, but it would be good to underscore *two original features* in this example.

On the one hand, there is in fact a historical novelty in this pragmatics of the opposition veracity/lie, if not in the essence of the lie. At issue here is a veracity or a *lie of state* determinable as such, on a stage of international law that did not exist before the Second World War. These hypotheses, in fact, are posed today with reference to juridical concepts, such as "crime against humanity," that are inventions and thus "performatives" unknown to humanity before this. These new juridical concepts imply international jurisdictions, contracts, and interstate charters, institutions and courts of justice that are in principle universal and that until now had no place to judge or even register such acts—which moreover were not identifiable as such. If all of this is historical through and through, it is because the problematic of the lie or of the confession, the imperative of veracity on the subject of something like a "crime against humanity," had no sense, either for individuals or for the State, before the definition of this juridical concept in Article 6c of the statutes of the International Military Tribunal at Nuremberg, and, in particular, as concerns at least France, unless I am mistaken, before these crimes were declared "imprescriptible" by a law dated December 26, 1964. Wherever the competence of the Nuremberg Tribunal is contested, the whole edifice that we are analyzing in this moment would be affected or even ruined. It is not necessary to insist on the difficulty and enormity of the stakes.

On the other hand, the objects in question, those on the subject of which a verdict is to be reached, are not natural realities "in themselves." They depend on interpretations, but also on performative interpretations. I am not speaking here of the act of performative language by which, confessing some culpability, a head of state produces an event and provokes a reinterpretation of all the utterances of his predecessors. Rather I mean to underscore above all the performativity at work in the very *objects* of these declarations: the legitimacy of a so-called sovereign state, the position of a boundary, the identification or attestation of a responsibility are performative acts. When performatives succeed, they produce a truth whose power sometimes imposes itself forever: the location of a boundary, the installation of a state are always acts of performative violence that, if the conditions of the international community permit it, create the law, whether durably or not, where there was none or no longer any law, where law did not yet impose itself or else was not yet strong enough. In creating the law, this performative violence—which is neither legal nor illegal—creates what is then held to be legal truth, the dominant and juridically incontestable public truth. Where today is the "truth" concerning boundaries in ex-Yugoslavia, in all its divided "enclaves" that are cleaved or enclaved in other enclaves, or in Chechnya, or in Israel, or in Zaire? Who tells the truth and who lies in these areas? For better and for worse, this performative dimension *makes the truth,* as Augustine says. It therefore imprints its irreducibly historical dimension on both veracity and the lie. This original "performative" dimension is not taken thematically into account, it seems to me, by either Kant or Hannah Arendt. I will try to show that, despite everything that divides or opposes them from another point of view, they share this misrecognition, or at least this insufficient explicitation, just as they both neglect the symptomal or unconscious dimension of these phenomena. Such phenomena cannot be approached without, at the very least, the combination of a "logic of the

speak-act theory

unconscious" and a theory of the "performative." This does not mean that the *current* and presently elaborated discourse of psychoanalysis or of speech act theory is sufficient to the task. It means even less that there is a ready articulation between them—or between them and a discourse on politics or the economy of tele-technological knowledge and power. We are defining here a task and the conditions of an analysis on the scale of these phenomena of "our time."

Rewriting history, lie, falsification, negation, and disavowal: all these questions point toward stakes that, because they can so easily be recognized, I did not think it useful to insist upon. I will do no more here than evoke or situate, in the immediate vicinity of a new problematic of the truth of state, the searing figures of revisionism and negationism. These figures proliferate endlessly; they are reborn from the ashes they would like to conjure away and to insult. How is one to fight them, which is to say, first of all, refute them, dispute them, recall them to the truth of their negationist and disavowed relentlessness? How to prove by bearing witness, if testimony remains irreducibly heterogeneous to proof? What is the best response, at once the most just, the most correct, the most critical, and the most reliable? Will this perversion be resisted by establishing by law a truth of state? Or rather, on the contrary, by reinitiating—interminably if necessary, as I believe it will be—the discussion, the recalling of evidence and witnesses, the work and discipline of memory, the indisputable demonstration of an archive? An infinite task, no doubt, which must be begun over and over again; but isn't that the distinctive feature of a task, whatever it may be? No state, no law of state, no reason of state will ever be able to take its measure. This does not mean that the state has to renounce its right or its law; but that one must remain vigilant to make sure it does not do disservice to the cause of a truth that, when left to itself, always risks getting perverted into dogmatism or orthodoxy.

II

Like everything that our tele-techno-mediatic modernity subjects to colossal amplification, either concentrated or dispersed, at accelerated and irregular rhythms, the effects of this performative power are difficult to measure. Simultaneously or successively, its consequences can be terrifying, major, interminable, superficial, slight, insignificant, or passing. Here, for example, is another, visibly minor sequence from the same story of a state confession. Because the media, as space of gathering, production, and archivation of public speech, must occupy a determining place in any analysis of the political lie and of falsification in the space of the *res publica*, it is not without interest to note that the *New York Times* wanted to report on Chirac's declaration. Concerned with truth and competence (let us assume that to be the case), it turned responsibility for the article over to a professor. The idea of competence is associated in our culture with the university and with university professors. Everyone assumes that professors know and say what is true. And that they do not lie. This professor presumed to know teaches in a great New York university. He even passes for an expert in matters of French modernity, at the crossroads of philosophy, ideology, politics, and literature. He is the author, as the *New York Times* recalls, of a book titled *Past Imperfect: French Intellectuals, 1944–1956*. So on July 19, 1995, the *New York Times* publishes an article with the title "French War Stories," by Mr. Tony Judt, Professor at New York University. Before applauding Chirac and concluding that, I quote, "It is well that Mr. Chirac has told the truth about the French past," the author of *Past Imperfect* had nonetheless denounced the shameful behavior of French intellectuals who, for a half-century, had been in his opinion too little concerned with this truth and with its public recognition. Sartre and Foucault, he claims, had been on this subject, I quote, "curiously silent." He chalks this up to their sympathy for Marxism. This explanation is somewhat amusing, especially in the case of Foucault, when one knows that the majority of the latter's most durable and best known "political commitments" were anything but Marxist, and sometimes they were even expressly anti-Marxist.

I will quote what Professor Judt then writes only in order to proliferate, by way of introduction, the examples of faults that will always be difficult to determine. There will always be several possibilities among which one must hesitate to choose. What exactly is the matter here? Incompetence? Lack of lucidity or analytic acuity? Good faith ignorance? Accidental error? Twilight bad faith falling somewhere between the lie and thoughtlessness? Or, to invoke Rousseau's three categories, imposture, fraud, calumny? The same *Reverie* speaks also of "counterfeit money." Shall we speak of compulsion and logic of the unconscious? An outright false witness, perjury, lie? These categories are no doubt irreducible to each other, but what is one to think of the very frequent situations in which, *in fact, in truth*, they contaminate one another and no longer lend themselves to a rigorous delimitation? And what if this contagion marked the very space of so many public discourses, notably in the media? Here, then, is what Professor Judt says in order to account for the silence, which in his view is guilty, of Sartre and Foucault:

Intellectuals, so prominent in post-war France, might have been expected to force the issue. Yet people like Jean-Paul Sartre and Michel Foucault were curiously silent. One reason was their near-obsession with Communism. While proclaiming the need to "engage," to take a stand, two generations of intellectuals avoided any ethical issue that could not advance or, in some cases retard the Marxist cause.

These declarations may appear merely a little confused and vague, especially where it is a question of the "Marxist cause" for Foucault. But Professor Judt does not stop there. After the subtitle "Shame of the Intellectuals" (a subtitle for which he must at least share responsibility with the newspaper, as we are unfortunately so often obliged to do whenever we think we have to write for the newspapers), the professor-journalist denounces the shame of intellectuals who have come *after* Sartre and who maintained, according to Mr. Judt, a guilty silence in the face of Vichy France's guilt and its "crimes against humanity": "No one stood up to cry 'J'accuse!' at high functionaries, as Emile Zola did during the Dreyfus affair. When Simone de Beauvoir, Roland Barthes, and Jacques Derrida entered the public arena, it usually involved a crisis far away—in Madagascar, Vietnam, or Cambodia. Even today, politically engaged writers call for action in Bosnia but intervene sporadically in debates about the French past."

Even if I am ready to concede a measure of truth in this accusation, I must declare that in the main it filled me with indignation. Not because, please believe this, it also concerns me personally, and because, along with others, I am the object of a veritable calumny. (This is not the first time that newspapers bearing the name of New York in their title say whatever they please and lie outright as concerns me, sometimes for months at a time and over several issues.) If I was particularly shocked, however, by this *contre-vérité*, as one calls it in French, it is not only for this reason, nor simply because, like others, I am among those who care about what Mr. Judt calls the "French past." It is especially because, with others, I have more than once made this known publicly, including on subjects other than this one (Algeria, for example), and because along with others I had signed an open letter to President Mitterrand asking him to recognize what Chirac has just recognized. Upon reading the *New York Times* and feeling discouraged in advance, which is, alas, too often the case, I had already given up any notion of answering and correcting this counter-truth become truth through the conjoined force of the presumed authority of an academic expert and a newspaper with a massive and international distribution (both American and European, for the same article was reprinted as is three days later in the European edition of the *International Herald Tribune*). Fortunately, four days later, the counter-truth was denounced in the same newspaper by another American professor whom I do not know but to whose competence and honesty I wish to pay grateful tribute: Kevin Anderson, who teaches at a more modest rank in a less celebrated university (he is Associate Professor of Sociology at Northern Illinois University). The *New York Times* was thus obliged to publish a letter "to the editor" from Kevin Anderson, under the title "French Intellectuals Wanted Truth Told." Such a letter is usually printed in an unobtrusive and sometimes unlocatable place, whereas the effect of truth, or rather counter-truth of the first article "properly speaking" remains ineffaceable for millions of readers, and especially for European readers of the *International Herald Tribune*, who will have never read the letter in question. Kevin Anderson criticizes the whole political analysis of Professor Judt (permit me to refer you to it), and he specifies in particular that:

On June 15, 1992, a petition signed by more than 200 mainly leftist intellectuals, including Mr. Derrida, Régis Debray, Cornelius Castoriadis, Mr. Lacouture and Nathalie Sarraute, noted that the French occupation government in 1942 acted "on its own authority, and without being asked to do so by the German occupier." It called on Mr. Mitterrand to "recognize and proclaim that the French state of Vichy was responsible for persecutions and crimes against the Jews of France."[19]

To my knowledge, but I don't know everything and it is not too late, Professor Judt has not yet acknowledged publicly that he did not tell the truth. You will have noticed that, in speaking of the *contre-vérité* of his article, I never said that Professor Judt had lied. Everything that is false cannot be imputed to a lie. The lie is not an error. Already Plato and Augustine insisted on this in unison. If the concept of lie has some resistant specificity, it must be rigorously distinguished from error, from ignorance, from prejudice, from faulty reasoning, and even from failure in the realm of knowledge or still again—and this is where things will soon have to get more complicated for us—from failure in the realm of action, practice, or technique. If the lie is neither the failure of knowledge and know-how, nor error, if it implies ill will or bad faith in the order of moral reason, not of practice but of pure practical reason, if it addresses belief rather than knowledge, then the project of a history of the lie should not resemble in the least what could be called, following Nietzsche in *The Twilight of the Idols*, the history of an error [*Geschichte eines Irrtums*].

No doubt, it would be necessary to keep a sense of proportion. But how is one to calculate proportion when the capitalistico-techno-mediatic power of an international newspaper can produce effects of worldwide truth or counter-truth, which are sometimes tenacious and ineffaceable, on the most serious subjects in the history of humanity, going far beyond the modest persons implicated in the recent example I have just given? Keeping everything in proportion, then, I will say that the history I have just recited would be neither the history of an error nor the history of a lie. In order to lie, in the strict and classical sense of this concept, one must know what the truth is and distort it intentionally. Thus, one must not lie to oneself. I am convinced that if Professor Judt had had a clear and distinct knowledge, if he had had a current consciousness of the fact that the intellectuals he accuses had signed that letter to Mitterrand, he would not have written what he wrote. I think it is reasonable to give him this much credit: he did not lie. Not really. He did not mean clearly and deliberately to deceive his reader and to take advantage of that reader's confidence or belief. Yet, is it simply, in all innocence, an error on his part or a simple lack of information? I do not believe that either. If Professor Judt did not seek to know more or enough about the subject, or everything that a historian and conscientious journalist should know before speaking, it is also because he was in a hurry to reach a conclusion and therefore to produce an "effect of truth" confirming at all cost his general theses on French intellectuals and politics, with which one may be familiar from his other writings—and which I am not alone in finding a little simplistic. We could show this if that were the subject of our lecture and if we were given the time. What I want to underscore here is that this counter-truth does not belong to the category of either lie or ignorance or error, doubtless not even to the category of self-deception that Hannah Arendt talks about. It belongs to another order and is not reducible to any of the categories bequeathed to us by traditional thinking about the lie, from Plato, Augustine, and Rousseau up to Kant and even up to Hannah Arendt, despite all the differences that separate all these thinkers from each other.

Here is the hypothesis that I wish to submit for your discussion: the concept of lie to oneself, of self-deception, for which Hannah Arendt has an essential need so as to mark the specificity of the modern lie as absolute lie, is a concept that is irreducible to what is called, in all classical rigor, a lie. But what I am calling here too quickly the classical rigor of the concept of lie also has a history, to which we are heirs and which in any case occupies a dominant place in our heritage and in our common language. The lie to oneself is not "bad faith," either in the ordinary sense or in the sense Sartre gives to it. It requires, therefore, another name, another logic, other words; it requires that one take into account both some mediatic techno-performativity and a logic of the *phantasma* (which is to say, of the spectral) or of a symptomatology of the unconscious toward which the work of Hannah Arendt signals but which it never deploys, it seems to me, as such. There are several signs in "Truth and Politics" that this concept of lie to oneself plays a determining role in the Arendtian analysis of the modern lie. To be sure, Arendt finds material to illustrate this lie to oneself in anecdotes or discourses from other centuries. We have known for a long time, she notes, that it is difficult to lie to others without lying to oneself, and "the more successful a liar is, the more likely it is that he will fall prey to his own fabrications" (TP, 254). But she assigns this possibility especially to modernity, from which she draws a very paradoxical consequence on the subject of democracy, as if this ideal regime were also the one in which deception were properly destined to become "self-deception." Arendt acknowledges, therefore, an "undeniable strength" in the arguments of "conservative critics of mass democracy":

Politically, the point is that the modern art of self-deception is likely to transform an outside matter into an inside issue, so that an international or inter-group conflict boomerangs onto the scene of domestic politics. The self-deceptions practiced on both sides in the period of the Cold War are too many to enumerate, but obviously they are a case in point. Conservative critics of mass democracy have frequently outlined the dangers that this form of government brings to international affairs—without, however, mentioning the dangers peculiar to monarchies and oligarchies. The strength of their arguments lies in the undeniable fact that under fully democratic conditions deception without self-deception is well-nigh impossible. (TP, 255–56)

I leave suspended the capital but far too difficult question of what can be understood here by "fully democratic conditions."

III

I do not know if she read it or knew it, but we have an obligation to the truth to say that these Arendtian theses fall directly in line with an article by Alexandre Koyré. Also published in New York, but years earlier, the article appeared in a 1943 issue of *Renaissance*, journal of the Ecole Libre des Hautes Etudes, with the title "Réflexions sur le mensonge," and a translation was published in June 1945 in the *Contemporary Jewish Record*, with the title "The Political Function of the Modern Lie." This remarkable essay has returned to France thanks to the review *Rue Descartes*, published by the Collège International de Philosophie.[20] It begins as follows: "Never has there been so much lying as in our day. Never has lying been so shameless, so systematic, so unceasing." All the Arendtian themes are already there, in particular that of the lie to oneself ("That man has always lied, to himself and to others, is indisputable") and of the modern lie:

Right now we want to concern ourselves with the contemporary lie, and even more strictly, with the contemporary political lie. We remain convinced that in this sphere, *quo nihil antiquius*, the present epoch, or more exactly, its totalitarian regimes, has created some mighty innovations. . . . Modern man—*genus totalitarian*—bathes in the lie, breathes the lie, is in thrall to the lie every moment of his existence.[21]

Among many other fascinating questions, which we will not have time to pursue, Koyré wonders in fact, which Arendt did not do, whether one still has, I quote, "the right to speak here of 'lie.'" In the strategy of his answer, which fills but a few lines, I would like to remark, no doubt too schematically, the stakes and the principal vein of a philosophical but also ethical, juridical, and political difficulty. What can be done with his response by anyone attempting to write a history of the lie and a genealogy of the concept of lie, as well as of the sacred veracity, of the *Heiligkeit* of the safe, the saintly, the healthy, or the safe and sound [*l'indemne*] that will always have linked the ethical to the religious?

In Koyré's strategy, to whose necessity and force I first want to pay tribute, I would be tempted to recognize at once a *limit* and an *opening*.

First, *the limit*. Koyré seems to suspect *any* question concerning the right to use the word "lie." He insinuates that such a question, already as a question, may be the first sign of a totalitarian perversion. He is not wrong, not simply wrong. The risk does in fact exist, and it remains a terrible one. One may wonder, however, whether this risk ought not to be treated otherwise, each time by taking into account, without any relativism, singular and novel historical situations, and especially by introducing into the analysis of these situations concepts that seem to be structurally excluded both by Koyré and by Arendt, and already before them by Kant, Augustine, and Plato, for essential reasons that have to do with the necessary and massive "frankness," as we were saying of this concept.

Koyré rightly recalls that the notion of "lie" presupposes that of veracity, of which it is the contrary or the negation, just as the notion of the "false" supposes that of the "true," the contrary remaining, let us not forget, ineluctable. He then adds a pertinent and grave warning, a warning that must never be overlooked, especially in politics, but that should not, all the same, halt us in our pursuit of a deconstructive genealogy of the concept of lie and therefore of veracity. How can one proceed with such a genealogy—so necessary for memory or critical lucidity, but also for all the responsibilities that remain to be taken today and tomorrow—in such a way that it does not consist in merely ruining or discrediting what it analyzes? How can one conduct the deconstructive history of the opposition of veracity and lie without discrediting this opposition, without threatening the "frankness" of a concept that must remain decidable, and without opening the door to all the perversions against which Koyré and Arendt will always have been right to warn us?

Here, then, is Koyré's warning. Keep in mind that it was written in 1943, both because of what was happening then and what has happened since, what is developing today more powerfully than ever; for his diagnoses concerning totalitarian practices of the period (for us it was yesterday) could be widely extended to certain current practices of so-called democracies in the age of a certain capitalistico-techno-mediatic hegemony:

The official philosophies of the totalitarian regimes unanimously brand as nonsensical the idea that there exists a single objective truth valid for everybody. The criterion of "truth," they say, is not agreement with reality [later on, Koyré will recall that there is a theory of the lie in *Mein Kampf* and that the readers of this book did not understand they themselves were being spoken of; and it is true that *Mein Kampf* deserves to be studied, today more than ever, not only for its practice of lying but in its explicit theorization of the lie and in particular of what Hitler calls "the colossal lie"], but agreement with the spirit of a race or nation or class—that is, racial, national or utilitarian. Pushing to their limits the biological, pragmatist, activist theories of truth, the official philosophies of the totalitarian regimes deny the inherent value of thought. For them thought is not a light but a weapon: its function, they say, is not to discover reality as it is, but to change and transform it with the purpose of leading us towards what is not. Such being the case, myth is better than science and rhetoric that works on the passions preferable to proof that appeals to the intellect.[22]

To avoid any misunderstanding, I repeat and underscore that what Koyré is saying here seems to me true, correct, necessary. One must begin by subscribing to it. An unfailing vigilance will always be necessary so as to be on guard against the danger he denounces. And yet, as you heard, what he condemns goes well beyond the biologism and the official philosophies of totalitarianism: he denounces all of what he calls "pragmatist" and "activist" interpretations of the truth, which is potentially quite a lot. This suspicion can touch on everything that exceeds, in more than one direction, the determination of truth as objectivity, as the theme of a constative utterance, or even as adequation; at the limit, it touches on any consideration of performative utterances. In other words, the same suspicion would be aimed at any problematic that delimits, questions, and *a fortiori* deconstructs the authority of the truth as objectivity or, this would be yet something different, as adequation or even as revelation (*aletheia*). The same suspicion would be aimed at any problematic that takes into account, for example, in the area of the political or rhetorico-techno-mediatic *res publica*, the possibility of institutive and performative speech (be it only *testimony*, which is always an act that implies a performative promise or oath and that constitutes the element, the medium of all language, including constative language). A problematic of this sort, which is so necessary, *both for the best and for the worst*, would therefore risk seeing itself disqualified or paralyzed in advance.

I underscore here two equally necessary precautions. *On the one hand*, I am not saying this in order to dismiss the suspicion that Koyré formulates: once again, this suspicion is indispensable and legitimate, it must watch over these new problematics, however urgent they may be. *On the other hand*, it is true that these same new problematics (of a pragmatico-deconstructive type) can in fact serve contradictory interests. This double possibility must remain open, as both a chance and a threat, for otherwise we would no longer be dealing with anything but the irresponsible operation of a programmatic machine. Ethical, juridical, or political responsibility, if there is any, consists in deciding on the strategic orientation to give to this problematic, which remains an interpretive and active problematic, in any case a performative one, for which truth, no more than reality, is not an object given in advance that it would be a matter of simply reflecting adequately. A problematic of testimony, as opposed to proof, seems to me to be necessary, but I cannot develop it here. The opposition veracity/lie is homogeneous with a testimonial problematic, and not at all with an epistemological one of true/false or of proof. (I specify also very quickly, since I do not have the time to say more, that I am using the word "performative" here a little facilely, setting aside many questions that I have formulated elsewhere on the opposition performative/constative, on the paradoxes and especially the limits of its pertinence and its purity. Austin having been the first to put us on guard against this alleged "purity," it is certainly not against him that I would attempt at top speed to restore it or reestablish its credit.)[23]

Such would be, in my view, a *limit* on Koyré's remarks in this article. I believe one encounters it again in Arendt. But Koyré also sketches a *step beyond this limit*, a step beyond that makes his interpretive strategy so acute and so necessary. It is this direction that I would have liked to pursue. Koyré suggests that totalitarian regimes and their analogues of all sorts have never gone *beyond* the distinction between truth and lie. In fact they have a vital need for this oppositional and traditional distinction. This is because they lie from within this tradition, which they therefore have every reason to want to maintain intact and in its most dogmatic form so as to operate the deception. The only difference is that they grant primacy to the lie within the old metaphysical axiomatics, thus contenting themselves with a simple reversal of the hierarchy, a reversal that Nietzsche says, at the end of "History of an Error" (and elsewhere), must not satisfy us.

We cite Koyré again at some length:

In their publications (even in those they call scientific), in their discussions, and of course in their propaganda, the representatives of totalitarian regimes are scarcely hampered by objective truth. More puissant than God Almighty, they change the past as well as the present according to their whim. [In this rewriting of the historical past they exceed even God, who, for his part, would be powerless to change the past: writing in 1943, during the Vichy regime, in a note that today could be extended infinitely, Koyré evokes "the historical teaching of totalitarian regimes" and even the "new history manuals of French schools."] One might conclude, as many have, that totalitarian regimes function outside the sphere of truth and lie.

We do not believe, however, that this is at all the case. The distinction between truth and lie, the fictitious and the real, remains altogether valid within totalitarian conceptions and regimes. Only their place and their role have been reversed: totalitarian regimes are founded on the *primacy of the lie*.[24]

At the time he was writing, Koyré had no difficulty illustrating this "primacy of the lie" in a totalitarian system (whether proclaimed or not), which more than any other needs a belief in the stable and metaphysically assured opposition between veracity and lie. We would have no trouble illustrating it today, whether we look close to home or far away. By definition the liar is someone who says that he says the truth (this is a law of structure and has no history), but the more a political machine lies the more it makes the love of truth into the watchword of its rhetoric. "I hate lies": Koyré quotes from memory and thus abbreviates the famous declaration by Marshall Pétain, who said, more precisely: "I hate the lies that have done you so much harm." Each word counts, and the tenses and the personal pronouns (*I . . . you*; I am speaking to you; I know the truth that I say to you; I know which lies have hurt you, they are hateful for that reason; and, moreover, that's finished, that's done, they have done you so much harm"). For my part, I would have liked to comment on another slogan from the Vichy period and its reactionary ideology of the return to the earth, as the surest locus of family and patriotic values, of the mother-fatherland: "La terre, elle, ne ment pas," "As for the earth, it does not lie," used to say Gustave Thibon, ideologue of the National Revolution who, after quoting Pétain, spoke also of a "realism of the earth" at the same time as "feminine realism," in another's phrase, was also feeding this conjoined celebration of the earthly and the feminine.[25]

One would have to privilege, it seems to me, two of the perspectives opened up in these pages by Koyré, and leave suspended there a serious question.

1. The first opening concerns the paradoxical perversion that consists in

second-degree lying: "the old Machiavellian technique," says Koyré, an art of which Hitler was a master and which consisted in saying the truth while knowing he would not be taken seriously by the uninitiated. The result is a sort of conspiracy "in broad daylight," in which Hannah Arendt also frequently recognizes the very figure of the modern lie: to tell the truth in view of deceiving those who believe they ought not believe it, the credulous ones who believe they are clever, skeptical, or experienced enough to know what has to be believed. Koyré is not the first to identify this ruse, any more than Freud before him, but he does indicate a concern with interpreting it as a modern political technique in the age of mass communications and totalitarianism.

2. The second perspective opens onto a *theory of the secret*. This political cryptology is in fact at the center of this article: its theme is not that of the secret society, but of a "society with a secret," whose structure permits a "conspiracy in broad daylight" that is not a "contradiction *in adjecto*."

The very original deployment of this modern crypto-politology is put in motion by an implicit concern and an implicit evaluation that might inspire a worry, about which I will say just a few words. Koyré seems to consider that any secret is in principle a threat to the *res publica*, indeed to democratic space. This is understandable and in overall conformity with a certain essence of *politeia* as absolute phenomenality. Everything must be made to appear in the transparency of the public space and its illumination. But I wonder if we do not see here signs of the inverse perversion of politicism, of an absolute hegemony of political reason, of a limitless extension of the region of the political. By refusing any right to secrecy, the political agency, most often in the figure of state sovereignty or even of reason of state, summons everyone to behave first of all and in every regard as a responsible citizen before the law of the *polis*. Is there not here, in the name of a certain type of objective and phenomenal truth, another germ of totalitarianism with a democratic face? I could not read without a certain indignant amazement one of Koyré's notes, which, by way of illustrating how one acquires training in secrecy, cryptic codes, and lying, launches a scattershot accusation at Spartans, Indians, Jesuits, and Marranos: "We cite at random the training in lying that was received by the young Spartan and the young Indian; the mentality of the Marrano or of the Jesuit."[26]

If one were to insist on an unconditional right to the secret against this phenomenalism and this integral politicism and if such an absolute secret had to remain inaccessible and invulnerable, then it would concern less the political secret than, in the metonymic and generalized figure of the Marrano, the right to secrecy as right to resistance against and beyond the order of the political, or even of the theologico-political in general. In the political order, this principle of resistance could inspire, as one of its figures, the right to what the United States names with that very fine phrase for the most respectable of traditions, in the case of *force majeure*, where the *raison d'état* does not dispense the last word in ethics: "civil disobedience." Which does not necessarily mean that one accepts with one's eyes closed the axiomatics of all the discourses that adopt this title, not even those of Thoreau, who forged the expression. Civil disobedience does not call one necessarily to disobey the law in general, as has too often been said recently, but to resist positive laws when, after some analysis, one judges that they are in contradiction not only with a superior law, a universal law (for example, human rights), or the spirit of a constitution, but in contradiction with themselves, with the law in which they claim to find their inspiration or their foundation and that therefore, through some lie or perjury, they already betray.

For lack of time, I must hasten these prolegomena toward their conclusion—and return to Hannah Arendt. Is a history of the lie possible, as such? I am less certain of it than ever. But supposing that one were still to attempt such a history, then one would have to take into account the whole oeuvre of Hannah Arendt and, more precisely, in the essays I have cited, a *double square* of motifs, of which one set seems propitious and the other unfavorable for such a project.

In conclusion, then, a program and two squares of four telegrams.

In the first place, several motifs seem propitious for such a history of the lie.

1. Arendt expresses clearly her concern to remove such a history from "moral denunciation."[27] Somewhat like Nietzsche, in a fashion that is both analogous and different, Arendt wants to treat these questions "in an extra-moral sense."

2. Arendt takes into account not only the development of the media but also a new mediatic structure that has transformed the status of the iconic substitute, of the image, and of public space.[28] This thematic appears to be absent from Koyré's remarks. Here one must remain cautious. There is indeed a technical transformation of the icon into a simulacrum

Civil disobedience

that then passes for the thing itself, ceases to represent it so as to replace it by destroying it, and becomes itself both the only archiving archive and the archived event. But this can give rise to phenomena that are structurally very different: *on the one hand*, to lies or mystifications of the classical kind, in other words, deliberate and intentional ones: for example, when television editing presents a speech by Fidel Castro, taken from another, archived source, as an exclusive interview granted to a French journalist.[29] Even in this case, moreover, things are not clear and French law, as we learned, remained powerless to determine that this mystification constituted a lie, that is, a harmful deception. It is not easy to demonstrate that this distortion harmed an addressee who could legally file a complaint, or even that anyone was in a position, as legal subject, to protest this abuse. But *on the other hand*, before and beyond any intentional or conscious mystification, this can also give rise to alterations that have no certain model, to distortions that don't even have a reliable enough referent to allow one to speak of a lie. The thing is thus at once less and more serious than the lie. Less serious because no one has, in bad faith, sought to deceive anyone else. More serious because the absence of any transcendent referent, or even of any meta-interpretive norm, makes the effect of the operation not only difficult to measure and to analyze, but fundamentally irreparable. One must here take into account the arti-factuality that presides over the constitution of images of so-called information, that is, those that are in principle subject to the principle of truth and veracity and that, all the same, through filtering, selection, editing, framing, substitution of the artifactual archive for the thing itself, "de-form" in order to "inform" without it being possible to assign or localize an intentional lie in the mind of a single individual or even in a delimitable group of individuals, albeit an international corporation. In the analysis of this causality, where it is entangled with the preceding one, that is, with intentional deception, the word and concept of the lie encounter their limits.

3. Arendt has the strongly marked intention to *delimit the order of the political*, to surround it with theoretical, practical, social, and institutional boundaries (which are in principle very strict, even if, as one can easily imagine, they remain difficult to draw, for noncontingent reasons). This is undertaken in two directions: *on the one hand*, by setting out that man, in his "singularity," in the "philosophical truth" of his solitary individuality, is "unpolitical by nature";[30] *on the other hand*, by assigning to the

order of the judiciary and the university, which is virtually independent
of the political, new missions and capital responsibilities in this delimitation of the political lie (TP, 260–61).

4. Finally, although the word is not used and there is not a sufficient or
determining development, Arendt sketches a problematic of the performativity of a lie whose structure and event would be linked in an essential manner to the concept of action and, more precisely, political action.[31] She often recalls that the liar is a "man of action," I would even
add: par excellence. Between lying and acting, acting in politics, mani-
festing one's own freedom through action, transforming facts, anticipat-
ing the future, there is something like an essential affinity. The imagination is, according to Arendt, the common root of the "ability to lie" and
the "capacity to act." Capacity to produce some image: productive imagination as experience of time, Kant or Hegel would have said. The lie is
the future, one may venture to say, beyond the letter of her text but without betraying Arendt's intention in this context. To tell the truth is, on the
contrary, to say what is or what will have been and it would instead prefer the past. Even if she insists on marking its limits, Arendt speaks of "the
undeniable affinity of the lie with action, with changing the world—in
short, with politics." The liar, says Arendt, needs no accommodation

> to appear on the political scene; he has the great advantage that he always is, so
> to speak, already in the midst of it. He is an actor by nature; he says what is not
> so because he wants things to be different from what they are—that is, he wants
> to change the world. . . . In other words, our ability to lie—but not necessarily to
> tell the truth—belongs among the few obvious, demonstrable data that confirm
> human freedom. (TP, 250)

Even if such utterances require some modalization and need to be
placed more prudently under a certain index of possibility (a translation
that we do not have the time to undertake now), it goes without saying
that not only do we have here, as illuminated by Arendt, the very idea of
a history of the lie but, more radically, the thesis according to which there
would be no history in general, and no political history in particular,
without at least the possibility of lying, that is, of freedom and of action.
And also of imagination and of time, of imagination as time.

In what way does the Arendtian discourse close or risk closing down
again what it opens up in this manner? This is what I would like to evoke
in conclusion or at least so as to have done with these modest prolegomena.

[margin handwritten note: the sea for the freedom, according to Hannah Arendt]

*[margin: *]*

In the second place, four motifs seem to me to have played an inhibiting, if not prohibiting role in the attempt to take such a history seriously.

1. The absence of a veritable problematic of testimony, witnessing, or bearing witness. Arendt is not interested in the history of this concept, as that which strictly distinguishes it from proof or the archive, even if in fact and not by chance an equivocation always blurs the limits between these radically heterogeneous possibilities. The distinction between "factual truth" and "rational truth," which forms the backbone of this whole discourse, appears to be insufficient here. Arendt herself acknowledges that she is using it only provisionally and for convenience (TP, 239). To be sure, she names testimony more than once (TP, 238, 243), but no more than for the lie, faith, or good faith does she make it the veritable theme of an eidetic analysis. Nor does Koyré, for that matter. Both of them proceed as if they knew what "lying" meant.

2. This is not unrelated to the concept of "lying to oneself" or "internal self-deception" (LP, 35), which plays a determining role in all these demonstrations by Arendt. Now, such a concept remains confused in the "psychology" it implies. It is also logically incompatible with the rigor of any classical concept of the lie and with the "frank" problematic of the lie. To lie will always mean to deceive the other *intentionally* and *consciously*, while *knowing* what it is that one is *deliberately* hiding, therefore while not lying to oneself. And the addressee must be other enough to be, at the moment of the lie, an enemy to be deceived in his belief. The *self*, if this word has a sense, excludes the self-lie. Any other experience, therefore, calls for another name and no doubt arises from another zone or another structure, let us say to go quickly, from intersubjectivity or the relation to the other, to the other in oneself, in an ipseity more originary than the *ego* (whether individual or collective), an enclaved ipseity, a divisible ipseity or one that is split by another oneself, and oneself as enemy.

Not that psychoanalysis or the analytic of *Dasein* (these two discourses that are no longer ordered principially around a theory of the ego or the self) are alone capable of taking the measure of the phenomena that Arendt calls lying to oneself or self-suggestion. I don't believe they would be (I will return to this elsewhere). But both Arendt and Koyré, at the point at which both of them speak of lying to oneself in politics, apparently do everything to avoid the least allusion to Freud and to Heidegger on these problems. Is this fortuitous? Is it fortuitous that they do not even mention the Marxist concept of *ideology*, if only to reelaborate it? Despite its fundamental obscurity, despite the philosophical or theoretical limits of the discourses that have sometimes deployed it, the concept of ideology all the same marks a *site*, the *place* of that which we are seeking to determine here. Even if this determination remains a sort of negative topology, it is very valuable. It takes us farther, beyond consciousness and intentional knowledge, at least in the plenitude of its self-presence or self-identity: in the direction of a locus of nontruth that is neither that of error, ignorance, or illusion nor that of the lie or of lying to oneself. Ideology, in the Marxist sense, in principle is none of these. Even if the word and concept of ideology risk remaining still inscribed in the space that they exceed, there is no doubt that they point toward the place of this problematic to come—which would be rooted in neither a truth of biblical revelation nor a philosophical concept of truth.

3. What seems to compromise, if not the project of such a history of the lie, at least its irreducible specificity, is an indestructible *optimism*. Such optimism is not to be accounted for by psychology. It does not reflect primarily a personal disposition, a habitus, a being-in-the-world, or even a project of Hannah Arendt. After all, to speak of our age as the age of the absolute lie, to seek to acquire the means to analyze it with lucidity, hardly shows optimism. But the conceptual and problematic apparatus here put in place or accredited is "optimistic." What is at stake is the determination of the political lie but also, above all, of the truth in general. The truth must always win out and end up being revealed because, as Arendt repeats frequently, in its structure it is assured stability, irreversibility; it indefinitely outlives lies, fictions, and images.[32]

This classical determination of the truth as indefinite survival of the "stable" (*bebaion* is Plato's and Aristotle's term)[33] seems to call not only for a great number of "deconstructive" questions (and not only in the Heideggerian style). By excluding even the possibility that a lie might survive indefinitely, it goes against experience itself. We know that the lie and its effect (for the concept of lie does not concern only an intention but a desired effect) can survive, must be able to last to infinity and never appear as such; and if one thinks that the effect of the lie, that is, of betrayed veracity, remains indestructible *as symptom* (which I don't believe, but this is a vast question that I leave suspended here), then, even in that case, one must recognize that the logic of the symptom can no longer be contained within an opposition between good faith and bad faith, the intentional and the nonintentional, the voluntary and the involuntary, and so forth—

in short, the lie. Here the task is still prescribed: for a postpsychoanalytic discourse to undertake a new delimitation between a symptomatology that would treat everything resembling the lie (the enormous range of all those betrayed truths that are the lapsus, the disavowal, the dream, all the rhetorical resources of the unconscious, and so forth) and the lie in the strict sense, for example, the one Freud speaks of in "Zwei Kinderlügen," where, moreover, this lie in the strict sense is itself treated as the revealing symptom, the avowal of another truth. *Mutatis mutandis*, an analogous and complementary task would await us as to the status of the lie in the strict sense in Heidegger's existential analytic, while following the path that starts in the 1923–24 seminar, which I indicated at the beginning.

By excluding the indefinite survival of mystification, Arendt makes of history, as history of the lie, the epidermic and epiphenomenal accident of a parousia of truth. Now, a specific history of the frank lie itself, including in Freud and Heidegger, should pass, at least, by way of the history of Christianization (via Paul, certain Church Fathers, Augustine and his *De mendacio*, and so forth), of the Greek thematic of *pseudos* (which, I repeat, means both the false, the fictive, and the untruthful, which does not simplify things or simplifies them too much), of the *eidōlon*, of the spectral *phantasma*, of rhetoric, of sophistics and the politically useful lie, according to Plato's *Republic*,[34] of the useful, curative, or preventive lie as *pharmakon*.

This radical Christianization is found, in the secularized state, so to speak, and in the age of Enlightenment, in the Kantian doctrine that condemns the lie as absolute decline, "human nature's capital vice," "negation of human dignity"; "the man who does not believe what he says is less than a thing," says Kant in his "Doctrine of Virtue."[35] One would be tempted to reply: Unless he does not cease thereby being less than a thing in order to become something and even someone, already something like a man, or even a *Dasein*, where *Dasein*, I cite once more the 1923–24 seminar, "bears within itself the possibilities for deceit and lying."

4. That is why, finally, one may always worry about the secondarization, relativization, or accidentalization, even the banalization of a theory or a history of the lie, if it is still dominated by the Arendtian certainty of a final victory and a certain survival of the truth (and not merely of veracity), even if one accepts its teleology as only a just regulating idea in politics or in the history of the human socius in general.

For me, it is not a matter of opposing to this risk the still Judeo-

Christiano-Kantian hypothesis of the lie as radical evil and sign of the originary corruption of human existence. That would remain within the same logic—a logic that it is not necessarily a matter of destroying but of trying to think, if that still means anything, by answering for its memory. And to begin to think it, is it not appropriate to note that without at least the *possibility* of this radical perversion and of its infinite survival and, especially, without taking into account *technical* mutations in the history of consciousness and the unconscious, in the structure of the simulacrum or the iconic substitute, one will always fail to think the lie itself, the possibility of its history, the possibility of a history that intrinsically involves it, and doubtless the possibility of a history, period?

However, to hasten to the conclusion, one must admit that nothing and no one will ever be able to prove, precisely—what is properly called to "prove," in the strict sense of knowledge, theoretical demonstration, and determinant judgment—the existence and the necessity of such a history as a history of the lie, and of the lie as such. This history cannot become an object of knowledge. It calls for knowledge, all possible knowledge, but it remains structurally heterogeneous to knowledge.

One can only say, beyond knowledge, what could or should be the history of the lie—if there is any.

Typewriter Ribbon: Limited Ink (2)

The Next to Last Word: Archives of the Confession

So here, it seems, is what came about—what happened *to them*, then came down to *us*.

And this was an event, perhaps an interminable event.

Here, they told us, is what happened to them before coming down to us. Both of them are sixteen years old. Several centuries, more than a millennium apart. Both of them happened, later, to confess their respective misdeed, the theft committed when each was sixteen. In the course of both the theft and the confession, there was at work what we could call in Greek a *mēkhanē*, at once an ingenious theatrical machine or a war machine, thus a machine and a machination, something both mechanical and strategic.

Both of these young men happened to become—this was their incredible destiny—the signatories of the first great works, to be called, in our Western Christian tradition, *Confessions*. Augustine and Rousseau not only wrote or confessed what thus happened to them. They confided in us or let us understand that if what happened had not happened that day when they were sixteen years old, if they had not stolen, they would probably never have written—or signed—these *Confessions*.

As if *I*, as if someone saying *I* got around to addressing you to say, and you would still be hearing it today: "Here is the most unjustifiable, if not the most unjust, thing that I ever happened to do, at once actively and passively, mechanically, and in such a way that not only was I able thus to let myself do it but also thanks to it, or because of it, I was able finally to say and to sign *I*."

How is that possible?

Before awakening this memory in its archive, before trying to understand what happened there, both the event and its *mēhkanē*, let us mark a pause and change speeds. Let us put in place the premises of our question.

Will this be possible for us? Will we one day be able, and in a single gesture, to join the thinking of the event to the thinking of the machine? Will we be able to think, what is called thinking, at one and the same time, *both* what is happening (we call that an event) *and* the calculable programming of an automatic repetition (we call that a machine)?

For that, it would be necessary in the future (but there will be no future except on this condition) to think *both* the event *and* the machine as two compatible or even indissociable concepts. Today they appear to us to be antinomic. Antinomic because what happens ought to keep, so we think, some nonprogrammable and therefore incalculable singularity. An event worthy of the name ought not, so we think, to give in or be reduced to repetition. To respond to its name, the event ought above all to *happen* to someone, to some living being who is thus is *affected* by it, consciously or unconsciously. No event without *experience* (and this is basically what "experience" means), without experience, conscious or unconscious, human or not, of what happens to the living.

It is difficult, however, to conceive of a living being *to* whom or *through* whom something happens without an affection getting *inscribed* in a sensible, aesthetic manner right on some body or some organic matter.

Why *organic*? Because there is no thinking of the event, it seems, without some sensitivity, without an *aesthetic* affect and some presumption of living organicity.

The machine, on the contrary, is destined to repetition. It is destined, that is, to reproduce impassively, imperceptibly, without organ or organicity, received commands. In a state of anesthesia, it would obey or command a calculable program without affect or auto-affection, like an indifferent automaton. Its functioning, if not its production, would not need anyone. Moreover, it is difficult to conceive of a purely machinelike apparatus without inorganic matter.

Notice I say *inorganic*. Inorganic, that is, nonliving, sometimes dead but always, in principle, unfeeling and inanimate, without desire, without intention, without spontaneity. The automaticity of the inorganic machine is not the spontaneity attributed to organic life.

This, at least, is how the event and the machine are generally conceived. Among all the incompatible traits that we have just briefly recalled, so as to suggest how difficult it is to think them together as the same "thing," we have had to underscore these two predicates, which are, most often, attributed without hesitation to matter or to the material body: the *organic* and the *inorganic*.

These two commonly used words carry an obvious reference, either positive or negative, to the possibility of an internal principle that is proper and *totalizing*, to a total form of, precisely, *organization*, whether or not it is a beautiful form, an aesthetic form, this time in the sense of the fine arts. This organicity is thought to be lacking from so-called inorganic matter. If one day, with one and the same concept, these two incompatible concepts, the event and the machine, were to be thought together, you can bet that *not only* (and I insist on *not only*) will one have produced a new logic, an unheard-of conceptual form. In truth, against the background and at the horizon of our present possibilities, this new figure would resemble a monster. But can one resemble a monster? No, of course not, resemblance and monstrosity are mutually exclusive. We must therefore correct this formulation: the new figure of an event-machine would no longer be even a figure. It would not resemble, it would resemble nothing, not even what we call, in a still familiar way, a monster. But it would therefore be, by virtue of this very novelty, an event, the only and the first possible event, because im-possible. That is why I ventured to say that this thinking could belong only to the future—and even that it makes the future possible. An event does not come about unless its irruption interrupts the course of the possible and, as the impossible itself, surprises any foreseeability. But such a super-monster of eventness would be, this time, for the first time, *also* produced by the machine.

Not only, I said, not only a new logic, not only an unheard-of conceptual form. The thinking of this new concept will have changed the very essence and the very name of what we today call "thought," the "concept," and what we would like to mean by "thinking thought," "thinking the thinkable," or "thinking the concept." Perhaps another thinking is heralded here. Perhaps it is heralded without announcing itself, without horizon of expectation, by means of this old word "thought," this homonym or paleonym that has sheltered for such a long time the name still to come of a thinking that has not yet thought what it must think, namely thought, namely, what is given to be thought with the name "thought," beyond knowledge, theory, philosophy, literature, the fine arts—and even technics.

As a still preliminary exercise, somewhat like musicians who listen to their instruments and tune them before beginning to play, we could try out another version of the same aporia. Such an aporia would not block or paralyze, but on the contrary would condition any event of thought that resembles somewhat the unrecognizable monster that has just passed in front of our eyes.

What would this aporia be? One may say of a machine that it is productive, active, efficient, or, as one says in French, *performante*. But a machine as such, however *performante* it may be, could never, according to the strict Austinian orthodoxy of speech acts, produce an event of the *performative* type. Performativity will never be reduced to technical performance. Pure performativity implies the presence of a living being, and of a living being speaking one time only, in its own name, in the first person. And speaking in a manner that is at once spontaneous, intentional, free, and irreplaceable. Performativity, therefore, excludes in principle, in its own moment, any machinelike [*machinale*] technicity. It is even the name given to this intentional exclusion. This foreclosure of the machine answers to the intentionality of intention itself. It is intentionality. Intentionality forecloses the machine. If, then, some machinality (repetition, calculability, *inorganic* matter of the body) intervenes in a performative event, it is always as an accidental, extrinsic, and parasitical element, in truth a pathological, mutilating, or even mortal element. Here again, to think *both* the machine *and* the performative event together remains a monstrosity to come, an *impossible* event. Therefore the only possible event. But it would be an event that, this time, would no longer happen without the machine. Rather, it would happen by the machine. To give up neither the event nor the machine, to subordinate neither one to the other, never to reduce one to the other: this is perhaps a concern of thinking that has kept a certain number of "us" working for the last few decades.

But who, "us"? Who would be this "us" whom I dare to speak of so carelessly? Perhaps it designates at bottom, and first of all, those who find themselves in the improbable place or in the uninhabitable habitat of this monster.

I owe you now some excuses, unless I must even ask your forgiveness for the *compromise* that I had to resolve to make in the preparation of this lecture. For several reasons, so as to save some time and energy, I had to reorient in the direction of this colloquium certain sessions of an ongoing seminar on *pardon*, *perjury*, and *capital punishment*. By analyzing the filiations of these concepts (on the one hand, the Abrahamic inheritance—that is, Jewish, Christian, or Muslim—and the Greek inheritance, on the other), by formalizing the aporetic logic that torments this history, these concepts, this experience, their present-day mutation on a geo-juridico-political scale in a world where scenes of public repentance happen more and more frequently, I insist in this seminar on a certain irreducibility of the *work*, that is, *l'oeuvre*. As a possible legacy from what is above all an event, *l'oeuvre* has a virtual future only by surviving or cutting itself off from its presumed responsible signatory. It *thereby* supposes that a logic of the machine is in accordance, however improbable that may seem, with a logic of the event. Hence, there will remain some traces, in the reflections I'm getting ready to submit to you, dare I say some visible archives, of this ongoing seminar and of its own context. This will not escape you, and I do not wish to hide it. In a certain way, I will be speaking solely about pardon, forgiveness, excuse, betrayal, and perjury—of death and death penalty. I have begun to do so already in order to attempt to excuse myself. But this will not necessarily betray the general contract of our colloquium. And I will speak neither of myself, nor of my texts on the scene of writing or archive fever, on signature, event, context, nor on the spirit, the virtual revenants and other specters of Marx, nor even directly of my seminar on forgiveness and perjury. I will speak only of this or that author: Augustine, Rousseau, Paul de Man, and a few others *à propos* of one or another of their works.

This first compromise was no doubt excessive and inexcusable. It became also unavoidable from the moment the title, program, or even protocol of this colloquium defined implacable imperatives. To save time, I ought not to undertake to read in its entirety this title, which I hold to be a masterpiece. Nevertheless, I reread it *in extenso*, for one must register everything about it, including its play with quotation marks—the word "Materiality" having been freed from quotation marks whereas, in the subtitle, care was taken to put the word "materialist" in the expression "'materialist' thought" (rather than materialist philosophy or theory) under the strict surveillance of quotation marks. I underscore this fact now because, much later, I will wonder à propos of de Man, what might be a thinking of machinistic materiality without materialism and even perhaps without matter. The generalization of quotation marks that then becomes necessary would in that case no longer mean in the least that one is citing an ulterior author or text; rather, and quite the contrary, it would mean that one is performatively instituting a new concept and a new contract with the word. One is thus inaugurating another word, in sum, a homonym that must be put forward cautiously between quotation marks. Another word-concept is thus staged whose event one causes to come about. The quotation marks signal in this case that one is citing only oneself at the moment of this invention or this convention, in a gesture that is as inaugural as it is arbitrary. I now reread, as promised, the complete title: "Culture and Materiality: A post-millenarian conference—à propos of Paul de Man's *Aesthetic Ideology*—to consider trajectories for 'materialist' thought in the afterlife of theory, cultural studies, and Marxist critique." This is an impressive series of transactions, which called for an equally impressive number of rhetorical performances or theoretical exploits: between culture and materiality, between a corpus or a proper name, Paul de Man, more precisely, a very particular place in the posthumous corpus, *Aesthetic Ideology* ("—à propos of Paul de Man's *Aesthetic Ideology*—"). Here, then, is an inheritance that is also a posthumous work of Paul de Man's to which we are invited to refer, between dashes, in the mode of an "à-propos" that set me to wondering. I wondered about this French idiom, which seems untranslatable and overdetermined enough that, I suppose, it was left like the foreign body it remains in your language.

Moreover, and à propos, I had for a moment dreamed of entitling my lecture: "*A propos* of A propos," à propos of all the meanings and all the uses of *à propos* and of the *à-propos* in French. As we know, "à propos" can be an adverb, *à propos*, or a noun, the *à-propos*. I had thus thought, but perhaps I will do it silently, of examining the modalities and figures of reference that are crossing in the inimitable and untranslatable expression "à propos"—which allies chance to necessity, contingency to obligation, machinelike association to the internal, intentional, organic link. When one says "à propos," "à propos de . . . ," there is, from a pragmatic point of view, always a mark of reference, a *reference-to . . .* , but it is sometimes a direct reference, sometimes indirect, furtive, passing, oblique, accidental, machinelike, also in the mode of the quasi avoidance of the unavoidable, of repression, or of the lapsus, and so forth. When one says "à propos," it is because one is at least pretending to leap at the opportunity to speak, metonymically, of something else altogether, to change the subject without changing the subject, or else to underscore that between what is being talked about and what someone wants to talk about there is either a link of organic, internal, and essential necessity or else, inversely, an insignificant and superficial association, a purely mechanical and metonymic association, the arbitrary or fortuitous comparison—"by accident"—of two signifiers. And yet one knows that, at that very moment, one touches on the essential, one at least brushes against the place of decision. That is where the thing happens, that is where it comes about. When Rousseau, after having stolen the ribbon, accuses Marion so as to excuse himself, it is because he denounced, he said, "the first object that presented itself [*le premier objet qui s'offrit*]."[1] Marion herself, or the name "Marion," being there by chance, by accident, it is as if he leaped on the opportunity and said, with *à-propos*: "A propos, it's Marion who gave it to me, I didn't steal it." The *esprit d'à-propos*, in French, is the art, the genius, but also the technique that consists in knowing how to grab an opportunity, to make the best of it, the best economy of contingency, and to make of the *Khairos* or the *Chaos* a significant, archivable, necessary, or even ineffaceable event.

So many other things still remained enormous and enigmatic for me in the "à propos" of this title—which says everything in advance, beginning with "post-millenarian" and "'materialist' thought" ("materialist" in quotation marks), not to mention everything that is put under the "umbrella" of some "afterlife" ("theory, cultural studies, and Marxist critique"). When I read this protocol, I asked myself which theoretical animal or which animal-machine of the third millennium could measure up to this inhuman program. If anyone could ever treat the subject in question, it will not be me, I said as I commanded myself to retreat: withdraw toward your own compromise on the subject of these untenable promises, but make every possible effort not to be too unworthy of the square you've landed on in this *jeu de l'oie* (a French board game that is something like a cross between Chinese checkers and Monopoly).

A propos of *Matière et mémoire*, this title that I confess to having stolen from Bergson and Ponge and that, still worse, I am preparing to disfigure or deport, good manners requires that it announce, as does a title, even a stolen title, some subject.

Regarding this presumed announced subject, and I beg you to excuse me also for this, in a certain way I will not treat it. Obviously not, not obviously not directly, certainly not head-on.

A propos, in his article "Excuses (Confessions)," à propos of Rousseau, de Man refers in a note to Austin's "A Plea for Excuses." A strange title, difficult to translate: "plea" is already an excuse, in some way, an allegation, an argument in the form of an appeal and that pleads—here for an excuse. That presents excuses. It is thus a question of a text that asks for or presents excuses, even as it argues on the subject of excuses asked for or presented. Paul de Man pays no attention to the fact that this text by Austin itself begins by presenting excuses and is thereby altogether enveloped, comprehended, included in the event of this first performative. Everything that Austin is going to say on the subject of the excuse will be at once comprehended and signed by the first gesture of the first sentence, by the performative event that is put to work, precisely, by the first words of "A Plea for Excuses." With the excuse that they implicitly present, these words of introduction make of this text an event, *une oeuvre*, something other than a purely theoretical treatise: "The subject of this paper, *Excuses*, is one not to be treated, but only to be introduced, within such limits."[2] Everything happens as if the title, "A Plea for Excuses," designated first of all and solely Austin's performative gesture, namely that of a lecturer himself presenting excuses and alleging limits (time, urgency, situation, context, etc.: "within such limits," he says). The title, "A Plea for Excuses," would thus be the name or the description of this cunning ruse or this rhetorical distress. It would designate an avowed simulacrum or failure, a prayer as well, rather than and before being the announced subject, a theme or a problem to be treated in a theoretical, philosophical, constative, or metalinguistic mode, namely, the concept or the usage of the word "excuses." This text constitutes a "Plea for Excuses," and it even does so in an exemplary fashion. So Austin excuses himself for not treating the excuse in a serious enough fashion. He excuses himself for falling short, or even for leaving his audience in ignorance on the subject of what is meant by "to excuse oneself." And this at the moment when (performative contradiction or not), having begun by excusing himself, by pretending to do so, or rather by pretending to pretend to do so, he undertakes to excuse himself for not treating the subject of the excuse. He must, nevertheless, know enough about what the word "excuse" means, he must presuppose enough on the subject of what his audience knows of the word "excuse" and understands about it in advance, in so-called ordinary language (which is moreover the real subject of this essay), to declare that he will not treat it—even as he introduces it.

Will he have treated it? Perhaps. It is for the reader to judge and for the addressee to decide if a lecturer will have treated, and treated well, the proposed subject. It is like the scene of the writing of a post card whose virtual addressee would in the future have to decide whether or not he or she will receive it and whether it is indeed to him or to her that it will have been addressed, in the singular or the plural. The signature is left to the initiative, to the responsibility of the other. At his or her discretion and to his or her work. Get to work. One will sign, if one signs, at the moment of arrival at a destination, rather than at the origin, at the moment of reading rather than of writing.

Did Austin, as well and already, allow himself to be enclosed in a "performative contradiction," as they say in Frankfurt? Did he do the contrary of what he claimed to do? This hypothesis and this suspicion could not have been formulated without him. May we thus be permitted to smile at it, along with his ghost? As if it were possible to escape all performative contradiction! And as if it were possible to exclude that an Austin would have had a little fun illustrating this inevitable trap!

Now it is not unthinkable that, in *Allegories of Reading* (a book published just before or even while the texts of *Aesthetic Ideology* were being prepared), the title chosen by de Man for his last chapter, "Excuses (*Confessions*)," also presents the excuses and confessions of the author, de Man himself, if I can put it that way, on some subject or another. It is possible that he played at this scene without playing, that he pretended to play at it, *à propos* of Rousseau's *Confessions* and *Reveries*. And perhaps, for example (this is only an example), inasmuch as he only "introduced" it, as Austin said, without really treating it—neither à propos of Rousseau nor in general.

I will add two subtitles to my title, namely, "machine" and "textual event." These are words de Man uses in "Excuses (*Confessions*)." I will thus propose that we interrogate together, at least obliquely, the use of these words, "machine" and "textual event," in *Allegories of Reading*. Their use as well as their supposed meaning. My hypothesis is that de Man reinvents and signs these words, in a certain way, even as he leads us, if we can still put it that way, toward the "thinking of materiality" that comes to light in *Aesthetic Ideology*. The coherent use, the performative inaugurality of these words ("machine" and "textual event"), their conceptual effects and the formalization that will follow, in semantics and beyond semantics, this is what will affect in a necessary fashion all of de Man's writing and thus the destiny of all the other words he put to work. For example, but these are only examples, despite their frequent occurrence in this book from 1979, the words "deconstruction" and "dissemination." My timid contribution would thus describe only a modest divergence in relation to the gigantic program proposed to us by Tom Cohen, Hillis Miller, and Andrzej Warminski. This displacement would remain discreet, micrological, infinitesimal—and literal. Perhaps it will be limited to underscoring "materiality," in place, so to speak, of "matter," then insisting on "thought of materiality," or even "material thought of materiality," in place, if I may put it this way, of "materialist" thought, even within quotation marks.

But we will see what happens when the moment comes.

There is a memory, a history, and an archive of confession, a genealogy of confessions: of the word "confession," of the rather late Christian institution that bears this name, but also of the works that, in the West, are registered under this title. Their status as works of literature remains to be decided. Augustine and Rousseau, both authors of *Confessions*, speak the language of excuse more often than that of pardon or forgiveness. Augustine speaks of the inexcusable (*inexcusabilis*), Rousseau of "excusing himself." I must recall, in this context, that in the course of his exemplary and from now on canonical reading of Rousseau's *Confessions*, de Man never speaks of Augustine and of this Christian history.[3] It is necessary to make at least some minimal reference to this because the sedimentation in question forms an interior stratum of the very structure of Rousseau's text, of its "textual event." It is not certain that a purely internal reading can legitimately neglect it, even supposing that the concept of "textual event," to quote once again these words of de Man, leaves standing the distinction between internal and external reading. For my part, I believe that if there is "textual event," this very border would have to be reconsidered.

Has anyone ever noticed, in this immense archive, that Augustine and Rousseau both confess a theft? And that both do so in Book 2 of their *Confessions*, in a decisive or even determining and paradigmatic place? That is not all: in this archive that is also a confession, both of them confess that, although it was objectively trifling, this theft had the greatest psychic repercussions on their whole lives. A propos, this apparently insignificant theft was committed by each of them at the precise age of sixteen. A propos, and on top of it all, each of them presents it as a useless theft. Their abusive appropriation did not take aim at the use value of the thing stolen: pears in the case of Saint Augustine, the famous ribbon in the case of Rousseau. Presuming that one can know with certainty the use value of a fetish, of the becoming-fetish of a thing, it so happens that they both insist on the fact that the use value was null or secondary. Augustine: "For I stole a thing of which I had plenty of my own and of much better quality. Nor did I wish to enjoy that thing which I desired to gain by theft, but rather to enjoy the actual theft and the sin of theft."[4] Rousseau will likewise speak of the trifling value, even the insignificance of the ribbon. We will see what fate de Man reserves for what he then calls the "free signifier" of a ribbon become available for a "system of symbolic substitutions (based on encoded significations arbitrarily attributed to a free signifier, the ribbon)."[5] Even though, at this point in his itinerary, de Man seems to expose, rather than countersign, a psychoanalytic or even self-analytic interpretation of the Lacanian type—he speaks of a "general economy of human affectivity, in a theory of desire, repression, and self-analyzing discourse" (ibid.)—everything seems to indicate that he does in fact consider the ribbon to be a "free signifier," thus indifferent as regards its meanings, like the purloined letter whose content, Lacan said, had no importance. I am less sure of this point myself in both cases, as I have shown elsewhere, and I will return to it. As you know, the first title de Man thought to give to this text was "The Purloined Ribbon."

No more than its immediate *use value*, Augustine and Rousseau likewise do not covet the *exchange value* of the stolen object, at least not in the banal sense of the term. The very act of stealing becomes the object of desire. If it is not the act itself, it is at least the equivalent of its metonymic value for a desire that we are going to talk about. Augustine thus confesses, in Book 2 (chap. 4, 9 ff.), the theft of pears. But to whom does he address his confession? In the course of this long confession and the prayer by which it is carried, he addresses the theft itself. As strange as it may seem, the addressee of the apostrophe is none other than the very gesture of stealing, as if the theft, the hiding itself were someone: "What was it that I, a wretch, loved in you [*Quid ego miser in te amavi?*] O my act of theft [*O furtum meum*], O my deed of crime done by night in the sixteenth year of my life [*O facinus illud meum nocturnum sexti decimi anni aetatis meae*]?" (chap. 6, 12).

Augustine himself thus archives his age at the time of the theft. He registers the age he was at the moment of the sin. To whom does he declare his age? To the theft itself. His addressee, the destination of his addressee, his address and his addressee is the theft. He addresses the sin in order to tell it two things, which he thereby archives and consigns: *both* its date, the date of the event of the theft, *and* his own age, the age of the thief at the moment of the misdeed. Theft, O theft, my theft (*O furtum meum*), know that I committed you, that I loved you, like a crime (*facinus*), theft, I loved you and I perpetrated you that night when I was sixteen years old.

Rousseau also speaks of his age in direct reference to this theft, at the precise moment when he writes: "This ribbon alone tempted me. I stole it. . . ." As always, he speaks of it *both* to clear himself *and* to add to his burden of guilt. "My age also should be taken into account. I was scarcely more than a child. Indeed I still was one" (89). That ought to clear him. But he right away adds: "In youth real crimes are even more reprehensible than in riper years." That ought to aggravate his fault. But he right away adds: "But what is no more than weakness is much less blameworthy, and really my crime amounted to no more than weakness." He does not say here that he was exactly sixteen years old at the time, but he had pointed it out earlier (I will cite this later) and, moreover, an easy calculation allows one to deduce without any risk of error that he too was just sixteen years old when, in 1728, during the summer and fall, he spent three months as a lackey in the house of Mme de Vercellis, where the affair of the ribbon took place. 1728: Jean-Jacques, son of Isaac Rousseau, was born in 1712; so he was 16 years old. Exactly like Augustine. And this theft, which is also confessed in Book 2 of the *Confessions*, was, by Rousseau's own admission, a determining event, a structuring theft, a wound, a trauma, an endless scarring, the repeated access to the experience of guilt and to the writing of the *Confessions*. This is true in both cases, even if the experience and the interpretation of guilt appear different, at first glance. As if, through a supplement of fiction in what remains a possible fiction, Rousseau had played at practicing an artifice of composition: he would have invented an intrigue, a narrative knot, as if to knot a ribbon around a basket of pears. This fabulous intrigue would have been but a stratagem, the *mēkhanē* of a dramaturgy destined to inscribe itself in the archive of a new, quasi literary genre, the history of confessions entitled *Confessions*, autobiographical stories inaugurated by a theft. And each time it is the paradigmatic and paradisiacal theft of forbidden fruit or a forbidden pleasure. Augustine's *Confessions* were written before the Catholic sacrament of confession was instituted; those of Rousseau, the converted Protestant, were written after this institution and, moreover, after his abjuration of Calvinism. As if it were a matter for Jean-Jacques of inscribing himself into this great genealogical history of confessions entitled *Confessions*. The genealogical tree of a more or less literary lineage that would begin with the theft, from some tree, in the literal or the figural sense, of some forbidden fruit. A tree with leaves or a tree without leaves that produced so many leaves of paper, manuscript paper and typing paper. Rousseau would have inscribed his name in the archival economy of a palimpsest, by means of quasi-quotations drawn from the palimpsestuous and ligneous thickness of a quasi-literary memory: a clandestine or encrypted lineage, a testamentary cryptography of confessional narration, the secret of an autobiography between Augustine and Rousseau, the simulacrum of a fiction right there where *both* Augustine *and* Rousseau claim truth, a veracity of testimony that never makes any concessions to the lies of literature (although fiction would not constitute a lie for Rousseau: he explains himself on this score with clarity and acuity in all his refined discourses on the lie, especially in the *Fourth Reverie*, precisely, where he confides to paper the story of the ribbon).

Let us not forget he had not forgotten that before reaching the age of sixteen, Rousseau had already stolen forbidden fruit, just as Augustine had done. More orthodox than Augustine, he had already stolen apples, rather than pears. He confesses it with delight, lightheartedness, and abundance in Book 1 of the *Confessions*. What is more, he stole constantly in his early youth: first asparagus, then apples. He's inexhaustible on the subject, and he insists on his good conscience, up until the theft of the ribbon. Since he was punished for all these earlier thefts, he began "to thieve with an easier conscience than before, saying to myself, 'Well, what will happen? I shall be beaten. All right, that's what I was made for [*Je me disais: qu'en arrivera-t-il enfin? Je serai battu. Soit: je suis fait pour l'être*]*" (43; 35). As if corporal punishment, physical injury, the automatic and justly repaid sanction exonerated him from any guilt, thus from any remorse. He steals more and more, and not only things to eat but also tools, which confirms him in his feeling of innocence. Rousseau, as you know, will have spent his life protesting his innocence and thus excusing himself rather than seeking to be forgiven: "Really the theft of these trifles [the master's tools] was quite innocent, since I only took them to use in his service: but I was thrilled to have these trifles in my power; I thought I was stealing the talent of his productions" (ibid.).

As if the most refined pleasure, at once the most innocent and the most guilty, was achieved in this way: steal the productive act rather than the product, the cause rather than the thing, the subject of origin rather than the secondary, derived, fallen, devalorized object.

"I thus learned that stealing was not so terrible as I had thought" (42). All these thefts predating the theft of the ribbon, before his sixteenth year, all these crimes engender no feelings of guilt; they have no repercussions, there is no common measure with the trauma that became something like the credits or the matrix of the *Confessions*. What was the phenomenal appearance of this trauma? As is well known, the appropriation of the ribbon was less serious as a theft than as a dissimulating lie. Rousseau allowed someone else to be accused, an innocent girl who did not understand what was happening to her: he accused her in order to excuse himself and he did it with the intention of misleading. This is what is evil.

Will one ever have access to the truth of this story of the ribbon in archives other than Rousseau's writings (the second book of the *Confessions* and the *Fourth Reverie*)? If, as I believe, Rousseau is the only testimonial source and the only archivist of the event, every hypothesis is possible, although I will abstain here from making any, regarding a pure and simple invention of the episode of the theft out of a compositional concern: at sixteen years old and in the second book of his *Confessions*, like the great ancestor of the *Confessions*, Augustine, with whom, in the ligneous lineage of the same genealogical tree bearing forbidden fruit, it would be a matter of sharing the titles of nobility. The same tree, the same wood, the same paper pulp. A delicate and abyssal problem of conscious or unconscious archivation.

Paul de Man does not speak of Augustine. No doubt his project allows him legitimately, up to a certain point, to dispense with talking about him. But Rousseau did read Augustine. And he talks about him. He does so, as you will hear, to avoid him. He at least alludes to him, precisely in the same Book 2 of his own *Confessions*. Let us be more precise, since it is a matter of the obscure relations between memory (either mechanical or not), archive, consciousness, the unconscious, and disavowal. Rousseau does not in truth admit that he had read Saint Augustine himself, in the text of his great corpus. He recognizes merely that he had nevertheless, without having read it, retained many passages from this text. He did not read it but he knew some passages by heart. Speaking of a priest who always gave everybody lessons, "young and a good speaker," "satisfied with himself if ever any Doctor ever was," Rousseau takes his revenge: "He thought he could floor me with Saint

Augustine, Saint Gregory, and the other Fathers, but found to his utter surprise that I could handle all the Fathers as nimbly as he. It was not that I had ever read them. Nor perhaps had he. But I remembered a number of passages out of my Le Sueur [author of a *History of the Church and the Empire up to the Year 1000*]" (70). The question remains as to what it means to "know by heart" certain passages cited from a secondary source, and whether the second book of Augustine's *Confessions* was included there. It all comes down once again to the faith one can put in a given word, be it a word of avowal or confession.

Another superficial reference to Saint Augustine appears at the end of the *Second Reverie*. This time things are in the open: Rousseau briefly names Augustine in order to oppose him. I will not do so here, but one could, "within such limits," reserve a structuring place for this objection and thus for this difference in the archive and the economy of a religious history of confession, but as well in the genealogy of autobiographies entitled *Confessions*. The place of the passage, at the end of the *Second Reverie*, is highly significant. Rousseau has just evoked humanity's "common plot" against him, what he calls the "universal agreement [*l'accord universel*]" of all men against him.[6] Here, then, is an agreement too universal and too "extraordinary to be purely fortuitous." Not a single accomplice has refused to cooperate with this plot, with this veritable *conjuration*, since the failure of just one accomplice would have caused it to fail. Rousseau evokes "the wickedness of men," a wickedness that is so universal that men themselves cannot be responsible for it, only God, only a divine secret: "I cannot prevent myself from henceforth considering as one of those secrets of Heaven impenetrable to human reason the same work that until now I looked upon as only a fruit of the wickedness of men [*Je ne puis m'empêcher de regarder désormais comme un de ces secrets du ciel impénétrables à la raison humaine la même* oeuvre *que je n'envisageois jusqu'ici que comme un fruit de la méchanceté des hommes*]" (21; 1010)

I underscore the word *oeuvre*. This "oeuvre," this fact, these crimes, this *conjuration*, this misdeed of men's *sworn* [conjurée] will would thus not depend on the will of men. It would be a trade secret of God, a secret impenetrable to human reason. For such a work of evil, only Heaven can answer. But since one cannot accuse heaven any more than human malevolence of such an extraordinary work of evil, since one cannot accuse the cunning, the *mēkhanē* of men of having produced this "universal conspiracy . . . too extraordinary to be a mere coincidence," thus the necessity of a machination, Rousseau must then at the same time turn toward God and put blind trust in God, in the secret of God: beyond evil and beyond the machination of which he accuses him. At this point he makes a brief allusion to Saint Augustine in order to oppose him. In the last paragraph of the *Second Reverie*, you will notice the at least *apparent* de-Christianization that would set adrift the filiation or inheritance, namely, the passage from Augustine's to Rousseau's *Confessions*:

I do not go as far as Saint Augustine who would have consoled himself to be damned if such had been the will of God. My resignation comes, it is true, from a less disinterested source [Rousseau thus confesses that his confessions obey an economy, however subtle or sublime it may be], but one no less pure and to my mind, more worthy of the perfect Being whom I adore. God is just; He wills that I suffer; and He knows that I am innocent [this takes us to the other extreme from Augustine, whose *Confessions* are made, in principle, so as to beg pardon for a confessed fault—God knows I am a sinner—whereas Rousseau confesses everything only so as to excuse himself and proclaim his radical innocence; at least at first glance, this will already mark the difference between the theft of the pears and the theft of the ribbon]. That is the cause of my confidence; my heart and my reason cry out to me that I will not be deceived by it. Let me, therefore, leave men and fate to go their ways. Let me learn to suffer without a murmur. In the end, everything must return to order, and my turn will come sooner or later. (21)

This "sooner or later," which signs the last words of the *Second Reverie*, is extraordinary—like other "last words" that are waiting for us: "In the end, everything must return to order, and my turn will come sooner or later." "Sooner or later": this patience of the virtual stretches time beyond death. It promises the survival of the work, but also survival *by* the work as self-justification and faith in redemption—not only the justification of myself but the justification of men and of Heaven, the justification, the theodicy of God whose order and indisputable justice will return. This act of faith, this patience, this passion of faith comes to seal in some way the virtual time of the work, of *une oeuvre* that will operate by itself. The work will accomplish its work of work, *son oeuvre d'oeuvre*, beyond its signatory and without his living assistance, whatever may be the time required, whatever may be the time to come; for time itself no longer counts in the survival of this "sooner or later." The time that this will take matters little, time is given, it is on my side, it is taken and has taken sides in advance, thus it no longer exists. Time no longer costs anything. Since it no longer costs anything, it is graciously given in exchange for the labor of the work that operates all by itself, in a quasi-machinelike fashion, virtually, and thus without the author's work: as if, contrary to what is commonly thought, there were a secret affinity between grace and the machine, between the heart and the automatism of the marionette, as if the excusing machine as writing machine and machine for establishing innocence worked all by itself.

This would be Rousseau's grace, but also Rousseau's machine. Grace as machine: *mēkhanē*, ruse, ingenious invention, machination and counter-machination. He pardons himself in advance. He excuses himself by giving himself in advance the time needed and that he therefore annuls in a "sooner or later" that the work bears like a machine for killing time and redeeming the fault. Such a fault seems therefore only apparent, whether this appearance be the malevolence of men or the secret of Heaven. Sooner or later, grace will operate in the work, by the work of the work at work, in a machinelike fashion. Rousseau's innocence will shine forth. Not only will he be forgiven, like his enemies themselves, but there will have been no fault [*il n'y aura pas eu de mal*]. Not only will he excuse himself, but he will have been excused. And he will have excused.

A propos of this extraordinary machine of the future (namely, a machine that by itself, in a machinelike fashion, machinates a future anterior plot to overturn the machination, the conjuration of all those who might have conspired against Rousseau, of all those enemies who would have universally sworn his demise), à propos also of this allusion to Augustine at the end of the *Second Reverie*, in a context that de Man no doubt, and perhaps rightly, considered *hors de propos*, extrinsic to his "propos," I would like to evoke the beginning of the *Fourth Reverie*. Allusion is made there to the theft of the ribbon, to the lie that followed it, and to the story of the one whom he will later call, in the same *Reverie*, "poor Marion." But one must also recognize or see put in place there a kind of machine that articulates among themselves events of a kind that ought to resist any mechanization, any economy of the machine, namely, oaths, acts of sworn faith: *jurer, conjurer, abjurer*, to swear, to conjure, to abjure or forswear.

In the beginning, there will have been the act and there will have been the word, and the two in one: the act of swearing. In the beginning, there will have been the act of swearing before heaven and taking heaven as one's witness in order to proclaim one's innocence. Very close by the word

"swear," very close to this act of speech that is a verb, very near the verb
"to swear," the word *délire* (folly, "irresponsible folly") will have the charge
of naming, above all, the extraordinary coincidence between, on the one
hand, the irrationality of the machine that is irresponsible or beyond my
control, the mechanism that caused me to do evil, and, on the other
hand, the absolute sincerity, the authentic innocence of my intentions.
On the one hand, the extreme self-accusation for an infinite crime, which
is incalculable in its actual and virtual effects (the "sooner or later" of
these effects, conscious or unconscious, known or unknown), the coincidence or the unheard-of compatibility between this feeling of properly infinite guilt, which is confessed as such, and, on the other hand, the just as
unshakable certainty in the absolute, virgin, intact innocence, which will
"sooner or later" appear, the declared absence of any "repentance," of any
"regret,' of any "remorse" for the fault, the theft, and the lie. "Repentance," "regret," "remorse" (*repentir, regret, remord*) are Rousseau's words,
on the same page, when he speaks of what he himself calls an "incredible
contradiction" between his infinite guilt and the absence of any guilty
conscience. It is as if he still had to confess the guilt that there is, and that
remains, in not feeling guilty, or better yet, in saying he is innocent, in
swearing his innocence in the very place where he confesses the worst. As
if Rousseau still had to ask forgiveness for feeling innocent. This theater
recalls the scene where Hamlet asks his mother to forgive him his own
virtue, to forgive him, in sum, for having nothing to forgive him for, to
forgive Hamlet for the fact that he has nothing to be forgiven for. Pardon
me my virtue, he says, in sum, to Gertrude: "Confess yourself to heaven;
Repent what's past. . . . Forgive me this my virtue" (III, iv). Perhaps one
also hears Rousseau address to his mother the same protest of accusatory
innocence.

The following day, having set off to carry out this resolution, the first idea which
came to me when I began to collect my thoughts was that of a dreadful lie I told
in my early youth, the memory of which has troubled me all my life and even
comes in my old age to sadden my heart again, already distressed as it is in so
many other ways. This lie, in itself a great crime, must have become an even
greater one because of its consequences—of which I have always been unaware,
but which remorse has made me suppose as cruel as possible. However, considering only how I was disposed when telling it, this lie was simply an effect of
mortification; and far from originating from an intention to harm her who was
the victim of it, I can swear by Heaven that in the very instant this invincible
shame tore it from me, I would joyfully have shed all my blood to turn the con-

sequences on myself alone. This is a delirium I can explain only by saying, and this is what I think and feel, that in that instant my timid natural temperament subjugated all the wishes of my heart.

The moment of this unfortunate act and the inextinguishable regrets it left me have inspired in me a horror for lying that should have preserved my heart from this vice for the rest of my life. (43–44)

This lie was surely a "great crime," but since it was devoid of any "desire [*intention*] to harm the girl who was its victim" (51), this crime in truth was not one, it was not even a lie if, at least, one follows the fascinating, impassioned, refined discussion that comes after this confession. For there is a veritable treatise on lying at the center of this *Reverie*. I note in passing that Rousseau twice has recourse to the lexicon of the machine ("My heart followed these rules *mechanically* before my reason had adopted them"; "Thus it is certain that neither my judgment nor my will dictated my reply, but that it was the *mechanical* effect of my embarrassment"; 51, 54, my emphases).

"I can swear by Heaven," "Je puis jurer à la face du ciel," says the *Fourth Reverie*. But he had abjured many years earlier. A few months before the theft of the ribbon (a theft and a lie, a perjury confessed more than a decade earlier in Book 2 of the *Confessions* but committed at the age of sixteen), Rousseau, then, abjures. At sixteen, he abjures Protestantism and converts to Catholicism. A few pages earlier, before the recital of the theft, he recounts how he was "led in procession to the metropolitan Church of Saint John to make a solemn abjuration" (73). This debate between Protestantism and Catholicism tormented the whole life of this citizen of Geneva, who shared, as he tells us in the same book of the *Confessions*, "that aversion to Catholicism which is peculiar to our city. It was represented to us as the blackest idolatry and its clergy were depicted in the most sordid colors" (67). Then, noting that he never made a decision, properly speaking, on this subject ("I did not exactly resolve to turn Catholic"), he writes: "Protestants are generally better instructed than Catholics, and necessarily so, for their doctrine requires discussion, where the Roman faith demands submission. A Catholic must accept a decision imposed on him; a Protestant must learn to decide for himself. They were aware of this but they did not expect from my age and circumstances that I should present any great difficulty to men of experience" (69).

Couldn't one say that Catholicism is less internal, more ritualistic, more machinelike, machinistic, mechanistic, and therefore more literalist? The Protestantism that Rousseau abjures would be freer, more intentionalist, more decisionist, less mechanistic, less literalist, and therefore more spiritual, *spiritualist*. Rousseau abjures and converts, therefore, mechanically to the Catholic mechanism; he abjures without having had the intention to abjure, he becomes a renegade without having resolved to do so, and what is more, and this is another mechanism, without being of an age to do so. Like an immature child, he mechanically pretends to abjure intentionalist and decisionist Protestantism; he feigns this event of rupture so as to convert to mechanistic and authoritarian Catholicism. He feigns mechanically to become mechanistic. But nothing happens in his heart; nothing happens. He converted mechanically, as if by chance, but opportunistically, for the circumstance, with *à-propos*, to a literalist and mechanistic religion of the *à-propos*.

A propos, remaining still on the edge of these things, on the barely preliminary threshold of what is going to interest us, since we have begun to wander or to rave deliriously à propos the kind of notations that seemed to me unavoidable upon a first rereading of these scenes, I also noticed something else, à propos of Catholicism and the debate, within Rousseau himself, between the Catholicism of his conversion and his original Protestantism. I say his *Catholicism of conversion*, I could say his *Catholicism of confession*—since one-on-one confession to a confessor and Protestantism are mutually exclusive; the word "confession," which means both the confession of sin and the profession of faith (another expression whose textual, semantic, and social history is too rich to be taken into account here, but all this refers back to the act of faith, to the oath and the experience of sworn faith that concerns us here). "Confession" did not come to designate a Catholic, rather than Protestant, institution until well after Augustine's time.

A propos of Catholicism and of a very à propos conversion to this religion of the à-propos, it so happens that the recital of the theft of the ribbon begins right after the recital of the death of Mme de Vercellis, in whose home the young Rousseau was both housed and employed, his "principal occupation" being, as he himself puts it, to "write [letters] at her dictation." Paul de Man, in "Excuses (*Confessions*)," devotes a note to this situation of the two accounts, to this linking of the two accounts, as well as to the two events recounted, the death of Mme de Vercellis, then the theft of the ribbon. At the point at which de Man is seeking, as he puts it, "another form of desire than the desire of possession" with which to explain "the latter part of the story," the part that "bears the main per-

formative burden of the excuse and in which the crime is no longer that
of theft," but rather of lying—and we will see in which sense, in particular for de Man, this crime excludes two forms of desire, the simple desire
or love for Marion and, second, a hidden desire of the Oedipal type—at
this point, then, de Man adds the following note: "The embarrassing
story of Rousseau's rejection by Mme de Vercellis, who is dying of a cancer of the breast, immediately precedes the story of Marion, but *nothing
in the text* suggests a concatenation that would allow one to substitute
Marion for Mme de Vercellis in a scene of rejection" (285; emphasis
added).

I have underscored the phrase "nothing in the text."

No doubt de Man is right, and more than once. No doubt he is right
to beware a grossly Oedipal scheme, and I am not about to plunge
headfirst into such a scheme in my turn (although there are more refined
Oedipal schemes). De Man may also be right to say that "*nothing in the
text* suggests a concatenation that would allow one to substitute Marion
for Mme de Vercellis in a scene of rejection."

But what does "nothing" mean here? And "nothing in the text"? How
can one be sure of "nothing" suggested in a text? Of a "nothing in a text"?
And if really "nothing" suggested this Oedipal substitution, how does one
explain that de Man thought of it? And that he devotes a footnote to it?
A propos, is not every footnote a little Oedipal? In pure à propos logic, is
not a footnote a symptomatic swelling, the swollen foot of a text hindered
in its step-by-step advance? How does one explain that de Man devotes an
embarrassed footnote to all this in which he excludes that the "embarrassing story," as he puts it, suggests an Oedipal substitution of Marion
for Mme de Vercellis, that is to say, first of all of Mme de Vercellis for
Maman? For Mme de Vercellis immediately succeeds Maman in the narrative, the same year, the year he turns sixteen. She succeeds Mme de
Warens, whose acquaintance Rousseau had made several months earlier—
and who had also recently converted to Catholicism, like the Calvinist
Jean-Jacques.

Moreover, soon after this meeting he travels on foot to Turin and finds
shelter at the hospice of the Holy Spirit, where he abjures. This episode is
told at the beginning of *The Creed of a Priest of Savoy*—a text we ought to
reread closely, in particular because it contains, at the end of its seventh
chapter, an interesting comparison between the respective deaths of
Socrates and Jesus. Both grant, but differently according to Rousseau, the

first his blessing and the second his forgiveness to his executioners, the first conducting himself as a man, the other as a God. The conclusion of *The Creed* recommends the wager of remaining in the religion of one's birth. Yes, the wager, in the quasi-Pascalian sense of the machine, because it is the best calculation, in case of error, with which to obtain the excuse or the forgiveness of God. Here is the argument, in which I underscore the lexicon of *excuse* and of *pardon* or *forgiveness*:

> You will feel that, in the uncertainty in which we find ourselves, it is an *inexcusable* presumption to profess another religion than the one in which you were born, and a falsehood not to practice sincerely the one you profess. If you wander from it, you deprive yourself of a great *excuse* before the throne of the sovereign judge. Will he not rather *pardon* the error in which you were reared than one which you dared choose yourself?[7]

Let us return now to our question concerning the substitution among all these women, who are more or less mothers and Catholics by more or less recent confession.

If one supposes that there is nothing, as de Man notes, "nothing" positive in the text to suggest positively this substitution, "nothing" in the content of the accounts, what is the meaning of the mere juxtaposition, the contiguity, the absolute proximity, the à propos of the association in the time of the narration, the simple linking of places, there where de Man says that "nothing in the text [what does "in" the text mean here?] suggests a concatenation that would allow one to substitute Marion for Mme de Vercellis in a scene of rejection"? (Moreover, let it be said in passing and à propos, I don't see the reason to speak here of rejection: there is no more a simple rejection of one than of the other.) The mere concatenation of places, the sequential juxtaposition of the two accounts is not nothing, if one wanted to psychoanalyze things. The juxtaposition of the two accounts, even if nothing but chronological succession seems to justify it, the mere mechanical association of an "à-propos" is not "nothing in the text." It is not a textual nothing even if there is nothing, nothing else, *in* the text. Even if nothing else were posed, nothing positive, a force would be at work there and thus a potential dynamic. From one woman to the other, from one attachment to the other, this topology of sequential juxtaposition, this à-propos, this displacement of the à-propos can by itself have a metonymic energy, the very force that will have suggested to de Man's mind the hypothesis of the substitution that he nevertheless excludes vigorously and with determination. In order to be excludèd, it must still present itself to the mind with some seduction. It must still be tempting. And the temptation suffices. We are talking here only about temptation and forbidden fruit. So even if there were nothing *in* the text of these two accounts, the simple topographic or sequential juxtaposition is "in the text," it constitutes the text itself and can be *interpreted*: it is *interpretable*. Not necessarily in an Oedipal fashion, but it is interpretable. One must and one cannot not interpret it; it cannot be simply insignificant.

Two series of arguments could confirm this interpretability. One concerns the *content* of the two accounts; the other, once again, their *form* and their place, their "taking place," their situation, their localization. I will not insist on the content. A large number of traits, stretching over many pages, describe the at once amorous and filial attachment that Rousseau feels for Mme de Vercellis, whose appearance succeeds the meeting with Mme de Warens in the second book of the *Confessions*. Mme de Vercellis, a widow without children, suffered from a "cancer of the breast." Rousseau comes back to this constantly. This illness of the maternal breast, "which gave her great pain," he writes, "prevented her from writing herself." Jean-Jacques becomes, by reason of this infirmity, her penholder. He holds her pen. Like a secretary, he writes in her place. He becomes her pen, her hand, or her arm, for "she liked writing letters." On the scenes of letters and testaments that follow, we could offer infinite glosses. We would be brought back to a topography of borders. Everything proceeds according to the substitution of one border for another. In such a parergonal composition, in this game of interlocking frames, we would find once again the mark of two limits. On the one hand, and the first thing at stake with the limit, is the memory of the abjuration, the crossing of the frontier between Protestantism and Catholicism; this is also the passage from childhood to adulthood, in a sort of internal history of the confessions, in the access to the institution called confession. On the other hand, also at stake with the limit, is what I will call *the last word*. And twice the last word. It is a matter of the last word *of the other* and the last word *of self*. A double silence on which a double episode closes: that of the theft-lie that wrongs Marion and that of the death of the stepmother, the childless widow, the very Catholic Mme de Vercellis.

Rousseau praises Mme de Vercellis even as he speaks ill of her. He also criticizes her insensitivity, her indifference, and, more precisely, her lack of mercy [*miséricorde*], of "commiseration": as if she had no mercy, no heart, or, for a mother, no breast. She is, moreover, going to die from that, from the illness that Rousseau calls literally "cancer of the breast." This cancer will have eaten away her breast. What good she does, she does mechanically, automatically, out of duty and not from the heart: "She always seemed to me to have as little feeling for others as for herself; and when she did a kindness to anyone in misfortune, it was in order to do something good on principle, rather than out of true commiseration" (84). Moreover, the breast is the heart and the place of commiseration, especially for Rousseau. Two pages after these allusions to the "cancer of the breast" and to the double expiration of Mme de Vercellis, who lacks commiseration, Rousseau writes the following, in which I underscore a certain "not even":

Nevertheless I have never been able to bring myself to relieve my heart by revealing this in private to a friend. Not with the most intimate friend, *not even* with Mme de Warens, has this been possible. The most that I could do was to confess that I had a terrible deed on my conscience, but I have never said in what it consisted. The burden, therefore, has rested till this day on my conscience without any relief; and I can affirm that the desire to some extent to rid myself of it has greatly contributed to my resolution of writing these *Confessions*. (88)

Twice a last word, I said. A double silence comes to seal the end. Irreversibly.

Here, first of all, are the first last words, in fact, therefore, the next-to-last words, which I will hesitate to place in the mouth of Mme de Vercellis, and you will see why:

She liked writing letters, which diverted her mind from her illness. But they put her against the habit, and got the doctor to make her give it up, on the plea that it was too tiring for her. On the pretense that I did not understand my duties, two great louts of chairmen were put in my place. In the end they were so successful that when she made her will I had not entered her room for a week. It is true that after that I went in as before. Indeed I was more attentive to her than anyone else, for the poor woman's suffering tore my heart, and the fortitude with which she bore it inspired me with the greatest respect and affection for her. Many were the genuine tears I shed in her room without her or anyone else noticing it.

Finally we lost her. I watched her die. She had lived like a woman of talents and intelligence; she died like a philosopher. I may say that she made the Catholic religion seem beautiful to me, by the serenity of heart with which she fulfilled its instructions, without either carelessness or affectation. She was of a serious nature. Towards the end of her illness she displayed a sort of gaiety too unbroken to be assumed, which was merely a counterpoise to her melancholy condition, the gift of her reason. She only kept her bed for the last two days, and continued to converse quietly with everyone to the last. Finally when she could no longer talk and was already in her death agony, she broke wind loudly. "Good," she said, turning over, "a woman who can fart is not dead." Those were the last words she spoke. (85–86)

After her ultimate silence or her last words have been verified, after it has been said "she could no longer talk," well, there she goes and farts again. She thus adds a living, surviving gloss to this after-the-last word: a fart. After these last words, these first "last words," what will now be the second and last "last word"?

It comes right at the end of the narration of the ribbon, which itself follows without transition on the double expiration of Mme de Vercellis. It comes, therefore, after this fart, after this last breath, at the end of this agony and these "last words she spoke" like a double expiration, a fart and a testamentary metalanguage on a next-to-the-last breath.

The moment having arrived for this absolute last word, it follows the narration of the stolen ribbon; it comes after the respect due to Marion will have been, like the young girl herself, violated. Violated both by the theft and by the lie, by the perjury, by the false testimony accusing Marion to excuse himself. This conclusion is inferred, as it were, by an allusion to the age of the guilty one. The allusion shows clearly that, even if Rousseau, at least at this point, does not say, like Augustine, "I was sixteen years old," he underscores the element of his age as an essential element of the story. And we can calculate that he was sixteen at the time. This element both accuses *and* excuses him, accuses and charges him, condemns him all the more but clears him of guilt by the same token, automatically. One can no longer decide between the two gestures: accusation and excuse.

My age also should be taken into account. I was scarcely more than a child. Indeed I still was one. In youth real crimes are even more reprehensible than in riper years; but what is no more than weakness is much less blameworthy, and really my crime amounted to no more than weakness. So the memory tortures me less on account of the crime itself than because of its possible evil consequences. But I have derived some benefit from the terrible impression left with me by the sole offense I have committed. For it has secured me for the rest of my life against any act that might prove criminal in its results. I think also that my loathing of untruth derives to a large extent from my having told that one wicked lie. If this is a crime that can be expiated, as I venture to believe, it must have been atoned for by all the misfortunes that have crowded the end of the life, by forty years of honest and upright behavior under difficult circumstances. Poor Marion finds so many avengers in this world that, however great my offense against her may have been, I have little fear of carrying the sin on my conscience at death. That is all I have to say on the subject. May I never have to speak of it again. (89)

He will speak of it again, of course, as if he had gotten a second wind in his turn. He will do so in the *Reveries*. There again, he will take pity on Marion, "poor Marion" (51). On the subject still of this age of sixteen years, what must one say? Rousseau proliferates remarks about his age in the first two books of the *Confessions*. He recalls it and specifies it with obsessional frequency. A propos, since we are talking about substitutions, that of Marion for Mme de Vercellis, Mme de Vercellis who succeeds Mme de Warens—and the logic of the à propos is also a logic of substitution—what is it we read in a self-portrait from some months earlier in the same year, 1728, in April, a few months before the death of Mme de Vercellis, therefore before the theft and the lie of the ribbon? Rousseau meets Mme de Warens. This is the beginning of his singular passion for Maman. Well, almost in the very sentence in which he notes the first meeting with Mme de Warens, like Saint Augustine he makes note of his age. And it is the same age. He was just sixteen years old:

Finally I arrived and saw Mme de Warens. This stage in my life has been decisive in the formation of my character, and I cannot make up my mind to pass lightly over it. I was half way through my sixteenth year and, without being what is called a handsome youth, I was well-made for my modest size, had a pretty foot, a fine leg, an independent air, lively features, a small mouth, black eyebrows and hair, and small, rather sunken eyes which sparkled with the fire that burnt in my veins. (54–55)

A same year, the year he was sixteen, decides his life twice. In the same second book of the *Confessions*, we see this decision that decides his life for him distributed over a single sequence of metonymic transitions. All along the same chain of quasi-substitutions, replacements, and supplements, it is literally a *succession*. A succession in the sense of the sequence of supplements and in the sense of temporal succession: the Catholic Mme de Warens is succeeded by the no less Catholic Mme de Vercellis, then comes "poor Marion" and the theft-lie of the ribbon. But this double *succession* (sequence of supplements and temporal consecution) is also a succession, as we'll see, in the sense of inheritance, testament, the last word as last will.

Let us not overstate this Marial chain of three women to whom a desire without desire links him as to the breast of a virgin mother—a Mary. Let us not speculate on the name of "poor Marion" so as to recognize the diminutive figure in a scene of passion and martyrdom. But who could deny that Jean-Jacques puts himself on a cross, even as he seems to de-Christianize the Augustinian confession? Sooner or later, "dans les siècles des siècles," as one says in Christian rhetoric, people will know he has suffered and expiated as an innocent martyr for all men, and at the hands of the wicked men who do not know what they do. And God the father is not to be accused of it.

Where the two authors of *Confessions* speak the language of the excuse, one of the "inexcusable [*inexcusabilis*]," the other of "excusing himself," they inscribe their avowals in the thickness of an immense Christian and, above all, Pauline, archive. With one and the other *Confessions*, we *inherit*: in yet another scene of succession, we inherit from a palimpsest of quotations and quasi-quotations, which moreover Augustine exhibits as such, notably in his borrowings from the Epistle to the Romans.[8] When, in Book 5 of his *Confessions*, Augustine recalls the errors of his Roman youth and his attraction to the Manicheans, the same palimpsest relies on the language of exchange between accusing and excusing. To return to oneself, to be oneself, to be what one is, as an indivisible whole, one must surmount, through confession, that is, through an act of faith, the division that consists in unloading blame onto another in oneself. Augustine calls this division of self impiety:

I loved to excuse myself, and to accuse I know not what other being that was present with me but yet was not I [*sed excusare me amabam et accusare nescio quid aliud, quod mecum esset et ego non essem*]. But in truth I was the one whole being, and my own impiety had divided me against myself [*uterum autem totum ego eram et adversus me inpietas mea me diviserat*]. . . . You had not yet "set a watch before my mouth, and a door" of continence "round about my lips," so that my heart would not decline "to evil words, to make excuses in sins with men that work iniquity" [*in verba mala ad excusandas excusationes*].[9]

This machinelike operation of the excuse divides and multiplies at the same time. A calculating machine, a multiplication—and division—table, it leads into error and drags the guilty one into the repetition of the "last word." Does not eschatology then become a genre, an inexhaustible eschatology of final words, in a word, a last word, a litany? ("Those were the last words she spoke," said Rousseau, then: "May I never have to speak of it again.")

Such an eschatology of last words seems as threatened by the litanical reproduction as is the unicity of the event, its irreplaceable and unforeseeable singularity.

What becomes, then, of what was nicknamed a moment ago "textual event"? And "succession"?

From what indefatigable writing machine will we still have to inherit? What will have been this legacy?

The Event Called "Ribbon": Power and Impower

I can say that what happened [*arriva*] to these two young men sixteen years old arrived to me [*m'arriva*].

The thing happened/arrived to me and it is still arriving to me.

Everyone can say, here, "It arrives to me." It arrives to me, right here. At least as a message addressed to me.

What happened to Augustine and Rousseau, the theft, the fault, and the avowal, this is still arriving to me; I inherit from it through an effect of succession, through the effect of complex writing and archiving machines. We must not disregard, like some accident without import, the ineradicable equivocation, which is ineradicably French, the untranslatable idiom that plays on the two senses or the two destinations of *arriver* (the event that *happens* to someone and the message that *arrives*—or doesn't arrive at destination, or even at some unforeseeable addressee).

This singular instability lends a movement, a mobility that is never spontaneously interrupted. It plays with its own automatism and offers us graciously perhaps a privileged access to this machine effect—to this effect of machinality or machination that concerns us.

Toward the end, over three pages, the second book of the *Confessions* multiplies the ends; it repeats its own ends. It divides them and doubles them. Two ends, and two times a last word: first, the double expiration of Mme de Vercellis ("Those were the last words she spoke"), then the very last word of the chapter, the end of the story of the ribbon ("May I never have to speak of it again").

The first "last words," attributed to the dying woman, belong to a sentence in the constative form, in the past. They recount or describe: this is what she said, Mme de Vercellis, in fact, and here in fact is what she did. The last last word, however, forms a performative sentence, at once a wish, a promise, a commitment, or a prayer in the first person: this is what I myself say, now, for the future. Although its grammar is such that, at least in French, the first person is not a subject, the "I" remains, despite the grammar, the true subject of this wish: "Qu'il me soit permis de n'en reparler jamais." The "I," moreover, reappears literally in the English translation: "May I never have to speak of it again."

Two occurrences, therefore, of a last word. They sink into the abyssal depths of another palimpsest, and not simply that of the Holy Scriptures, of Saint Paul or the Psalms. Taking into account the limits of these lectures ("Within such limits," Austin might say once again), we will not have time to reinscribe them in the endless archive of last words that are not words of the end: from Socrates' last word in an apologetic scene in the *Hippias Minor* to Blanchot's *Le Dernier Mot* (1935), passing by way of Austin's "A Plea for Excuses"—this address that speaks to us also of machines and of a "complicated internal machinery," even as it explains in passing that, although ordinary language is not the last word, it is in any case the first: "Ordinary language is *not* the last word: in principle it can be supplemented and improved upon and superseded. Only remember, it *is* the *first* word."

The question of "ordinary language" is perhaps, à propos, the real question of "A Plea for Excuses."[10] At a certain moment, Blanchot's *Le Dernier Mot* takes the figure of the French expression *il y a*. I would have been tempted to relate this moment to the long meditation by Levinas on the *il y a*. For this problematic of the *il y a* (in ordinary, which is to say, untranslatable French) has a pertinence for our remarks. But I treat this elsewhere and must leave it aside here.

One could also reread the whole de Manian interpretation of the purloined ribbon as the displacement of a "last word." The last word of the *Confessions* on this subject, the ultimate decision, which he would like never to have to go back on ("May I never have to speak of it again"), was, according to de Man, only the next to last. Rousseau will have to reiterate this confession many years later, in the *Reveries*. Only this text delivers the last last word, the extreme eschatology. One of the many interesting and original things about de Man's analysis is that it takes into account this difference between the very last word and the next to last, and it mobilizes what seems necessary in order to explain the history and the mechanism that transforms the last into the next to last, the motor that regresses from the final to the penultimate.

If I insist on this paradoxical instance of the "last word," it is because forgiveness or pardon, the excuse, and the remission of sin, absolute absolution, are always proposed in the figure, so to speak, of the "last word." A pardon not granted with the assurance, the promise, or, in any case, the meaning of a last word or an end of history (even if it is according to the virtualizing logic of the "sooner or later"), would that still be a pardon? Hence the disturbing proximity the pardon maintains to the last judgment—which, nevertheless, it is not. A pardon does not judge; it transcends all judgment, whether penal or not. Foreign to the courtroom, it nevertheless remains as close as possible to the verdict, to the *veridictum*, by the irresistible and irreversible force it has as, precisely, "last word." *I forgive you* has the structure of the last word, hence its apocalyptic and millenarian aura; hence the sign it makes in the direction of the end of time and the end of history. We will later get around to this concept of history, which de Man wants to link no longer to time ("History is therefore not a temporal notion," as he will say in "Kant and Schiller"; it has nothing to do with temporality)[11] but to "power," to the "event," and to the "occurrence." It corresponds to "the emergence of a language of power out of a language of cognition" (ibid.). I tried to show elsewhere that what I call *le mal d'archive* has to do with this destiny: always finite and therefore selective, interpretative, filtering, and filtered, censuring, and repressive, the archive always figures a place and an instance of power.[12] Destined to the virtuality of the "sooner or later," the archive produces the event no less than it records or consigns it.

After having analyzed two long series of possible readings, de Man explains, then, these two times of the end: after a certain failure of the confession in the *Confessions* (begun in 1764–65, the second part completed at the latest in 1767 and the whole in 1770), after this first last word, Rousseau was to write the *Fourth Reverie* (in 1777, therefore at least ten years later). The last word of the *Confessions* would thus have marked a failure. After the avowal, the vow ("May I never have to speak of it again"), but the vow does not succeed in sealing an authentic last word signing the end of the story or of history. According to de Man, this failure, this becoming next-to-last of the last is what motivated, compulsively, the writing of the *Fourth Reverie* and the return, let us not say the repentance, the rewriting of the confession in the form of excuse.

But the text offers further possibilities. The analysis of shame as excuse makes evident the strong link between the performance of excuses and the act of understanding. It has led to the problematics of hiding and revealing, which are clearly problematics of cognition. Excuse occurs within an epistemological twilight zone between knowing and not-knowing; this is also why it has to be centered on the crime of lying and why Rousseau can excuse himself for everything provided he can be excused for lying. When this turns out not to have been the case, when his claim to have lived for the sake of truth (*vitam impendere vero*) is being contested from the outside, the closure of excuse ("qu'il me soit permis de n'en reparler jamais") becomes a delusion and the *Fourth Reverie* has to be written.[13]

How is one to understand this incessant passage, which transports and deports beyond the last word of excuse, from the *Confessions* to the *Reveries*, for example? De Man himself here calls upon a logic of *supplementarity* at work between excuse and guilt. Far from effacing guilt, far from leading to the "without-fault" or the "without-defect," excuses add to it; they engender and augment the fault. The *plus de faute*, "no more fault" (innocence) becomes right away the *plus de faute*, all the more fault (endless guilt).[14] The more one excuses oneself, the more one admits that one is guilty, and the more one feels guilt. Guilty of excusing oneself. By excusing oneself. The more one excuses oneself, the less one clears oneself. Guilt is thus an inscription that is *ineffaceable*. This is also de Man's word. Ineffaceable and thus, I would say, inexorable and inexorable because inexonerable. The *written* excuse produces guilt. It ineffaces the guilty deed. The inscription of the work, *l'oeuvre*, the event of a text in its graphic body generates and capitalizes a sort of interest (I won't be so bold as to say surplus value) of guilt. It overproduces this shame, it archives it instead of effacing it. I underscore *effacing* or *exonerating*, and *inexonerable* guilt, for two reasons of unequal importance. Here, first, is the passage where all of these threads are knotted together in the most visible and tightly wound fashion:

Excuses generate the very guilt they *exonerate*, though always in excess or by default. At the end of the *Reverie* there is a lot more guilt around than we had at the start: Rousseau's indulgence in what he calls, in another bodily metaphor, "*le plaisir* d'écrire" [the phrase occurs at the end of the *Fourth Reverie*], leaves him guiltier than ever. . . . Additional guilt means additional excuse. . . . No excuse can ever hope to catch up with such a proliferation of guilt. On the other hand, any guilt, including the guilty pleasure of writing the *Fourth Reverie*, can always be dismissed as the gratuitous product of a textual grammar or a radical fiction: there can never be enough guilt around to match the text-machine's infinite power to excuse.[15]

The "text-machine" has just arrived on stage. We will let it wait for a moment.

I announced two unequal reasons for underscoring the verb "exonerate" (which de Man's translator renders in French by *effacer*, to efface or erase), but also the figure of an ineffaceable guilt that the excuse, instead of effacing, aggravated, tattooed in a more and more indelible fashion onto the body of the archive. The first reason is *objective*; the other is, in some way, for de Man and for me, if I may say so, *auto-biographical*.

The objective reason first: de Man will have wanted to show that from the *Confessions* to the *Reveries* the guilt (with regard to one and the same event, of course, the theft of the ribbon) has been displaced from the written *thing* to the *writing* of the thing, from the referent of the narrative writing (the theft and the lie) to the act of writing the account, from the written confession to the inscription of the confession. The second time it is no longer the theft or the lie, as the thing itself, the fault itself, the perjury itself, that becomes guilty; the fault is now with the writing or the account of the thing, the pleasure taken in inscribing this memory, in archiving it, setting it down in ink on paper. The fault of this pleasure cannot be effaced because it is reprinted and rewritten while it is being confessed. It is aggravated and capitalized; it grows heavier, becomes more onerous, more costly; it overproduces itself, becomes pregnant with itself by confessing itself. De Man writes: "The question takes us to the *Fourth Reverie* and its implicit shift from reported guilt to the guilt of reporting, since here the lie is no longer connected with some former misdeed but specifically with the act of writing the *Confessions* and, by extension, with all writing" (290). The excuse does not merely accuse; it carries out the verdict: "Excuses not only accuse but they carry out the verdict implicit in their accusation" (293).

One must hear the weight of this sentence as carried by the "carry out," this execution of the verdict, this performance of the judgment and its ap-plication, its "enforcement." There is not only accusation and judgment in the confession or in the excuse itself; there is already the executioner, the carrying out of the sentence—but here of the sentence endured in the very pleasure of writing, in the ambiguous enjoyment at the heart of the terrible and severe jubilation of the inscription. The fault is committed right on the trace left now for the "sooner or later," but enjoying now al-ready, virtually, the retrospection of the "sooner or later." One steps up to the cashier right away to collect interest on a capital that will assume value only "sooner or later," perhaps after my death, in any case, in my absence.

Structurally ineffaceable guilt no longer has to do with this or that mis-deed, but with the confession itself, with confessional writing. The first and last fault would be the public *mise en oeuvre* of self-justification, of self-disculpation, and of the shameful pleasure that the body finds there—still or already. Guilt can no longer be effaced because it has to do with the body of the confession, with its literal inscription. It is the pulse of the confession. It is compulsively linked to the drive [*pulsion*] dedicated to confessing the fault in writing—contradicting or disavowing thereby the avowal at the heart of the avowal.[16]

The second reason I underscore the lexicon of the inexonerable as ineffaceable is minor and modestly autobiographical. Its importance, if it has any, derives from a strange experience of the date and the trace of a sig-nature. In this case, it is a matter of the archive of a dedication, of an "in-scription," as one says in English. Will I dare to cite it? On my inscribed copy of *Allegories of Reading*, dated November 1979, I could read: "Pour Jacques, en ineffaçable amitié, Paul" ("For Jacques, in ineffaceable friend-ship, Paul"). This "inscription" in ink was followed, in pencil, by two last words: "lettre suit." Yes, "lettre follows." You know at least something of the rest, the posthumous continuation. De Man died four years later, in 1983, leaving us with the well-known painful legacies for a virtually inde-terminable "sooner or later." Letter follows: this was also the continuation of a history in which certain people believed they could reproach de Man, not so much for having done this or that, but especially, or even solely, for having dissimulated, for not having admitted what he ought to have ad-mitted, for not having publicly confessed what he had one day written—precisely, during the war. His fault will also have consisted in writing. This is enough to make one dream aloud—about the "sooner or later" of archives, about machines in general, and about confession machines. We know quite well that there are machines for making people confess. And there are those who like these things. The police, the inquisition, inquisitors, prosecutors, and torturers throughout history have been very familiar with these machines for extracting confessions. They also know the jubilatory pleasure to be had in the handling of these machines, in the forced confession, in the forcing of the confession more than in knowing what is true, more than in knowing to what the confession, or so one supposes, refers. In this familiar and ageless tradition, those who manipulate these confessing machines care less about the fault committed than about the pleasure they take in extracting or even dictating the confession. What they realize only rarely, however, what de Man in any case knew, and this is one of the themes of his text, is that confession, for the addresser *as well as* the addressee, is always in itself, in the act of its inscription, guilty—more *and* less, more *or* less guilty than the fault it is a question of confessing. The confession, in a word, on both sides, is never innocent. This is a first machine, the implacable and repetitive law of an undeniable program; this is the economy of a calculation inscribed in advance. The undeniable, here as always, is what one can only disavow.

A moment ago, we met the expression "text-machine." The whole of this demonstration is played out around the text-machine, around the work, the *oeuvre* of a writing machine. The concept of a textual machine is both produced by de Man and, as it were, found, discovered, *invented* by him in Rousseau's text. One also speaks of the invention of the body of Christ to designate an experience that consists in discovering, in an inaugural fashion, to be sure, but all the same a body that was already there, in some place or other, and that had to be found, discovered, *invented*. Even though it unveils the body of what was already there, this invention is an event. De Man invents the text-machine by discovering and citing, so as to justify his expression, a certain passage of the *Fourth Reverie* that speaks in fact of a "machinelike effect," an *effet machinal*. But there are also, in Rousseau, many other examples of machines—both prosthetic and mutilating machines. We will keep them waiting as well.

This must be placed in a network of relations with the whole work of de Man, with his style, and with the axioms of what he calls, after "Blindness and Insight," in this article and elsewhere while insisting upon it more and more, a "deconstruction." This always implies reference to a certain machinality, to the automaticity of the body or of the automaton corpus. The allusion, in the essay "Excuses," to Kleist's marionettes refers us back to other references to Kleist (for example, in "Phenomenality and Materiality in Kant," in *Aesthetic Ideology*). "Excuses (*Confessions*)" is also the theater of Rousseau's marionettes (which de Man never associates, to my great surprise, with the name "Marion"):

By saying that the excuse is not only a fiction but also a machine one adds to the connotation of referential detachment, of gratuitous improvisation, that of the implacable repetition of a preordained pattern. Like Kleist's marionettes, the machine is both "anti-grav," the anamorphosis of a form detached from meaning [somewhat like the neutral, anonymous, and insignificant *il y a* in Blanchot and Levinas] and capable of taking on any structure whatever, yet entirely *ruthless* in its inability to modify its own structural design for nonstructural reasons. The machine *is like* the grammar of the text when it is isolated from its rhetoric, the merely formal element without which no text can be generated. There can be no use of language which is not, within a certain perspective thus radically formal, i.e. mechanical, no matter how deeply this aspect may be concealed by aesthetic, formalistic delusions.[17]

Why this resemblance ("is like")? And why "ruthless"? Why would a text-machine be ruthless? Not mean but ruthless in its effects, in the suffering it inflicts? What relation is there between the ruthlessness of this "text-machine" and what de Man calls, at the end of the trajectory, the "textual event"? This is another way of repeating my initial question: How is one to think together the machine *and* the event, a machinelike repetition *and* what happens? What happens to what? To whom? For our question about the machine and the event is also a question about who and what, between the "who" and the "what."

De Man speaks of excuse; he almost never names "pardon" or "forgiveness." He seems to exclude the specific problem of forgiveness from his field of analysis. First of all, no doubt, because both Rousseau and Austin, who are the guiding references here, also speak massively of excuse rather than forgiveness. Unless de Man considers, perhaps like Rousseau and like Austin, that whatever one says about the excuse is valid as well for forgiveness. That remains to be seen. Two hypotheses in this regard.

First hypothesis: de Man sees no essential difference between forgiveness and excuse. This argument can be made, but it leaves aside enormous historical and semantic stakes. The very possibility of this distinction is not problematized. I therefore set it aside.

The other hypothesis would concern Austin as much as de Man. The only pragmatic or performative modality that interests them is what happens on the side of the one who has committed the misdeed, never on the other side, the side of the victim. What they want to analyze is the act that consists in saying "I apologize" rather than "I ask forgiveness," "I beg your pardon," and, above all, "I forgive" or "I pardon." Rather than the possibility of forgiving or even of excusing, both of them are interested only in what one *does* when one *says*, in the performative mode, "excuse me" and, more precisely, "I apologize." They believe they can consider only the modality of the excuse and that the rest is beyond the limit of the field of their analysis. So, unless I am mistaken, de Man almost never speaks of forgiveness, except in passing, as if it were no big deal, on two occasions. One concerns what is, he says, "easy to forgive" since "the motivation for the theft becomes understandable." But here as well, de Man keeps to the side of the one who excuses himself and thinks that it's "easy to forgive":

The allegory of this metaphor, revealed in the "confession" of Rousseau's desire for Marion, functions as an excuse if we are willing to take the desire at face value. If it is granted that Marion is desirable, or Rousseau ardent to such an extent, then the motivation for the theft becomes understandable and easy to forgive. He did it all out of love for her, and who would be a dour enough literalist to let a little property stand in the way of young love? (284)

The other occurrence of the word "forgiveness" is found in a passage that carries the only reference to Heidegger, whose definition of truth as revelation-dissimulation remains determinant in this whole strategy. And de Man's quasi Heideggerian strategy at least resembles that of Lacan to this extent. At the end of the seventies, de Man inscribes, in fact, his own deconstructive gesture and his own interpretation of dissemination—I mean his appropriation of these two insistent words, *deconstruction* and *dissemination*, which are everywhere and foregrounded in this essay—in a highly ambiguous double proximity: proximity to a certain Lacanianism, readable in what is said both about repression as "one speech act among others," about desire and language, and even in the recourse to truth according to Heidegger. But there is the proximity as well, despite this Lacanianism, to a certain Deleuzianism from the period of the *Anti-Oedipus*, in what links desire to the machine, I would almost say to a desiring machine. How is one to sort out all these threads (disseminal deconstruction, Lacanianism, and Deleuzianism) in de Man's original signature? That is what I would like to be able to do, without being sure in the least that I will manage it today. But it remains true that all my questions concern obliquely the Lacanian and Deleuzian discourses, where, despite all the apparent oppositions and differences, they are still crossing. In one of its places, de Man's discourse would be situated at this point of Heideggeriano-Lacano-Deleuzian crossing; it would attest to this possibility.

Here is the allusion to the guilt that is "forgiven":

Promise is proleptic, but excuse is belated and always occurs after the crime; since the crime is exposure, the excuse consists in recapitulating the exposure in the guise of concealment. The excuse is a ruse which permits exposure in the name of hiding, not unlike Being, in the later Heidegger, reveals itself by hiding. Or, put differently, shame used as excuse permits repression to function as revelation, and thus to make pleasure and guilt interchangeable. Guilt is forgiven because it allows for the pleasure of revealing its repression. It follows that repression is in fact an excuse, one speech act among others. (286)

Unless I have missed something, these are the only borrowings from the lexicon of forgiveness, in what is a strong genealogy of excuse. The scene of the excuse would be an economic ruse, a stratagem and calculation, either conscious or unconscious, in view of the greatest pleasure in the service of the greatest desire. We will later get around to the complication of this desire, of its writing machine as a mutilating machine.

If there is a proper eventness that is of a performative type in the moment of the avowal and also in the moment of the excuse, can one distinguish the avowal from the excuse, as de Man attempts to do? Can one distinguish between, on the one hand, the confession as avowal (namely, a truth revealed-dissimulated according to the Heideggerian scheme that is here accredited) and, on the other, the confession as excuse? At the beginning of his text, de Man proposes clearly isolating from each other the two structures and the two moments. He claims to discern between the two modes of confession, the avowal and the excuse, with regard to referentiality, that is, their reference to an event—extraverbal or verbal. The distinction that is thereby proposed is alone capable of accounting for, in his view, the divergence, within the repetition, between the two texts, the *Confessions* and the *Fourth Reverie*. Separated by ten years, these two confessions refer to the same event, the theft of the ribbon and the lie that followed it. But they refer to it differently. The confession "stated in the mode of revealed truth" has recourse to "evidence" that is, according to de Man, "referential (the ribbon)," whereas the "evidence" for the confession "stated in the mode of excuse" could only be "verbal" (280). This is the beginning of a difficult analysis. I must confess that it often leaves me perplexed. I am not sure, for example, that, if there is reference to an avowal that admits a misdeed, this reference consists here, as de Man asserts very quickly, in "the ribbon": "the evidence . . . is referential (the ribbon)," he says. The reference of the avowal, the fault, is the theft of the ribbon and not the ribbon, and above all, more gravely, the lie that followed, and the verbal act that accused "poor Marion." Even if de Man is right to recall that "To steal is to act and includes no necessary verbal elements" (281), the reference of the avowal is not only the theft but also the lie that followed.

De Man thus proposes here a distinction that is at once subtle, necessary, and problematic. It seems fragile to me, in a process that, at any rate, is of the order of event, doubly or triply so, in the sense of memory, archive, and the performative: *first*, for memory, it is of the order of event by reference to an irreversible event that has already happened; *second*, it produces moreover some technical event, some archivation, an inscription or a consignment of the event; and finally, *third*, it is of the order of an event in a mode that is each time performative and that we must clarify. The distinction proposed by de Man is thus useful but needs to be further differentiated. If there is indeed an allegation of truth to be revealed, to be made known, thus a gesture of the theoretical type, a cognitive or, as de Man says, epistemological dimension, a declaration of Rousseau's regarding the theft of the ribbon is not a confession or admission except on a strict condition and to a determined extent. It must in no case allow itself to be determined by this cognitive dimension, reduced to it, or even analyzed into two dissociable elements (one de Man calls the cognitive and the other, the apologetic).

To make known does not come down to knowing and, above all, to make known a *fault* does not come down to making known anything whatsoever; it is *already* to accuse oneself and to enter into a performative process of excuse and forgiveness. A declaration that would bring forward some knowledge, a piece of information, a thing to be known would in no case be a confession, even if the thing to be known, even if the cognitive referent were otherwise defined as a fault: I can inform someone that I have killed, stolen, or lied without that being at all an admission or a confession. Confession is not of the order of knowledge or making known.

That is why Augustine wonders why he must confess to God, who already knows everything. Answer: confession does not consist in making known, informing, apprising the other, but in excusing oneself, repenting, asking forgiveness, converting the fault into love, and so forth. For there to be a confessional declaration or avowal, it is necessary, indissociably, that I recognize that I am guilty in a mode of recognition that is not of the order of cognition, and also that, at least implicitly, I begin to accuse myself—and thus to excuse myself or to present my apologies, or even to ask for forgiveness. There is doubtless an irreducible element of "truth" in this process but this truth, precisely, is not a truth to be known or, as de Man puts it so frequently, revealed. Rather, as Augustine says, it is a truth to be "made," to be "verified," if you will, and this order of truth is not of a cognitive order. Such a truth remains to be rethought there where it does not reveal some knowledge. It is not a revelation. In any case, this revelation, if one insists on that term, does not consist only in lifting a veil so as to present something to be seen in a neutral, cognitive, or theoretical fashion. A more probing and patient discussion (I admit that I don't see things clearly enough here) would therefore have to focus on what de Man calls "verification." This notion allows him, if I have understood correctly, to dissociate the confession of the *Confessions* from the excuses of the *Reveries*:

The difference between the verbal excuse and the referential crime is not a simple opposition between an action and a mere utterance about an action. To steal is to act and includes no necessary verbal element. To confess is discursive, but the discourse is governed by a principle of referential verification that includes an extraverbal moment: even if we confess that we *said* something (as opposed to *did*) [and this is also what happens with Rousseau, as I recalled a moment ago: he confessed what he *said* as well as what he *did*], the verification of this verbal event, the decision about the truth or falsehood of its occurrence, is not verbal but factual, the knowledge that the utterance actually took place. No such possibility of verification exists for the excuse, which is verbal in its utterance, in its effects and in its authority: its purpose is not to state but to convince, itself an "inner" process [this is an allusion to Rousseau's "inner feeling"] to which only words can bear witness. As is well known at least since Austin, excuses are a complex instance of what he termed performative utterances, a variety of speech acts. (281–82)

This series of affirmations does not seem to me always clear and convincing. The "inner process" can also be, it is even always the object of a reference, even in testimony; and testimony is never simply verbal. Inversely, if there is determination of the "factual" and of the factual occurrence of something that has actually taken place, it always passes by way of an act of testimony, whether verbal or not.

I am all the more troubled by these passages inasmuch as de Man seems to hold firmly to a distinction that he will later, in fact right after, have to suspend, at least as regards the example he considers, Rousseau, but in my opinion throughout. In the very next sentence, the distinction is in fact suspended, thus interrupted, by an "as well" ("performatively as well as cognitively") that describes, de Man says, "the interest of Rousseau's text"—I would say the interest of Rousseau period and even, by radicalizing the thing, all "interest" in general: "The interest of Rousseau's text is that it explicitly functions performatively as well as cognitively, and thus gives indications about the structure of performative rhetoric; this is already established in this text when the confession fails to close off a discourse which feels compelled to modulate from the confessional into the apologetic mode." (282) Yes, but I wonder if the confessional mode is not already, always, an apologetic mode. In truth, I believe there are not here two dissociable modes and two different times, in such a way that one could modulate from one to the other. I don't believe even that what de Man names "the interest of Rousseau's text," therefore its originality, consists in having to "modulate" from the confessional mode to the apologetic mode. Every confessional text is already apologetic. Every avowal begins by offering apologies or by excusing itself.

Let's leave this difficulty in place. It is going to haunt everything that we will say from here on. We'll return to what de Man calls "the distinction between the confession stated in the mode of revealed truth and the confession stated in the mode of excuse" (280). This distinction organizes, it seems to me, his whole demonstration. I find it an impossible, in truth undecidable, distinction. This undecidability, moreover, is what would make for all the interest, the obscurity, the nondecomposable specificity of what is called a confession, an avowal, an excuse, or an asked-for forgiveness. But if one went still further in this direction by leaving behind the context and the element of the de Manian interpretation, it would be because we are touching here on the equivocation of an originary or preoriginary synthesis without which there would be neither trace nor inscription, neither experience of the body nor materiality. It would be a question of the equivocation between, *on the one hand*, the truth to be known, revealed, or asserted, the truth that, according to de Man, concerns the order of the pure and simple confessional and, *on the other*, the truth of the pure performative of the excuse, to which de Man gives the name of the apologetic. Two orders that are analogous, in sum, to the constative and the performative. By reason of this equivocation itself, which invades language and action at their source, we are always already in the process of excusing ourselves, or even asking forgiveness, precisely in this ambiguous and perjuring mode.

Following a path whose necessity neither Austin nor de Man failed to perceive, we may say that every constative is rooted in the presupposition of an at least implicit performative. Every theoretical, cognitive utterance, every truth to be revealed, and so forth, assumes a testimonial form, an "I myself think," "I myself say," "I myself believe," or "I myself have the inner feeling that," and so forth; "I have a relation to myself to which you never have immediate access and for which you must believe me by taking my word for it." Therefore, I can always lie and bear false witness, right there where I say to you, "I am speaking to you, me, to you," "I take you as my witness," "I promise you," or "I confess to you," "I tell you the truth." By reason of this general and radical form of testimoniality, whenever someone speaks, false witness is always *possible*, as well as equivocation between the two orders. No one will ever be able to demonstrate, moreover, no one will ever be able to point to properly theoretical proof that someone has lied, that is, did not believe, in good faith, what he was saying. The liar can always allege, without any risk of being proved wrong, that he was in good faith when he spoke, even if it was in order to say something untrue. The lie will always remain *improbable*, even where, in another mode, one is certain of it.

In my address to another, I must always ask for faith or confidence, beg to be believed at my word, there where equivocation is ineffaceable and perjury always possible, precisely unverifiable. This necessity is nothing other than the solitude, the singularity, the inaccessibility of the "as for me," the impossibility of having an originary and internal intuition of the proper experience of the other ego, of the alter ego. The same necessity is necessarily felt on both sides of the address or the destination (on the side of the addresser and of the addressee) as the place of an always possible violence and abuse for which the apologetic confession is already at work, *à l'oeuvre*. I say "apologetic confession" to use two de Manian notions that are here indissociable, always indissociable. And not only in Rousseau.

But this is also why Rousseau is interesting. He endured in an exemplary fashion this common fate. This fate is not only a misfortune, a trap, or a curse of the gods. It is also the only possibility of speaking to the other, of blessing, saying, or making the truth. Since I can always lie and since the other can always be the victim of this lie, since he or she never has the same access that I do to what I myself think or mean to say, I always begin, at least implicitly, by confessing a possible fault, abuse, or violence, an elementary perjury, an originary betrayal. I always begin by asking forgiveness when I address myself to the other and precisely in this equivocal mode, even if it is in order to say to him or her things that are as constative as, for example: "You know, it's raining."

This is why, in the last phase of his interpretation, the one that is most important to him and that concerns the leap from the *Confessions* to the *Fourth Reverie*, when de Man evokes at that point a "twilight zone between knowing and not-knowing," I feel so much in agreement with him. I would even raise the stakes: I don't believe such a twilight obscures only an initial clarity or covers only the passage from the *Confessions* to the *Reveries*. This twilight seems to me consubstantial, from the origin, with confession—even in the element that de Man would like to retain within the order of knowledge: a purely cognitive, epistemological dimension, a moment of revealed truth. De Man argues, in the following lines, for the necessity of a passage, that is, also a transformation or a displacement, from the *Confessions* to the *Fourth Reverie*. But this seems to me already valid for the *Confessions*. If I am right, that would make it difficult to maintain the allegation of a change of register between the two, at least in this regard.

But the text offers further possibilities. The analysis of shame as excuse makes evident the strong link between the performance of excuses and the act of understanding. It has led to the problematics of hiding and revealing, which are clearly problematics of cognition. Excuse occurs within an epistemological twilight zone between knowing and not-knowing; this is also why it has to be centered on the crime of lying and why Rousseau can excuse himself for everything provided he can be excused for lying. When this turns out not to have been the case, when his claim to have lived for the sake of truth (*vitam impendere vero*) is being contested from the outside, the closure of excuse ("qu'il me soit permis de n'en reparler jamais") becomes a delusion and the *Fourth Reverie* has to be written. (286)

If "the closure of excuse," at the end of the avowal in the *Confessions*, later "becomes a delusion," it is indeed because it is already there, in the

Confessions. And it will remain a delusion after the *Fourth Reverie*. Later on we will consider the consequence of this.

Let us return to this value of event. The event affects the "who" and the "what." It affects and changes singularities of all sorts, even as past event, inscribed or archived. Irreducible eventness of the event in question, which, then, must be retained, inscribed, traced, and so forth, can be the thing itself that is thus archived, but it must also be the event of the inscription. Even as it consigns, inscription produces a new event, thereby affecting the presumed primary event it is supposed to retain, engram, consign, archive. There is the event one archives, the *archived* event (and there is no archive without a body—I prefer to say "body" rather than "matter," for reasons that I will try to justify later), and there is the *archiving* event, the archivation. The latter is not the same thing, structurally, as the archived event, even if, in certain cases, it is indissociable from it or even contemporary with it.

In his reading of Rousseau, de Man is concerned with what he himself calls a "textual event." An admirable reading, in fact a paradigmatic interpretation of a text that it poses as paradigmatic, namely, Rousseau's confession and excuse, whether one considers them to be successive, as de Man wants to do, or as simultaneous and indissociable in both their moment and their structure. A double paradigm, therefore, paradigm on paradigm. For if de Man's reading is exemplary, and from now on canonical, because of its inaugural character as the first rigorous elaboration, with regard to this famous passage, of certain theoretical protocols of reading (in particular, although not only, of a theory of the performative whose Austinian complications I had followed and aggravated elsewhere), such a reading itself declares that it bears on a "paradigmatic event" (these are de Man's terms) in the work of Rousseau:

We are invited to believe that the episode [of the stolen ribbon] was never revealed to anyone prior to the privileged reader of the *Confessions* "and . . . that the desire to free myself, so to speak, from this weight has greatly contributed to my resolve to write my confessions." When Rousseau returns to the *Confessions* in the later *Fourth Reverie*, he again singles out this same episode as paradigmatic event, the core of his autobiographical narrative. (278–79)

It is then, in the second paragraph of his introduction, that de Man uses the expression "textual event," an expression that will reappear on the last page of the same essay. He continues: "The selection [of the theft of the ribbon and the lie that followed as paradigmatic episode] is, in itself, as arbitrary as it is suspicious, but it provides us with a *textual event* of undeniable exegetic interest: the juxtaposition of two confessional texts linked together by an explicit repetition, the confession, as it were, of a confession" (279; my emphasis).

That this selection is held by de Man to be "as arbitrary as it is suspicious" is a hypothesis that must be taken seriously, even if one is not prepared to subscribe to it unreservedly. For it subtends in a definitive way de Man's whole interpretation, notably his concepts of grammar and machine. At the end of the text, he will speak of the "gratuitous product of a textual grammar" (299), or yet again, still à propos of this structure of machinelike repetition, of "a system that is both entirely arbitrary and entirely repeatable, *like* a grammar" (300). Once again I underscore "like," this index of analogy.

The expression "textual event" is found again in conclusion, very close to the last word. It is no longer a matter of the last word of a chapter, but of a book, since this is, in de Man's corpus, the last chapter of the last book he will have published and reread during his lifetime.

Now, it both is and is not the same "textual event"; it is no longer the one in question at the beginning of the text. Apparently, it would be the same, to be sure, because it is still a matter of what happens with the paradigmatic passage in the *Confessions*. But now this event has been analyzed, determined, interpreted, localized within a certain mechanism, namely— and we will come back to this later—an anacoluthon or a parabasis, a discontinuity or, to quote de Man's conclusion, "a sudden revelation of the discontinuity between two rhetorical codes. This isolated textual event, as the reading of the *Fourth Reverie* shows, is disseminated throughout the entire text and the anacoluthon is extended over all the points of the figural line or allegory" (300).

How does this "textual event" inscribe itself? What is the operation of its inscription? What is the writing machine, the typewriter, that both produces it and archives it? What is the body, or even the materiality that confers on this inscription both a support and a resistance? And, above all, what essential relation does this textual event maintain with a scene of confession and excuse?

Since we are getting ready to speak of matter or, more precisely, of the body, I note in the first place that de Man, very curiously, pays almost no attention, for reasons that he doubtless considers justified and that in my view are only partially so, to either the matter and body of the ribbon or its use, because he holds it to be "devoid of meaning and function," circulating "symbolically as a pure signifier" (283). Everything happens as with the purloined letter, at least as it is interpreted by Lacan—to whom I objected a long time ago that if the content of the letter appeared indifferent, it is because each of the protagonists, and each reader, knew that it signified at least perjury and betrayal of a sworn faith. Likewise, I would observe here that the ribbon is not such a free or undetermined signifier: it has at least the sexualizable signification of ornament and fetish; and by the same token it has perhaps several others.

De Man is not interested either in the intermediary paragraph between the account of the death of Mme de Vercellis from a cancer of the breast (her double expiration, her last word) and the beginning of the confession of the misdeed that afflicts Rousseau with the "unbearable weight of a remorse" from which he cannot recover any more than he can ever console himself for it. The paragraph neglected by de Man describes nothing less than a scene of inheritance. It is a question of the will left by Mme de Vercellis, of whom de Man nevertheless says, as you recall, that there is no reason to "substitute" Marion for her ("nothing in the text," he says, suggests such a "concatenation") and thus *a fortiori* no reason to replace her with Mme de Warens—of whom de Man speaks only once in this context, and concerning whom I recall that Rousseau had met her for the first time the same year, a few months earlier, their meeting coinciding more or less with their common abjuration, their almost simultaneous conversion to Catholicism.

This scene of inheritance is once again a scene of *succession*, in the third sense of this word that we discerned the last time. It seems to me significant, in this place, for countless reasons that I will not develop and to which, astonishingly to me, de Man pays no attention. One must take into account there, by essence or par excellence, as in every scene of inheritance, laws of *substitution*—that is, the law period, namely, responsibility, debt, or duty, thus guilt and forgiveness. Substitution of persons and things, of "who" and of "what," in the domains of the law governing persons and the law governing things, for one must not forget that the ribbon belongs more or less clearly to this scene and to the patrimony of things and valuables left as legacies. Even if it is a thing without value, as we will see, an old and used thing, its exchange value is caught up in the logic of substitution constituted by the inheritance. And we will once again have to reckon with more than one substitution—those of which de Man speaks and those of which he says nothing.

So that this may be more concrete in your eyes, here are the lines which seem not to interest de Man:

She had left one year's wages to each of the under-servants. But not having been entered on the strength of her household I received nothing. . . . It is almost inevitable that the breaking up of an establishment should cause some confusion in the house, and that various things should be mislaid. But so honest were the servants and so vigilant were M. and Mme Lorenzi that nothing was found missing when the inventory was taken. Only Mlle Pontal lost a little pink- and silver-colored ribbon, which was quite old [*un petit ruban de couleur de rose et argent déjà vieux*]. (86; 84)

These two little words "quite old," *déjà vieux*, are also omitted by de Man, I don't know why, in his quotation of this phrase, which he extracts therefore from its context and without having cited the preceding paragraph, which I would call *testamentary*. No doubt the inventory in the course of which the disappearance of the ribbon was remarked is not the moment of the inheritance itself, but it is something like its inseparable continuation; and Mlle Pontal, who "lost" (*perdit*) the "little ribbon" had received 600 *livres* in inheritance, twenty times more than all the servants, who had each received, in addition, individual legacies. Rousseau inherited nothing, and he complains about it. These scenes of inheritance and inventory, which de Man does not evoke, are not the scenes that Rousseau describes before recounting the death of Mme de Vercellis, in a passage where it is already a question of legacies: the entourage of Mme de Vercellis, already thinking about the legacy, had done everything to get Rousseau out of the way and "banish [him] from her sight," as he puts it. No doubt it is to this paragraph preceding the account that de Man refers in the note that had surprised me somewhat: "The embarrassing story of Rousseau's rejection by Mme de Vercellis, who is dying of a cancer of the breast, immediately precedes the story of Marion, but nothing in the text suggests a concatenation that would allow one to substitute Marion for Mme de Vercellis in a scene of rejection." Curiously, de Man does not believe this substitution should be credited. Curiously because, inversely, his whole text will put to work in a decisive fashion a logic of substitution. In a later passage, which is not, it is true, his last word on the subject, he talks abundantly of a substitution between Rousseau and Marion and even of "two levels of substitution (or displacement) taking place: the ribbon substituting for a desire which is itself a desire for substitution" (284). Summing up the facts, he writes: "The episode itself is one in a series of stories of petty larceny, but with an added twist. While employed as a servant in an aristocratic Turin household, Rousseau has stolen a 'pink and silver colored ribbon'" (279).

Why does he cut the sentence, mutilating it or dismembering it in this way, and in such an apparently arbitrary fashion? Why does he amputate two of its own little words before the period: "quite old," *déjà vieux*? I have no answer to this question. I say mutilation, amputation, dismemberment, or even arbitrary cut to qualify the violence of a surgical operation. A phrase is thus deprived of two of its little words and interrupted in its organic syntax. I underscore this violence both because that's the way it is, no doubt, and the phenomenon is as strange as it is remarkable (it is indeed an apparently arbitrary amputation and dissociation, and arbitrariness is, like gratuitousness and chance, a major motif of de Man's essay),[18] but also because the general interpretation by de Man of the "textual event" in question will put to work, in a determinant fashion, these motifs (mutilation and dismemberment), as well as the operation of a machinery, as we will see. I underscore these motifs for another reason. The words "matter" and "materialism" are not yet uttered, in 1979, in *Allegories of Reading* and this essay, "Excuses (*Confessions*)," although a certain lodging seems to be made ready for the welcome de Man will extend to them in later publications. Among the significations that will later structure the de Manian concept of materiality or material inscription, one finds once again, besides the significations of mute literality and body, those of discontinuity, caesura, division, mutilation, and dismemberment or, as de Man often says here, dissemination. Whether one is talking about the body in general, the body proper, or, as in the example of Kleist's *Marionettentheater* read by de Man, of the linguistic body of phrases and words in syllables and letters (for example, from *Fall* as case or fall to *Falle* as trap),[19] these figures of dismemberment, fragmentation, mutilation, and "material disarticulation" play an essential role in a certain "materialist" signature (I leave the word in quotation marks) that insists in the last texts of de Man. How does the concept of materiality or the associated concept of "materialism" get elaborated in the later texts ("Phenomenality and Materiality in Kant" and "Kant's Materialism," both in *Aesthetic Ideology*)? This is a question we can keep in view in this interpretation of Rousseau.

We must also keep in view a certain concept of *history*, of the historicity of history, so as to trace its intersection with this logic of the textual event as material inscription. When it is a matter of this structure of the text, the concept of historicity will no longer be regulated by the scheme of progression or of regression, thus by a scheme of teleological process, but rather by that of the event, or occurrence, thus by the singularity of the "one time only." This value of occurrence links historicity not to time, as is usually thought, nor to the temporal process but, according to de Man, to power, to the language *of* power and to language *as* power. Hence the necessity of taking into account performativity, which defines precisely the power *of* language and power *as* language, the excess of the language of power or of the power of language over constative or cognitive language. In "Kant and Schiller" (a lecture delivered at Cornell the year of his death, in 1983, and collected in *Aesthetic Ideology* on the basis of notes), de Man speaks of thinking history as *event* and not as *process*, progress, or regression. He then adds: "There is history from the moment that words such as 'power' and 'battle' and so on emerge on the scene. At that moment things *happen*, there is *occurrence*, there is *event*. History is therefore not a temporal notion, it has nothing to do with temporality, but it is the emergence of a language of power out of a language of cognition" (133). This hyperbolic provocation, in the style of de Man, certainly does not negate all temporality of history. It merely recalls that time, temporal unfolding is not the essential predicate of the concept of history: time is not enough to make history.

De Man distinguishes the eventness of events from a dialectical process or from any continuum accessible to a process of knowledge, such as the Hegelian dialectic. No doubt he would have said the same thing of the Marxist dialectic, I presume, if the heritage and the thought of Marx could be reduced to that of the dialectic. He also specifies that the performative (the language of power beyond the language of knowledge) is not the negation of the tropological but remains separated from the tropological by a *discontinuity* that tolerates no mediation and no temporal scheme. It remains the case that the performative, however foreign and excessive it may be in relation to the cognitive, can always be reinscribed, "recuperated" is de Man's word, in a cognitive system. This discontinuity, this event as discontinuity, is important for us if only because it will allow us to go beyond the excuse and come closer to the event of forgiveness, which always supposes irreversible interruption, revolutionary caesura, or even the end of history, at least of history as teleological process.

Moreover, one may note with equal interest that, in the same text ("Kant and Schiller"), de Man constructs his concept of event, of history as the eventness of events rather than as temporal process, on the basis of two determinations that are equally important for us: that of irreversibility (forgiveness and excuse suppose precisely that what has happened is irreversible) and that of inscription or material trace.

When I speak of irreversibility, and insist on irreversibility, this is because in all those texts and those juxtapositions of texts, we have been aware of something which one could call a progression—though it shouldn't be—a movement, from cognition, from acts of knowledge, from states of cognition, to something which is no longer a cognition but which is to some extent an *occurrence*, which has the materiality of something that actually happens, that actually occurs. And there, the thought of material occurrence, something that occurs materially, that leaves a trace on the world, that does something to the world as such—that notion of occurrence is not opposed in any sense to the notion of writing. But it is opposed to some extent to the notion of cognition. I'm reminded of a quotation in Hölderlin—if you don't quote Pascal you can always quote Hölderlin, that's about equally useful—which says: "Lang ist die Zeit, es ereignet sich aber das Wahre." Long is time, but—not truth, not *Wahrheit*, but *das Wahre*, that which is true, will occur, will take place, will eventually take place, will eventually occur. And the characteristic of truth is the fact that it occurs, not the truth, but that which is true. The occurrence is true because it occurs; by the fact that it occurs it has truth, truth value, it is true. (132)

But then why did de Man forget, omit, or efface those two words ("quite old," *déjà vieux*), which qualify a certain materiality of the enigmatic thing called a ribbon? Was it to save space, as one sometimes does by not citing a text integrally, by omitting passages that are less pertinent for the demonstration under way? Perhaps, but it is difficult to justify doing so for two little words ("quite old") that come just after the words quoted and before the final period. I recall the sentence and underscore certain words: "La seule Mlle Pontal *perdit* un petit ruban couleur de rose et argent *déjà vieux*," "Only Mlle Pontal lost a little pink- and silver-colored ribbon, which was quite old." I underscore in passing that Rousseau says of this ribbon that she "lost it," *le perdit*. On the preceding page, it was said of Mme de Vercellis: "Nous la *perdîmes* enfin. Je la vis expirer." "Finally we lost her. I watched her die."
Might there be a relation of substitution between the two losses signi-

fied by the same verb in the same tense, the *passé simple* or preterite that says—but what does it thereby say and mean to say?—*nous la perdîmes, elle perdit?* I would not swear to such a relation of substitution, but we'll leave it at that.

Excluding a concern for economy and the possibly inconsequential abbreviation of two little words, can one speak of a pure and simple omission by mechanical distraction? If one supposes that such a thing exists, it is all the more puzzling why it would have struck these two words from which de Man, instead of letting them drop, could have drawn an argument or with which he could have reinforced his own argument. To lend coherence to his hypothesis of substitution (between Rousseau and Marion, the desire of Rousseau and Marion, desire and the desire of substitution), the ribbon had to be a "free signifier," a simple exchange value without use value. Moreover, if indeed theft is a sin, then no one ever steals anything but exchange values, not use values. If I steal in order to eat, my theft is not really a crime, an evil for the sake of evil. In order to speak of misdeed, the profit must not be located in the usefulness of the fault, the crime, the theft, or the lie, but in a certain uselessness. One has to have loved the crime for itself, for the shame that it procures, which supposes some "beyond use" of the immediate or apparent object of the fault. But, in relation to immediate use, the beyond use does not mean absolute insignificance and uselessness. Augustine and Rousseau understood that very well. They both emphasize that they stole something for which they had no need and no use. Moreover, a little further on (and this explains my astonishment), de Man does allude to the fact that the ribbon must be beyond use, "devoid," as he puts it, "of meaning and function," in order to play the role it plays. In the first stage of his analysis, at the level he himself calls elementary, when he is describing one of the ways the text functions (among others, which he will exhibit later), de Man specifies forcefully that the desire for gift and possession, the movement of representation, exchange, and substitution of the ribbon supposes that it not be, I would say, a "use value" but an exchange value or even, I would say again (but this is not de Man's term), already a fetish, an exchange value whose body is fetishizable; one never steals the thing itself, which, moreover, never presents itself. Let us read:

Once it is removed from its legitimate owner, the ribbon, being in itself devoid of meaning and function, can circulate symbolically as a pure signifier and become the articulating hinge in a chain of exchanges and possessions. As the ribbon changes hands it traces a circuit leading to the exposure of a hidden, censored desire. Rousseau identifies the desire as his desire for Marion: "it was my intention to give her the ribbon," i.e., to "possess" her. At this point in the reading suggested by Rousseau, the proper meaning of the trope is clear enough: the ribbon "stands for" Rousseau's desire for Marion or, what amounts to the same thing, for Marion herself.

Or, rather, it stands for the free circulation of the desire between Rousseau and Marion, for the reciprocity which, as we know from *Julie*, is for Rousseau the very condition of love; it stands for the substitutability of Rousseau for Marion and vice versa. Rousseau desires Marion as Marion desires Rousseau. . . . The system works: "I accused Marion of having done what I wanted to do and of having given me the ribbon because it was my intention to give it to her." The substitutions have taken place without destroying the cohesion of the system, reflected in the balanced syntax of the sentence and now understandable exactly as we comprehend the ribbon to signify desire. Specular figures of this kind are metaphors and it should be noted that on this still elementary level of understanding, the introduction of the figural dimension in the text occurs first by ways of metaphor. (283–84)

Now think of the *word* "ribbon," but also of this figure of a narrow band of silk, velvet, or satin, which one wears on one's head, in one's hair, or like a necklace around the neck. The uncertain origin of the word *ribbon* probably links the motifs of the *ring* (it appears the word is *ringhband* in Middle Dutch), thus the circular link, the annular, or even the wedding band, and *band*, namely, once again the link, as *bind* or *Bund*. The ribbon thus seems to be, in itself, doubly enribboned, *ring* and *band*, twice knotted, banded, or banding, *bandé* or *bandant*, as I might say in French. A ribbon perhaps figures therefore the double bind *en soie*, in itself, its own silky self. The silk ribbon, the double silk ribbon [*ruban à soie*] that will never have been the self's own ribbon [*ruban à soi*].

By renaming the renown of this ribbon, I've been led to associate, almost inadvertently, without expecting it but no doubt not fortuitously, Marion's ribbon with the typewriter ribbon. De Man has little interest in the material of the ribbon, as we have just seen, for he takes the thing "ribbon" to be a "free signifier." But he is also not interested in the verbal signifier or the word "ribbon." Yet this lost piece of finery from the eighteenth century, the ribbon that Mlle Pontal "lost" after we "lost"

Mme de Vercellis, was also, once stolen and passed from hand to hand, a formidable writing machine, a ribbon of ink along which so many signs transited so irresistibly. This ribbon was a skin on which or under which so many words will have been printed. This *ringhband* exposes itself, it unrolls and rolls itself up like a phantasmatic body through which waves of ink will have been made to flow. An affluence or confluence of limited ink, to be sure, because a typewriter ribbon, like the ink cartridge of a computer printer, has only a finite reserve of coloring substance. The material potentiality of this ink remains modest, true, but it capitalizes, virtually, for the "sooner or later," an impressive superabundance: not only a great flux of liquid, good for writing, but a growing flux at the rhythm of a capital—on a day when speculation goes crazy in the capitals of the stock markets. And when one makes ink flow, figuratively or not, one can also figure that one *causes* to flow or *lets* flow all that which, by spilling itself this way, can invade or fertilize some cloth or tissue. Mlle Pontal, who lost poor Marion's ribbon, will not have worn it up till the end, but it will have supplied the body and the tissue and the ink and the surface of an immense bibliography. A virtual library, national and international.

I would have been tempted, but I will not have the time, to sketch other itineraries for this ink flow: for example, to pass from the figural ink of this ribbon of ink across a text of Austin's that I treated elsewhere, in *Limited Inc* (and it is also a text on excuse and responsibility, an analysis that, moreover, complements "A Plea for Excuses"). Austin analyzes there the possibilities of a bad thing one does intentionally or unintentionally, deliberately or by accident, by inadvertence—which is what one can always claim in order to excuse oneself. This text is titled "Three Ways of Spilling Ink," by reason of the à propos of a first example: a child spills some ink and the schoolmaster asks him, "Did you do that intentionally?" or "Did you do that deliberately?" or "Did you do that on purpose (purposely)?"[20] The question of the à-propos resonates again in this last formulation.

This ribbon will have been a subject, to be sure, but also more or less than a subject. It was originally a material support, both a subjectile on which one writes and the piece of a machine thanks to which one will never have done with inscribing: discourse upon discourse, exegesis on top of exegesis, beginning with those of Rousseau. In the universal *doxa*, this typewriter ribbon has become by substitution the ribbon of "poor

Marion," whose property it never was and to whom it was therefore never given or returned.

Imagine what she might have thought, "poor Marion," if someone had told her what was going to happen sooner or later to her ghost, that is to say, *to* her name and *in* her name over the centuries, thanks to Rousseau or by "Rousseau's fault," on the basis of the act to which she was perhaps one day barely the witness, only the poor victim who understands nothing of what is happening, the innocent girl who is perhaps as virginal as Mary. Will one ever know what she was able or might have been able to think, feel, love, hate, understand, or not understand about what was happening to her without happening to her? Could one know it, could one even form a hypothesis about it without the archive of the violent writing machine?

With or without annunciation, Marion will have been fertilized with ink through the ribbon of a terrible and tireless writing machine that is now relayed, in this floating sea of characters, by the apparently liquid element of computer screens and from time to time by ink cartridges for an Apple printer, just the thing to recall the forbidden fruit and the apples stolen by the young Jean-Jacques. Almost everything here will have passed by way of a written confession, without living addressee and within the writing of Rousseau, between the *Confessions* and the *Reveries* dreaming the virtual history of their "sooner or later."

As piece of a tireless writing machine, this ribbon gave rise—which is why I began with the event, with the event that is archivable as much as it is archiving—to what de Man twice calls, at the beginning and the end of his text, a "textual event." The second time it is in order to recognize there, as you heard, a dissemination of the textual event called anacoluthon; the first time it is to recall that this event has already the structure of a repetitive substitution, a repetition of the confession in the confession.

Among all the remarkable merits of de Man's great reading, there is first of all this reckoning with the works of Austin. I say purposely, and vaguely, the "works" of Austin because one value of these works is to have not only resisted but marked the line of resistance to systematic work, to philosophy as formalizing theorization, absolute and closed, freed of its adherences to ordinary language and to so-called natural languages.

There is also, and this is another advance, an elaboration and an original complication of Austinian concepts. De Man cites "Performative Utterances" and "A Plea for Excuses" precisely at the point at which he writes: "As is well known at least since Austin, excuses are a complex instance of what he termed performative utterances, a variety of speech acts" (281–82). To illustrate the complexity of this "complex example," he specifies right away that "the interest of Rousseau's text is that it explicitly functions performatively and thus gives indications about the structure of performative rhetoric" (282). Now, the opposition between "performative" and "cognitive" rhetoric was evoked in the first lines of the chapter, which apparently mark the passage from temporality to historicity that we were speaking of a moment ago. This passage is all the more paradoxical in that it goes from a more political text, the *Social Contract*, to a less political one, the *Confessions* or the *Reveries*. The phenomenon of this appearance must be analyzed. If, de Man says, "the relationship between cognition and performance is relatively easy to grasp in the case of a temporal speech act such as a *promise*—which, in Rousseau's work, is the model for the *Social Contract*—it is more complex in the confessional mode of his autobiographies" (278).

In other words, the performative mode of the promise would be simpler than that of the confession or the excuse, notably as regards the distinction between cognition and performance, knowledge and action, constative and performative, and so forth. In the preceding chapter, de Man had treated the promise setting out from the *Social Contract*. He thus goes from the *Social Contract* to the *Confessions* and to the *Reveries*, from the simpler to the more complex, where, precisely, the complexity can no longer be undone, and the distinction can no longer operate (at least as I see it, because de Man wants to maintain this distinction even when it seems difficult to do so). In the preceding chapters on Rousseau, in particular, in the chapter on the *Social Contract*, one finds the premises of the chapter we are now reading, "Excuses (*Confessions*)." I retain at least three of these premises:

1. A concept or an operation of *deconstruction*: "A deconstruction always has for its target to reveal the existence of hidden articulations and fragmentations within assumedly monadic totalities" (249), within "a binary metaphorical system" (258), or in "metaphorical patterns based on binary models" (255). Nature becoming a "self-deconstructive term" (249), one will always be dealing with a series of deconstructions: deconstructions of deconstructions of figures.

2. A concept of the "machine" indissociable from this deconstruction. A text whose grammaticality is a logical code obeys a machine. No text is

conceivable without grammar, and no grammar, thus no machine, would be conceivable without the "suspension of referential meaning." In the order of the law (and this is valid for any law, it is the law of the law), what does this mean? Well, this: "Just as no law can ever be written unless one suspends any consideration of applicability to a particular entity, including, of course, oneself, grammatical logic can function only if its referential consequences are disregarded. On the other hand, no law is a law unless it also applies to particular individuals. It cannot be left hanging in the air, in the abstraction of its generality" (269).

3. A concept of *originary injustice*, or of *unjust justice*. De Man interprets this contradiction or this incompatibility (the law suspends referential application even as it requires it as verification) in a striking fashion, in particular, in the passage from the *Social Contract* (read here from the viewpoint of the *promise*) to the *Confessions* or to the *Reveries* (read here from the viewpoint of the *excuse*). One can overcome this contradiction or this incompatibility only by an *act of deceit*. The violence of this deception is a *theft*, a theft in language, the theft of a word, the abusive appropriation of the meaning of a word. This theft is not the appropriation of just any word whatsoever. It is the absolute substitution, the theft of the subject, more precisely, of the word *chacun*, "each one," inasmuch as it says at once the "I," the singularity and the generality of every "I." Nothing is in fact more irreducibly singular than "I," and yet nothing is more universal, anonymous, and substitutable. This deception and this theft consist in appropriating the word *chacun*. "S'approprier le mot 'chacun'" are Rousseau's terms. "Deceit" and "theft" are de Manian translations, which are at once brutal and faithful: when one appropriates, one always steals, and when one steals, one deceives, one lies, especially when one denies it. This deceit and this theft, therefore, would be constitutive of justice (which is both without reference and applicable, thus with a reference: *without and with* reference). De Man is then led to say that "justice is unjust." This extraordinary formula is one I must have retained while forgetting it, while forgetting that I stole it in this way because afterwards, and very recently, I took it up on my own account and ventured it in another context, without making reference to de Man. The context was an interpretation of Levinas, of the logic of the third party and of perjury, namely, that all justice is unjust and begins in perjury, which is what I tried to show, using a very different argument, in *Adieu à Emmanuel Levinas*.[21]

Having confessed this involuntary theft, so as to excuse myself for it, I underscore this reference to theft in the chapter preceding the one we are concerned with at present on the excuse, which thus serves as a premise for it.

Here are several lines, but to be fair, one would have to reconstitute the whole context:

> The preceding passage makes clear that the incompatibility between the elaboration of the law and its application (or justice) can only be bridged by an act of deceit. "S'approprier en secret ce mot *chacun*" is to steal from the text the very meaning to which, according to this text, we are not entitled, the particular *I* which destroys its generality; hence the deceitful, covert gesture "en secret," in the foolish hope that the theft will go unnoticed. Justice is unjust; no wonder that the language of justice is also the language of guilt and that, as we know from the *Confessions*, we never lie as much as when we want to do full justice to ourselves, especially in self-accusation. (268)

The substitution of the "I" for the "I" is also the root of perjury: I (the I) can always, by addressing myself/itself to (a [you]), each one to each one, substitute the other same "I" for this here "I" and change the destination. (An) "I" can always change the address in secret at the last moment. Since every "I" is an "I" (the same and altogether other: *tout autre est tout autre*, every other is altogether other as the same), since every other is altogether other, (the) I can betray, without the least appearance becoming manifest, by substituting the address of one for the address of the other, up to the last moment—in amorous ecstasy or in death, one or the other, one and the other.

Let us end today with a postscript or a footnote, since it is a matter of the foot. And of what comes down to walking on the foot. On the foot of another.

A propos of "Performative Utterances" and "A Plea for Excuses," attention is sometimes drawn to several strategic and, in my view, important gestures. De Man does not remark them, but I do because they cross the paths we are following in perhaps an ironic way. You should know that de Man was a great theorist of irony, of all the traditional interpretations of irony, as experience or as trope, from Fichte and Schlegel to Kierkegaard and Benjamin.[22]

First of all, just for laughs, a strange association: the second example of "performative utterances," in the text with that title, is "I apologize" when you step on someone's foot. Now, how does this example come up? Is it symptomatic (a question one must always ask when Englishmen seem to exercise their wit by choosing at random arbitrary, insignificant, joking, or trivial examples)? The text had begun with irony, as always with Austin, when, in what is precisely a decisive and performative fashion, he baptizes "performative" what will be defined as performative. Why this word, "performative"? Beyond the theoretical or semantic justifications for this terminological choice of an expression consecrated to a regulated use, this choice includes a performative dimension: I decide to propose that utterances of this type be called *performatives*. Austin has decided thus—and *it works, it will have worked* [ça marche, ça aura marché], it has been imprinted on all typewriter ribbons, more or less correctly, because the rigorous definition of the performative is infinitely problematic. But the word is now ineffaceable.

So Austin begins his text as follows:

You are more than entitled not to know what the word "performative" means. It is a new word and an ugly word, and perhaps it does not mean anything very much. But at any rate there is one thing in its favour, it is not a profound word. I remember once when I had been talking on this subject that somebody afterwards said: "You know, I haven't the least idea what he means, unless it could be that he simply means what he says." Well, that is what I should like to mean.[23]

(This reminds me of my experience with the "ugly" and "new" words "deconstruction" and "differance" in 1967 at Oxford, when I gave a lecture titled "Difference." The thing was not very well received: icy consternation, rather than objection and critique, but an angry outburst from Ayer, the only one to lose his cool there among Ryle, Strawson, and so forth. Whenever I have misadventures at Oxford, where Austin taught [or later at Cambridge, even when things turn out all right], I always think of him.)

The second major example of "performative utterance" will thus be "I apologize" when I step on someone's foot. This example comes up right after the example of the "I do" in the marriage ceremony, the "I do" that marks clearly that I do what I say by saying what I do. Austin has just said that with certain utterances, one says that the person is in the process of doing something rather than saying something: "Suppose for example, that in the course of a marriage ceremony I say, as people will, 'I do' (sc. take this woman to be my lawful wedded wife). Or again [this "Or again" is sublime] suppose that I tread on your toe and say 'I apologize.' Or again . . . " (235). This linking by additive contiguity, without transition ("Or again") from the marriage ceremony to the excuse when I tread on another's toes makes me think irresistibly of an Algerian Jewish rite. According to common and more or less superstitious custom, the wedded couple is advised, at the precise moment when their marriage is consecrated in the synagogue, to hurry up and place a foot on the other's foot so as to guarantee for himself or herself power in their conjugal life. One has to hurry and take the other by surprise. One must create the event. The first one who places his or her foot on the other's will have the upper hand during the rest of their life together, until the end of history: history as occurrence and power, de Man would say.

As if, right after the paradigmatic "I do" of the wedding ceremony, one had to excuse oneself or ask forgiveness from the other for this first *coup d'état*, for the power that is thus violently appropriated by a *coup de force*—or even a kick, a *coup de pied*. "I do take you for husband (or wife), oh, excuse me, sorry," followed perhaps by an "it's nothing," "no problem," *y a pas d'mal*. At any rate, whatever the response might be to a marriage proposal, it would be necessary to excuse oneself or ask forgiveness. "Marry me, I want to marry you." Response: "Yes, I beg your pardon" or "No, I beg your pardon." In either case, there is fault and thus forgiveness to be asked—and it is always as if one were treading on the other's toes.

The "One Certain Monument": Of a Materiality Without Matter

As if . . .

Not *it was* as if, but *I was* as if.

How can one say "I was as if . . ."?

For example: "I was as if I had committed incest." Not *it was* as if, but *I was* as if, *I* became as if, *I* will have been as if. The "I" seems to come to be, as the other used to say, there where it was, there where the neutral, impersonal "it," the *ce*, the *ça*, ought to have been—or stay what it will have been. We have here perhaps come very close to the theft of the "I" that we were speaking of yesterday. Moreover, one always robs someone, one never steals something without robbing someone: one never steals a "what" without stealing, or even raping, a "who," a woman, a child, a man.

This sentence, "J'étais comme si j'avais commis un inceste," is now part of my archive, or even my corpus, but it never belonged to me. I inscribed it more than thirty years ago as epigraph to the whole second part of *Of Grammatology*, devoted to Rousseau. Signed Rousseau, the "I was as if . . ." comes from the *Confessions*. Rousseau describes himself with these words in a passage around the famous and scabrous sexual initiation by Maman. At the beginning of the paragraph, we read the narration of a commitment. The account (in the descriptive or constative mode, therefore) recounts a commitment (in the performative mode). It is thus the story, the constative memory of a performative act of sworn faith. The commitment consists in a promise and, as always, a profession of veracity: "The day came at last, more dreaded than desired. I promised all and did not break my word [*Ce jour-là, plustot redouté qu'attendu, vint enfin. Je promis tout, et je ne mentis pas*]." Further in the same paragraph: "No; I tasted pleasure, but I knew not what invincible sadness poisoned its charm. I was as if I had committed incest [*Non, je goûtai le plaisir. Je ne sais quelle invincible tristesse en empoisonnait le charme. J'étois comme si j'avais commis un inceste*]." As for Maman, in the aftermath of the more or less shared experience of the same pleasure, she knew no remorse: "As she was not at all sensual and had not sought for gratification, she neither received sexual pleasure nor knew the remorse that follows [*Comme elle était peu sensuelle et n'avoit point recherché la volupté, elle n'en eut pas les délices, et n'en a jamais eu les remords*]" (189; 197). She did not come, so there was no fault, no remorse for her. Not only did she know no remorse, but she had, like God, the virtue of mercy [*miséricorde*], forgiving without even thinking that there was some merit in forgiveness. So Maman never knew any remorse for this quasi-incest, and Rousseau justifies her in every regard, he excuses her with all his well-known eloquence. Now, you know, and Rousseau knew better than we do, how many lovers the lady he called "Maman" had had. He nevertheless wrote, as if he were speaking of himself: "All her faults, I repeat, came from her lack of judgment, never from her passions. She was of gentle birth, her heart was pure" (190). Several pages later, he is still speaking of her, as if he were speaking of himself: "She loathed duplicity and lying; she was just, equitable, humane, disinterested, true to her word, her friends, and what she recognized as her duties, incapable of hatred or vengeance and not even imagining that there was the slightest merit in forgiveness" (191). So she forgave graciously, without difficulty, without forcing herself. She was mercy itself and forgiveness itself. The following sentence, however, still attempts to excuse the least excusable: "Finally, to return to her less excusable qualities, though she did not rate her favors at their true worth, she never made a common trade in them; she conferred them lavishly but she did not sell them, though continually reduced to expedients in order to live; and I would venture to say that if Socrates could esteem Aspasia, he would have respected Mme de Warens."

Maman forgives infinitely, like God. As to her faults, she can be excused, which is what the son sets out to do. One could follow the occurrences of the word "forgive," "first *jouissance*," that of this quasi-incest, and especially this oath: "I can swear that I never loved her more tenderly than when I so little desired to possess her" (189).

A few years ago, when I was rereading these pages of Rousseau for a seminar on forgiveness and perjury, a prodigious archive had just been exhumed, in Picardy, and then deciphered. In layers of fauna and flora were found, protected in amber, some animal or other (which would be nothing new), but also the cadaver of an insect surprised by death, in an instant, by a geological or geothermal catastrophe, at the moment at which it was sucking the blood of another insect, some fifty-four million years before humans appeared on earth. Fifty-four million years before humans appeared on earth, there was once upon a time an insect that died, its cadaver is still visible and intact, the cadaver of someone who was surprised by death at the instant it was sucking the blood of another! But it would suffice that it be but two hours before the appearance of any living being or other, of whoever would be capable of referring to this archive as such, that is, to the archive of a singular event at which this living being will not have been, itself, present, yesterday, an hour ago—or fifty-four million years before humans appeared, sooner or later, on earth.

It is one thing to know the sediments, rocks, plants that can be dated to this timeless time when nothing human or even living signaled its presence on earth. It is another thing to refer to a singular event, to what took place one time, one time only, in a nonrepeatable instant, like that animal surprised by catastrophe at the moment, at some instant, at some stigmatic point of time in which it was in the process of taking its pleasure sucking the blood of another animal, just as it could have taken it in some other way, moreover. For there is also a report of two midges immobilized in amber the color of honey when they were surprised by death as they made love: fifty-four million years before humans appeared on earth, a *jouissance* took place whose archive we preserve. It arrives/happens to us again, it is still arriving to us. We have there, set down, consigned to a support, protected by the body of an amber coffin, the trace, which is itself corporeal, of an event that took place only once and that, as semelfactive event, is not at all reducible to the permanence of elements from the same period that have endured through time and come down to us, for example, amber in general. There are many things on earth that have been there since fifty-four million years before humans. We can identify or analyze them, but rarely in the form of the archive of a singular event and, what is more, of an event that happened to some living being, affecting a kind of organized individual, already endowed with a kind of memory, with project, need, desire, pleasure, *jouissance*, and aptitude to retain traces.

I don't know why I am telling you this. Perhaps because this discovery is itself an event, an event on the subject of another event that is thus archived. Perhaps because we are in the process of interrogating the relation between, on the one hand, impassive but fragile matter, the material depository, the support, the subjectile, the document and, on the other, singularity, semelfactivity, the "one time only," the "once and for all" of the event thus consigned, to be confided without any guarantee that is not aleatory, incalculably, to some resistant matter, here to amber.

Perhaps one begins to think, to know and to know how to think, to know how to think knowing, only by taking the measure of this scale: for example, fifty-four million years before humans appeared on earth. Or yesterday, when I was not there, when an "I" and above all an "I" saying "me, a man" was not there—or, tomorrow, sooner or later, will not be there any longer. On this scale, what happens to our interest for archives that are as human, recent, micrological but just as fragile as confessions or reveries, as some "I apologize" and some asked-for pardons in a history of literature that, even on the very small scale of human history, is barely a child born yesterday, being only a few centuries old or young, namely, a few fractions of a second in the history of life, earth, and the rest?

Let us now recall the two beginnings of the *Confessions*, for there are two of them. Let us go back toward the duplicity of these two beginnings, of the first word and the before-the-first word. These two beginnings both begin by saying that what is beginning there begins for the first and last time in the history of humanity. No true archive of man in his truth before the *Confessions*. Unique event, without precedent and without sequel, event that envelops its own archivation: "This is the only portrait of a man, drawn precisely from nature and in all its truth, that exists and that will probably ever exist. [*Voici le seul portrait d'homme, peint exactement d'après nature et dans toute sa vérité. Qui existe et qui probablement existera jamais*]" (15; 3). This is found in the preamble, which has a strange status that I will talk about in a moment. On the following page, with the opening of the first Book and therefore with what one may call the first word of the *Confessions*, Rousseau repeats more or less the same thing: "I have resolved on an enterprise that has no precedent, and which, once complete, will have no imitator. My purpose is to display to my kind a portrait in every way true to nature, and the man I shall portray will be myself. [*Je forme une entreprise qui n'eut jamais d'exemple, et dont l'exécution n'aura point d'imitateur. Je veux montrer à mes semblables un homme dans toute la vérité de la nature; et cet homme ce sera moi*]" (17; 5).

As if, after more than fifty-four million years, one were witnessing in nature, and according to nature, the first pictorial archive of man worthy of that name and in all his truth: the birth if not of man, at least of the exhibition of the natural truth of man. Listen to it again: "I have resolved on an enterprise that has no precedent, and which, once complete, will have no imitator. My purpose is to display to my kind a portrait in every way true to nature, and the man I shall portray will be myself."

I didn't know, a moment ago, why I was telling you these stories of archives: archives of a vampire insect, archives of animals making love fifty-four million years ago—and archives as *Confessions*. But yes, I think I remember now, even though it was first of all unconscious and came back to me only after the fact. It is because in a moment I am going to talk to you about effacement and prostheses, about falsifications of the letter, about the mutilation of texts, of bodies of writing exposed to cutting no less than insects are (and "insect," *insectum*, as you know, means "cut," "sectioned," and, like "sex," *sexus*, *sectus*, it connotes section, separation, and so forth). Now—and here you'll just have to believe me because I am telling you the truth, as always—when I quoted Rousseau in *Of Grammatology* in 1967 and wrote as an epigraph for the whole section (almost the whole book) that I devoted to Rousseau, "J'étois comme si j'avais commis un inceste," "I was as if I had committed incest," well, the first proofs of the book came back to me with a typographical error.

I was tempted, for a moment, not to correct it. The compositor in fact had set: "J'étois comme si j'avais commis un *insecte*," "I was as if I had committed an *insect*." Perhaps the typo was meant to protect from incest, but to protect whom or what? A perfect anagram (*incestel insecte*) that, in order to respect the grammatical machine, I had to resolve to rectify and to normalize. I thus returned from insect to incest, retracing the whole path, the fifty-four million years that lead from the blood-sucking animal to the first man of the *Confessions*, an Oedipal man as first man (in Hegel's expression) or as last man (in Nietzsche's expression), Oedipus dictating there the first, here the last word of man.

We are seeking in this way to advance our research on the subject of that which, in forgiveness, excuse, or perjury, *comes to pass, is done, comes about, happens, arrives* and thus that which, as event, requires not only an operation, an act, a performance, a *praxis*, but an *oeuvre*, that is, at the same time the result and the trace left by a supposed operation, an *oeuvre* that survives its supposed operation and its supposed operator. Surviving it, being destined to this sur-vival, to this excess over present life, the *oeuvre* as trace implies from the outset the structure of this sur-vival, that is, what *cuts* the *oeuvre* off from the operation. This *cut* assures it a sort of archival independence or autonomy that is quasi-machinelike (not machinelike but *quasi*-machinelike), a power of repetition, repeatability, iterability, serial and prosthetic substitution of self for self. This cut is not so much effected by the machine (even though the machine can in fact cut and repeat the cut in its turn) as it is the condition of production for a machine. The machine is *cut* as well as *cutting* with regard to the living present of life or of the living body. The machine is an *effect of the cut* as much as it is a *cause of the cut*. And that is one of the difficulties in handling this concept of machine, which always and by definition structurally resembles a *causa sui*. And where one says *causa sui*, the figure of a god is not far off. Question of the technical as question of the theological. Question of the "machine for making gods" in which Bergson recognizes, at the end of *The Two Sources of Morality and Religion*, the "essential function of the universe . . . on our refractory planet."

Forgiveness and excuse are possible, are called upon to go into effect only where this relative, quasi-machinelike survival of the *oeuvre*—or of the archive as *oeuvre*—takes *place*, where it constitutes and institutes an event, in some manner taking charge of the forgiveness or the excuse. To say in this way that the *oeuvre* institutes and constitutes an event is to register in a confused way an ambiguous thing. An *oeuvre* is an event, to be sure; there is no *oeuvre* without singular event, without textual event, if one can agree to enlarge this notion beyond its verbal or discursive limits. But is the *oeuvre* the trace of an event, the name of the trace of the event that will have instituted it as *oeuvre*? Or is it the institution of this event itself?

I would be tempted to respond, and not only so as to avoid the question: both at once. Every surviving *oeuvre* keeps the trace of this ambiguity. It keeps the memory of the present that instituted it, but, in this present, there was *already*, if not the project, at least the essential possibility of this cut—of this cut in view of leaving a trace, of this cut whose purpose is survival, of this cut that sometimes assures survival even if there is not the purpose of survival. This cut is at once a wounding and an opening, the chance of a respiration, and it was in some way already there at work, *à l'oeuvre*. It marked, like a scar, the originary living present of this institution—*as if* the machine, the *quasi*-machine were already operating, even before being produced in the world, if I can put it that way, in the vivid experience of the living present.

This is already a terrifying aporia. But why *terrifying*? And for whom? This question will continue to haunt us. A terrifying aporia because this fatal necessity engenders automatically a situation in which forgiveness and excuse are both automatic (they cannot not take place, in some way independently of the presumed living "subjects" that they are supposed to involve) and therefore null and void, since they are in contradiction with what we, as inheritors of these values, either Abrahamic or not, think about forgiveness and excuse: automatic and mechanical pardons or excuses cannot have the value of pardon and excuse. Or, if you prefer, one of the formidable effects of this machinelike automaticity would be to reduce every scene of forgiveness not only to a process of excuse but to the automatic and null efficacy of an a priori "I apologize," I disculpate myself and justify myself a priori or a posteriori, with an a posteriori that is a priori programmed, and in which, moreover, the "I" itself would be the "I" of anyone at all, according to the law of "deceit" or "theft" we have discussed. One always robs *someone* even when one steals *something* from him: usurpation of the singular *I* by the universal *I*, ineluctable substitution and subterfuge that makes all "justice" "unjust."

A question of technics: mechanical, machinelike, automatic forgiveness and excuse self-destruct without delay—and lose their meaning, even their memory, more radically still than the recorded tapes on "Mission Impossible," which self-destruct instantly, annihilating their own archive after having been heard just once.

Why would it be terrifying, this self-destructive, suicidal, and automatic neutralization, which both *produces* and *is produced by* the scene of forgiveness or the apologetic scene? Why fear its effects? One could use other words, more or less grave. In any case, it would be a matter of naming a negative affect, the feeling of threat, but a threat at the heart of the promise. For what threatens is also what makes possible the expectation or the promise, for example, the anticipation of a forgiveness or an excuse that I could not even desire, expect, or see coming without this cut, without this survival, without this beyond-the-living-present. Right there where automaticity is effective and disculpates "me" a priori, it threatens me, therefore. Right there where it reassures me, I can fear it. Because it cuts me off from my own initiative, from my own origin, from my originary life, therefore from the present of my life, but also from the authenticity of the forgiveness and the excuse, from their very meaning, and finally from the eventness—of both the fault and its confession, the forgiveness or the excuse. As a result and by reason of this quasi-automaticity or quasi-machinelike quality of the sur-viving *oeuvre*, one has the impression that one is dealing only with quasi-events, quasi-faults, quasi-excuses, with ghosts of excuses, or with spectral silhouettes of pardons. Before any other possible suffering or any other possible passion, there is the wound, which is at once infinite and unfelt, anesthetized, of this neutralization by the "as if," by the "as if" of this *quasi*, by the limitless risk of becoming a simulacrum or a virtuality without consistency— of everything.

Is it necessary and is it possible to give an account of this wound, of this trauma, that is, of the desire, of the living movement, of the proper body, and so forth, given that the desire in question is not only injured or threatened with injury by the machine, but produced by the very possibility of the machine, of the machine's expropriation? Giving an account becomes impossible since, once again, the condition of possibility *is* the condition of impossibility. This is, it seems to me, the place of a thinking that ought to be devoted to the virtualization of the event by the machine, to a virtuality that, in exceeding the philosophical determination of the possibility of the possible (*dynamis*, power, *Möglichkeit*), exceeds by the same token the classical opposition of the possible and the impossible.

One of our greatest difficulties, then, would be to reconcile with the machine a thinking of the event, that is, a thinking of what remains real, undeniable, inscribed, singular, of an always essentially *traumatic* type, even when it is a happy event: an event is always traumatic, its singularity interrupts an order and rips apart, like every decision worthy of the name, the normal fabric of temporality or history. How, then, is one to reconcile, *on the one hand*, a thinking of the event, which I propose withdrawing, despite the apparent paradox, from an ontology or a metaphysics of presence (it would be a matter of thinking an event that is undeniable but without pure presence), and, *on the other hand*, a certain concept of machineness [*machinalité*]? The latter would imply at least the following predicates: a certain materiality, which is not necessarily a corporeality, a certain technicity, programming, repetition or iterability, a cutting off from or independence from any living subject—the psychological, sociological, transcendental, or even human subject, and so forth. In two words, how is one to think together the event *and* the machine, the event *with* the machine, this here event *with* this here machine? In a word and repeating myself in a quasi-machinelike fashion, how is one to think together the machine *and* the event, a machinelike repetition *and* that which happens/arrives?

In the perspective opened by this repetitive series of questions, we began to read what de Man wrote one day, what he inscribed one day, apparently *à propos* of an "excuse me" of Rousseau's—which was perhaps only an "excuse me" of de Man's, just as we read an "excuse me" of Austin's at the moment he was getting ready to talk about the excuse in general and excused himself for not doing so, contenting himself apparently with excusing himself, "within such limits."

I say indeed an "excuse me" of Rousseau's. Instead of the excuse in general, or even some generality in general, de Man apparently intends this *here* "excuse me" of this *here* Rousseau, even if, we are getting to this, with the example or the index of this *here* "excuse me," he appeals to what he himself says he "calls text" ("What we call text," he will have written, a phrase that is followed by a definition of the text in general that places the word "definition" in quotation marks). There is, to be sure, a general thematics or problematics in play in these very rich texts. But at the point of the reference, what is at stake, in my opinion, is the singularity of a certain "excuse me" by Rousseau that is, moreover, double, according to the at once ordinary and ambiguous French grammar of this verb (*s'excuser*), which appears at least twice in Rousseau, in strategic places, in the same paragraph of the *Confessions* concerning the theft of the ribbon.

The two occurrences are the object of a very active interpretation by de

Man. One of the reasons the use of *s'excuser* is sometimes deemed improper in French culture is that it can mean either to "offer apologies" or else to clear oneself in advance, to wash one's hands of the confessed fault, which, in truth, since it was not a fault, does not even have to be confessed, still less excused or forgiven, all of this thereby becoming, as event itself, simulacrum or feint, fiction or scene of quasi-excuse. And the machineness of this *s'excuser* draws in like a magnet the whole field of the de Manian analysis.

These two occurrences fall within the space of three sentences, in the paragraph that concludes the second book of the *Confessions* and the episode of the ribbon. In a fashion somewhat analogous to the scene, at once naive and perverse, in which Austin seems, in "A Plea for Excuses," to excuse himself in advance for not being able to treat the announced subject, namely, the "excuse," Rousseau begins, in a passage that does not appear to interest de Man, by excusing himself for having not even succeeded in excusing himself. He excuses himself for having been unable to clear himself of his crime. As if, at bottom, one had always to excuse oneself for failing to excuse oneself. But once one excuses oneself for failing, one may deem oneself to be, as one says in French, *d'avance tout excusé* or, on the contrary, condemned forever, irremediably, irreparably. It is the madness of this machine that interests us.

1. Here is the first occurrence of the *s'excuser* in the last paragraph of the second book of the *Confessions*:

I have been absolutely frank in the account I have just given, and no one will accuse me, I am certain, of palliating the heinousness of my offense [thus, I have surely not convinced you that I was in no way at fault or that my fault was minor, and this is my fault: I have failed, and I am at fault; but—for there is a "but" and it is the "but" that is going to interest us—but, as Rousseau is going to explain to us right away, I believe I must explain to you, while justifying myself, why I believed I must do it, that is, excuse myself, excuse myself for excusing myself for excusing myself]. But I should not fulfill the aim of this book if I did not at the same time reveal my inner feelings and hesitated to put up such excuses for myself as I honestly could. [*Mais je ne remplirois pas le but de ce livre si je n'exposois en même tems mes dispositions intérieures, et que je craignisse de m'excuser en ce qui est conforme à la vérité*]. (88; 86)

De Man quotes this last sentence, as we have just done, in the original French *and* in translation. But he then undertakes a surprising operation, which has been pointed out by his French translator and for which I can find neither justification nor necessity. He adds within brackets a word to the text, an expletive *ne*. An expletive *ne* in French is a pleonastic *ne*. One may either inscribe it or not in a sentence as one wishes. For example (and this example, which is given in all the dictionaries, is all the more interesting in that it uses a verb found in Rousseau's sentence as changed or augmented by the useless expletive prosthesis that de Man nevertheless utilizes), I can say "il craint que je sois trop jeune" or, just as well and with the same meaning, "il craint que je *ne* sois trop jeune." These two sentences are strictly equivalent in French. Now, what does de Man do? Where Rousseau writes: "Mais je ne remplirois pas le but de ce livre si je n'exposois en même tems mes dispositions intérieures, et que je craignisse de m'excuser en ce qui est conforme à la vérité" (which is perfectly clear for a French ear and means "if I feared to excuse myself," and so forth), de Man adds a *ne* between brackets in his quotation of the French— which is not at all serious and can always be done, pleonastically, without changing the meaning, all the more so because the brackets signal clearly de Man's intervention. But what he also does, and what seems disturbing to me because more serious, because it even risks inducing or translating a misinterpretation in the mind of Anglophone readers or in de Man's own mind, is that he then translates, so to speak, this expletive *ne* into English but without brackets, and he translates it as a "not" that is no longer at all expletive. As a result one reads, in de Man's own translation: "But I would not fulfill the purpose of this book if I did not reveal my inner sentiments as well, and if I did *not* fear" (here, de Man neither underscores nor brackets the second "not" that he adds even before he quotes the French in parentheses; he assumes only the fact of having himself italicized the French *excuser* and "excuse" in English) "to excuse myself by means of what conforms to the truth."

I do not know how to interpret this confusion. It risks making the text say exactly the opposite of what its grammar, its grammatical machine, says, namely, that Rousseau does not fear, he does not want to fear, he does not want to have to fear to excuse himself. He would not fulfill the aim of his book if he did not reveal his inner feelings and if he feared to excuse himself with what conforms to the truth. So the correct translation would be exactly the opposite of the one proposed by de Man: "But I would not fulfill the purpose of this book if I did not reveal my inner sentiments as well and if I did fear [or "if I feared" and not as de Man writes, "if I did *not* fear"] to excuse myself by means of what conforms to the truth." Naturally, de Man might claim, and this is perhaps what he has in mind when he proceeds to comment at length on this motive of fear, that Rousseau says he does not fear or he must not fear *because* in fact he does fear, and all of this is disavowal by means of an expletive ruse.[24] If de Man had wanted merely to make audible the ruse of this disavowal, he would have said that, one can be sure, more clearly.[25]

Let's leave this aside. But, *à propos*, as it has been and will often be a question of what *happens* to texts, injuring them, mutilating them, adding prostheses to them (de Man himself mentions the word "prosthesis" at one point),[26] I point out this little thing, just as I pointed out, *à propos*, de Man's omission of the two little words *déjà vieux* in relation to a rather old ribbon, rather aged and marked and damaged by a scene of succession. As if, to take up again the example of the dictionary I quoted a moment ago, de Man feared that the ribbon *ne fusse (ou fusse) déjà vieux ou qu'il craignisse au contraire qu'il fût ou ne fût "trop jeune"* (as if de Man feared that the ribbon were too old or, on the contrary, as if he feared that it were "too young").

A propos of this first occurrence of the *m'excuser*, the imperative to which Rousseau here seems to submit everything so as to justify the gesture that consists in excusing himself, in not fearing to excuse himself, even if he does not succeed in doing so in a convincing way, this imperative is, not just the truth itself, not just the truth in itself, but his *promise* before the truth, more precisely, his sworn promise to write in a truthful and sincere fashion. What counts here is less the truth in itself than the oath, namely, the written promise to write this book in such and such a way, to sign it in conformity with a promise, not to betray, not to perjure the promise made at the beginning of the *Confessions* or in any case at the beginning of the first book of the *Confessions*.

Of a first book that is not, as we will see right away, the absolute beginning of the work. I will recall only these few lines—which de Man, of course, supposes are familiar to everyone, but which he does not reinscribe in their necessity of principle that determines the general structure and the whole chain of the *Confessions*. But I refer you to this whole first page of Book I, a page that is at once canonical and extraordinary and whose first version was much longer.

This immense little page would call for centuries of reading by itself alone, as would the reactions that it has incited. What counts, it seems to me, is the scene of the oath not to betray, of the performative promise not to perjure or abjure. This appeal seems to me more important than the theoretical or constative dimension of a truth to be revealed or known. I underscore this point so as to mark once again that the criterion by which de Man distinguishes confession from excuse, as well as an epistemic moment from an apologetic moment, remains problematic in my view. At any rate, the moment said to be epistemic, the content of knowledge, truth, or revelation, *already* depends, from the first line of the book, on a performative promise: the promise to tell the truth, including the truth of the faults and indignities that are going to be mentioned right after, the indignities of someone who declares "I may not be better, but at least I am different [*si je ne vaux pas mieux, au moins je suis autre*]" and adds that he does not know "whether nature did well or ill in breaking the mold in which she formed me [*si la nature a bien ou mal fait de briser le moule dans lequel elle m'a jetté*]," that is, left his example without possible imitation or reproduction. He does not know, but as for the reader, he or she, sooner or later, will judge. I recall the beginning of the *Confessions*. The paragraphs are numbered.

1. I have resolved on an enterprise which has no precedent, and which, once complete, will have no imitator. My purpose is to display to my kind a portrait in every way true to nature, and the man I shall portray will be myself.

2. Simply myself. I know my own heart and understand my fellow man. But I am like no one in the whole world. I may be no better, but at least I am different. Whether Nature did well or ill in breaking the mould in which she formed me, is a question which can only be resolved after the reading of my book.

3. Let the last trump sound when it will [here is the call to appear before the last word], I shall come forward with this book in my hand, to present myself before the Sovereign Judge, and proclaim aloud: "Here is what I have done, what I have thought, what I have been." I have said the good and the bad with the same frankness. (17; 5)

Commitment to the future, toward the future, promise, sworn faith (at the risk of perjury, promising never to commit perjury), all these gestures present themselves as exemplary. The signatory wants to be, he declares himself to be at once singular, unique, *and* exemplary, in a manner analogous to what Augustine did in a more explicitly Christian gesture. Rousseau also addresses God, he invokes God, and like Augustine he uses the familiar *tu* form of address. He addresses his fellow men through the intermediary of God, he apostrophizes them as brothers: sons of God. The scene of this virtual "sooner or later" remains fundamentally Christian.

But taken for myself alone (*moi seul*: Rousseau insists on both his solitude and his isolation, forever, without example, without precedent or sequel, without imitator), the same oath also commits, beginning at the origin, all others yet to come. It is a "without example" that, as always, aims to be exemplary and therefore repeatable. It will not be long before Rousseau apostrophizes others: in a defiant tone, he calls them to imitation, to compassion, to community, to sharing what cannot be shared, as if he were appealing to them not only to judge whether nature did well in breaking the mold in which she formed him, but also to see to it that this mold be not forever broken. This appeal to others and to the future belongs to the same time, to the same moment as the "myself alone," the only portrait "that exists and that will *probably* ever exist." I underscore "probably."

"Myself alone," the "only portrait . . . that exists and that will *probably* ever exist": this is what the prebeginning will have said, at which we will arrive in a moment. "This is the only portrait of a man, drawn precisely from nature and in all its truth, that exists and that will probably ever exist." This "probably" says the aleatory, the nonprobable, nonprobable space or time, improbable, thus delivered over to uncertainty or to the wager, virtual space or time, the incalculability of the absolute *perhaps* in which the contradiction between the *without example* and the exemplary will be able to insinuate itself, slip in, and survive, not surmount itself but survive and endure as such, without solution but without disappearing right away. A little further down, in the same opening movement of Book I of the *Confessions*, the apostrophe or the invocation is addressed directly to God:

Eternal Being, let the numberless legion of my fellow men gather round me, and hear my confessions. Let them groan at my depravities, and blush for my misdeeds. [So everyone should be ashamed and confess with him, for him, like him, provided that one reads and understands him.] Let each of them in turn reveal his heart at the foot of Thy throne with equal sincerity [what counts, therefore, is not the objective truth, referred to the outside, but veracity referred to the inside, to the internal feeling, to the adequation between what I say and what I think, even if what I think is false] and then let any man say if he dares: "I was better than he" [*je fus meilleur que cet homme-là*, a formula one finds very frequently in Rousseau]. (Ibid.)

A propos of this act of sworn faith, in the final form of the work this beginning is only a *quasi*-opening. It is preceded by another little page, still shorter and without title, something like an *avant-propos*, a before-the-first-word that would also call for an infinite analysis. I will have to be content, within such limits, with signaling one or two little things. This before-the-first-word of the *Confessions* is found *only* in the Geneva manuscript, as it is called, and it is in a different handwriting from that of the *Confessions* (the handwriting is larger and looser, says the editor of the Pléiade edition, in a note that in effect concerns the material body of the archive or the ribbon of textual events). This before-the-first-word announces, repeats, or anticipates the first words of the *Confessions*, to be sure. One reads there, in fact, right away with the first words, the challenge whose hubris I have just recalled: "This is the only portrait of a man, drawn precisely from nature and in all its truth, that exists and that will probably ever exist." But in the logic of this challenge, the little phrase is followed by something else altogether that will not appear on the actual first page, although the two pages resemble each other in many other ways. The following sentence *convokes* and *conjures* every reader to come, sooner or later. It asks whoever might be in a situation to do so *not to destroy* this document, this archive, this subjectile, the support of this confession—literally a notebook, a *cahier*.

Here then, for once, one time only, is something that precedes and conditions the confession. Here is something that comes before the virtually infinite oath that assures the performative condition of truth. What precedes and conditions the performative condition of the *Confessions* is thus another performative oath or, rather, another performative appeal *conjuring, beseeching* others to swear an oath, but this time regarding a body, a *cahier*, this *here cahier* of this *here* body in a single copy, a single *exemplaire*: unique and authentic.

This copy or *exemplaire* can be reproduced, of course, but it is first of all reducible to a single original and authentic copy, without other example. This body of paper, this body of destructible, effaceable, vulnerable paper is exposed to accident, mutilation, cutting, censoring, falsification, or revenge. Rousseau is going to *conjure* (that is his word, for this appeal is another performative, another recourse to sworn faith, in the name "of my misfortunes," "by my misfortunes," Rousseau says). But he is going to conjure also "in the name of all humankind." He is going to conjure, that is, beseech men unknown to him, men of the present and of the future, not to "annihilate," sooner or later, his work. This *cahier*, which he confides to future generations, is at once "unique" and, in that it is an original archive, the "one certain *monument*." This document, this *cahier* is a "monument" (a sign destined to warn and to recall in the form of a thing exposed in the world, a thing that is *at the same time* natural and artifactual, a stone, amber, or another substance). Here is this appeal of the before-the-first word, before any preface and any foreword. It comes just after the first sentence, the one that is more or less equivalent to the first paragraph of the *Confessions*:

Whoever you are whom my destiny or my confidence has made the arbiter of the fate of *this* "*cahier*" [I underscore the deictic, "this here *cahier*," which functions only if the *cahier* in question has not been destroyed, *already* destroyed], I beseech you [*je vous conjure*] by *my* misfortunes, by *your* entrails, [it would be necessary to analyze this series of things in the name of which he swears and guarantees this act of swearing and conjuring: he adjures, he swears by calling upon others to swear with him, he conjures/beseeches them] and in the name of the whole human race [here, the guarantor in the name of which Rousseau swears, conjures, adjures, and calls on others not to abjure is almost infinite: after my misfortunes and your entrails, it is the "sooner or later" of the whole human race, past, present, and to come] not to annihilate a unique and useful work, which can serve as the first piece of comparison for the study of men, a study that is certainly yet to be begun [so, although it is unique and concerns me alone, it is exemplary for the study of men in general, a study to come for which this document will be the instituting arch-archive, something like the first man caught in absolute amber], and not to remove from the honor of my memory the *only* certain document of my character that has not been disfigured by my enemies [I underscore "only" because if this monumental document is vulnerable, it is because it is the only one and irreplaceable]. (3)[27]

This page was published only in 1850, based on a copy of the Moultou manuscript, as it is called, made by Du Peyrou in 1780. In its inspiration, it is comparable to many analogous and well-known things Rousseau wrote when he began to fear that *Emile* had fallen into the hands of the Jesuits, who would seek to mutilate it. What is very quickly termed his persecution complex was fixated, as you know and as many texts attest, on the fate of the manuscripts or the original copies, on the authentic arch-archive, in some fashion (*Rousseau juge de Jean Jaques, 1772, Histoire du précédent écrit, 1776*). Concerning this whole problematic, I refer you to the splendid and well-known chapters that Peggy Kamuf devotes to Rousseau, to this Rousseau, in her *Signature Pieces*.[28]

The end of this adjuration explicitly announces the time when, sooner or later, none of those who is called upon to swear, adjure, conjure in this way will still be alive: "Finally, if you yourself are one of these implacable enemies, cease being so with regard to my ashes and do not carry over your cruel injustice to the time when neither you nor I will any longer be alive."

What is the logic of the argument? And its strategy? It consists, to be sure, in calling on others to save this *cahier*. They should promise not to destroy it. But not only for the future; rather, in truth and first of all, so that they may now bear witness to themselves, in the present, to their generosity, more precisely, so that they may bear witness that they have been able to forswear vengeance—thus that they have been able to substitute a movement of justice, understanding, compassion, reconciliation, or even forgiveness for a passion of retaliation and revenge. Even though, Rousseau suggests, everything is still to be decided for the future, in the future when neither you nor I will still be there, you can nevertheless right away *today* have the advantage, realize a benefit, a profit *at present*, from the anticipation *now* of this future perfect; you could right now look yourself in the eye, love yourself, and honor yourself, beginning at this very instant, for what you will have done tomorrow for the future—that is, for me, for this here *cahier* that by itself tells the first truth of man. That is the present chance offered to you already today, if you read me and understand me, if you watch over this manuscript, this *cahier*: you will thus be able to honor yourself, love yourself, bear witness to yourself that you will have been good—and just—"at least once."

This offered chance is also a wager, a logic and an economy of the wager: by wagering on the future, the future of this *cahier*, you will win at every throw, since you draw an immediate benefit, that of bearing witness in your own eyes to both your goodness and your justice, that of having thereby a good image of yourself right away, without waiting, and of enjoying it no matter what happens in the future. Logic and economy of a wager whose import cannot be exaggerated for all our calculations and our whole relation to time, to the future and to survival, to the work [*l'oeuvre*] and to the work of time. De Man does not analyze this logic of the wager in Rousseau. He did so, *mutatis mutandis*, à propos of Pascal, in "Pascal's Allegory of Persuasion" (I take advantage of this remark to recall the superb essay that Geoffrey Bennington has devoted to this read-ing, precisely around a certain machine: "Aberrations: De Man (and) the Machine").[29]

At least once, launches Rousseau's apostrophe, here is the chance I offer you. I beseech you to seize it. For once at least, you will not have been guilty, you will be able to forgive yourself. Better than that, for once at least, you will not even have virtually to excuse yourself or ask forgiveness for having done wrong, for having given in to "cruel injustice," for hav-ing been "wicked and vindictive." This end of the before-the-first-word is sculpted by the multiplicity of these temporal modes (almost all of them are there) and by all the possible blows of this "at least once," which plays on all these virtualities of time, of the "sooner or later" of yesterday and tomorrow: "*to the time* when neither you nor I will any longer be alive; so that you *may* at least once bear the noble witness to yourself of *having been* generous and good when you *could have been* wicked and vindic-tive—if it *is* the case that the evil one *bears* a man [myself] who *has never done any can be called* vengeance."

A propos of this *avant-propos*—we should devote to it an abyssal devel-opment and carefully archive this strange phenomenon of archivation. We should also recognize and then establish its contours with the minute gestures of an archaeologist who does not want his instrument to damage the exhumed monument. For the treatment undergone by the document of this before-the-first-word, this little page of the Geneva manuscript, will have been exceptional. *On the one hand*—again the cut and the in-sectuous caesura—the sheet was *cut* (this is the word used by the editors of the *Confessions* in the Pléiade edition: "The sheet has been imperfectly cut about halfway up," they say).[30] *On the other hand*, right on the cut sheet, one can see "traces" (once again, this is the editors' term) of a dozen additional lines that have been effaced, but that remain as vestiges of the effacement. They remain, but as illegible traces ("The page must have had another dozen lines whose traces can be seen, but the sheet has been im-perfectly cut about halfway up"). This confirms the vulnerability of the effaceable document. The archive is as precarious as it is artificial, pre-cisely in the very place where the signatory puts on guard, appeals, be-seeches, warns against the risk of whatever might come along, as he says, "to annihilate this work." Even if he is the one who erased the dozen ad-ditional lines and cut the sheet, this demonstrates a priori that he was right to worry: the archived document is transformable, alterable, even destructible, or, in a word, falsifiable. The authentic integrity is, in its very body, in its proper and unique body, threatened in advance. Sooner or later, virtually, the worst can happen to it. Although it is presented as the only "certain monument," the little document could have not been there. After these contingent ups and downs, these *après-coups*, these recompositions, here it is now at the head of the *Confessions*, before the exordium and the self-presentation in the form of the exemplary promise addressed at once to you, "Eternal Being," and to all of you, "the crowd of my fellow men." The "I beseech you" not to "annihilate" this *cahier* is not only a before-the-first-word; it is the performative eve of the first performative, an arche-performative before the performative. Younger or older than all the others, it concerns the support and the archive of the confession, its subjectile, the very body of the event, the archival and auto-deictic body that will have to consign all the textual events engendered *as* and *by* the *Confessions*, the *Reveries*, *Rousseau juge de Jean Jaques*, or other writings in the same vein. Arch-performative, the arch-event of this sequence adjures one to save the body of the inscriptions, the *cahier* without which the revelation of the truth itself, however unconditional, truthful, sincere it may be in its promised manifestation, would have no chance of coming about and would be in its turn compromised.

Perhaps we have here, à propos (but this would deserve long and careful analyses), a historical difference between Augustine's *Confessions* and those of Rousseau, whatever Christian filiation they no doubt share, but in a quite different way. Why is it so difficult to imagine this archival protocol at the beginning of Augustine's *Confessions*? This question would require that we articulate many problematics of different styles among themselves. One of these, which I take more and more to heart, would concern the paradoxical antinomy of performativity and event. It is often said, quite rightly, that a performative utterance produces the event of which it speaks. But one should also know that wherever there is some performative, that is, in the strict and Austinian sense of the term, the mastery in the first person present of an "I can," "I may" guaranteed and legitimated by conventions, well, then, all pure eventness is neutralized, muffled, suspended. What happens, by definition, what comes about in an unforseeable and singular manner, couldn't care less about the performative. And here, for example, no performative warning, no "I beseech you," no "I appeal to you," and so forth suffices to prevent what can happen, like an unanticipatable accident, to the body of the original manuscript. The vulnerability, the finitude of a body and of a corpus is precisely the limit of all performative power, thus of all assurance. And of all bibliophilic preservation in all our libraries.

2. We were in the process of reciting the two occurrences of Rousseau's *s'excuser* in the last paragraph of the second book of the *Confessions*. The second occurrence of the "I excused myself" comes several lines after the first. After having said "I would not fulfill the purpose of this book if I did not reveal my inner sentiments as well, and if I feared *to excuse myself* by means of what conforms to the truth," he continues:

Never was deliberate wickedness further from my intention than at that cruel moment. When I accused that poor girl, it is strange but true that my friendship for her was the cause. She was present in my thoughts, and I *excused myself* on the first object that presented itself [je m'excusai *sur le premier objet qui s'offrit*]. *I accused her* of having done what I intended to do myself. I said that she had given the ribbon to me because I meant to give it to her. (88; 86)

Despite the proximity in the text, despite the semantic or grammatical analogy, this "I excused myself" does not refer to the same object or the same time as the first occurrence ("if I feared to excuse myself"). The first occurrence refers to an ulterior event, the last in time since it is a matter of excusing oneself *by writing* or *while writing* the *Confessions*. The second occurrence refers to an earlier time: what Rousseau did, that day, by accusing Marion. In other words, Rousseau does not want to fear to excuse himself in the *Confessions* by telling how and why he already excused himself, so many years earlier, at the time of the theft of the ribbon. Without forcing things too much, one could perhaps say that the first "excuse oneself" (the first event in the order of the text and according to the time of the *Confessions*) is a first "excuse oneself" on the subject of the second "excuse oneself," even though this second "excuse oneself" refers, in the order of real events, as we say, to an anterior or first moment. Unlike the first, the second "excuse oneself" recalls a past anterior to the writing of the *Confessions*. Rousseau first of all excused himself by means of the first object that offered itself and he must now, and in the future, without fear, excuse himself on the subject of this past excuse. He must not fear to excuse himself on the subject of a fault that consisted in excusing himself by lying. And he has moreover just recognized that he risks being less convincing with excuse number two (in the *Confessions*) than excuse number one (at the moment of the crime).

Having arrived at this point, I submit to you in conclusion a few hypotheses or interpretations whose performative imprudence I assume, à propos of the extraordinary event constituted by de Man's reading of Rousseau, a reading to which I above all wanted to pay tribute by recognizing everything I owe to it. It is as a testimony of gratitude that I believe I should offer here a few supplementary footnotes.

De Man does not treat this couple of excuses, this excuse on the subject of an excuse, as I am doing here. I will nevertheless venture to assert, while attempting then to demonstrate, that his whole interpretation fits between these two times, which are also two events and two regimes of the "excuse oneself." Not, as seems to be the most manifest appearance, and as he says and wants to say himself, between the excuses of the *Confessions* and those of the *Reveries*, but between the two times of the excuse already in the *Confessions* itself. Approaching the second phase of his reading, the one that interests him the most, he declares, moreover:

> We have, of course, omitted from the reading the other sentence in which the verb "excuser" is explicitly being used, again in a somewhat unusual construction; the oddity of "que je craignisse de m'excuser" is repeated in the even more unusual locution: "Je m'excusai sur le premier objet qui s'offrit" ("I excused myself upon the first thing that offered itself," as one would say "je me vengeai" or "je m'acharnai sur le premier objet qui s'offrit" . . .).[31] Because Rousseau desires Marion, she haunts his mind and her name is pronounced almost unconsciously, as if it were a slip, a segment of the discourse of the other . . . the sentence is phrased in such a way as to allow for a complete disjunction between Rousseau's desires and interests and the selection of this particular name. . . . She [Marion] is a free signifier, metonymically related to the part she is made to play in the subsequent system of exchanges and substitutions. She is, however, in an entirely different situation than the other free signifier, the ribbon, which also just happened to be ready-at-hand, but which is not in any way itself the object of a desire [I mentioned my reservations on this subject earlier, but de Man goes a little further]. . . . But if her nominal presence is a mere coincidence, then we are entering an entirely different system in which such terms as desire, shame, guilt, exposure, and repression no longer have any place.
>
> In the spirit of the text, one should resist any temptation to give any significance whatever to the sound "Marion." For it is only if the act that initiated the entire chain, the utterance of the sound "Marion," is truly without any conceivable motive that the total arbitrariness of the action becomes the most effective, the most efficaciously performative excuse of all. (288–89)

Here is a disarticulatable articulation of allusions to contingency, to the "almost unconsciously," not only to the discourse of the other, but to the "segment of the discourse of the other," to the discourse of the other as sectioned, fragmented discourse, therefore mutilated, half-effaced, redistributed, deconstructed, and disseminated as if by a machine. This disarticulated articulation of allusions is relayed, in the whole text, by a number of analogous motifs: the machine, the arbitrary, mutilation, prosthesis, and so forth.

I do not find Rousseau's constructions as "strange" as de Man twice says they are; I have explained why on the subject of the expletive added by de Man in French and transmuted in advance into a pure and simple negation in English. As for "sur le premier object qui s'offrit," the thing is very clear in French even if de Man is right to say that this *may* in fact make one think of "je me vengeai" or "je m'acharnai sur le premier objet"—yes, or as well, I would say, one might think of "à propos, je me précipitais sur le premier objet qui s'offrit," "à propos, I leaped on the first object that presented itself," "je me jetai sur le premier objet qui s'offrit à propos," "I threw myself on the first object that presented itself à propos."

Since we cannot reread together, step by step, de Man's whole text, here are a few hypotheses or interpretations.

In the first place, de Man also analyzes Rousseau's text as "the first object that offered itself." As many of his formulations clearly show, he constantly supposes that the text (here à propos of *s'excuser*) is exemplary, that is, at once singular (therefore an irreplaceable event) and yet, according to the very machine described here, valid for every text—and thus, as de Man said in the preceding chapter on the *Social Contract*, for everything that "we call text." The performative formulation of this "we call text" is assumed as such—and I want to reread it. The phrase appears just after the passage in which it is a question of the "theft," of stealing "from the text the very meaning to which, according to this text, we are not entitled": "We call *text* any entity that can be considered from such a double perspective: as a generative, open-ended, non-referential grammatical system and as a figural system closed off by a transcendental signification that subverts the grammatical code to which the text owes its existence. The 'definition' of the text also states the impossibility of its existence and prefigures the allegorical narratives of this impossibility" (270).

I commented on and interpreted these words "We call *text*" ("text" in italics) and these quotation marks around "definition" in *Mémoires for*

Paul de Man.[32] If what is said here about what we "call" text (followed by a "definition" in quotation marks) is valid for every text, exemplarily and metonymically (*metonymically* is my addition; in any case it is not metaphorically, for de Man is explaining here the displacement of the metaphor, including the metaphor of the text, especially of the text as body, into something else), then it is valid as well for de Man's text, which includes itself, by itself, in what he "calls" and "defines" in this fashion. I do not think de Man would have rejected this consequence: his writings can and should be read as also politico-autobiographical texts. They also figure a long, machinelike performative, at once confessional and apologetic, with all the traits that he himself, in an exemplary way, trains on this object that offers itself and that is called, for example, and "à propos," Rousseau. It is true that even if there were, for de Man as for Rousseau, other objects on other stages, one may wonder why Rousseau gave such emphasis and privilege to this theft and this perjury, when he was sixteen years old, in the genesis of the *Confessions*; and why de Man hounds him, *s'acharne sur lui*, so lovingly, as if he were *after him* in this trace.

Without any doubt, many passages would demonstrate, in their very letter, that Rousseau's text, however singular it may be, serves here as exemplary index. Of what? Of the text *in general*, or more rigorously (and this makes a difference that counts here) of "what we call *text*," as de Man says, playing with the italics and with the "definition" that he gives by putting the word "definition" in quotation marks. These are literal artifices that mark at the same time (1) that de Man assumes the performative and decisional character of the responsibility he takes in this appellation and this "definition" and (2) that one must be attentive to every detail of the letter, the literality of the letter defining here the place of what de Man will call materiality. The literality of the letter situates this materiality not so much because it would be a physical or sensible (aesthetic) substance, or even matter, but because it is the place of prosaic resistance (cf. "Phenomenality and Materiality in Kant" in *Aesthetic Ideology*, where de Man concludes with the words "prosaic materiality of the letter") to any organic and aesthetic totalization, to any aesthetic form. And first of all, I would say for my part, a resistance to every possible reappropriation. Perhaps in a fashion that is analogous (notice I do not say identical) to the "referential function" whose "trap" would be "inevitable," according to the phrase of de Man's that Andrzej

Warminski inscribes in epigraph to his luminous introduction to *Aesthetic Ideology*. The materiality in question—and one must gauge the importance of this irony or paradox—is not a thing, it is not *something* sensible or intelligible; it is not even the matter of a body. As it is not something, as it is nothing and yet it works, *cela oeuvre*, this nothing therefore operates, it forces, but as a force of resistance. It resists both beautiful form and matter as substantial and organic totality. This is one of the reasons that de Man never says, it seems to me, *matter*, but *materiality*. Assuming the risk of this formula, although de Man does not do so himself, I would say that it is a materiality without matter. This materiality without matter allies itself very well, moreover, with a formality without form (in the sense of the beautiful synthetic and totalizing form) and without formalism. In his thinking of materiality, de Man, it seems to me, is no more materialist than he is formalist. To be sure, on occasion he uses these two words to accentuate and accompany a Kantian movement, an original reading of Kant. At the end of "Kant's Materialism," he speaks of an "absolute, radical formalism," and while taking all possible precautions regarding this performative nomination and appellation, regarding this act of calling, he adds: "To parody Kant's stylistic procedure of dictionary definition: the radical formalism that animates aesthetic judgment in the dynamics of the sublime is *what is called* materialism."[33]

I have added emphases to suggest that this "what is called" gives a good measure of the audacity in this materialist interpretation of the sublime. De Man does not himself assume, it seems to me, a philosophical or metaphysical position that one might complacently call materialism. At work here is a force of resistance without material substance. This force derives from the dissociative, dismembering, fracturing, disarticulating, and even disseminal power that de Man attributes to the letter.[34] To a letter whose dissociative and inorganic, disorganizing, disarticulating force affects not only nature but the body itself—as organic and organized totality. From this point of view, even though the word "matter" is not pronounced, or even the word "materiality," concerning which I just said that it designates a materiality without matter or material substance, this thinking of the materiality of the letter already silently marks the chapter of *Allegories of Reading* that we are in the process of reading and that attributes a determinant role to dismemberment, mutilation, disfigurations, and so forth, as well as to the contingency of literal signifiers. The textual event is inseparable from this formal materiality of the letter. I say "formal materiality" or "literality" because what one might call in quotation marks or italics "materialism"—it would be better to say the re-noun, the re-naming, the re-nomination of materiality—requires a consistent reckoning with formality. You heard it at the end of the text on "Kant's Materialism."

Valid for what de Man calls text, this becomes just as pertinent for *his* text, this very text of his—which thus becomes a case of what he is talking about and does not fail to present itself in that fashion, more or less ironically. Just one example. It says something about the values of machine, mechanicity, and formality toward which I will then turn, after having left under construction an endless task, the project not only of showing the politico-performative autobiographicity of this text of de Man's, but of reapplying to it in a quasi-machinelike way what he himself writes on one of the first objects that offered itself, namely, the text of Rousseau—and of a few others. If the confession of the *Confessions*, even after one distinguishes it as a moment of truth from the apologetic text of the *Reveries*, cannot be a text of pure knowledge, if it includes an irresistible and irreducible performativity in its cognitive structure, well then, likewise, the performativity of the de Manian text prohibits one from reducing it to an operation of pure knowledge. Here, then, is an exemplary passage: à propos of Rousseau's text, its object is the text and language *in general*, in its law, in a law that is itself without individual reference or application, as grammar of political law—the notion of *grammar* is to be understood with reference to the *trivium* and the *quadrivium* (as Warminski shows very clearly in his indispensable study), but also as a machine of the letter (*gramma*), a letter machine, a *writing machine* [*machine à écrire*, typewriter]. Exemplarity in general is this difficult marriage between the event and the typewriter. He writes: "The machine is *like* [I would be tempted to insist heavily, perhaps beyond what de Man would himself have wanted, on this word "like," which marks an analogy, the "like" of a resemblance or of an "as if," rather than an "as"] the grammar of the text when it is isolated from its rhetoric, the merely formal element without which no text can be generated" (294).

It is not said that the machine *is* a grammar of the text. Nor that the grammar of the text *is* a machine. One is *like* the other once grammar is isolated from rhetoric (performative rhetoric or cognitive rhetoric, the rhetoric of tropes, according to another distinction). The machine is determined on the basis of grammar and vice versa. Isolated from its rhetoric, as suspension of reference, grammar is purely formal. This is valid in general: no text can be produced without this formal, grammatical, or machinelike element. No text and no language. De Man right away adds, speaking of *language* after having spoken of *text*, and here they amount to the same thing: "There can be no use of language which is not, within a certain perspective, thus radically formal, i.e. mechanical, no matter how deeply this aspect may be concealed by aesthetic, formalistic delusions. The machine not only generates, but also suppresses, and not always in an innocent or balanced way" (ibid.).

We see here, already (but dare I say *already* without teleological illusion?), the insistence on the formal, on formality, in truth on grammatical or machinelike formality, in opposition to aesthetic illusions but also formalist illusions in the philosophy of art or the theory of literature. De Man deploys this gesture and this strategy in a systematic way in *Aesthetic Ideology*.

My only ambition would thus be, on the basis of this text from *Allegories of Reading*, to sketch out a kind of deduction, in the quasi-philosophical sense, of the concept of materiality (without matter). It is not present here in that name but I believe one can recognize all its traits. In the texts gathered under the title *Aesthetic Ideology*, the concept will be thematized in that name.

Despite the association of materiality and the machine, why are we not dealing here with a mechanistic materialism? No more than with a dialectical materialism? It is because the de Manian concept of materiality is not, dare I say to his credit, a *philosophical* concept, the *metaphysical concept of matter*; it is, it seems to me, the name, the artifactual nomination of an artifactual figure that I will not dissociate from the performative signature I spoke of a moment ago. It is a sort of invention by de Man, one could say, almost a fiction produced in the movement of a strategy that is at once theoretical and autobiographical and that would need to be analyzed at length.

To say it is a fiction (in the de Manian sense) does not mean that it is without theoretical value or philosophical effect, or that it is totally arbitrary. But the choice of the word "materiality" to designate "that" seems in part arbitrary, in part necessary in relation to an entire historical space (the history of philosophy and, for example, of the diverse possibilities of philosophies of matter, the history of literary theory, political history, ideological camps, and so forth), in short, in relation to a contextualized world, to a worldwide context in which de Man is calculating his strategy. And placing his bets.

To attempt the deduction I've just described on the basis of this text, I will take into account, much too quickly, the different predicates (which are so many *predicaments*, de Man, who liked this word a lot, might say), the different predicating traits that constitute inseparably and irreducibly this concept of materiality. Without having yet been named, this *concept of materiality*, in *Allegories of Reading* and no doubt in *The Rhetoric of Romanticism*, plays a role that I will not call organizing, for obvious reasons, but rather trenchant, decisive. I insist once again and heavily: it is a question of the *concept of materiality* and not of *matter*. This is not easily said and I leave intact the problem of the choice of this word "materiality," which brings with it a high essentializing, ontologizing risk there where it should exclude, in its interpretation, any semantic implication of matter, of substratum or instance called "matter," and any reference to some content named "matter," in order to signify only "effect of matter" without matter. This concept of materiality thus determines the concept of textual event that, as you recall, is named as such at least twice, and twice associated with what de Man, for his part, *calls* in his fashion, but literally and often in this text, "deconstruction" and "dissemination."

I will cut out several motifs that are ultimately indissociable in what is at bottom one and the same perspective, one and the same performative strategy.

1. *First motif.* First of all, the inscription of the textual event—and this will later be one of the traits of the materiality of matter—involves a machinelike deconstruction of the body proper. This is why I said, using a formulation that is not de Man's, that *materiality* becomes a very useful generic name for all that resists appropriation. De Man declares, moreover, from another point of view, in "Promises (*Social Contract*)": "There is nothing legitimate about property, but the rhetoric of property confers the illusion of legitimacy" (262). He also analyzes the "fascination of . . . *proper* names" in Proust (ibid.). Materiality is not the body, at least the body proper as organic totality. This machinelike deconstruction is also a deconstruction of metaphor, of the totalizing metaphorical model, by a dissociative metonymic structure (a gesture that, I suggested, has some affinity with a certain Lacanianism allied with a certain Deleuzianism). The preceding essay on the *Social Contract* analyzed with insistence the

necessity of a "deconstruction of the metaphorical model" (259), the "deconstruction of metaphorical totalities" (260), the "deconstruction of metaphorical patterns based on binary models" (255) wherever "the attribute of naturalness shifts from the metaphorical totality to the metonymic aggregate" (259).

This movement becomes more precise in the essay on the *Confessions*. In the context of an analysis of the *Fourth Reverie*, de Man writes, for example: "But precisely because, in all these instances, the metaphor for the text is still the metaphor of text as body (from which a more or less vital part, including the head, is being severed), the *threat* remains sheltered behind its metaphoricity" (297). I underscore "threat" because a little further on, the allusion to a threat returns: "Only when Rousseau no longer confronts Tasso's or Montesquieu's but his own text, the *Confessions*, does the metaphor of text as body make way for the more directly *threatening* alternative of the text as machine" (ibid.). I underscore "threatening" once again. The word will come back later ("The deconstruction of the figural dimension . . . threatens the autobiographical subject"; 298). Why such a threat? What is a threat? This question reactivates the one we were asking on the subject of cruelty. From the preceding text to this one, one passes from the promise to the excuse, to be sure, as from one performative to another, but also from the promise to the threat, to fear in the face of a cruel menace. As I have tried to show elsewhere,[35] this threat is also and already constitutive of any promise, and is not at all, as good sense and the theorists of speech acts would have it, irreducibly opposed to the promise. For them, who rely on good sense to ground all their supposed knowledge, the promise may in fact seem to be able to promise only something good: one does not promise something threatening, but a benefit, a fidelity, a gift; one does not promise to kill or wound, for that would be a threat. I elsewhere dispute the simplicity of this opposition, but I'll not do so again here.

Paul de Man again raises the stakes of the threat. To the same *menacing* machination of the body proper and its metaphor, he adds the "loss of the illusion of meaning":

But in what way are these narratives threatening? As instances of Rousseau's generosity they are . . . more inept than convincing. They seem to exist primarily for the sake of the mutilations they describe. But these actual, bodily mutilations seem, in their turn, to be there more for the sake of allowing the evocation of the machine that causes them than for their own shock value; Rousseau lingers complacently over the description of the machine that seduces him into dangerously close contact: "I looked at the metal rolls, my eyes were attracted by their polish. I was tempted to touch them with my fingers and I moved them with pleasure over the polished surface of the cylinder" (1036). In the general economy of the *Reverie*, the machine displaces all other significations and becomes the raison d'être of the text. Its power of suggestion reaches far beyond its illustrative purpose, especially if one bears in mind the previous characterization of unmotivated fictional language as "machinal." The underlying structural patterns of addition and suppression as well as the figural system of the text all converge towards it. Barely concealed by its peripheral function, the text here stages the textual machine of its own constitution *and* performance, its own textual allegory. The threatening element in these incidents then becomes more apparent. The text as body, with all its implications of substitutive tropes ultimately always retraceable to metaphor, is displaced by the text as machine and, in the process, it suffers the loss of the illusion of meaning. (298)

This loss of the illusion of meaning threatens also sometimes, as passage from metaphor to metonymy and as fiction, to produce the loss of the illusion of reference: "In fiction thus conceived the 'necessary link' of the metaphor has been metonymized beyond the point of catachresis, and the fiction becomes the disruption of the narrative's referential illusion" (292).

2. *Second motif.* The word "machine" is here singled out, apparently, in the text of Rousseau: "It is certain that neither my judgment, nor my will dictated my reply, but that it was the automatic result [*l'effet machinal*] of my embarrassment" (quoted by de Man, 294). But the word and the concept of machine are found again, reelaborated, and redistributed everywhere: in Kleist, Pascal, and already in the *Social Contract* when Rousseau speaks of what there is "in the wheels of the State [*dans les ressorts de l'Etat*]," namely an "equivalent of the principle of inertia in machines" (272). This word-concept "machine" is thus inseparable from motifs of suspended reference, repetition, the threat of mutilation, and so forth— and from interpretation as the de Manian practice of deconstruction-dissemination.

3. *Third motif.* This deconstruction implies a process of de-metaphorization and also, by the same token, of machinelike dis-figuration. Another example allows one to deduce this third motif of the concept of materiality, namely, a mechanical, machinelike, automatic independence

in relation to any subject, any subject of desire and its unconscious, and therefore, de Man doubtless thinks, any psychology or psychoanalysis as such.

This point remains to be discussed. Where is one then to situate the affect of desire and especially of threat and cruelty? Is there not a force of nondesire in desire, a law of desubjectivation in and as the subject itself? These are so many questions that I would have liked to deploy before this magnificent text, which I find sometimes too Lacanian, sometimes insufficiently Lacanian, in any case insufficiently "psychoanalytic." I believe one can hear this ambivalent resistance to psychoanalysis, notably Lacanian psychoanalysis, at the very point where de Man comes closest to it in passages like this one:

The deconstruction of the figural dimension is a process that takes place independently of any desire; as such it is not unconscious but mechanical, systematic in its performance but *arbitrary* in its principle, *like a grammar*. This threatens the autobiographical subject not as the loss of something that once was present and that it once possessed, but as a radical estrangement between the meaning and the performance of any text." (298; my emphasis)

Once again, "like" in the phrase "like a grammar" has a status that is as difficult to pin down as Lacan's "like a language": "The unconscious is structured *like* a language." As difficult and no doubt very close, even in its implicit protest against psychology—or against psychoanalysis as psychology, be it that of desire.

This deconstruction *should be*, according to him, independent of any desire, which, although I can only say it quickly, seems to me both defensible and indefensible, depending on the concept of desire one puts to work. For this reason, de Man goes beyond his first attempts at interpretation of the purloined ribbon: the logic of Rousseau's desire for Marion, substitution between Rousseau and Marion, symbolic circulation of the ribbon that, as "pure signifier," is substituted for a desire that is itself "desire for substitution," both desires being "governed by the same desire for specular symmetry" and so forth.

Because this logic of desire seems to him to be, if not without pertinence, at least unable to account for the textual event, de Man wants to go further. On two occasions, within an interval of two pages, he declares: "This is not the only way, however, in which the text functions" (284) or "But the text offers further possibilities" (286). He then goes from the

Confessions to the *Reveries*, from the excuse for what happened to the excuse for the writing of the excuse, for the pleasure taken in writing what happened and thus for the pleasure taken in excusing himself. And, in fact, Rousseau clearly suspects what he calls his "pleasure in writing" at the end of the *Fourth Reverie*.

4. *Fourth motif.* Beyond this logic and this necessity of desire, materiality would imply the effect of *arbitrariness*. The systematic recourse to this machinelike value of the *arbitrary* (relayed by a series of equivalents, notably the *gratuitous*, the *contingent*, the *random*, or the *fortuitous*), whether one is talking about "the gratuitous product of a textual grammar" (299), the "random lie in the Marion episode" (291), the "absolute randomness of language," the "arbitrary power play of the signifier" (296), the "gratuitous improvisation, that of the implacable repetition of a preordained pattern. Like Kleist's marionettes" (294), the fortuitous proximity of the ribbon and Marion (293), the "excuse of randomness in the *Confessions*" (291), the "total arbitrariness" (291) of "the sound 'Marion'" (289)—a name that, despite its alleged contingency and even though de Man makes no remark to this effect, we can now no longer separate from either Marie/Mary or marionette. The Marion of the ribbon will have been the instant, the blink of an eye of a fictive generation, just the time of a literary Passion and Pietà, the intercessor in a marriage of reason between the Virgin Mary and all her marionettes. Or, if you prefer, Marion the intercessor remains also in the literary archives of Christian Europe like the sister-in-law of all the automatic virgins that still amble about between the Gospels and Kleist.

Even though de Man does not say it, at least not in this way, the eventness of the event requires, if one wants to think it, this insistence on the arbitrary, fortuitous, contingent, aleatory, unforeseeable. An event that one held to be necessary and thus programmed, foreseeable, and so forth, would that be an event? But then this arbitrariness undoes the power and the force of a performative, which, as I was suggesting earlier, tends always to neutralize the event it seems to produce. De Man associates this feeling of arbitrariness with the experience of threat, cruelty, suffering in dismemberment, decapitation, disfiguration, or castration (the abundance of whose figures he isolates in Rousseau). What conclusions should be drawn from this?

There is the conclusion that de Man himself draws, namely, that this suffering is in fact what happens and is lived, but "from the point of view of the subject": "This more than warrants the anxiety with which Rousseau acknowledges the lethal quality of writing. Writing always includes the moment of dispossession in favor of the arbitrary power of the play of the signifier and *from the point of view of the subject* [my emphasis], this can only be experienced as a dismemberment, a beheading, or a castration" (296).

De Man therefore wishes to describe what it is in deconstruction-dissemination, in what "is disseminated," he says, as "textual event" and as anacoluthon "throughout the entire text" (300), that operates independently of and beyond any desire. Deconstruction, he says, is a "process that takes place independently of any desire" (298). The materiality of this event as textual event is what is—or makes itself—independent of any subject or any desire.

It is a logic that has something irrefutable about it. If, on the one hand, the event supposes surprise, contingency, or the arbitrary, as I emphasized a moment ago, it also supposes, on the other hand, this exteriority or this irreducibility to desire. And therefore it supposes that which makes it radically inappropriable, nonreappropriable, radically resistant to the logic of the proper. What I have elsewhere called *exappropriation* concerns this work of the inappropriable in desire and in the process of appropriation. Unless nondesire haunts every desire and there is between desire and nondesire an abyssal attraction rather than a simple exteriority of opposition or exclusion.

Without being able to develop it here, I would draw another consequence that no doubt goes beyond what de Man himself says or would say. It is this: By reason of this unforeseeability, this irreducible and inappropriable exteriority for the subject of experience, every event as such is *traumatic*. Even an event experienced as a "happy" one. This does, I concede, confer on the word "trauma" a generality that is as fearsome as it is extenuating. But perhaps we have here a double consequence that must be drawn in the face of the speculative inflation to which the word is today subject. Understood in this sense, trauma is that which makes precarious any distinction between the point of view of the subject and what is produced independently of desire. It makes precarious even the use and the sense of all these words. An event is traumatic or it does not happen, does not arrive. It injures desire, whether or not desire desires or does not desire what happens. It is that which, within desire, constitutes it as possible and insists there while resisting it, as the impossible: some outside, irreducibly, as some nondesire, some death, and something inorganic, the becoming possible of the impossible *as* im-possible. Inappropriability of the other.

On this stage, no doubt, arise the questions of the unforgivable, the unpardonable, the inexcusable—and of perjury.

There you are, pardon me for having spoken too long. I cut things off here, arbitrarily.

But not without saluting once again the spirit, I mean the ghost of my friend. One day, de Man wrote this: "Whatever happens in Derrida, it happens between him and his own text. He doesn't need Rousseau, he doesn't need anybody else."[36] As you have seen quite well, this is of course not true. De Man was wrong. I needed Paul de Man. And Rousseau and Augustine and so many others. But perhaps in order to show in my turn, many years later, that maybe he, Paul de Man, had no need of Rousseau in order to show and to demonstrate, himself, what he thought he ought to confide in us. That is what I was suggesting by insisting on the exemplarity, and for example, the exemplarity of de Man's autobiographico-political texts *à propos* of Rousseau, materiality, and other similar things.

I am so sad that Paul de Man is not here himself to answer me and to object. But I can hear him already—and sooner or later his text will answer for him.

That is what we all call a machine.

But a spectral machine.

By telling me I am right, it will tell him he is right.

And sooner or later, our common innocence will not fail to appear to everyone's eyes, as the best intentioned of all our machinations.

Sooner or later and virtually already, always, here now.

§ 3

"Le Parjure," *Perhaps*: Storytelling and Lying

("abrupt breaches of syntax")

"You will write it, won't you? Much better than I could ever do! Because I can't! Impossible! Way beyond my means! But you!"[1]

The passage in Proust has to do with storytelling (in the double sense of lying and of narration), with memory as a precarious support of narrative continuity, and with anacoluthon's function in both storytelling and lying. Anacoluthon doubles the story line and so makes the story probably a lie. A chief evidence for the middle's perturbation is the small-scale details of language. This means that close reading is essential to reading narrative: "To tell the truth, I knew nothing that Albertine had done since I had come to know her, or even before." (to be continued)[2]

By "the ethics of reading," the reader will remember, I mean the aspect of the act of reading in which there is a response to the text that is both necessitated, in the sense that it is a response to an irresistible demand, and free, in the sense that I must take responsibility for my response and for further effects, "interpersonal," institutional, social, political, or historical, of my act of reading, for example as that act takes the form of teaching or of published commentary on a given text. What happens when I read *must* happen, but I must acknowledge it as *my* act of reading, though just what the "I" is or becomes in this transaction is another question.[3]

What Is Called Not Thinking?

"Just imagine, I was not thinking about it" [*Figurez-vous que je n'y pensais pas*].

Let us begin with a quotation. And a response. They come from a narrative. A narrative that remains forever a fiction. They will never cease returning to it, returning to it and belonging to it. Yes, response, for legibly this sentence is addressed to someone in the grammar of the imperative ("Just imagine . . . " "Figurez-vous . . . "), even as it *already* refers to something *already* defined: "I was not thinking about it."

Imagine the scene, now, yourself. Imagine this exchange. You hesitate between believing and not believing. You no longer know whether you must believe someone or believe *in* someone, which is not the same thing, or yet again believe what someone says when he responds without really responding: "Just imagine, I was not thinking about it."

What would you reply, you in turn, to the man (for it is a man) who said that to you, in response to an accusation of perjury, at the moment you reminded him of some proof, a fact, even a testimony? In the cited text, the friend reminds the perjurer accused of bigamy: "My dear Stéphane, I'm not the one, after all, who had a little lapse of memory the day you got married" (134). Another way of saying, I paraphrase: "But all the same you are a perjurer [*parjure*], you committed *perjury* [*parjure*], you lied, you dissimulated, you knew that you were lying and perjuring." [I have asked my translator friends to keep the word "parjure" in French because many things are going to depend on it, almost everything, in truth. The same word, *parjure*, in French means both the act of perjuring, the crime of perjury, in sum, and the author of the perjury, the guilty one, the perjurer.] How would you react, and with what interpretation, faced with someone who then responded to you: "That's true. Just imagine, I was not thinking about it. Thank you." For the character in the novel will have surrounded this strange proposition (imperative, demand, suggestion, remark: "Just imagine," "Figurez-vous") with an acquiescence that is not just any one ("That's true") and with a sign of gratitude that is literally unfathomable ("Thank you"). What truth is in question here? For what exactly does he say he is grateful? What does he recognize with gratitude [*reconnaissance*]?

I have extracted the quotation ("It's true. Just imagine, I was not thinking about it. Thank you.") from a novel by Henri Thomas, *Le Parjure*.[4] As the cover of the book rightly confirms, we are indeed talking of a "novel," thus of a *fiction* and a *literary* fiction. We shall not forget this and will return to it, but only after a long detour.

"I was not thinking about it" does not mean simply "I forgot." Beyond the *fact* of amnesia, or even of omission, which is not a simple loss of memory, beyond the failure that is noted in the official record [*constat*], it is already the confession of some breach of duty: I was not thinking about it although, as you have just reminded me, I *should* have thought of it. That was my duty; I was supposed not to be ignorant of this law. More precisely, this confession resembles an avowal that disculpates itself; thus, it also resembles a neutral description no less than a confession, a strange avowal of innocence, that of someone who, disavowing his avowal, in some way pleads guilty and not guilty at the same time for having believed, innocently, that he did not have to remember, that he did not have the duty to remember, for not having thought *what* was necessary, for not having thought *that* it was necessary, that it would have been necessary to think of it—and first of all, before this or that, of the imperative to think of it, to think of remembering to think of it, to think of thinking of it—and thus to think of being faithful to a commitment, of avoiding perjury: I did not think that I *had* to remember, I did not think that I had a duty of memory, that I had to not forget, not forget myself, not forget my identity as subject, my identity with myself. I was not thinking, I forgot; it's a fact that, like the self-identity of the subject, memory *is* or rather *must, should* be an ethical obligation: infinite and at every instant.

Can one commit perjury "without thinking about it"? In a moment of distraction? Not as an active transgression, but through forgetting or because it's not the moment to think about it? One wonders if there is here an excuse to be found, an attenuating circumstance. And whether it can be deemed forgivable to "not think about it"—to forget to think of everything, of all the presuppositions and implications of what one does or says. If there is no thinking without the risk of forgetting oneself, if forgetting to think, if forgetting to think *of it* is a fault, if such an interruption, such an intermittence is a failure, then what is called thinking? And forgetting? What is called not thinking? Not thinking to think *of it?* There is nothing more banal, in a certain way. After all, one cannot reasonably expect a finite subject to be able, at every instant, in the same instant, or even merely at the desired moment, to remember actively, presently, in an act, *continuously*, without interval, to *think of all* the ethical obligations for which, in all fairness, he should answer. That would be inhuman and indecent.

As a result, the *figurez-vous* oscillates between a strong sense and a weak one. Let us translate. On the one hand: you can easily imagine that my mind was elsewhere; I couldn't think of everything; I was occupied, a priori, with other pressing matters or other laws, other commitments, or someone else—who, for reasons that are no less ethical, called for and deserved no less attention. On the other hand: even though it is difficult to imagine, make an effort of imagination or figuration to understand me, to understand this singular thing that has happened to me. It's as if I was not the same, as if "I" was not identical at several moments of history, of the story to be recounted or recalled, or even at several instants of the day or the night, awake or asleep, conscious or unconscious, or even with different persons, with all the others to whom I am tied finally by different commitments, all equally imperious, all equally just but incomparable, untranslatable into each other.

Miller says it so well, precisely, so justly: "Just what the 'I' is or becomes in this transaction is another question."

Let us leave this question waiting, along with the other one that has to do with the situation of the tête-à-tête or face-to-face between two men, two friends, two accomplices, perhaps, or two acolytes, one of whom asks the other to understand him ("Just imagine, I . . . ") and thus to begin by putting himself in his place, by identifying with him. The space of an at least virtual "we" is already supposed by this exchange—as it is by any exchange, no doubt. We will come back to this at length.

A supplementary connotation here: the one addresses himself to the other to ask him to understand him, to put himself in his place, thus already to substitute himself for the other. What about the *we* in this scene of undecidable confession, of ironic confiding, of postulated substitution? Even before one comes to the determined "perjury," to the content or the act of the perjury in question in the "Just imagine, I was not thinking about it," is there not already an initial perjury haunting the exchange to which the "Just imagine" belongs?

It remains to be seen how "we" can perjure and say "we"—more precisely, while saying "we," and while thinking to think *we* and to avow or disavow *us*, and to ask or give *us* forgiveness. It remains to be seen how we can tell ourselves the truth and the truth of "us," but also how we can then, without delay, betray, disavow, perjure, disclaim, renounce, abjure this supposed truth of the *we*.

"Probably," "Maybe," Perhaps":
The Ethical Rigor and Inventions of J. Hillis Miller

How to go about it? How to speak? I would like to withdraw this text from the law of the genre "text in homage," even if sincere, and from the well-known academic scene: a long-time colleague and friend devotes an essay to a friend and eminent colleague, to an influential and distinguished professor whose work—one of the richest and most impressive that he has been given to know and respect in the course of his life—he wishes, along with others, to salute. Moreover, I don't feel capable, in a few pages, of measuring here my admiration for and gratitude to Hillis Miller, still less of recounting a shared history, I will say a companionship—most of whose major features are known anyway: thirty years of untroubled friendship, of work in common, of making our way side by side—"teaching" and "reading," as the passage cited from *Ethics of Reading* in epigraph says—in the same institutions (Johns Hopkins, Yale, UC Irvine), so many private and public encounters, so many colloquia, and, throughout all of that, such a profound agreement about what Hillis Miller calls "the ethics of reading" and perhaps, if I dare to say it, "ethics," period.

Therefore, after weighing things for a long time, I thought it was more just to make the following choice: to propose to Hillis Miller, to give him to read and to judge, the most demanding interpretation possible, but the most trembling as well, of a certain "story" or "history," and to do this while taking inspiration from the lesson that, like so many others, I have learned from him. This "story" is not just any one. It was not unrelated to our own, to that which, the one who was "between us," I mean the other friend, Paul de Man. This story is the oblique object of a *récit*, let us say of a *narration*. A literary narration, a "fiction," as one tends to say with too much facility. Yes, for the moment let's keep the rather neutral word "narration." Let's keep it for *three reasons*. First, I am told that the texts collected here are supposed to take "narrativity" as their leitmotiv. Second, Hillis Miller has renewed magisterially, among other things, the reading and the thinking of narration—and not only as literary fiction and not only in so-called Victorian fiction. Finally and above all, because the work I am preparing to take as example, *Le Parjure*, appears to be narrative, of course, in its structure (its cover, I repeat, bears the term "novel") but poses formidable problems in its relation to so-called "real" history (that of Paul de Man, which will thus have traversed our own, so to speak, and very closely, that of Hillis Miller and myself, among others), in its relation to *fiction*, to *witnessing*, in short to all the "unknowns" that today can be inscribed under the words *truth* and *reality*, but also *sincerity, lying, invention, simulacrum, perjury,* etc.

To justify my choice, before I even begin, I will reconstitute again a few premises. At least three, whose *configuration* is also a *conjunction* of dated events or apparently irreversible sequences. In the three cases, it is a matter of figuring out what "to remember" means—and thinking *of* remembering: not forgetting to remember, not forgetting to keep memory, but also thinking of remembering, which also means in its French syntax: to think *because, insofar as, as long as, inasmuch as* one remembers, thought as memory and first of all as memory of self, memory of the other in the self. I think of that English word, I remember "to re-mind," whose enigma has always fascinated me: to not forget to put back in memory, to remind someone, to think of reminding, warning, with a sign, a crib note, a memento, a reminder. Already a mnemotechnics at the heart of and not outside the thinking of thought.

1. First reminder: a moment in Hillis Miller's work. A few years ago, as we know, Miller began to elaborate a new problematic: at the unfathomable depths of an abyssal staging, at the beating heart of what is so blithely called literary fiction, to decipher the still invisible vein of a question believed to be ageless, the great and inexhaustible history of the lie, that is, of perjury. Every lie is a perjury, every perjury implies a lie. Each betrays a promise, that is, an at least implicit oath: I owe you the truth from the moment I speak to you. A certain number of recent essays, often devoted to Proust, testify to this.[5] Daringly engaged on the path of what Miller proposes to call—the neologism is his—"polylogology," this problematic opens up the space to an at least implicit multiplicity of voices, narrative or narrating origins, in order to take rigorous account of them. These voices are so many legitimating sources, sources of authority or legitimacy ("the implicit multiplicity of the authorizing source of the story"[6]). As soon as there is more than one voice in a voice, the trace of perjury begins to get lost or to lead us astray. This dispersion threatens even the identity, the status, the validity of the concept—in particular the concept of perjury, but also and equally the word and the concept "I."

Miller gives several names to this multiplicity of voices or "consciousnesses." He recognizes in them several figures, either himself signing and forging a new term (for example, "polylogology," or even "alogism"), or borrowing it and granting it a new destiny, another working out, as, for example, following Friedrich Schlegel, "permanent parabasis of irony." But I would like to insist on the most striking and no doubt the most productive of these figures, the one that assures a powerful general formalization even as it remains rooted and forever inscribed in the fictional singularity of a corpus that *already* produces it in itself, like a sort of general theorem, like a generalizable theoretical fiction, if I can put it that way, like a fiction having the value of theoretical truth and an ethical dimension: it is that of *anacoluthon*. Doubtless more than a figure of rhetoric, despite appearances, it signals in any case toward the *beyond* of rhetoric *within* rhetoric. Beyond grammar *within* grammar. With a gesture whose necessity and elegance I have always admired, it is in the text of Proust himself that Miller finds what he *invents*: namely, a noun and a concept that he will then put to work in a productive, demonstrative, generalizable fashion—well beyond this unique literary root, well beyond this *oeuvre*.

But we are already involved in the difficulty that seemed to loom once the theoretical concept is itself part of the fiction, once it *finds itself* at work in the work studied. It *is part* of the narrative fiction that thus comprises it at the very moment it allows one to comprehend it in turn. The concept is more powerful than the work, which is more powerful than the concept. This theoretical generalization does not happen only after the fact. Miller was looking for it. Because he was looking for it, because he anticipated it even as he felt its necessity, he discovered and invented it at the same time in Proust. He found it where it was to be found. He *invented* it in the other, in the two senses of the term: produced and revealed. He caused it to arise, in an inaugural gesture, there where its body was already to be found, at once visible and invisible. The long quotation that I will dare to extract from "The Anacoluthonic Lie" continues the one placed in epigraph. The underlined words will translate what I must select for my purposes, without further justification, without other authorization than that given me or imposed on me by the configural conjunction I was speaking of a moment ago. It will be a matter of what is at stake ethically in the interruption of a memory. The essential finitude of a discontinuous anamnesis inscribes ellipses and eclipses in the identity of the subject. It permits anyone to respond, in a manner that is at once responsible and irresponsible, as serious as it is insolent, undecided between provocative irony and disarming sincerity, perhaps in truth disarmed: "It's true. Just imagine, I was not thinking about it. Thank you."

The passage in Proust has to do with storytelling (in the double sense of lying and of narration), with memory as a precarious support of narrative continuity, and with anacoluthon's function in both storytelling and lying. Anacoluthon doubles the story line and so makes the story *probably* a lie. A chief evidence for the middle's perturbation is small-scale details of language. This means that close reading is essential to reading narrative:

To tell the truth, I knew nothing that Albertine had done since I had come to know her, or even before. But in her conversation (she might, had I mentioned it to her, have replied that I had misunderstood her) there were certain contradictions, certain embellishments which seemed to me as decisive as catching her red-handed [*qui me semblaient aussi décisives qu'un flagrant délit*], but less usable against Albertine who, often caught out like a child, had invariably, by dint of sudden, strategic changes of front, stultified my cruel attacks and retrieved the situation. Cruel, most of all, to myself. She employed, not by way of stylistic refinement, but in order to correct her imprudences, abrupt breaches of syntax not unlike the figure which the grammarians call anacoluthon or some such names [*de ces brusques sautes de syntaxe ressemblant un peu à ce que les grammairiens appellent anacoluthe ou je ne sais comment*]. Having allowed herself, while discussing women, to say: "I remember, the other day, I . . . ," she would suddenly, after a semi-quaver rest, change the "I" to "she": it was something that she had witnessed as an innocent spectator, not a thing that she herself had done. It was not she who was the subject of the action [*Ce n'était pas elle qui était le sujet de l'action*]."[7]

Miller continues at length the quotation of this passage, which he deems to be of an "admirably graceful subtlety." He then fits it with an analysis, which is itself subtle and admirable, that extends and generalizes the "theoretical" scope, in some way, of this singular example. It is as if, extending and generalizing, the analysis were *inventing* it in some way. I believe I must prefer here this word "invention" because it *hesitates perhaps* between *creative* invention, the production of what is not—or was not earlier—and *revelatory* invention, the discovery and unveiling of what *already* is or finds itself to be there. Such an invention thus hesitates *perhaps*, it is suspended undecidably between fiction and truth, but also between lying and veracity, that is, between perjury and fidelity. Whence, it seems to me, the essential role played by the discreet but decisive intervention of the mark of the undecidable that is the "perhaps" in "The Anacoluthonic Lie," precisely, in the definition of the anacoluthon. Two examples:

A passage of an admirably graceful subtlety! The anacoluthon, or failure to follow a single syntactical track, for example in the shift from first to third person in the middle of a sentence, creates a narrative line that does not hang together. That shows, to anyone who notices it, that the story is—*may be*—a lie, a fiction. How could the same story apply at once to the teller and to someone else? The difficulty is in noticing the discrepancy, since memory, for Proust, far from being total and continuous, is intermittent and discontinuous. Our memories are out of our control. We remember only what our memories, acting on their own, happen to think it worthwhile to save. Lying and fiction, as Albertine's anacoluthons show, come to the same thing since both are forms of language that cannot be returned to a single paternal, patronizing logos or speaking source. . . . Who is the liar here, Albertine as the example of the eternal feminine, evasive and unpossessable, in this case betraying Marcel in covert lesbian liaisons? Or is the prime liar Marcel Proust himself, who has displaced into a misogynist fiction his own experience of betrayal in a "real life" homosexual liaison?[8]

Though we can notice that something has gone wrong with the narrative sequence, we can no longer remember the beginning well enough to see for certain the incoherence of the story and so *perhaps* discover the truth hidden behind the lie.

I say "perhaps" because for Proust it is impossible ever to be sure whether or not someone is lying. This is because, contrary to what seems common sense, a lie is a performative, not a constative, form of language. Or, rather, it mixes inextricably constative and performative language.[9]

Unlike the recent "Fractal Proust," Miller's earlier essays on Proust do not refer directly to de Man or explicitly to de Man's readings of Proust. But it seems to me at every moment obvious that these texts are pursuing an *explanation* with de Man, in the sense of *Auseinandersetzung*. There is always, at least implicitly, it seems to me, an active reading, an interpretation, and a discussion of de Man's theses: his theses concerning Proust and reading, of course, but also his theses concerning all that which, in the question of lying or truth, is eminently ethical, ethical in general and ethical in the sense of an ethics of reading. The passage I placed in epigraph is drawn from a chapter of *The Ethics of Reading*, which bears as epigraph a long quotation from *Allegories of Reading*. One reads there in particular provocative utterances such as:

The ethical category is imperative (i.e., a category rather than a value) to the extent that it is linguistic and not subjective. Morality is a version of the same language aporia that gave rise to such concepts as "man" or "love" or "self," and not the cause or the consequence of such concepts. The passage to an ethical tonality does not result from a transcendental imperative but is the referential (and therefore unreliable) version of a linguistic confusion. Ethics (or, one should say, ethicity) is a discursive mode among others.[10]

Within the scope of this essay, I will not be able to discuss these propositions, but I do not think they are unquestionable, either in my view or in Miller's. I recall them merely in order to reconstitute the configuration or the conjunction in which I am preparing to approach the eminently ethical question of perjury (that is, a species of lie or, inversely, the genus of which lying is a species) and the book *Le Parjure*. It is an indissolubly ethico-literary question of testimonial narration and of fiction.

2. Second reminder, a memory: Toward the end of the seventies, at Yale, Paul de Man said to me one day something like this (I do not recall what led to this remark, but we must have been talking, as we often did, of Paris, probably of Henri Thomas, one of the friends of my friend Paule Thévenin): "If you want to know a part of my life, read 'Hölderlin en Amérique.' Henri Thomas, whom I knew here, in America after the war, published this text in *Mercure de France*, and it was reprinted or augmented as a novel, at Gallimard, *Le Parjure*." I confess that I did not rush out looking for the book. I never found the issue of the *Mercure de France*. But years later, at a bookseller's in Nice where I was on vacation, I came upon *Le Parjure*. I read it very quickly, but very quickly I understood that the principal character of the fiction, Stéphane Chalier, resembled in certain features the real person of Paul de Man and that it was a matter, to say things once again much too quickly, of the story of a second marriage, in the United States, while a first marriage in Europe had not ended in legal divorce. Hence the accusation of bigamy and perjury. The novelist-narrator-witness-character tells the moving and agitated story of a young Belgian-American couple: "Hölderlin in America," hospitalized and almost blind, finds himself, with his new young wife, the object of legal proceedings or threatened with legal proceedings. He is being pursued by both the first wife and the American authorities.

After my reading, I remember that I wrote to Paul de Man, a few words, as discreetly as possible, in conformity with the customary tone of our exchanges, saying that I had been *bouleversé*, bowled over. We never spoke about it again. Just as I never spoke about it with Henri Thomas, whom I didn't know at the time and whom I nevertheless telephoned, years later, in 1987 (he lived in Brittany) to hear his response to what some friends (including Hillis Miller) and myself had just discovered about the past of the young Belgian journalist that Paul de Man was during the war and that we right away decided to make public and accessible to discussion. Some may still recall perhaps what was hastily called the "de Man affair" by some newspapers, avid for this kind of merchandise, and some university professors, who for a long time had been poisoned by the impotence of resentment. It was *their* affair, but I will not go back over this by now abundantly "documented" episode, concerning which I have said what I felt at length and publicly.[11] I recall merely that Henri Thomas's testimony was at the time that of a trusting and admiring friend, without the least reservation.[12]

3. Third reminder: It so happens that last year, in the course of a seminar on forgiveness and perjury, I reread more attentively, as if for the first time, Thomas's book in order to test a certain number of schemas and hypotheses. Hillis Miller was present at this seminar, at UC Irvine. He thus shared this strange experience of which, in many ways, we are, if not the only witnesses, at least privileged witnesses—to attempt, as he put it,

a response to the text that is both necessitated, in the sense that it is a response to an irresistible demand, and free, in the sense that I must take responsibility for my response and for further effects, "interpersonal," institutional, social, political, or historical, of my act of reading, for example as that act takes the form of teaching or of published commentary on a given text. What happens when I read *must* happen, but I must acknowledge it as *my* act of reading, though just what the "I" is or becomes in this transaction is another question.[13]

For, however trembling and undecidable, however suspended remained and still remains today the novel's and the fictional "character's" reference to our friend de Man, we could not not be haunted by the memory we still had of him. We could not not know that we were in some way being observed internally by him, by the spectral vigilance of his gaze, even if this quasi "presence" in no way limited our freedom. In truth, it even sharpened our responsibility.

Hölderlin in America: The Oath of a Madman

In the course of this seminar, I insisted at length on a first given of history: a separate study ought in fact to be devoted to the multiple and tangled reasons for which the crime of perjury, inscribed to be sure in all legal codes of the European tradition, finds nevertheless in the United States the zone of its most intense gravity. It is in the United States, to my knowledge, that perjury is named and tracked, by that name, with the greatest frequency, with an obsessional insistence. Although I have not done an inventory, it seems to me that the occurrence of the word "perjury" is much more frequent in the United States than in any other Western country, as threat of legal action against the "perjurer," in official documents, wherever a commitment or declaration is made, and practically everywhere a signature is required. Much more frequent than, for example, in France (where the word "perjury" remains rare, somewhat specialized, certainly unintelligible to the ordinary population) are the equivalents or nearby words, such as *faux témoignage, contrefaçon* (false witness or testimony, forgery, counterfeit). In the United States, one cannot sign a public document without having to read, without being supposed to have read, officially, legally, that perjury is strictly punishable by law. Which is in fact completely consistent, since this practice merely thematizes, and thus in principle makes undeniable, a universal implication of the law and the Western social contract: on the condition, of course, that the legal subject understands the language and *knows how to read* what he or she is being reminded of in this fashion, namely, that no one is assumed to be ignorant of the law before which one is in advance obligated and obligated to appear; truth, veracity, and good faith are owed by whoever promises it, beginning with the veracity of the promise. A promise whose structure is thereby vertiginously complicated, because it is engaged even before any explicit formulation, and even in the case where I would declare, with a negation, denegation, or disavowal, that I do not commit myself. Such a complication is reinvested and capitalized in the act of perjury. For if I perjure myself, if I lie while making what is called a false testimony, I have perhaps already lied (not necessarily or always but *perhaps*), I have *perhaps* previously lied by promising (seriously, it is understood) to tell the truth: I have already lied by promising *veracity* (and one must always specify *veracity* rather than *truth* [vérité]: lying or perjury does not involve saying what is false or untrue but saying something other than what one thinks; it is not making a mistake or an error, but misleading the other deliberately). I have perhaps *already* lied by promising to tell the truth, lied before lying in not telling the truth.

Thus we see the time of perjury is divided from the very first moment. When I accuse myself of perjury or when I accuse someone of perjury, this accusation can take one or two directions at once: I can accuse the other (or myself) of having betrayed, *in a second moment*, a sincere promise that would not have been kept, thus the betrayal *follows*, like a second original moment, a commitment that was first of all honest and in good

faith, authentic; or else (or even at the same time) I can accuse the perjurer, the other or myself, of having lied *from the first moment*, of having
perjured by promising to tell the truth, thus by swearing an oath to begin
with, of having perjured or forsworn by swearing [*d'avoir parjuré en ju-
rant*]. One can thus perjure oneself *after* having sworn, but one can also
forswear by swearing. These two temporalities or these two structural
phases seem after the fact to envelope one another. Hence the gulf of amnesia, the interruption, the possibility of anacoluthic discontinuity that
we were talking about earlier, the "Just imagine, I was not thinking about
it." I can always say, whether or not one believes me, whether or not one
takes it into account: "I sincerely promised to tell the truth, or I promised
this or that, promised to be faithful to my promise, promised to be faithful to my given word, swore to be faithful, period, and *then later*, for some
reason or other, or for no other reason than the return of my wickedness,
my malice, or even my loss of love, or even a transformation of myself, or
even the sudden arrival of another person, another obligation, or even
forgetfulness or distraction, I had to betray. But this betrayal comes about
only in a second moment: when I promised-swore, I was sincere, in good
faith, I was not perjuring myself. Not yet."

These two moments are at once rigorously distinct and strangely in-
discernible. But this difference of the times is inscribed under the law of
a contract, under a contracted, contracting, and sacral, sacramental law.
This law, and no doubt it is the Law itself, the origin of the Law, is destined to annul precisely temporal difference. The essential destination, the
structural signification of the oath or the given word, is to commit oneself not to be affected by time, to remain the same at moment B, whatever may happen, as the one who swears previously, at moment A. This
sublating negation of time is the very essence of fidelity, of the oath, and
of sworn faith. The essence or the truth of the Law. But the perjurer, the
one who perjures himself or herself, can always seek to be excused, if not
forgiven, by alleging, on the contrary, the unsublatable thickness of time
and of what it transforms, the multiplicity of times, instants, their essential discontinuity, the merciless interruption that time inscribes in "me" as
it does everywhere. That is the ultimate resource, or even the fatality, of
the anacoluthon. The typical allegation, justified or not, undecidably veracious or lying: "I sincerely promised in the past, but time has passed,
precisely, passed or surpassed, and the one who promised, long ago or in
the past, can remain faithful to his promise, but it is no longer me, I am

no longer the same me, I am another, *I* is another, I have changed, everything has changed, the addressees of the promise as well. For example: I was in love, I am in love no longer in the same way, I love someone else, and I am unable to account for that, myself, ask the other who decides this for me within me."

One could appeal here to a psychology of the self, even a basic but still difficult to dispute psycho-phenomenology. It attests that in certain cases, someone, me, a me, can sincerely, seriously commit himself or herself under oath to tell the truth, the whole truth, nothing but the truth, and then, in a second moment, for one reason or another, show that he or she is not worthy of the promise, incapable of keeping it or capable of betraying it, of perverting it, abjuring, disavowing, and so forth. According to the same psycho-phenomenology, the unfolding of this process, namely, the drama of this diachrony, would be distinct from another scenario: someone is *already* lying, he perjures himself *already* at the moment of the oath and the promise. This bifid structure is not without effect on the scene of repentance and forgiveness. To ask for forgiveness or offer excuses may consist in confirming the sincerity of the first commitment and of *attenuating* the betrayal ("attenuating circumstances"), if not as an inessential accident, at least as a second moment of fall, a second or even secondary and above all unforeseeable corruption: I was sincere when I promised this or that, when I promised fidelity, but I could not foresee this change, these events, everything *that* has happened, I could not foresee *who, the other who* has arrived in the interval, the other who may be another, a third party, or else myself.

Is it necessary to insist? Our lives are made up of such stories. The psycho-phenomenology of the self, the egology that is in general tied to it, seems to be indisputable. And yet the essence of the oath, the vocation of the promise, the very idea of sworn faith or fidelity, the Law, are *made in view of* causing the laws of the just mentioned psycho-phenomenology of the self to lie. In their concept, in their horizon, which is itself a promise, they are *destined* to defeat, to undo, to put to rout the *logos* of this psycho-phenomenology itself, the reason and the identity of the psyche. They happen so as to prove wrong, if not to lay blame on the psyche, *logos*, phenomenality, the ego. An oath is sufficiently mad to put these "authorities" in the wrong or to destine them in turn to madness. Which is madder, *psyche, logos, ego,* the phenomenon—or the oath?

This expression, this metonymy, the periphrasis of this nickname,

"Hölderlin in America," was first of all something like the oath of a madman. He was not joking when he said one day to his father: "You are mistaken, father; it will be *Hölderlin in America* and I will go write it over there," then insisted again, going right to the bottom of things: "At bottom I am not joking. It will be *Hölderlin in America*, and I am going to pack my bags to go write it over there."

Project or challenge ("It will be *Hölderlin in America*, and I am going to pack my bags to go write it over there"), these words *commit*. They appear in the first pages of Henri Thomas's novel, *Le Parjure*. Let us recall that in the *Mercure de France*, before the publication of the book, the fragment was titled "Hölderlin in America." The person a part of whose story was something like the referent of what remains forever a fiction—and let us not forget that—was, then, my friend Paul de Man, who, I repeat, confided to me one day that he had also been Henri Thomas's friend and that, if I wanted to know something of his life, I ought to read this "Hölderlin in America."[14]

Let us return to what remains forever a literary fiction, to the novel-play titled *Le Parjure*. Everything begins in Belgium with a strange story of letters. Letters that are more or less purloined or detoured in their destination, between the father, "a specialist in the great Romanticism," and the son who will become "Hölderlin in America" and who gets called a "little romantic" while he is studying *Penthesilea*. Because his father, specialist in the great Romanticism, treats him as a "little romantic," because his father says of him "Stéphane has not yet found his way," the son protests, and I quote him again: "You are mistaken, father; it will be *Hölderlin in America*, and I will go write it over there."

In this novel within the novel *Le Parjure*, *Hölderlin in America* is first of all the title of a novel or a play that the young man Stéphane Chalier, the principal character, plans to go write there, in America. It is, in effect, as if the play or the novel, as if the *writing* of the play or the novel was meant to be confused with his *way* [voie], with the voyage or the path of his existence, with that "way" that his father used to say he had not yet found, the way of his exile or his adventure in America. He decided to leave Belgium after the war for the United States, in an infinitely overdetermined personal and political situation, but as a challenge thrown up to the father, his father or the Father: "You are mistaken, father; it will be *Hölderlin in America*, and I will go write it over there."

Stéphane Chalier thus leaves for America, having "fled after a last quarrel with father Chalier" (11), the "specialist in the *great* Romanticism" (13) who often called his son a "little romantic," the son who was never sure whether "this was blame or praise" (12). At the same time, Stéphane leaves his wife Ottilia and his two children. He had, moreover, been annoyed by Ottilia's working for father Chalier, whose "brilliant student" she had been. Her study, *Les Bijoux dans la poésie symboliste*, "had aroused the enthusiasm of the elder Chalier" (21).

This remark appears in a sequence that puts on stage the triangle of great and little romanticism (father/son/daughter-in-law) at the same time as the moment of the oath ("You are mistaken, father; it will be *Hölderlin in America*, and I will go write it over there"). But the *present* of this oath (which is, moreover, sealed, signed, as we will see, by an "it is now") presents itself in truth, like any self-respecting oath, in the future of what is coming: here, in the grammar of three futures, three commitments, or three promises. To be kept beginning now. These three performatives are not just any ones; they are carried by verbs such as "to be," "to go," "to know": "it will be," "I will go," "I will know." Such grave oaths remain nevertheless rather mad or rather rash because they do not correspond to any plan. They are not only improvised but, as it were, imposed on Stéphane. He surprises himself, he lets himself be surprised, therefore, in an apparently aleatory or unforeseeable and therefore irresistible fashion, by the strange force of another law, by the pull or impulsion of one knows not what necessity coming from the other. *Hölderlin in America*: Will that be the title of a work to come, as everything seems to indicate? Or else, by means of the work, the proper name, barely a metonymy, at bottom the autograph of his own becoming to come? Will not he, himself, be Hölderlin in America?

That evening father Chalier had modified somewhat his formula, while speaking to Jaubert: "*Stéphane has not yet found his way . . .* "

"You are mistaken, father; it will be *Hölderlin in America*, and I will go write it over there."

Everyone had laughed, but gently. Jaubert had clarified: "It's not what you say that amuses us, but your manner of saying it!"

"I hope so, because at bottom I am not joking. It will be *Hölderlin in America*, and I am going to pack my bags to go write it over there."

He was not thinking about this ten minutes before he spoke; at the moment at which he blurted out these words, he really had no plan. He had never had any desire to see the United States. The hills of Bohemia, Andalusia, Crete, everything attracted him, except that country whose accent he found so ugly. But neither was it the first time that he surprised himself by speaking in this way, as if by chance, and always against someone, he who was otherwise so gentle, so docile. As if something in him from time to time tried to leap out, in words. In words alone, this could have gone on for a long time, speaking didn't change anything in life over there, the father and Ottilia also spoke, the breach closed up again. Ottilia had laughed along with the other two:

"I can't see you as an emigrant. You don't know what it's like."

She knows. She fled the Rumania of the Iron Guard, and by way of the Black Sea no less, and Turkey, and the Greek freighter! With all that, a brilliant student of father Chalier; as for her, she chose her way rapidly. *Les bijoux dans la poésie symboliste* had aroused the enthusiasm of the elder Chalier.

Stéphane merely replied: *I will know it,* and dinner ended as if nothing had happened. And yet everything is clear from that moment on. Stéphane is loathe to form a clear idea of what he was before; too many things are involved, it's too close to adolescence. But from that moment on, well, it is like now, it is now. (20–21)[15]

Untranslatable Title: *Le Parjure*

Like the "reality" it fictionalizes, *Le Parjure* opposes an infinite or abyssal resistance to any meta-narrative. Henri Thomas was the friend of the "real" character, Paul de Man, whom he met in America after the war. In the novel, the narrator, who is not the author, is also the friend of the principal character, Stéphane Chalier. But in what does the narrative core consist, that which seems to support the title, the event designated by *Le Parjure*? Where is it situated? This magnificent title, *Le Parjure*, is a *chef d'oeuvre* in itself. It exceeds any interpretive decision. There are at least three ways of reading and interpreting it, three ways of situating its thematic referent, but each of the three haunts the others. Each of the three thus raises the number of titles (3 + n), to be sure, but each also makes apparent the title's intrinsic multiplicity. Each recalls as well its divisibility, without possible end, its essential dissociation, its internal interruption.

1. In the first place, *le parjure* could always be, for a somewhat vigilant and patient reader, the fiction, the novel itself, its signature, if you will, the manner in which the novelist, *at work* in his act of writing, but also the narrator, in the novel, which is still something else, betrays his friend by unveiling, by taking his confession (it is constantly question of a con-

fession and an avowal in the novel), by publishing this confession, namely, a story of perjury, or even by falsifying it. That is a first possible perjury. The narrator *causes to avow and disavows* his friend. The title could thus designate, *already*, the double perjury of the narrator or the novelist who betrays the truth confided to him by his friend or the truth of which he was the privileged and secret witness. *Le Parjure* would *already* sign the perjury, betrayal, fault, and would do it doubly, like a double signature, since both the novelist and the narrator accuse themselves with it. It is in the open, described, or prescribed space of such a title that what Miller calls "storytelling" comes about: "storytelling (in the double sense of lying and of narration), with memory as a precarious support of narrative continuity, and with anacoluthon's function in both storytelling and lying."

2. Without contradicting but by complicating the first, by overdetermining it *en abyme*, a second reading of the title *Le Parjure* (and thus of the book that bears this title) might also concern the betrayed, failed, unfulfilled promise, by the hero of the novel this time, to go make or write "Hölderlin in America." With regard to the scene I have just read and commented on (promise, commitment, threat, challenge: "I am not joking. It will be *Hölderlin in America*, and I am going to pack my bags to go write it over there"), has there been perjury or not? Perhaps. Who will ever know? It is true that the real character, my friend, was someone who not only wrote a lot on Hölderlin, in France and in America, but who thought at least to change something or invent something new in the interpretation of the thinking poetry of Hölderlin. The stakes of this may be considerable, or even in-finite, if one follows out the implication in a certain way. This friend, then, would have in a certain way introduced Hölderlin in America, through and beyond a field of literary theory. Which is also true of the perjury and the lie in the *Confessions* of Rousseau, especially around the stolen or "purloined" ribbon.[16] One of the important motifs in his reading of Hölderlin concerned, moreover, the question of the true (*das Wahre*, rather than *die Wahrheit*, the truth) and of the event. This question haunts *Le Parjure*, as we will verify. No one will ever know whether or not "Hölderlin in America" has taken place, whether the promise has been kept or whether some perjury has betrayed it. Perhaps.

3. But the third sense of the title, which is also its first referent or its principal theme, its most obvious sense, the most common, the most

massive, is the one that refers to the central narrative, namely, the perjury
as such, the legal perjury, the perjury in the eyes of positive law, *le parjure*
committed by *le parjure*, the perjury committed by the perjurer—since in
French alone, as we must once again underscore, "le parjure" is certainly
the act of perjuring (perjury), or even the content and the object of this
act (again perjury), but also the author of the perjury, the perjurer. This
is only possible in French, where one can say: you are a *parjure* or you
committed a *parjure*. To this immeasurable extent, *Le Parjure* remains untranslatable. With all the consequences one can imagine, its economy in
any case resists the other language. And thus perhaps it resists the passage
across the frontiers of one nation, from one nation-state to another.

Here *le parjure* is thus, first of all, the hero of a novel and/or the offense
that he committed in the eyes of the American justice system: he had
been married, he had two children in Belgium, he remarried in the
United States, a few years later, while omitting to declare his former and
still valid marriage (he had not divorced) or while declaring that he was
not married. Before this second marriage, before the perjury itself,
Stéphane and Judith (who will be his second wife, his American wife) become bound to each other in a situation or at a moment in which, as
Henri Thomas (or in any case the narrator, the witness, who will be like
the witness of this second marriage and of the *parjure*) recalls, they were
still placed under the sign and in the memory of Hölderlin.

The One Who Did Not Accompany Me:
The Truth of the Acolyte

So here is Hölderlin in the restaurant of a motel. It is before the perjury,
before the second marriage, the one that Hölderlin would have somehow
incited or blessed, before a perjury that is, in a certain way, consummated
in advance of having taken place. Hölderlin in America, topometonymy,
is also, as we'll see, Hölderlin in France. Everything seems to be suspended from a metonymy, a quotation, a quasi anacoluthic change of
subject. Interruption in the obvious, the shadow at the heart of the light,
painting, snapshot. Let us observe first, in this love scene, the painting of
light itself: illustration of the lighting, clarification of the clearing, elucidation of the truth. The painting tells a story of brightness. There is here
a logic, a poetics, a rhetoric of narration. What it is trying to show hangs
from a hair (the hair of the perjurer) but is not as farfetched as it appears:

The light was bright in the dining room, the shadow of hands played over the pink paper tablecloth, and Stéphane's heavy mop of blond hair shone as he lowered his head. He did this often, it was almost a tic with him. When he laughed, when he had just said something a little bizarre, he bent his head so as to hide for a moment in the shadow. While laughing between the words, so that she had not grasped it all, he had just said:

> *The lines of life are different,*
> *What we are here below . . .*

And he was still talking, his head bent, laughing, when she plunged her right hand into the golden, somewhat dirty mop that was there beneath her eyes. Her roughly scarred palm clung to it. The people from the motel had almost never witnessed such gestures in the dining room. There was no longer any doubt: these young people were not married. Stéphane then did something no one had ever seen in this place in America, and that no one perhaps will never see again: he grabbed the wrist of the hand that was stirring in his hair, he pulled it out, and held it before him, its palm open and its fingers moving more slowly. Then he bent down over it and kissed it for a long time in several places. His hair was touching her wrist and he was laughing once again, his face hidden in this hand. Then raising his head, he continued in a joking manner:

> *What we are here below, only a god can complete it.*

He held Judith Samson's hand in both of his now, hiding the palm that he had just kissed. She looked at him with a dreamy attention, an absent look, then she asked:

"What were you saying a moment ago?"

"Hölderlin," he said. "Two lines of Hölderlin."

"Who was Hölderlin?"

"A man like me . . . yes, well, with all the differences. What made me think of it? Oh, it's very simple."

The high price of the meal they were finishing was due chiefly to the bottle of wine Stéphane had ordered. He turned it so the girl could see the label.

"Bordeaux," he said. "You see? He went to Bordeaux on foot, from Germany, and he made the return trip the same way."

"All alone?"

"Yes . . . or rather, no, that is, not really all alone. The people who met him saw him alone, naturally, no one was walking beside him. Yet, listen, a lady who lived in the center of France, about a third of his way home, told how one morning when she opened the shutters she saw a man standing in the garden, not moving, except that he was passing his glance over the flowers, the trees. He saw the lady and smiled. What astonished her, besides the smile that she found charming, was the color of the man's hair, a very light blond, what we call platinum now. And long hair, falling onto his shoulders. Light blue eyes, the pure Nordic type, if you will." (42–43)

Reading these descriptions, it seems already, but we will specify this, that the narrator is also a little in love with Stéphane-Hölderlin-the perjurer. He identifies both with him and with the woman in love. In truth, he identifies with everyone, and this would be one of the inextricable knots that keeps the title at the bottom of its own abyss. Witness and friend of Stéphane-Hölderlin, the narrator is also an *acolyte*, that is, someone who accompanies. According to both etymology and usage, the acolyte accompanies with an eye to following and assisting. He is an attached subject, who follows the other, listens to him, and is joined to him like his shadow. He *assists* in a double sense: he is present and he aids, he supplements. The suppleant can be the one who aids a priest in church (service of the *akoluthia*), the most frequent sense. He can also become the accomplice in a suspicious or even guilty act, even if, to take up again Proust's phrase quoted by Miller, he is not himself the "subject of the action." In this role of the substitute, which is both necessary and contingent, essential and secondary, the acolyte is an accomplice, a second, a suppleant who accompanies, but without accompanying altogether, in any event, at a certain distance. He is someone who, repeatedly, *assists*, but not without giving someone the slip a little [*non sans fausser quelque peu compagnie*].[17] The companion thus becomes, simultaneously, "the one who did not accompany," to parody Blanchot's title.

In a structural and regular fashion, the acolyte thereby takes on, as we will verify, an *anacolytic* figure. *Anakolouthia* designates generally a rupture in the consequence, an interruption in the sequence itself, within a grammatical syntax or in an order in general, in an agreement, thus also in a set, whatever it may be, in a community, let's say, or a partnership, an alliance, a friendship, a being-together: a company or a guild [*compagnonnage*]. But since the acolyte assists without being absolutely identical or in agreement, therefore not fully present to the person, the subject, or the community that he supplements, he represents not only his contrary, an anacolytic figure, but also, by himself, an *analytic* figure. His place is as much that of the analyst as of the breach, the fission reaction, the interruptive dissociation. There is no need to mobilize all the resources of semantics or etymology in order to associate the figure of the *acolyte*, which accompanies, with its negative, the *anacoluthon*, which does not accompany. Think, for example, of the definition that Fontanier gives of the anacoluthon. It is more grammatical than rhetorical. Moreover, he classes the anacoluthon among the figures of speech "other than tropes," among the "non-tropes." This definition itself banks on the figure of accompaniment, and speaks, in what is finally a rather pathetic and human manner, of "letting stand alone a word that calls out for another as companion. This missing companion is no longer a *companion*." (We would be tempted to compare this definition, which speaks of lack, solitude, aloneness, mourning in the language, to the one given by the OED for *anacoluthon*: "a wanting sentence"):

Here is a figure whose existence Beauzée does not deny, but that he finds useless to distinguish by a special name. Nevertheless, it is a very particular species of ellipsis, which has nothing in common with the other species except that it belongs to the same genus. *It consists in implying, and always in conformity with usage or without contravening it, the correlative, the* companion *of an expressed word; it consists, I say, in letting stand alone a word that calls out for another as companion.* This missing companion is no longer a *companion*; it is what in Greek is called *Anacoluthon*, and this name is also that of the figure.[18]

When he reflects the scene he has just described, the narrator also reflects the light, the elucidation of the lights and shadows. Doing so, he avows, he confesses. But he confesses the failure of a "witness" or a "narrator," his powerlessness to avoid perjury, in effect, to tell the truth: his dependent situation, the place from which he witnesses, his attachment, his love or friendship, his assistance, his *compagnonnage*, let us say his subjection as supplement to the beings he is speaking of: all this deprives him of the truth, or even of the promised veracity. Thus of a certain light. He cannot keep his word as witness. He is party to the drama that he must recount, before the law. While showing, must he show *himself* in the light of day or not? In either case, he betrays. He must, *in the same light*, hide where it is a matter of showing, but also he must show where he would like to hide, first all, to hide himself. He must expose while dissimulating, encrypt while unveiling, stifle a "great secret" even as he tells it, and finally betray, precisely because he is a witness, denounce, disavow the very thing and those whom he accompanies as witness (virtually a witness at a marriage ceremony). He gives them the slip [*Il leur fausse compagnie*].

This tragedy of testimonial narration is admirably inscribed by Thomas in the essence of a "light," a same light, the light but also the shadow whose physical or literal play he has just described, in the preceding scene, in an apparently naïve or conscientiously pictorial fashion. This light bears its shadow within itself and it now reveals its essence as "philosophical light," the light of a truth that hides by revealing, gathering and dispersing, moreover, through the turning of its tropes (metonymy, synecdoche, anacoluthon) the whole story of Hölderlin in America—which from now on neither the narrator nor any of us will ever again behold like a stranger, an insensitive, impassive witness. The perverse light of this anacoluthon: this time, the instantaneous substitutions to which it gives rise thanks to the ruptures in construction still conceal from us the "subject of the action," but while leaving us undecided between the narrator-witness "subject" (too implicated in the narration) and the "subjects" whose story he is telling. Here then, on the side of the narrating narration and not only on the side of the narrated narration, the anacoluthon gives rise to fictions or *perhaps*, even, to lies by the narrator himself. He is already and he is going to become, more and more, the assistant, the auxiliary, the partner, even the double, and we should say, so as to remain within the anacoluthic family, the companion, the accomplice, the *acolyte*, Conrad's "secret sharer," in sum,[19] of the principal perjurer, of the criminal, here of Stéphane Chalier. (I point out here that Hillis Miller will have taken into account the structural possibility of this anacoluthon, namely, that of an undecidable lie or perjury that must never be excluded on the part already of the narrator, or even the author.[20] This possibility thus traverses, and in truth institutes all the couples of acolytes, if I may say that, beginning with those whose positions we are studying here: narrated narration / narrating voice and/or narrative voice, character/narrator and/or author):

And yet I who am in that time when one drags oneself through all sorts of obstacles with less and less strength, what would I be without them? Still another question that will remain unanswered, because I cannot be without them. . . . Oh this misery of the witness, whether one calls him a narrator or chronicler or teller of imaginary tales! If he shows himself, he hides what he wants to uncover for you; if he shows only the things he wants to say, he stifles a great secret, himself, his link to all this, the flash that unites them all in a same world, that *philosophical light around the window* of a small room in Heidelberg, in summer, which Stéphane Chalier was thinking about because of the indirect lighting behind the motel's dwarf palms. This light emanating from a distant reading had also shone in the wine of origin before spreading out bizarrely beneath the little palms and becoming all the paleness of the prairie where they stopped, several hours after the motel. (43–44)

We—in the University

"I cannot be without them," says the narrator, the acolyte who, to adapt Fontanier's phrase, "calls out for another as companion." Here, then, arises an ordeal putting to the test this tie, this alliance, this "being together," this complicity of the acolyte, let us say this uneasy friendship. In 1964, the narrator reports on the "Chalier affair," without knowing, of course, without the author suspecting that one day there will be, in the same country, and in "reality," other affairs, for example, a "de Man affair," in the course of which, however, a question will often be asked whose form was already to be found, literally, in *Le Parjure*: "*What was known about his years before America?*" (138–39). Neither the author nor the narrator could foresee that in years to come, just as in this first "Chalier affair," it was going to be necessary to pay attention, as we will in a moment, to the most vulgar forms of media violence (already the link between television, the University, and "American law"). The narrator wonders whether it was Ottilia (the name he gives to Chalier's first wife, in memory, I suppose, of Goethe and *Elective Affinities*) who, hunting down her husband in the U.S., "herself advised the Immigration Committee of the fact that Chalier had made a false declaration before entering into his second marriage" (111). At the university where he is teaching, Chalier receives a letter convoking him to Washington, before an authority charged with such matters. Everything therefore begins with a letter and a letter received *at the university*, for everything we are talking about is set in the theater of the academy, beginning with father Chalier, a distinguished university professor, his daughter-in-law, who is carrying out research under his direction, and Hölderlin in America (a possible subtitle for this book: of perjury in the university, between Europe and America). Everything begins with the reading of this letter, a letter brought by this *facteur de la vérité* that is the narrator, but it is a letter for a blind man, if I may put it that way, a letter that his two acolytes, his wife and his witness, give to "Hölderlin" and read to him since his eyesight is so bad he cannot do it himself. It is unnecessary to recall the challenge to the father in order to think that, "almost blind," in the narrator's words, this "Hölderlin" is a very oedipal figure. The anacoluthon finds here its first lodging.

The letter had been addressed to him at the University, where he had not gone for several days. He was hesitating at the time about having the operation (a question of money once again), and it is quite possible that this letter made him decide to enter the hospital the next day. The man whom I now know would have willingly remained blind in one eye, just as he had given up almost his entire inheritance. The most docile thing to do, obviously, would have been to go to Washington, in his poor state of health, unable to read, seeing everything in a blur. He would perhaps have done it if we had not been there, Judith and I. I had brought him the letter, and it was Judith who read it to him. That is how I learned that Chalier had been guilty of taking a false oath in front of an American magistrate before marrying Judith Samson. He had declared under oath that he had not been previously married or divorced. The letter from the Committee mentioned this fact briefly, but also gave the date of the marriage with a numerical reference proving that an investigation had taken place—and above all it mentioned additional information concerning his marriage in Europe and the two children born from it. Stéphane Chalier was requested to present himself within a week at a certain office of the Department of the Interior, where he would be interviewed by the person who had signed the letter. It was a woman, more precisely, a middle-aged Miss. For the police to have convoked Chalier to an office in Washington, and not in New Hampshire, meant that the affair was very serious, but it might also mean that no one wished, for the moment, to put him in an awkward position vis-à-vis the University and the New Hampshire authorities. The affair was delicate: an investigation of the winner of the first fellowship awarded by the Papaïos Foundation risked setting off a scandal like that of the Sorrows affair—the highly respected professor who had cheated on a television quiz show, for several months running, while amassing a fortune. But the infraction of American law was obvious, indisputable; there was even something brutal about it that impressed me at the time like an unexpected gesture—the claw stroke of a peaceful cat, a rock thrown by a child. (112–13)[21]

Now begins the narrator's torment, the avowal of his aversion in the face of this incredible offense (a bottomless perjury, before the law of the state, to be sure, but first of all as regards the sworn faith of the first marriage and above all, above all, as regards the betrayed innocence of the first children!); now begins the movement to renounce a friendship incompatible with perjury/the perjurer, to disavow it, to *accompany* Chalier no longer and yet, right away, the belief in the unbelievable, then, finally, apparently, the reaffirmed fidelity, however damaged and ambivalent it remains.

I could not be indignant that he had been convoked to Washington, I could not feel sorry for him, but neither could I tell him that he had asked for all this and let him sort things out for himself. It was necessary to choose, however. I don't mean I had to choose how to conduct myself with him, because it was not a question of leaving him there, he who was almost blind—but in my feeling: if he was guilty, it was not only of perjury before the American authorities, but of abandoning his first family, especially his children; I am, I must say, excessively sensitive in that regard— and there could no longer be any question of friendship between us. But if he was not guilty? What an idea! Of course, he was guilty! Bigamist! What a ridiculous word. I never dared use it when speaking with him. So he was guilty, I had no doubt of that, nor did he, moreover. Judith herself had her share of guilt since she was aware of the first marriage; if she had expected the letter from Washington she could not have remained more calm after having read it. (113–14)

The anacoluthon becomes generalized. It thus cleaves or causes to trem-ble *all* the "subjects" of the action and the enunciation: *at once* the charac-ters of the novelistic fiction, the narrator, *and* their supposed models re-ferred to in real life, the author and his friends. So many acolytes. The anacoluthon passes, by definition, the border between fiction and reality, between literature and testimonial document. Even if, finally, it erases all these borders, this generalization without decidable limit supposes at least a highly significant structural fold: the duel of friendship, the companion-ship that strangely links the narrator and the perjurer/perjury, or, if you prefer, the witness of the perjurer/perjury and the perjurer/perjury himself or itself. The narrator is constantly tormented by a disturbance of identi-fication. He wonders at what moment and even whether he will ever have had the right to say "us." Later, much later (we will get to this), he writes: "Now I can say 'us'" (163). Question of the "us," which can be extended to the whole scene of forgiveness and perjury. Is there, at what moment, and in what modalities, an "us" that, with a single signature, gathers together the victim and the guilty one, the accuser-prosecutor and the offender, the person from whom one asks forgiveness and the person before whom or to whom the confession is confided? Here, at what moment can the narrator say and thus sign an "us" that unites him to the principal character, to the perjurer, that is, moving from one to the next, to Hölderlin in America, in the same "philosophical light," that is, in the anacoluthic metonymy? This metonymy blurs or complicates all the frontiers; it instigates all possible substitutions: between characters, between the narrator and the characters, between the fiction and reality, between the secret and the manifest, between the private and the public, and so forth.

This question is dramatized in countless ways, but I will highlight only one of them. Hölderlin in America, alias Stéphane Chalier, alias Paul de Man, finds himself in an "ophthalmologic clinic" for a problem of partial blindness (which makes one think also of Blanchot's *Madness of the Day*). He asks his friend, his companion the narrator, who relates it to us, to take his place and to write for him, who because of his partial blindness cannot write, the confession required, in a very American style, by the Washington committee. Even though apparently, in all conscience, he is completely innocent of what has happened, the narrator begins to feel guilty. Hölderlin in America does everything to make him feel guilty and thus responsible for the awaited confession, to make him sign it, in some way, in his place, or to countersign it.

The "Report-Confession," the Unique Impossible / Impossible Unique

What would the narrator-friend-witness-companion be guilty of? Well, of having wanted to defend Hölderlin, of having intervened in his favor, of having been a witness for the defense, a witness for him, and for having thereby provoked the demand for a confession on the part of the committee and its Quaker lady president. The structural fold is formed, or rather becomes more manifest than ever, at the moment of this inversion of roles, when the guilty one accuses the witness and makes him bear responsibility for the offense. The anacoluthic catastrophe finds one of its privileged places in this fold. Here is one of the most extraordinary passages of the book. The narrator-witness has gone to the clinic to see his friend the perjurer. Together they evoke the process that led to the demand for this report-confession by the "Quaker lady president." I will emphasize a few words in this sequence, which includes the "Just imagine, I was not thinking about it." (I leave the interested, and informed, reader free to make all the transpositions possible between the protagonists of "the Chalier affair" and those of "the de Man affair." There is no relation between them, but all relations are also possible between them.)

"The idea of this report didn't come from me."

At this point I received the only reproach that he ever addressed to me:

"If you had not thought it was right to intervene in this committee, with a letter from Dr. X—I know because he told me about it himself—the Quaker lady president would never have gotten the idea."

I was annoyed; I was upset to the point of not knowing what to say except: "Yes, that's true." *I felt guilty*, and there must have been something in my voice, or in my silence—how do I know?—that informed him exactly of my state, he who was listening to me in the dark, with a *pitiless* attention, for he played on it and said to me only what was sure to disconcert me even more. He laughed—carefully, since the least tug on the edges of his bandaged eye caused him pain. He said:

"Well, you will just have to follow through with your initiative, all the way to the end. It is you who will write my complete confession to the Quaker lady of the high Commission."

He thus meant to make me feel I had committed an error, an offense—that I was . . . guilty. Well, really! The time it had taken me, all the maneuvers, to reach this lady! And he was reproaching me, whereas I had never reproached him. *If I was guilty*, what about him? Was he without fault and without clumsiness?

I swear that not even for a second did I mean to reply spitefully, even as the strongest gust of resentment broke over me and my throat tightened as when one holds back tears. I could do nothing but remain silent or say something terrible, as I now perfectly well realize. But he, for his part, did not want me to keep silent! He wanted the answer:

"You will write it, won't you? Much better than I could ever do! Because I can't! Impossible! Way beyond my means! But you!"

It is then that I said:

"My dear Stéphane (and this was the first time I called him by his first name, quite naturally, instinctively, out of great friendship!), my dear Stéphane, I'm not the one after all who had a little lapse of memory the day you got married." (132–34; my emphasis)

Before listening to the response from Stéphane (a first name that Henri Thomas, who was a specialist in English-language literature and a great translator, chose perhaps while thinking of the figure of the rebellious son represented by Stéphane Chalier, alias Stephen in *Ulysses*), let us note that behind the good sense of the denegation ("I'm not the one after all who . . ."), a muffled anxiety impels the protest: what if, basically, I were he?

He said:

"That's true. Just imagine, I was not thinking about it. Thank you. I think the visit is over. You needn't bother to come back."

He held out his hand to me, at random. I could do nothing but shake it, and then I left. (134)

What if, basically, I were he? said I, commenting in a certain way on the narrator's denegation ("I'm not the one after all who . . . ," that is, the perjurer is not me) and letting it be understood that the anacoluthic substitution of the subject, the replacement of the acolyte, could be at once the motor, the motivation, and the dramatic emotion of this narrative. A generalized anacoluthon would make of the narrator, of any narrator no doubt, an acolyte of his "character" or of his "friend." An identificatory substitution would harbor, in sum, the betrayal and the perjury at the heart of every narration, every *récit*, every confession, every "relation" or "report" [*rapport*]. It would wreak havoc with the very truth or veracity of which it is all the same the condition. No meta-discourse, no meta-narrative would escape unscathed from this devastating perjury, which is all the more destructive in that it serves the most sincere desire for truth.[22] And in fact, in *Le Parjure* the narrator's denegation ("I'm not the one after all who . . . ," that is, the perjurer is not me) proves rather insistent. It is repeated. This assiduous obstinacy confirms that the narrator, the unconscious subject, if you like, or the narrative voice of the narrator *whispers* the contrary and smuggles it into the narrative: yes, yes, on the contrary, it is indeed *you* who . . . it is indeed *you*, thus it is indeed *me* the perjurer, and you are lying once again, and I am lying, and you betray all the time, you disavow, I betray and disavow on the pretext of fidelity. You do it, I do it, you make me confess it, I make you confess it and at the same time as you, I disavow it.

Some ten pages further, the same denegative form recurs, this time in the past, heavily underscored by a "what I said was true" that could well be merely one more perjury, lie, or mystification. "I am not Chalier," he will say a little after that (147), in a manner that is less and less convincing. In a different sense, yet another disavowal at the heart of the avowal. A "what I say is true" is inevitably inscribed in the scene and even in the signature of every lie. I emphasize:

When I said to Chalier that *I'm not the one after all who had a memory lapse*—I was speaking like other people. And, so? *What I said was true.* They will say that Sorrows, since we're talking about him, was irreproachable in his behavior toward his wife and his three children—that this no doubt finally explains the committee's indulgence toward him. Sorrows cheated the idiotic television audience, and the petition from the students insisted on that: the stupidity of the quiz show audience. . . . Chalier, on the other hand, how to put it? He is cheating the administration, which is not idiotic like the public; it puts faith in *the sworn word of honor*—he abandons a wife and two children. . . . And then he thinks it's funny that the lady head of the committee suggests he explain himself freely in writing. He breaks with the only friend he has, I don't mean just in Westford, but in the whole United States, in the whole world; he remains alone in his hospital bed, still unable even to write to his wife, his wife who is not his wife. How can one not agree with everyone on all this? The more I thought about it, the more I saw it thus and not otherwise. Ever since things had started going wrong for Chalier, people must have ended up forgetting something. *What was known about his years before America?* Or even, in which city in California or Arizona did he sign that damned oath of honor? I had to find out, myself, before I began writing for the lady. (138–39)

"What I said was true," declares the witness-narrator. A question of the truth, therefore, or rather of veracity, of light—and thus, from one to the next, a question of the meaning of what I am *doing* here, myself, by writing, and what *we* are doing together, you and me, I who seem to be speaking as analyst, interpreter, but also as narrator, friend, and witness, for example, of Paul de Man, my friend and the mutual friend of Hillis Miller and myself. This question of veracity is knotted up in an inextricable and vertiginous fashion with that of the *us* in this confession, in this report-confession of repentance. Moreover, the expression *rapport-confession*, which the narrator uses all the time, has been well chosen by Henri Thomas to mark the troubling indissociability of an objective report that merely reports *constatively*, for the American administration, the reality of what was, on the one hand, and, on the other, the confession that is an avowal and already a repentance, thus a performative disavowal, a denunciation of oneself, of the evil one has done that is more than a mistake. The American administration requires *one and the other at the same time*, the report and the confession, the report as confession, the report-confession.

Hölderin in America asks his friend, the narrator, the acolyte, to write the report-confession for the administration in his place, since it's his friend's fault that the process got started. The narrator feels this to be not a punishment but an impossible assignment, the order to do the impossible. This impossible, whose law we are going to follow, becomes something both more and other than the report-confession, more and other than the impossible avowal as disavowal: the most impossible impossible becomes the narrator himself, the friend, the acolyte, the countersignatory, the one who says "I" and that an absolute anacoluthon dislodges forever from its proper place: disavowed identity.

He had accepted the principle of the report-confession, while I was looking at my chestnut tree and was accepting to write this report myself, but not at all because the idea had come from me and as punishment for my initiative—but because I knew as well as Chalier did that this report-confession was impossible. But impossible in a strange, I would even say unique way. (145)

This impossibility of the impossible is thus unique. It is unique by reason of a certain essence of time, more precisely, of the having been, of the past, of the "outmoded" [*dépassé*]. The lexicon of the "past" and especially of the *dépassé* or "outmoded" brings together a whole argument on the subject of the impossible confession—and of an *impossible* that becomes at once the report-confession, the confessed, and the confessor, the one who avows, makes one avow, and disavows. The *dépassé* is not unrelated to the amnesia or distraction of the "Just imagine, I was not thinking about it." Moreover, we will soon hear an "it escaped me" from the mouth of the narrator, which strangely resembles the "I was not thinking about it." It recalls, it brings back nonmemory to memory, the possibility of an essential amnesia, the threat or the chance of a (active or passive) forgetting, the effects of an irreducible distraction at the heart of finite thought, a discontinuity, an interruptibility that is at bottom the very resource, the ambiguous power of the anacoluthon: the disappearing at work, a passive work, in the very essence of seeming [*paraître*], in the very phenomenality of appearing [*apparaître*]. The argumentation is all the more troubling in that Hölderlin in America, in "real" life if we can still say that, will have shown some years later, notably with the example of Rousseau, why confession is in a certain manner impossible. This demonstration has become one of the canonical points of reference in certain American university milieus.

We can follow the movement by which the friend-witness-narrator, the acolyte who accompanies without accompanying, prepares not only to say "us" on the subject of the offense and the report-confession, but to become himself, and to admit the fact, the report-confession that is awaited and that is effaced in the writing, having become impossible and forever "outmoded" in the process. Himself and this book, *Le Parjure*, become in effect the report-confession that he agreed to write even though it was impossible. All of this is the narrative of a *disappearance*, a signature that gets erased at the moment it enters literature. Here is the rest of the passage we just quoted. Besides the work on *passer-dépasser*, that is, to pass, to overtake, we will also follow the play in the semantic transformation of the word *rapport* ("report," "relation").

But impossible in a strange, I would even say unique way. There are perhaps those who would understand this immediately; for the others, I will try to explain. One often says, today, that this or that idea, some scientific or philosophical theory is outmoded [*dépassée*]. It is still taken into account, like the rung of a ladder for climbing higher, but one must not tarry on it. No longer believing in them, one is necessarily no longer really interested in these ideas. I mention this well-known process so as to clearly show the difference between what was happening to us and what happens to all reasonable beings in the modern world. We had gone beyond [*dépassé*] the idea of sending a report-confession to the Quaker lady and, at the same time, the idea he had had, that it was up to me to write it—but this is the most difficult point to speak of—the point on which we were in perfect agreement since our almost silent quarrel had happened. Here it is, or rather I am there, but I cannot manage to stay there in a way so as to understand clearly. It escaped me, as if my mind were turning in a dance around a landscape without stopping. A confession by Chalier to the Quaker lady to explain his false declaration—I had believed this was possible, I admit! And I would be the one to write it, I had accepted this, I had already taken some mental notes. Well, there would be no report-confession, that had been decided. No visit to the committee lady. Those intentions were outmoded [*dépassées*], I would say—it's a question I teach—like classical tragedy; but no, that would seem to say we had good reasons for moving [*passer*] on to another means for getting out of it, and I do not see any such good reason. The intentions had been overtaken [*dépassées*] in a far simpler way: by movement, the true, the only movement—by disappearing. And there is one thing that I understood clearly, perhaps the only thing in this whole race to nowhere: disappearing was effectively the only true response that Chalier could make to the committee, to the entire government, to society as a whole. But to disappear is not to respond to a precise question (the false oath)! There is no relation [*rapport*] between the two; they are two different orders of things! That is what I also assert—and if I don't just leave things there, that's because I am not Chalier, merely someone close to him, and because I can offer an explanation to the extent that my situation is not altogether his—it will thus be only an approximate explanation. All the same, I am also aware of what was absolutely clear in Chalier's story, or rather absolutely direct. Without that, I could not even begin to defend him. But equally because of that, I realize that my "plea for the defense" is really nothing but a stopgap when compared with what is obvious and needs no defending by anyone.

How right Chalier was when he said that it was my responsibility to write the report! He was more right than he thought (for he spoke in anger and did not remember when I reminded him of it). I do not have to write this report, for I find
I am myself the report, the relation [*rapport*] between my Chalier (if he read this,
what a wicked little smile he would have!) and the others, beginning with their
various committees. . . . " (145–48)

   At the moment he says "I am myself the *rapport*," a *rapport* that had
just seemed impossible, the impossible itself, the word *rapport* changes
meaning, even as it remains, on the spot, what it is. It turns on itself like
a trope, in the manner of a strophe. It is far from exhausted by its value
as "report to be written on the subject of," testimony, countersigned confession, and so forth. The word *rapport* gets charged with a far graver and
more impossible mission. It *becomes*, but in the past it *will have become*
the relation to others, a relation that is just as impossible, a relation without relation, Blanchot would say, the relation between persons, between
someone, his friend, and others, the anonymous crowd or the institutional authority before whom one must appear, co-appear—or disappear.
Here then is the narrator-friend-witness-countersignatory, the acolyte
who does not accompany, accusing himself again—this time of playing on
words, on the word *rapport*, but not only on words:

What am I saying with that! I am playing on words and things at the same time.
And after all! There are days when I am tempted to run to Washington, to search
out the lady, if she is still in the same position (she's probably been promoted),
or her replacement, and to say to her: It's about the Chalier affair, five years ago.
I am the report that you were waiting for, the report-confession! I will tell all I
know, and then I will say: "Now I efface myself; from here on, I know nothing
more, there is something else." What would they do? (148)

The Truth Without Us:
"Which Father are we talking about?"

Narrator, witness, the friend has thus himself become, with and without
a translatable play on words, an *impossible report/relation*, the impossible-
rapport in the triple sense of narrative or administrative report, of confession ("report-confession"), and of relation to the other, between one and
the other, one and others, the ones and the others. The anacoluthon has
not only operated, to dissociate, disjoin, interrupt, at the heart of the

word "rapport," at the very inside of language and discourse, as does a trope in general. The anacoluthon has also done its work in things themselves, if one can say that, here in the "subjects of the action," across and beyond the grammatical "I." Transmutation of the whole "rapport," of all the bearings [*portées*] and all the analogies of this *rapport*. This transmutation is neither active nor passive; it takes place like the obscure alchemy that precipitates out an "us." In the novel and no doubt everywhere that an "us" takes form, always in the shelter of/ from [*à l'abri de*] some sober and inevitable perjury (I mean to let this "in the shelter of/from" be delivered over to the dark powers of the equivocal; they are what I am talking about: we guard ourselves from the perjury that we inhabit, that inhabits us and keeps watch over us at the very moment we think we have posted guards against it, at the instant we are warned, by the perjury itself, against the betrayed truth).

Here, between the narrator and Hölderlin in America, there is now this *us* of the perjury. The perjuring-perjured *us* maintains from now on a strange relation to the truth of the true. A truth that, by reason of this disappearance of the subject, is there *without us* who are I no longer know where most of the time. "Yes, yes, that is true," says a narrator who is more than ever destined to the disavowing avowal, to denegation, to perjury, to the most devoted abjuration. Unable as I am, in the limits of this essay, to reconstitute the whole weave in which I must cut and select, I ask the reader not to measure the richness of this book, *Le Parjure*, by the shreds extracted from it, in a supplemental betrayal, for the needs of the current demonstration. An immense work remains to be done, I am convinced, beginning with the "impossible" translation of this book into English. The passage that I lift out here (the appearance of the *us*, of a desperate *us*, the "now I can say *us*") says, above all, something about finitude, the failure of memory, the amnesia essential to the movement of truth for finite and mortal beings, "finished in advance," as the narrator says. Earlier we proposed recognizing this finitude at the origin of the anacoluthic interruption, of discontinuity and divisibility in general, of the disjunction that makes *relation* at once possible and impossible.

We are much too small, much too finished in advance, much too dead. I had begun to understand this during the first stop, but it was in the form of a kind of despair, all muddled with fatigue. Now I can say *us*. I caught up with it precisely there, in the despair into which we had fallen. What a distressing subjection, to have to vacillate between happiness and unhappiness, without end, and more and more dry and hollow with oneself, in this movement of a pendulum. One has to believe it, since no exception has ever been found: this movement continues until immobilized by exhaustion. Yes, yes, it is true. The child already knew this when he looked at his father from the other side of the table, in the dining room at Gijon.

If the guests, if the gentleman and the lady sitting at the same table had awakened *us* at that moment by bursting into laughter and saying, "But here is our little orphan!"—well, then I would not be here trying to master a fantastic truth, which is constantly changing in some silly detail or another, silly but true in its manner, the historical manner, that of father Chalier. (163–64)

To what do these final allusions refer ("Yes, yes, it is true. The child already knew this when he looked at his father from the other side of the table, in the dining room at Gijon"), as well as the "we are . . . much too dead"? They recall and follow a passage that shows the perjurer (Stéphane) as symbolic *orphan* of a father whose honesty consisted in *knowing himself to be dead*. And the son knew this knowledge, he knew himself to know that his father knew himself to be dead, dead in his lifetime, dead in advance. Stéphane was constituted, he knew himself to be instituted, instructed, formed by such a knowledge of knowing, by such a knowing-oneself knowing this knowledge of self of his dead father (the death in advance of the said father); he knew it and he followed this knowledge that followed him everywhere. This knowledge pursued him in advance, chasing him as far as his movement of "Hölderlinian" flight to America, as far as the conjugal perjury. I am, I follow this knowledge of the knowing-oneself dead of my father, he might have said, and everything follows from there.

Upon arriving in Washington, the next morning, I knew in any case this: you remember the town where the Chalier family used to spend their vacations in Spain, at Gijon? Little Chalier begging with the other kids at the exit from the station? *Orphan!* In the dining room, that evening, the father was as always, as he had been lately, as he was at present. Stéphane Chalier, at ten years old, already knew what today, in the carefreeness of his release from the clinic, he had thought he was inventing. I don't mean to say that he invented, for the pleasure of talking in the breeze of the highway, the fact that his father had been extraordinarily honest; that was pure truth, of which the ten-year-old child had no knowledge— but this honesty consisted in knowing himself to be, he told me—did he really pronounce the word?—*dead*. I made him say that, a moment ago, and there I've underscored the word. Now I believe he said this word once, in a low but distinct voice, and right after he laughed his little laugh that sets him apart from everything. (161–62)[23]

This *us* will never be the *us* reached by a phenomenology of mind in the figure of a *knowing-itself* of absolute knowledge. Basically, the anacoluthon interrupts forever the relation to self, the possibility of a relation to self, or even of an absolute and absolutely absolved confession of self, a report-confession. We are not present to the truth of this *us* and when we are present, the truth is not there. No one says this better, more consistently, than the acolyte, a little after this extraordinary ellipsis (ellipsis on the very eclipse of the "us"). This ellipsis plays on a discreet and once again untranslatable homonymy between the *suis* of the verb *être* ("to be") and the *suis* of the verb *suivre* ("to follow"). (Once more, for lack of space, I extract it brutally from a long development that the interested reader can reconstitute if he wishes):

Even their death is false. When the father died, in the time of the Father, what a sudden abyss, what distress, and then what presence of the Father. . . .

Yes, I know, you are feeling a little pity for us. Which Father are we talking about? Be precise! . . . To whom can we say it, since those we love are forever dispersed? Certainly not to the Quaker lady! The *report* is excluded once and for all. Oh eternal life, to whom? First of all, the question is posed only for me, in this moment; it is a fact, I am alone, I was before meeting Chalier, and in this moment Chalier is far from this country. . . . No one followed him, except possibly me at present, who am [*suis*] also with him, I said it: *us*. . . . We face the truth, from time to time; ten, fifteen years can pass before a movement puts us once more face to face with it, not necessarily in a flash of light; it can be darkest night, there may be a smoking blaze—and walls of rocks and walls of books—nothing can stand in the way: thus, it is not just from time to time that the truth is there, but we only who are I don't know where most of the time. (167–74)[24]

Yes, "Much too dead"

Le Parjure is a story of the truth, in sum, of the truth without knowledge, without absolute knowledge—*this* story of *this* truth, of the eclipse of the *us* in which is produced its light, the remaining [*restance*] without substance of its remains. Toward the end of the book: "They were very small marks of the truth, the minimal trace, almost nothing. Today I am no longer laughing—I need all my attention to distinguish what separates this 'almost nothing' from 'nothing'" (221–22).

Where ethics and the law demand what is owed them, where judges would call for some sanction, the narrator takes the responsibility to respond: "In sum, it was punishment for carelessness and lack of foresight rather than for perjury—and the punishment came down to very little, since we are alive at this moment, like everybody" (222).

For us, for me who is writing and for you who are reading, they are dead today, both of them. The two wives survive. So do we. Alive, they still used to say, in a single voice, which remains that of the narrator, the witness, the friend, the acolyte signing and countersigning with what should have been the same seal:

Yes, like you, like everybody, as much you like. You show me the seal that is on all the living, that covers us all exactly; each word, each gesture, the least polite smile allows me to touch it, and I contradict nothing. Chalier and I, we never thought to escape from this seal: we are docile living beings, and that is why what we used to say made us laugh; it was our way of bearing what happened to us—the almost nothing, the nothing: how can one not laugh about it? We were out of danger, he said. (Ibid.)

The anacoluthon introduces a maddening irregularity; it dislocates, disperses, denegates, disavows in advance every "us" and every "you" we have just read, the "us" of the couple of friends and the "you" (namely, "us" the reader or supposed addressees, sometimes included in, sometimes excluded from the "us" of the acolytes). How to decide who is "us" and "you"? Rereading them, I emphasize these personal pronouns, I underscore every "us" and "you," including the "he" that sends everybody back, first of all, the one who is speaking, to his or her absolute solitude—within and in spite of the "you"-"us."

Yes like *you*, like everybody, as much *you* like. *You* show me the seal that is on all the living, that covers *us* all exactly; each word, each gesture, the least polite smile allows me to touch it, and I contradict nothing. Chalier and I, *we* never thought to escape from this seal: *we* are docile living beings, and that is why what *we* used to say made *us* laugh; it was our way of bearing what happened to *us*—the almost nothing, the nothing: how can one not laugh about it? *We* were out of danger, *he* said.

Confirmation, seal, signature: near the very last ending of the novel, the narrator declares: "For me to be able still to say *us*, I had to remain alone, at present" (242).

The last paragraphs break with *he, she*, or *us*, with the third and the first persons. This is so as to address now a second person plural who, this time, does not intend us, the readers, addressees, interpreters (or even the other friends—or enemies—of Chalier alias Paul de Man). The narrator apostrophizes the couple for and by the love of whom all this has happened, "you," Judith and Stéphane: "Judith, Stéphane, listen to me" (245).

None of this would have happened without this couple, without the event of this encounter, the encounter between Judith and Stéphane before the encounter with the narrator himself. Consequently, everything becomes indebted to what has, there, irreducibly, undeniably, ineffaceably, *come about*: this is the true. Everything becomes indebted to this true. Am I forcing things by interpreting in this, precisely, *symbolic* manner the fact that the last pages of the book, very close to the ultimate signature, say something about the *debt*, precisely, a debt that remains unpaid by the narrator even as it is a question of the money that he was supposed, that he ought to have lent them or given them, the money that he owed them for having failed in his duty to give it to them?

The last scene of the perjury is a scene of asked-for forgiveness. As always—and this is why the seminar to which I referred at the beginning never dissociated, from its title on, perjury and forgiveness. Speaking to the original couple, the couple who were at the origin of the story, the couple of the perjury, the narrator asks forgiveness for an unpaid debt. They had asked him for money before leaving, and he says to them: "Judith, Stéphane, listen to me. Earlier, faster, I couldn't. Money, quite simply. I had sent you three-fourths of all I had available. . . . I should have. . . ." (245).

Forgive me for not having done what I should have done, in sum, he says, he says to them, he says to us, we say to us.

Everything then seems to become descriptive again, realistic, "matter-of-fact" in order to depict the last moments before the final separation, the calm wrenching apart of the departure. The couple has left the island. The last paragraph names a kind of *idiocy* of man, of the two men who have understood nothing, the two acolytes, the perjurer and his witness, sleeping in the same body in some way, whereas the woman, meanwhile, the second wife keeps watch, is stirring about, making decisions, and so on. One feels an accusation on the horizon: a couple of men united as one, "a single idiot," brothers, in sum, seems to denounce the woman.

An impassive and at bottom inaccessible woman. The other, the only one to decide, when you get down to it. It is she who, when the last word is addressed to her, keeps it, this last word. She is its only guardian and the only survivor. Note that she keeps watch; it's her turn to keep watch. "At the end of the night." "Without saying a word."

You left Halifax without seeing me again, and without telling me where you were going. It is you, Judith, who acted, without consulting anyone, without hesitating, as you did on the island when you left to go get the boat, although nothing had been decided yet and it was merely your turn to keep watch, at the end of the night. And we were sleeping, Stéphane and me, like a single idiot, and it was the children that you meant to awaken first. Quick, leaving everything behind, but not your bits of wood, your sea eagle, your dolls—quick, climb into the boat, without saying a word, and you so calm. (244–45)

P. S. Signature Event Context

A last accompanying note for all these acolytes who do not accompany. As you will no doubt have noticed, they are all, by profession, professors. Like us. All these professors *have*, they learn and teach the fatal experience of perjury—within the profession, within the profession of faith, within the sworn faith. I am speaking of the men and not the women: Paul de Man, Henri Thomas, Stéphane Chalier, Father Chalier, the narrator, Hillis Miller, myself. All professors.

For these reasons, and a few others, it would be consistent (consistent with the responsibility of a signature) to recall once again, however briefly, the *academic* context in which this narrative will have had to be inscribed. Including this text whose narrative framework is more or less obvious. In the seminar to which I have made more than one allusion, it was a question not only of Hölderlin in America, of perjury and forgiveness in America (North and South, because we also evoked Clinton and Pinochet and his sons, etc.). It was also a matter of leading things back to the place par excellence of perjury: the family, marriage, the sexual relation according to sworn faith, the relation that *is* or *is not* sexual, depending on how, as Clinton said one day, you say or you understand "what 'is' is." Clinton and Hölderlin in America are accused of having publicly perjured themselves, before a committee, before the law. But before being public and brought before positive law, their perjury concerned, in its content, a domestic and private betrayal, namely, infidelity to a first sacrament of marriage. While reading Kafka's *Letter to the Father,* we linked the question of forgiveness to that of the impossible marriage, on the one hand, and to literature, on the other. Through the sacrifice of Isaac, we followed a sort of rupture of marriage, an infidelity to Sarah, to whom Abraham says not a word at the moment of taking the life of his son, their son. This is also what happens in *Le Parjure*, where the relation to Father Chalier seems determinant, where marriage seems at once too possible (twice) and thus impossible since it was forgotten, denegated, taken lightly, the question of the twice perjured "us" that we followed between Hölderlin and his witness-acolyte thus being posed first of all between the two members of the conjugal couple. They do not manage to say *us* with a sufficiently sworn *us*, so that the innocence or the offense might be shared. By following the rupture of his engagement with Regina, we could have found in Kierkegaard interminable discussions of this impossible "us," be it the us of a common repentance. The madness of marriage, therefore. The madness of the oath, as we were saying above.

If one recalls what Kafka's *Letter to the Father* said about marriage as "madness," one will be equally struck by certain Kierkegaardian echoes. Kierkegaard excludes shared repentance—one always repents alone—even while declaring that, if it commands one to marry, then Christianity is a form of madness. The logic of the argument: One cannot suffer *together* from an unhappy love. One cannot say "us" while declaring "us" to be unhappy together from an unhappy love. One cannot say, it has no sense: *We* are unhappy from the same unhappiness, *we* are living together an unhappy love, *we* repent.

> To wish to proceed along that path in union would be to repeat that dreadful incongruity . . . that in union we should mourn an unhappy love. That cannot be. What likeness is there between her sorrow and mine, what fellowship between guilt and innocence . . . ? I can sorrow in my way; if she is to sorrow, she must do it on her own account. . . . it is unethical for her and me to sorrow thus in union [*sorge*: that we share the same care, the same affliction, the same solicitude, the same grief, all possible meanings of the word *sorg*, which plays in Kierkegaard, as in Heidegger, a determining role].[25]

Is this not the fundamental logic of "Hölderlin in America"? If one credits him with having considered his first marriage or his first love unhappy, it was broken off by itself and he could no longer share even this unhappiness with Ottilia, the first wife. Everything that happens before the public law, especially in a foreign country, then becomes secondary, superficial with regard to this private, secret, singular truth. The first commitment warranted forgetting or distraction when new love arose: "Just imagine, I was not thinking about it."

Elsewhere Kierkegaard also writes: "The life of such a sinner is rigorous. For example, he cannot marry. Or should he perhaps fall in love and unite with a girl in order to repent together, this should be the significance of the marriage. And if one's only passion is repentance—then to give a child life, a child who should innocently rejoice in life and have the right to do so. No, he will say, if Christianity commanded marriage it would be madness."[26]

This Christian marriage, this madness, would consist in giving the nuptial consecration its sense as the constitution of an us, of an alliance of repentance, of a community in expiation, the sworn faith of two sinners who unite to ask for forgiveness together, in the unique passion of repentance for a sin that, if it is serious, must be mortal. Marriage would be a machine of death, a machine for giving oneself death even as one pretends to give oneself life, to give oneself to life, and to give life to one's children. This madness of the alliance, in the form of Christian marriage, would be at the center of the whole question of perjury and forgiveness.

Doesn't this happen each time a Christian marriage takes place? Each time a constitution, whether democratic or secular in appearance, takes up the burden of the madness of a Christian marriage? Each time politics is married with Christianity? Conclusion: one ought *never* to get married, *whether or not one is Christian*. Marriage is a madness in Christian lands, but it has no absolute sacramental sense outside of Christianity. Or yet again, which comes down to the same thing, one ought never to marry more than once, like Hölderlin in America. One does not marry twice, and if one can marry twice, that's because marriage is impossible or destined to perjury, to the impossibility of repenting together. Whether it takes place once or twice, marriage would be that madness. Impossible to decide if it is more mad to lose one's senses in a Christian land or a non-Christian land. But it is perhaps even more impossible today to decide where the frontiers of Christian lands are drawn.

§ 4
The University Without Condition

This will no doubt be *like* a profession of faith: the profession of faith of a professor who would act *as if* he were nevertheless asking your permission to be unfaithful or a traitor to his habitual practice.

Before I even begin to follow in fact a torturous itinerary, here is the thesis, in direct and broadly simple terms, that I am submitting to you for discussion. It will be distributed among a series of propositions. In truth, it will be less a thesis, or even a hypothesis, than a declarative engagement, an appeal in the form of a profession of faith: faith in the university and, within the university, faith in the Humanities of tomorrow.

The title proposed for this lecture signifies first that the modern university *should* be *without condition*.[1] By "modern university," let us understand the one whose European model, after a rich and complex medieval history, has become prevalent, which is to say "classic," over the last two centuries in states of a democratic type. This university demands and ought to be granted in principle, besides what is called academic freedom, an *unconditional* freedom to question and to assert, or even, going still further, the right to say publicly all that is required by research, knowledge, and thought concerning the *truth*. However enigmatic it may be, the reference to truth remains fundamental enough to be found, along with light (*lux*), on the symbolic insignias of more than one university.

The university *professes* the truth, and that is its profession. It declares and promises an unlimited commitment to the truth.

No doubt the status of and the changes in the value of truth can be discussed ad infinitum (truth as adequation or truth as revelation, truth as the object of theoretico-constative discourses or as poetico-performative events, and so forth). But these are discussed, precisely, *in* the university and in departments that belong to the Humanities.

Let us leave these enormous questions suspended for the moment. We will underscore merely by way of anticipation that this immense question of truth and of light, of the Enlightenment—*Aufklärung, Lumières, Illuminismo*—has always been linked to the question of man, to a concept of that which is proper to man, on which concept were founded both Humanism and the historical idea of the Humanities. Today the renewed and reelaborated declaration of "human rights" (1948) or, as we say in French, "des Droits de l'homme," the rights of man, and the institution of the juridical concept of "crime against humanity" (1945) form the horizon of *mondialisation* and of the international law that is supposed to keep watch over it. (I am keeping the French word *mondialisation* in preference to "globalization" or *Globalisierung* so as to maintain a reference to the world—*monde, Welt, mundus*—which is neither the globe nor the cosmos.) The concept of man, of what is proper to man, of human rights, of crimes against the humanity of man, organizes, as we know, such a *mondialisation* or worldwide-ization.

This *mondialisation* wishes to be a humanization.

If this concept of man seems both indispensable and always problematic, well—and this will be one of the motifs of my thesis, one of my theses in the form of profession of faith—it can be discussed or reelaborated, as such and without conditions, without presuppositions, only within the space of the *new* Humanities.

I will try to specify what I mean by the "new" Humanities. But whether these discussions are critical or deconstructive, everything that concerns the question and the history of truth, in its relation to the question of man, of what is proper to man, of human rights, of crimes against humanity, and so forth, all of this must in principle find its space of *unconditional* discussion and, without presupposition, its legitimate space of research and reelaboration, *in* the university and, within the university, above all *in* the Humanities. Not so that it may enclose itself there, but, on the contrary, so as to find the best access to a new public space transformed by new techniques of communication, information, archivization, and knowledge production. (Although I must leave this aside, one of the serious questions that are posed, and posed here, between the university and the politico-economic outside of its public space is the question of the marketplace in publishing and the role it plays in archivization, evaluation, and legitimation of academic research.)

The horizon of truth or of what is proper to man is certainly not a very determinable limit. But neither is that of the university and of the Humanities.

This university without conditions does not, *in fact*, exist, as we know only too well. Nevertheless, in principle and in conformity with its declared vocation, its professed essence, it should remain an ultimate place of critical resistance—and more than critical—to all the powers of dogmatic and unjust appropriation.

When I say "more than critical," I have in mind "deconstructive." (Why not just say it directly and without wasting time?) I am referring to the right to deconstruction as an unconditional right to ask critical questions not only about the history of the concept of man, but about the history even of the notion of critique, about the form and the authority of the question,[2] about the interrogative form of thought. For this implies the right to do it *affirmatively* and *performatively*,[3] that is, by producing events (for example, by writing) and by giving rise to singular *oeuvres* (which up until now has not been the purview of either the classical or the modern Humanities). With the event of thought constituted by such *oeuvres*, it would be a matter of making something happen to this concept of truth or of humanity, without necessarily betraying it, that is, to the concept that forms the charter and the profession of faith of all universities.

This principle of unconditional resistance is a right that the university itself should at the same time reflect, invent, and pose, whether it does so through its law faculties or in the new Humanities capable of working on these questions of right and of law—in other words, and again why not say it without detour, the Humanities capable of taking on the tasks of deconstruction, beginning with the deconstruction of their own history and their own axioms.

Consequence of this thesis: such an unconditional resistance could oppose the university to a great number of powers, for example, to state powers (and thus to the power of the nation-state and to its phantasm of indivisible sovereignty, which indicates how the university might be in advance not just cosmopolitan, but universal, extending beyond worldwide citizenship and the nation-state in general), to economic powers (to corporations and to national and international capital), to the powers of the media, ideological, religious and cultural powers, and so forth—in short, to all the powers that limit democracy to come.

The university should thus also be the place in which nothing is beyond question, not even the current and determined figure of democracy, not even the traditional idea of critique, meaning theoretical critique, and not even the authority of the "question" form, of thinking as "questioning." That is why I spoke without delay and without disguise of deconstruction.

Here, then, is what we could call, in order to call upon it, the unconditional university or the university without condition: the principial right to say everything, even if it be under the heading of fiction and the experimentation of knowledge, and the right to say it publicly, to publish it. This reference to public space will remain the link that affiliates the new Humanities to the age of Enlightenment. It distinguishes the university institution from other institutions founded on the right or the duty to say everything, for example, religious confession and even psychoanalytic "free association." But it is also what fundamentally links the university, and above all the Humanities, to what is called literature, in the European and modern sense of the term, as the right to say everything publicly, or to keep it secret, if only in the form of fiction. This allusion to confession, which is very close to the profession of faith, could link my remarks to the analysis of what is happening today, on the worldwide scene, that resembles a universal process of confession, avowal, repentance, expiation, and asked-for forgiveness. One could cite innumerable examples, day after day. But whether we are talking about very ancient crimes or yesterday's crimes, about slavery, the Shoah, apartheid, or even the violent acts of the Inquisition (concerning which the Pope announced not long ago that they ought to give rise to an examination of conscience), repentance is always carried out with reference to the very recent juridical concept of "crime against humanity."

Because we are preparing to articulate together Profession, the Profession of faith, and Confession, I note in passing and in parentheses (for this would require a long development) that in the fourteenth century it was possible to organize the confession of sins according to social and professional categories. The *Summa Astesana* from 1317 prescribes that the penitent in confession be interrogated with reference to his socio-professional status: princes about justice; knights about plunder; merchants, officials, artisans, and laborers about perjury, fraud, lying, theft, and so forth; bourgeois and citizens in general about usury and mortgages; peasants about envy and theft, and so forth.[4]

One must insist on this again: if this unconditionality, in principle and *de jure*, constitutes the invincible force of the university, it has never been in effect. By reason of this abstract and hyperbolic invincibility, by reason of its very impossibility, this unconditionality exposes as well the weakness or the vulnerability of the university. It exhibits its impotence, the fragility of its defenses against all the powers that command it, besiege it, and attempt to appropriate it. Because it is a stranger to power, because it is heterogeneous to the principle of power, the university is also without any power of its own.

That is why we are speaking here of the *university without condition*.

I say "the university" because I am distinguishing here, *stricto sensu*, the university from all research institutions that are in the service of economic goals and interests of all sorts, without being granted in principle the independence of the university; I also say "without condition" to let one hear the connotation of "without power" and "without defense." Because it is absolutely independent, the university is also an exposed, tendered citadel, to be taken, often destined to capitulate without condition, to surrender unconditionally.

Yes, it gives itself up, it sometimes puts itself up for sale, it risks being simply something to occupy, take over, buy; it risks becoming a branch office of conglomerates and corporations. This is today, in the United States and throughout the world, a major political stake: to what extent does the organization of research and teaching have to be supported, that is, directly or indirectly controlled, let us euphemistically say "sponsored," by commercial and industrial interests? By this logic, as we know, the Humanities are often held hostage to departments of pure or applied science in which are concentrated the supposedly profitable investments of capital foreign to the academic world.

A question is then posed and it is not merely economic, juridical, ethical, or political: Can the university (and if so, how?) affirm an unconditional independence, can it claim a sort of *sovereignty* without ever risking the worst, namely, by reason of the impossible abstraction of this sovereign independence, being forced to give up and capitulate without condition, to let itself be taken over and bought at any price?

What is needed, then, is not only a principle of resistance, but a force of resistance—and of dissidence. The deconstruction of the concept of unconditional sovereignty is doubtless necessary and under way, for this is the heritage of a barely secularized theology. In the most visible case of the supposed sovereignty of nation-states, but also elsewhere (for it is at home, and indispensable, everywhere, in the concepts of subject, citizen, freedom, responsibility, the people, etc.), the value of sovereignty is today in thorough decomposition. But one must beware that this necessary deconstruction does not compromise, not too much, the university's claim to independence, that is, to a certain very particular form of sovereignty that I will try to specify later.

This would be what is at stake in political decisions and strategies. This stake will remain on the horizon of the hypotheses or professions of faith that I submit to your reflection. How can one deconstruct the history (and first of all the academic history) of the principle of indivisible sovereignty even as one claims the unconditional right to say everything, or not to say anything, and to pose all the deconstructive questions that are called for on the subject of man, of sovereignty, of the right to say everything, therefore of literature and democracy, of the worldwide-ization under way, of its techno-economic and confessional aspects, and so forth?

I will not claim that, in the torment threatening the university today, and within it some disciplines more than others, this force of resistance, this assumed freedom to say everything in the public space, has its unique or privileged place in what is called the Humanities—a concept whose definition it will be advisable to refine, deconstruct, and adjust, beyond a tradition that must also be cultivated. However, this principle of unconditionality *presents itself*, originally and above all, in the Humanities. It has an originary and privileged place of *presentation*, of manifestation, of safekeeping in the Humanities. It has there its space of discussion and of reelaboration as well. All this passes as much by way of literature and languages (that is, the sciences called the sciences of man and culture) as by way of the nondiscursive arts, by way of law and philosophy, by way of critique, questioning, and, beyond critical philosophy and questioning, by way of deconstruction—where it is a matter of nothing less than rethinking the concept of man, the figure of humanity in general, and singularly the one presupposed by what we have called, in the university, for the last few centuries, the Humanities. From this point of view at least, deconstruction (and I am not at all embarrassed to say so and even to claim) has its privileged place in the university and in the

Humanities as the place of irredentist resistance or even, analogically, as a sort of principle of civil disobedience, even of dissidence in the name of a superior law and a justice of thought.

Let us call here *thought* that which at times commands, according to a law above all laws, the *justice* of this resistance or this dissidence. It is also what puts deconstruction to work or inspires it *as* justice.[5] We would have to open a space without limit for this law, this right founded on a justice that surpasses it and thus authorize ourselves to deconstruct all the determined figures that this sovereign unconditionality may have assumed throughout history.

For this, we will have to enlarge and reelaborate the concept of the Humanities. To my mind, it is no longer a matter simply of the conservative and humanist concept with which most often the Humanities and their ancient canons are associated—canons which I believe ought to be protected at any price. This new concept of the Humanities, even as it remains faithful to its tradition, should include law, "legal studies," as well as what is called in this country, where this formation originated, "theory" (an original articulation of literary theory, philosophy, linguistics, psychoanalysis, and so forth), but also, of course, in all these places, deconstructive practices. And we will have to distinguish carefully here between, on the one hand, the principle of freedom, autonomy, resistance, disobedience, or dissidence, the principle that is coextensive with the whole field of academic knowledge and, on the other hand, its privileged place of *presentation*, of reelaboration, and of thematic discussion, which in my opinion would more properly belong to the Humanities, but to the transformed Humanities. Why insist on linking all of this not only to the question of literatures, to a democratic institution that is called literature or literary fiction, to a certain simulacrum and a certain "as if," but also to the question of the profession and of its future? It is because throughout a history of *travail* (usually translated as "work" or "labor," but I will leave it in French for the moment), which is not only trade or craft, then a history of trade or craft, which is not always profession, then a history of the profession, which is not always that of professor, I would like to connect this problematic of the university without condition to a pledge, a commitment, a promise, an act of faith, a declaration of faith, a profession of faith. In an original way, this profession of faith articulates faith to knowledge in the university, above all in the place of the self-presentation of unconditionality that will go by the name "Humanities."

To link in a certain way faith to knowledge, faith in knowledge, is to articulate movements that could be called performative with constative, descriptive, or theoretical movements. A profession of faith, a commitment, a promise, an assumed responsibility, all that calls not upon discourses of knowledge but upon performative discourses that produce the event of which they speak.

One will therefore have to ask oneself what "professing" means. What is one doing when, performatively, one professes, but also when one exercises a profession, and singularly the profession of professor? I will thus rely often and at length on Austin's now classic distinction between performative speech acts and constative speech acts. This distinction will have been a great event in this century—and it will first have been an academic event. It will have taken place *in* the university. In a certain way, it is the Humanities that made it come about and that explored its resources; it is to and through the Humanities that this happened, and its consequences are incalculable. Even while recognizing the power, the legitimacy, and the necessity of the distinction between constative and performative, I have often had occasion, after a certain point, not to put it back in question but to analyze its presuppositions and to complicate them.[6] I will do so once again today, but this time from another point of view, and after having made this pair of concepts count for a lot, I will end up designating a place where it fails—and must fail.

This place will be precisely *what happens*, what comes to pass, that at which one arrives or that which happens to us, arrives to us, the event, the place of the taking-place—and which cares as little about the performative, the performative power, as it does about the constative. And this can happen, this can arrive in and by the Humanities.

Now I am going to begin, at once at the end and at the beginning. For I began with the end *as if* it were the beginning.

I

As if the end of work were at the origin of the world.

Yes, "as if," I indeed said "as if. . . . "

At the same time as a reflection on the history of work, that is, *travail*, I will also no doubt propose to you a meditation on the "as," the "as such," the "as if."

And perhaps on a politics of the virtual.

Not a virtual politics but a politics *of the* virtual in the cyberspace or cyberworld of worldwide-ization. One of the mutations that affect the place and the nature of university work today is a certain delocalizing virtualization of the space of communication, discussion, publication, archivization. It is not the virtualization that is absolutely novel in its structure, for as soon as there is a trace, there is also some virtualization; these are the abc's of deconstruction. What is new, quantitatively, is the acceleration of the rhythm, the extent, and the powers of capitalization of such a virtuality. Hence the necessity to rethink the concepts of the possible and the impossible. This new technical "stage" of virtualization (computerization, digitalization, virtually immediate worldwide-ization of readability, telework, and so forth) destabilizes, as we have all experienced, the university habitat. It upsets the university's topology, disturbs everything that organizes the places defining it, namely, the territory of its fields and its disciplinary frontiers as well as its places of discussion, its field of battle, its *Kampfplatz*, its theoretical battlefield—and the communitary structure of its "campus." Where is to be found the communitary *place* and the social bond of a "campus" in the cyberspatial age of the computer, of tele-work, and of the World Wide Web? Where does the exercise of democracy, albeit a university democracy, have its *place* in what Mark Poster calls "CyberDemocracy"?[7] One has the clear sense that, more radically, what has been upset in this way is the topology of the event, the experience of the singular taking place.

What, then, are we doing when we say "as if"?

Notice that I have not yet said, "*It is* as if the end of work were at the origin of the world." I have not said anything whatsoever and I have not said it in a principal clause. I left suspended, I abandoned to its interruption a strange subordinate clause ("as if the end of work were at the origin of the world"), as if I wanted to let an example of the "as if" work all by itself, outside any context, to attract your attention. What are we doing when we say "as if"? What does an "if" do? We are acting *as if* we were responding to at least one of several of the possibilities that I am going to begin to enumerate—or to more than one at a time.

1. *First possibility*: By saying "as if," are we abandoning ourselves to the arbitrary, to dream, to imagination, to utopia, to hypothesis? Everything I am preparing to say will tend to show that the answer cannot be so simple.

2. Or, *second possibility*: With this "as if," are we putting to work certain

types of judgment, for example, the "reflective judgments" that Kant regularly said operated "as if" (*als ob*) an understanding contained or comprehended the unity of the variety of empirical laws or "*as if* it were a lucky chance favoring our design [*gleich* als ob *es ein glücklicher unsre Absicht begünstigender Zufall wäre*]."[8] In Kantian discourse, the gravity, seriousness, and irreducible necessity of the "as if" points to nothing less than the finality of nature, that is, a finality whose concept, Kant tells us, is among the most unusual and difficult to pin down. For, he says, it is neither a *concept of nature* nor a *concept of freedom*. Therefore, although Kant does not say as much in this context, and for good reason, this "as if" would itself be something like an agent of deconstructive ferment, since it in some way exceeds and comes close to disqualifying the two orders that are so often distinguished and opposed, the order of nature and the order of freedom.

The opposition disconcerted by a certain "as if" is the very one that organizes all our fundamental concepts and all the oppositions in which they are determined and in which they determine, precisely, what is proper to man, the humanity of man (*phusis/tekhnē*, *phusis/nomos*, nature *versus* humanity, and, within this humanity, which is also that of the Humanities, one finds sociality, law, history, politics, community, and so forth, all set within the same oppositions). Kant also explains to us, in effect, that the "as if" plays a decisive role in the coherent organization of our experience.

Now, Kant is also the philosopher who attempted, in an extremely complex fashion, both to justify and to limit the role of the Humanities in teaching, culture, or the critique of taste.[9] This was recalled and analyzed in a magisterial fashion by two of my friends and colleagues to whom I owe a lot: Sam Weber in what is in many ways an inaugural book, one that is very dear to me, *Institution and Interpretation*,[10] followed recently by a remarkable article, "The Future of the Humanities,"[11] and Peggy Kamuf, who treats the same text of Kant in her admirable book *The Division of Literature, or the University in Deconstruction*.[12] Sam Weber and Peggy Kamuf say decisive things, and I refer you to them, concerning what is happening between deconstruction, the history of the university, and the Humanities. What I am trying to explore here would be another avenue on the same site, another path through the same landscape. And if my trajectory appears different here, I will doubtless cross their tracks at more than one intersection—for example, in the reference to Kant. There is nothing surprising in the fact that the *Third Critique* comes back with such insistence in the United States in all the discourses on the institutions and the disciplines tied to the Humanities, on the problems of professionalization that are posed there. Kant has a whole set of propositions on this subject, notably on work, craft, and the arts, both the liberal arts and the salaried, mercenary arts, but also on the conflict of the faculties—something I discussed many years ago in "Economimesis" and "Mochlos."[13]

This recurrent appeal to Kant may be especially remarked, in fact, in the United States, where, for reasons that should be analyzed, the term "Humanities" has known a particular history and still appears at this century's end in the figure of a problem, with a semantic energy, a conflictual presence and resonance that it has doubtless never had or that it lost in Europe and no doubt everywhere else in the world where American culture is not yet prevalent. There are certainly interwoven reasons for this, in particular that of the effects of the worldwide-ization under way, which always passes in an unavoidable and visible fashion by way of the United States, its political, techno-economic, and techno-scientific power.

3. Finally, *third possibility*: Does not a certain "as if" mark, in thousands of ways, the structure and the mode of being of all objects belonging to the academic field called the Humanities, whether they be the Humanities of yesterday or today or tomorrow? I will not hasten for the moment to reduce these "objects" to fictions, simulacra, or works of art, while acting as if we already had at our disposal reliable concepts of fiction, of art, or of the work. But if one were to follow common sense, couldn't one say that the modality of the "as if" appears appropriate to what are called *oeuvres*, singularly *oeuvres d'art*, the fine arts (painting, sculpture, cinema, music, poetry, literature, and so forth), but also, to complex degrees and according to complex stratifications, all the discursive idealities, all the symbolic or cultural productions that define, in the general field of the university, the disciplines said to be in the Humanities—and even the juridical disciplines and the production of laws, and even a certain structure of scientific objects in general?

I have already quoted two of Kant's "as if's." There is at least one more. I would not subscribe to it without reservation. With it, Kant seems to me to place too much confidence in a certain opposition of *nature* and *art*, at the very moment when the "as if" makes it tremble, just as we saw happen a moment ago to the opposition of *nature* and *freedom*. But I recall this remark *for two reasons.* On the one hand, I would suggest that what is perhaps at issue here is changing the sense, the status, the stake of the Kantian "as" and "as if," which would be a subtle displacement but one whose consequences seem to me limitless; on the other hand, I am preparing to cite an "as if" that describes an essential modality of experiencing works of art, in other words, that which, to a large extent, defines the field of the classical Humanities insofar as it concerns us here this evening. Kant says that "in a product of beautiful art, we must become conscious that it is art and not nature; but yet the purposiveness in its form must seem to be as free from all constraint of arbitrary rules *as if* it were a product of mere nature."[14]

In a provisional way, so as to introduce from a distance my remarks, my hypotheses, or my profession of faith, I want to draw your attention to this troubling thing we do when we say "as if" and to the connection this troubling thing, which looks like a simulacrum, might have with the questions I am preparing to address, the conjoined questions of profession and confession, of the university with or without condition—of the humanity of man and of the Humanities, of work [*travail*] and of literature.

What I would like to attempt with you is this apparently impossible thing: to link this "as if" to the thinking of an event, that is, to the thinking of this thing that *perhaps* happens, that is supposed to *take place*, that is supposed to find its place—and that *would* happen—here, for example, to what is called *le travail* ("work"). It is generally believed that, in order to happen, to take place, an event must interrupt the order of the "as if," and therefore that its "place" must be real, effective, concrete enough to belie the whole logic of the "as if." What happens, then, when the place itself becomes virtual, freed from its territorial (and thus national) rootedness, and when it becomes subject to the modality of an "as if"?

I will speak of an event that, without necessarily coming about tomorrow, would remain perhaps—and I underscore *perhaps*—to come: to come *through* the university, to come about and to come *through* it, *thanks* to it, *in* what is called the university, assuming that it has ever been possible to identify an *inside* of the university, that is, a *proper essence of the sovereign university*, and within it, something that one could also identify, properly, under the name "Humanities." I am thus referring to a university that would be what it always should have been or always should have represented, that is, from its inception and in principle: autonomous, unconditionally free in its institution, in its speech, in its writing, in its thinking. In a thinking, a writing, a speech that would not be only the archives or the productions of *knowledge* but also performative works, which are far from being neutral utopias. And why, we will wonder, would the principle of this unconditional freedom, its active and militant respect, its effective enactment, its *mise en oeuvre*, be confided above all to the new "Humanities" rather than to any other disciplinary field?

By putting forward these questions, which still resemble virtual desires taken for realities, or at best barely serious promises, I seem to be professing some faith. It is as if I were engaging in a profession of faith. Some would say, perhaps, that I am dreaming out loud, while already engaging in a profession of faith.

Assuming that one knows what a profession of faith is, one may then wonder who is responsible for such a profession of faith. Who would sign it? Who would profess it? I do not dare ask who would be its professor, but perhaps we should analyze a certain inheritance, in any case, a certain proximity between the future of the academic profession, that of the profession of professor, the principle of authority that derives from it, and the profession of faith.

In sum, what does it mean *to profess*? And what stakes are still hidden in this question as concerns *travail*, work, career, trade, craft (whether professional, professorial, or not), for the university of tomorrow and, within it, for the Humanities?

This word of Latin origin (*profiteor, professus sum, eri; pro et fateor*, which means to speak, from which also comes "fable" and thus a certain "as if"), to "profess" means, in French as in English, *to declare openly, to declare publicly*. In English, says the OED, before 1300 it had only a religious sense. "To make one's profession" then meant "to take the vows of some religious order." The declaration of the one who professes is a *performative* declaration in some way. It pledges like an act of sworn faith, an oath, a testimony, a manifestation, an attestation, or a promise. It is indeed, in the strong sense of the word, an *engagement*, a commitment. To profess is to make a pledge [*gage*] while committing one's responsibility. "To make profession of" is to declare out loud what one is, what one believes, what one wants to be, while asking another to take one's word and believe this declaration. I insist on this performative value of the declaration that professes while promising. One must underscore that constative utterances and discourses of pure knowledge, in the university or elsewhere, do not belong, as such, to the order of the profession in the strict sense. They belong perhaps to the craft, career, the *métier* ("competence, knowledge, know-how"), but not to the profession understood in a rigorous sense. The discourse of profession is always, in one way or another, a free profession of faith; in its pledge of responsibility, it exceeds pure techno-scientific knowledge. To profess is to pledge oneself while declaring oneself, while *giving oneself out to be*, while promising this or that. *Grammaticum se professus*, Cicero tells us in the *Tusculanes* (2, 12), is to give oneself out to be a grammarian, a master of grammar. It is neither necessarily to be this or that nor even to be a competent expert; it is to promise to be that, to pledge oneself on one's word to be that. *Philosophiam profiteri* is to profess philosophy: not simply to be a philosopher, to practice or teach philosophy in some pertinent fashion, but to pledge oneself, with a public promise, to devote oneself publicly, to give oneself over to philosophy, to bear witness, or even to fight for it. And what matters here is this promise, this pledge of responsibility, which is reducible to neither theory nor practice. To profess consists always in a performative speech act, even if the knowledge, the object, the content of what one professes, of what one teaches or practices, remains on the order of the theoretical or the constative. Because the act of professing is a performative speech act and because the event that it is or produces depends only on this linguistic promise, well, its proximity to the fable, to fabulation, and to fiction, to the "as if," will always be formidable.

What relation is there between professing and working? In the university? In the Humanities?

II

From my first sentence, as soon as I began to speak, I named *le travail*, work, by saying, "*As if* the end of work were at the beginning of the world."

What is work, that is, *le travail*? (I believe we will have to keep this word in French here.) When and where does *un travail* take place, its place? For lack of time, I will have to renounce right away a rigorous semantic analysis. Let us recall at least *two traits* that concern the university. *Le travail* is not merely action or practice. One can act without working and it is not certain that a *praxis*, in particular a theoretical practice, constitutes, *stricto sensu*, *un travail*. Above all, whoever works is not necessarily granted the name or status of worker, *travailleur*. The agent or the subject who works, the operator, is not always called a *travailleur* (*laborator*), and the sense seems to be modified when one goes from the verb to the noun: the *travail* of whoever *travaille* in general is not always the labor of a *travailleur*. Thus, in the university, among all those who in one way or another are supposed to be working there (teachers, staff or administrators, researchers, students), some, notably students, as such, will not ordinarily be called *travailleurs* as long as a salary (*merces*) does not regularly compensate, like a commodity in a market, the activity of a craft, trade, or profession. A fellowship or scholarship will not suffice for this. The student may very well work a lot, but he will be considered a *travailleur*, a worker, only on the condition of being on the market and only if in addition he performs some task, for example, here in the U.S., that of the teaching assistant. Inasmuch as she studies, purely and simply, even if she works a lot, the student is not held to be a *travailleur*. Even if, and I will insist on this in a moment, every craft, trade, or career is not a profession, the worker is someone whose work is recognized as a craft, trade, or profession in a market. (All of these social semantics are rooted, as you know, in a long socio-ideological history that goes back at least to the Christian Middle Ages.) One may thus work a lot without being a worker recognized as such in society.

Another distinction will count for us more and more, which is why I pay it considerable attention right away: one can work a lot, and even work a lot *as a worker*, a *travailleur*, without the effect or the result of the work (the *opus* of the operation) being recognized as a "work," this time in the sense not of the productive activity but of the product, *l'oeuvre*, that which *remains* after and beyond the time of the operation. It would often be difficult to identify and objectify the product of very hard work carried out by the most indispensable and devoted workers, the least well treated workers in society, the most invisible ones as well (those who dispose of the trash of our cities, for example, or those who control air traffic, more generally, those who guarantee the mediations or transmissions of which there remain only virtual traces—and this field is enormous and growing steadily). There are thus workers whose work, and even whose productive work, does not give rise to substantial or real products, only to virtual specters. But when work gives rise to real or realizable products, one must then introduce another essential distinction within the immense variety of products and structures of products, within all the forms of materiality, of reproducible ideality, of use and exchange values, and so forth.

Certain products of this working activity are held to be objectivizable use or exchange values without deserving, it is believed, the title of *oeuvres*. (I can say this word only in French.) To other works, it is believed one can attribute the name *oeuvres*. Their appropriation, their relation to liberal or salaried work, to the signature or the authority of the author, and to the market are of a great structural and historical complexity, which I will not analyze here. The first examples of *oeuvres* that come to mind are *oeuvres d'art* (visual, musical, or discursive, a painting, a concerto, a poem, a novel). But since we are interrogating the enigma of the concept of *oeuvre*, we would have to extend this field as soon as we tried to discern the type of work proper to the university and especially to the Humanities. In the Humanities, one no doubt treats in particular *oeuvres* (*oeuvres d'art*, either works of discursive art or not, literary or not, canonical or not). But in principle the treatment of works, in the academic tradition, depends on *a knowledge that itself does not consist* in *oeuvres*. To profess or to be a professor, in this tradition, which is, precisely, undergoing mutation, was no doubt to produce and to teach a knowledge even while professing, that is, even while promising to take a responsibility that is not exhausted in the act of knowing or teaching. But, in the classical-modern tradition that we are interrogating, to know how to profess or to profess a knowledge or even how to produce a knowledge is not to produce *oeuvres*. A professor, as such, does not sign an *oeuvre*. His or her authority as professor is not that of the author of an *oeuvre*, a work. It is perhaps this that has been changing over the last few decades, encountering the frequently indignant resistance and protestations of those who believe they can distinguish, in writing and in language, between criticism and creation, reading and writing, the professor and the author, and so forth. The deconstruction under way is no doubt not unrelated to this mutation. It is even its essential phenomenon, a more complex signal than its detractors admit, one we must take into account. In principle, if we refer to the canonical state of certain conceptual distinctions, and if we rely on the massive and widely accepted distinction between performatives and constatives, we may deduce from it the following propositions.

1. All work, all *travail* (work in general or the work of the worker) is not necessarily performative, that is, it does not produce an event. It does not make this event, it is not by itself, in itself, the event; it does not consist in the event it speaks of, even if it is productive, even if it leaves a product behind, whether or not this product is an *oeuvre*.

2. Every performative doubtless produces something; it makes an event come about. But what it *makes* in this way and *makes come about* in this way is not necessarily an *oeuvre*; it must always be authorized by a set of conventions or conventional fictions, of "as if's" on which an institutional community is founded and to which it agrees.

3. Now, as traditionally defined, the university would be a place identical to itself (a nonsubstitutable locality, rooted in the ground, limiting the substitutability of places in cyberspace), a place, a single place, which gives rise only to the production and teaching of a *knowledge* [savoir], that is, of knowledges [*connaissances*] whose form of utterance is not, in principle, performative but theoretical and constative, even if the *objects* of this knowledge are sometimes of a philosophical, ethical, political, normative, prescriptive, or axiological nature, and even if, in a still more troubling fashion, the structure of these objects of knowledge is a structure of fiction obeying the strange modality of the "as if" (poem, novel, *oeuvre d'art* in general, but also everything that, in the structure of a performative utterance—for example, of the juridical or constitutional type—does not belong to the realist and constative description of what is, but produces the event on the basis of the qualified "as if" of a supposedly established convention). In a classical university, in conformity with its accepted definition, one practices the study, the *knowledge* of the normative, prescriptive, performative, and fictional possibilities that I have just enumerated and that are more often the object of the Humanities. But this study, this knowledge, this teaching, this *doctrine* ought to belong to the theoretical and constative order. The act of *professing* a doctrine may be a performative act, but the *doctrine* is not. This is a limitation concerning which I will say that *one must* indeed, at the same time, conserve it *and* change it, in a nondialectical mode.

A. On the one hand, one must reaffirm it because a certain neutral theoreticism is the chance for the critical and more-than-critical (deconstructive) unconditionality that we are talking about and that, in principle, we all uphold, we all declare to uphold, in the university.

B. On the other, one must change while reaffirming this limitation because it must be admitted, and professed, that this unconditional theoreticism will itself always suppose a performative profession of faith, a belief, a decision, a public pledge, an ethico-political responsibility, and so forth. Here is found the principle of the unconditional resistance of the university. One may say that, from the point of view of this classical auto-definition of the university, there is no place in it, no essential, intrinsic, proper place either for nontheoretical work, for discourses of a performative type, or, *a fortiori*, for those singular performative acts engendering *today*, in certain places in the Humanities today, what are called *oeuvres*. The classical auto-definition and auto-limitation that I have just evoked characterized the academic space reserved formerly for the Humanities, even where the *contents, objects, and themes* of these produced or taught forms of knowledge were of a philosophical, moral, political, historical, linguistic, aesthetic, anthropological nature, that is, belonged to fields where evaluations, normativity, and prescriptive experience are admitted and sometimes constitutive. In the classical tradition, the Humanities define a field of knowledge, sometimes of knowledge production, but without engendering signed works or *oeuvres*, whether these are works of art or not.

I will once again invoke Kant in order to define these classical limits assigned to the traditional Humanities by those who demonstrate their necessity. Kant sees there first of all a "propaedeutic" to the Fine Arts rather than a practice of the arts. "Propaedeutic" is his word. The *Critique of Judgment* specifies that this pedagogic preparation, this simple introduction to the arts, will come at the point in the order of knowledge (the knowledge of what *is* and not of what *ought to be*) where it must not involve any "prescriptions" (*Vorschriften*). The Humanities (*Humaniora*) must prepare without prescribing: they would propose forms of knowledge that remain merely preliminary (*Vorkenntnisse*). And without bothering, in this text, with considerations of the long and sedimented history of the word "Humanities," Kant discerns there solely the study that favors legal communication and sociability among men, what gives the taste of the common sense of humanity (*allgemeinen Menschensinn*). There is, then, a theoreticism here, but also a Kantian humanism that privileges the constative discourse and the form "knowledge." The Humanities are and must be sciences. Elsewhere, in "Mochlos," I tried to lay out my reservations on this subject even as I saluted the logic one finds at work in *The Conflict of the Faculties*. This theoreticism limits or forbids the possibility for a professor to produce *oeuvres* or even prescriptive or performative utterances in general. But it also permits Kant to withdraw the faculty of philosophy from any outside power, notably from state power, and guarantees this faculty an unconditional freedom to say what is true and to conclude concerning the subject of truth, provided that it does so *in the inside* of the university. This final limitation (to say *publicly* all that one believes to be true and what one believes one must say, but only *inside* the university) has never been, I believe, either tenable or respectable, in fact or by law. And the transformation under way in public cyberspace, which is public on a worldwide scale, beyond state-national frontiers, seems to render it more archaic and imaginary than ever.

And yet I maintain that the idea of this space of the academic type has to be symbolically protected by a kind of absolute immunity, as if its interior were inviolable; I believe (this is *like* a profession of faith that I address to you and submit to your judgment) that this is an idea we must reaffirm, declare, and profess endlessly—even if the protection of this academic immunity (in the sense in which we speak of biological, diplomatic, or parliamentary immunity) is never pure, even if it can always develop dangerous processes of auto-immunity, even if and especially if it must not prevent us from addressing ourselves to the university's outside—without any utopic neutrality. This freedom or immunity of the university and par excellence of its Humanities is something to which we must lay claim, while committing ourselves to it with all our might. Not only in a verbal and declarative fashion, but in work, in act, and in what we make happen with events.

Against the horizon of these preliminary reminders and these classic definitions, one may see certain questions taking shape. They have at least *two forms*, for the moment, but we might see them change and become more specific as we go along.

1. First, if this is indeed the way things are, if in the classical and modern academic tradition (up through the nineteenth-century model) normative and prescriptive performativity, and *a fortiori* the production of *oeuvres*, must remain foreign to the field of university work, even in the Humanities, foreign to their teaching, that is, in the strict sense of the word, to their theory, to their theorems as discipline or doctrine (*Lehre*), then what does it mean "to profess"? What is the difference between a trade or craft and a profession? And then between any profession and the profession of the professor? What is the difference between the different types of authority granted to craft or trade, to profession, and to the profession of the professor?

2. Second, has something happened to this classical-modern university and to these Humanities? Is there something happening to it or promising to happen to it that upsets these definitions, either because this mu-

tation transforms the essence of the university, and in it the future of the Humanities, or because it consists in revealing, through the seismic activities under way, that this essence has never conformed to these definitions, however obvious and indisputable they are? Here once again the question "What does it mean for a professor 'to profess'?" would be the fault line of this seismic activity underway or still to come. What happens not only when one takes into account the performative value of "profession" but when one accepts that a professor produces *oeuvres* and not just knowledge or preknowledge?

To make our way toward the definition of the type of particular performative action that is the act of professing, and then the act of profession of a professor, and then finally of a professor of Humanities, we must pursue further our analysis of the distinctions between *acting, doing, producing, working, work in general, and the work of the worker.*

If I had the time, I could recall once again and discuss some conceptual distinctions Kant makes between art and nature, *tekhnē* and *phusis*, as well as between *tun* (*facere*), on the one hand, and, on the other, acting (*Handeln*), realizing (*wirken*) in general (*agere*), or between the product (*Produkt*) as oeuvre (*Werk, opus*), on the one hand, and effect (*Wirkung, effectus*) on the other.[15] In the same passage, Kant distinguishes between art and science, art and craft (*Handwerke*), liberal art (*freie Kunst*) and mercenary art (*Lohnkunst*). Let us return for a moment to my equivocal expression: *the end of work.* It may designate the suspension, the death, the term of the activity called "work." It can also designate the object, the aim, the product, or the *oeuvre* of the work. All action, all activity, as we were saying, is not work. Work is no more reducible to the activity of the act than it is to the productivity of the production, even if, out of confusion, these three concepts are often linked. We know better than ever today that a gain in production can correspond to a diminishing of work. The virtualization of work has always, and today more than ever, been able to complicate infinitely this disproportion between production and work. There are also activities, even productive activities, that do not constitute work. The experience of what we call work, *travail*, signifies also the passivity of a certain affect; it is sometimes the suffering and even the torture of a punishment. *Travail*, is that not *tripalium*, an instrument of torture? If I underscore this doloristic figure of punishment and expiation, it is not only in order to recognize the biblical legacy ("In the sweat of thy face shalt thou eat bread"). It is Kant, once again, who sees in this expiatory dimension of work a universal trait that transcends biblical traditions.[16] If I underscore this expiatory interpretation of work, it is also so as to *articulate* or in any case interrogate *together* two phenomena that I am tempted today to gather into the same question: Why is it that, on the one hand, we are witnessing throughout the world a proliferation of scenes of repentance and expiation (there is today a theatrical *mondialisation* of the confession, of which we could cite many examples) and, on the other hand, a proliferation of all sorts of discourses on the end of work?

Work supposes, engages, and situates a living body. It assigns it a stable and identifiable place even where the work is said to be "nonmanual," "intellectual," or "virtual." Work thus supposes a zone of passivity, a passion, as much as it does a productive activity. Moreover, we must also distinguish between social work in general, craft or trade, and profession. All work is not organized according to the unity of a craft or a statutory and recognized competence. As for "crafts" or "trades," even where they are gathered under these names by legitimate institutions or by corporations, not all of them are called, not all of them can easily be called, in our languages, "professions," at least when these languages remember their Latin. Even if this were not impossible, one would not easily speak of the profession of the seasonal farm worker, the priest, or the boxer, since their know-how, their competence, and their activity suppose neither the permanence nor the social responsibility granted by the in principle secular society to someone who exercises a profession by freely committing himself to accomplish a duty. One would more easily and above all speak of the profession of physician, lawyer, professor, as if profession, linked more to the liberal and nonmercenary arts, implied a pledge of responsibility freely declared, very nearly under oath—in a word, *professed*. In the lexicon of "professing," I will emphasize less the authority, the supposed competence, and the guarantee of the profession or of the professor than, once again, the pledge to be honored, the declaration of responsibility. For lack of time, I must leave aside the long history of the "profession," of "professionalization," that leads to the current seismic activity. Let us retain, all the same, one essential trait. The idea of profession supposes that beyond and in addition to knowledge, know-how, and competence, a testimonial commitment, a freedom, a responsibility under oath, a sworn faith obligates the subject to render accounts to some tribunal yet to be defined. Finally, all those who exercise a profession are not professors. We will thus have to take account of these sometimes hazy distinctions: between work, activity, production, trade or craft, profession, professor, the professor who dispenses a knowledge or professes a doctrine, and the professor who can as well, as such, sign *oeuvres*—and who is perhaps already doing so or will do so tomorrow.

III

As if, we were saying at the outset, the end of work were at the origin of the world.

Let us indeed say "as if": *as if* the world began where work ends, as if the *mondialisation du monde* (which is what I call in French the *mondialisation du monde,* the worldwide-ization of the world, in short, what the Anglo-Saxon countries call "globalization," in German, *Globalisierung*) had as both its horizon and its origin the disappearance of what we call *le travail.* This old word, painfully laden with so much meaning and history (*work, labor, travail,* and so forth), has not only the sense of an activity; it designates an actual activity. By that let us understand real, effective (*wirklich*) and not virtual. This actual effectivity seems to ally it to what we generally think of as event. What happens or comes about in general, we still believe, cannot be virtual. This is where, as we'll see, things are certain to get complicated.

By beginning or by pretending to begin with an "as if," we are neither in the fiction of a possible future nor the resurrection of a historical or mythical past, still less of a revealed origin. The rhetoric of this "as if" belongs neither to the science fiction of a utopia to come (a world without work "at the end without end," *in fine sine fine* of an eternal sabbatical rest, a Sabbath without evening, as in St. Augustine's *City of God*) nor to the poetics of a nostalgia turned toward a golden age or an earthly paradise, toward the moment in Genesis when, before there is sin, the sweat of laboring brows would not yet have begun to flow, either in man's toil and plowing or in woman's labor of childbirth. In these two interpretations of the "as if," science fiction or memory of the immemorial, it would be *as if* in fact the beginnings of the world originarily excluded work; there would *not yet* or *no longer* be work. It would be *as if,* between the concept of world and the concept of *travail,* there were no originary harmony, thus no given accord or possible synchrony. Original sin would have introduced work into the world and the end of work would announce the terminal phase of an expiation.

The logical skeleton of this proposition in "as if" is that the world and work cannot coexist. One would have to choose the world or work, whereas according to common sense, it is difficult to imagine a world without work or some work that is not *of the world* or *in the world*. The Pauline conversion of the Greek concept of *cosmos* introduces into the Christian world, among many other associated meanings, the assignation to expiatory work.

I recalled a moment ago that the concept of *travail*, work, is laden with meanings, history, and equivocations, and that it is difficult to think it beyond good and evil. Although it is always associated simultaneously with dignity, life, production, history, the good, freedom, it connotes no less often evil, suffering, pain, sin, punishment, servitude. The laborious is painful, this pain [*peine*] can be that of a physical suffering but also of a penality. The concept of world is no less obscure, in its European, Greek, Jewish, Christian, Islamic history, between science, philosophy, and faith, whether the world is wrongly identified with the earth, with the humans on earth here below, or with the heavenly world above, the cosmos, the universe, and so forth. Successful or not, Heidegger's project, beginning with *Sein und Zeit*, will have sought to remove the concept of world and of being-in-the-world from these Greek or Christian presuppositions. It is difficult to put any faith in the word "world" without careful prior analyses, especially when one wants to think it with or without work, a work whose concept branches out into notions of activity, of the doing or *making* of technics, on the one hand, and into passivity, affect, suffering, punishment, and passion, on the other. Whence the difficulty of understanding the "as if" with which we began: "As if the end of work were at the origin of the world." Once again, let us keep this phrase in French. Unlike "globalization" or *Globalisierung*, *mondialisation* marks a reference to this notion of world that is charged with a great deal of semantic history, notably a Christian history: the world, as we were saying a moment ago, is neither the universe, nor the earth, nor the terrestrial globe, nor the *cosmos*.

No, this "as if" should not signal either toward the utopia or the improbable future of a science fiction or toward the dream of an immemorial or mythological past *in illo tempore*. This "as if" takes into account, in the present, two commonplaces of today, and it puts them to the test: on the one hand, there is a lot of talk about the end of work, and, on the other, there is just as much talk about a "globalization," a worldwide-ization of the world, a becoming-world of the world. These are always associated with each other. I borrow the expression "end of work" from the title of a recent and already well-known book by Jeremy Rifkin, *The End of Work: The Decline of the Global Labor Force and the Dawn of the Post-Market Era.*[17]

As you also know, this book gathers up a fairly widespread sort of *doxa* concerning the effects of what Rifkin calls the "Third Industrial Revolution." This revolution has the potential, in his opinion, to be "a powerful force for good and evil," and the "new information and telecommunication technologies have the potential to both liberate and destabilize civilization" (xviii).

I don't know if it is true that, as Rifkin claims, we are entering "a new phase in world history": "Fewer and fewer workers will be needed to produce the goods and services for the global population." "*The End of Work,*" he adds, naming thus his own book, "examines the technological innovations and market-directed forces that are moving us to the edge of a near workerless world" (xvi).

What would be the consequences of this from the viewpoint of the university? To know whether these propositions are literally "true," one would have to agree about the meaning of each of these words ("end," "history," "world," "work," "production," "goods," etc.). I have neither the means, the time, nor, therefore, the intention to discuss directly this book or this serious and immense problematic, notably the concepts of world and work mobilized there. Whether or not one adopts the premises and the conclusions of a discourse like Rifkin's, one must recognize at least (this is the minimal consensus from which I will set out) that something serious is indeed happening or is about to happen to what we call "work," "tele-work," virtual work, and to what we call "world"—and therefore to the being-in-the-world of what is still called "man." We must also admit that this depends to a large degree on a techno-scientific mutation that, in the cyberworld, in the world of the Internet, of e-mail, and of cellular telephones, affects tele-work, the virtualization of work, and, at the same time as the communication of knowledge, at the same time as any putting-into-common and any "community," the experience of place, of taking place, of the event, and of the *oeuvre*: of that which happens, comes about, or, as I would prefer to say, that which *arrives*.

This problematic of the "end of work" was not altogether absent from certain texts of Marx or Lenin. The latter associates the progressive reduction of the workday with the process that would bring about the complete disappearance of the state.[18] As for Rifkin, he sees in the third technological revolution now under way an absolute mutation. The first two revolutions, that of steam, coal, steel, and textiles (in the nineteenth century) and then that of electricity, petroleum, and the automobile (in the twentieth century), did not radically affect the history of work. Both freed up a sector where the machine had not penetrated. Human labor, nonmachine and nonsubstitutable by the machine, was still available.

After these two technical revolutions would come ours, therefore, the third one, that of cyberspace, micro-computing, and robotics. Here, no fourth zone where the unemployed can be put to work seems to exist. A saturation by machines heralds the end of the worker, thus a certain end of work. End of *Der Arbeiter* and his age, as Jünger might have said. Rifkin's book treats teachers and, more generally, what he calls the "sector of knowledge" as a special case within the mutation underway. In the past, when new technologies replaced workers in some sector or another, new spaces appeared to absorb the laborers who lost their jobs. But today, when agriculture, industry, and services lay off millions because of technological progress, the only category of workers spared would be that of "knowledge," an "elite of entrepreneurs, scientists, technicians, computer programmers, professional educators, and consultants."[19] But this remains a narrow sector, unable to absorb the mass of the unemployed. Such would be the dangerous singularity of our age. Rifkin does not speak of unemployed teachers or aspiring professors, in particular in the Humanities. He pays no attention to the growing marginalization of so many part-time employees, all underpaid and marginalized in the university, in the name of what is called flexibility or competitivity.

I will not treat the objections one could make to these kinds of discourse, in their generality, neither as concerns the "end of work" nor with regard to so-called *mondialisation*. In both cases, which are, moreover, closely linked, if I had to treat them head-on, I would try to distinguish, in a preliminary fashion, between the massive and hardly contestable phenomena that these words register, on the one hand, and, on the other, the use people make of these words without concept. In fact, no one will deny that something is indeed happening to work in this century, to the reality and to the concept of work—active or actual work. What is happening is indeed an effect of techno-science, with the worldwide-izing virtualization and delocalization of tele-work. What is happening indeed accentuates a certain tendency toward the asymptotic reduction of work time, as work in real time and localized in the same place as the body of the worker. All of this affects work in the classic forms we have inherited, in the new experience of borders, of the nation-state, of virtual communication, of the speed and spread of information. This evolution goes in the direction of a certain worldwide-ization; it is undeniable and fairly well known.

But these phenomenal indices remain partial, heterogeneous, unequal in their development; they call for close analysis and no doubt new concepts. Moreover, between these obvious indices and the doxic use—others might say the ideological inflation—the rhetorical and often hazy complacency with which everyone gives in to the words "end of work" and "globalization," there is a gap. I do not wish to bridge this gap in a facile way, and I believe one must severely criticize those who forget it is there. For they attempt thereby to induce forgetfulness of zones in the world, of populations, nations, groups, classes, individuals who, massively, are the excluded victims of the movement called "the end of work" and "globalization" or *mondialisation*. These victims suffer either because they lack the work they would need or else because they work too much for the salary they receive in exchange on a worldwide market that is so violently inegalitarian. This capitalistic situation (where capital plays an essential role between the actual and the virtual) is more tragic in absolute figures than it has ever been in the history of humanity. Humanity has perhaps never been further from the worldwide-izing or worldwide-ized homogeneity of "work" and "without work" that is often alleged. A large part of humanity is "without work" where it would like to have more, more work, and another has too much work where it would like to have less, or even to be done with a job that is so poorly paid on the market.

This history began a long time ago. It is interwoven with the real and semantic history of "craft," "trade," and "profession." Rifkin is acutely conscious of the tragedy that could also ensue from this "end of work" that does not have the sabbatical or dominical sense it has in the Augustinian *City of God*. But in his moral and political conclusions, when he wants to define the responsibilities to be assumed in the face of "the technological storm clouds on the horizon," in the face of "a new age of global markets and automated production," he comes back to—and I believe this is neither fortuitous nor acceptable without examination—the Christian language of "fraternity," of "qualities not easily reducible to or replaceable by machines," of "renewed meaning and purpose in life," of "renewal of community life," of "rebirth of the human spirit"; he even envisions new forms of charity, for example, "providing shadow wages for volunteering time, imposing a value-added tax on the products and services of the high-tech era to be used exclusively to guarantee a social wage for the poor in return for performing community service," and so forth (291–93).

If, precisely, our time were not limited here, I would no doubt still have insisted, while taking frequent inspiration from the research of Jacques Le Goff, on the time of work. In the chapter "Temps et travail" in his *Un autre Moyen Age*, he shows how, in the fourteenth century, demands for prolonging and demands for reducing the duration of work already coexisted.[20] We have here the premises for workers' rights and a right to work in the form in which they will later be inscribed in human rights.

The figure of the humanist is a *response* to the question of work. The humanist responds to the question that is *posed* to him on the subject of work. He poses himself as humanist in the responsible exercise of this response. In the theology of work that dominated the period and that is no doubt not yet dead today, the humanist is someone who begins to secularize the time of work and the monastic time schedule. Time, which is no longer just a gift of God, can be calculated and sold. In the iconography of the fourteenth century, the clock sometimes represents the attribute of the humanist[21]—the same clock that I am obliged to watch and that keeps a strict watch over the lay worker that I am here.

I would have liked to speak to you for hours about the *hour*, about that purely fictional countable unit, about this "as if" that regulates, orders, and makes time (*fiction* is what *figures* but also what *makes*), the time of work outside and within the university, where everything, courses, seminars, lectures, is counted by hourly segments. The "academic quarter hour" is itself regulated by the hour.

Does not deconstruction also put the hour in question, put in crisis the unit called "hour"? It would also have been necessary to follow the trace of the tripartite classification that, beginning in the ninth century, divided society into the three orders of clerks, warriors, and workers (*oratores, bellatores, laboratores*), and then the hierarchy of crafts (noble or servile, licit or illicit, *negotia illicita, opera servilia*, forbidden on Sunday). Le Goff shows well how the unity of the world of work, as distinct from the world of prayer and the world of war, "did not last very long"—"if it ever existed," says Le Goff in passing, with necessary caution that, in my view, is at least as important as the assertion it thus suspends.[22]

After the "contempt for the crafts . . . a new frontier of contempt is laid down that passes through the middle of new classes, and even the middle of the professions" (102). Although he does not distinguish, it seems to me, at least not with any insistence, between "craft" and "profession" (as I believe one must do), even though he frequently associates "crafts and professions" (159) and also uses the category "socio-professional groups" (103, for example), Le Goff also describes the process that gave birth in the twelfth century to a "theology of work" and to the transformation of the tripartite schema (*oratores, bellatores, laboratores*) into "more complex" schemas. This transformation is explained by "the growing differentiation of economic and social structures as an effect of the growing division of labor" (165). In the twelfth and thirteenth centuries, the "scholarly craft" appeared as the hierarchy of *scolares* and *magistri* that would be the prelude to universities. Abelard had to choose between *litterae* and *arma*. He sacrificed *pompa militari gloriae* for *studium litterarum*.

I would be tempted to situate the profession of the professor, in the strict sense, at this highly symbolic moment of the pledge by which, for example, Abelard assumed the responsibility to respond to the injunction or the appeal *tu eris magister in aeternum* (179), even if, as Le Goff underscores, he continued to describe his career in military terms, dialectics remaining an arsenal and the *disputationes* battles. It is often the figure and the name of *philosopher* (181), of the professor *as* philosopher, that becomes necessary in a new situation. The university is thought and represented from the privileged place of the philosophical: within and outside the Humanities. There is nothing surprising in Kant's granting such a privilege to the faculty of philosophy in his architecture of the university.

If, to a certain extent at least, philosophy is at once a privileged reference, a resource, *and* a target for deconstruction, this may no doubt be explained in part by this dominant tradition. In the twelfth and thirteenth centuries, scholarly life became a craft or trade (*negotia scholaria*). One then spoke of *pecunia* and *laus* to define what compensated the work and research of new students and scholars. Salary and glory between them articulated economic functioning and professional conscience.

With these few historical indications, I wish to suggest that one of the tasks of the Humanities to come would be, ad infinitum, to know and to think their own history, at least in the directions that we have just seen open up: the act of professing, the theology and the history of work, knowledge and the faith in knowledge, the questions of man, of the world, of fiction, of the performative and the "as if," of literature and *oeuvre*, and so forth, and then all the concepts that we have just articulated with them.

This deconstructive task of the Humanities to come will not let itself be contained within the traditional limits of the departments that today belong, by their very status, to the Humanities. These Humanities to come will cross disciplinary borders without dissolving the specificity of each discipline into what is called, often in a very confused way, "interdisciplinarity" or into what is lumped with another good-for-everything concept, "cultural studies." But I can very well imagine that departments of genetics, natural science, medicine, and even mathematics will take seriously, in their work itself, the questions that I have just evoked. Besides medicine, this is especially true—to make one last reference to the Kant of *The Conflict of the Faculties*—of law schools and departments of theology or religious studies.

IV

I must now hasten to my conclusion. I will do so in a dry and telegraphic manner with seven theses, seven propositions, or seven professions of faith. They remain altogether programmatic. Six of them will have only a formalizing value as reminders or by gathering things up. They will recapitulate. The seventh, which will not be sabbatical, will attempt a step beyond the six others toward a dimension of the *event* and of the *taking place* that I have yet to speak of.

Between the first six theses—or professions of faith—and the last, we will get a foothold in preparation for a leap that would carry us beyond the power of the performative "as if," beyond even the distinction between constative and performative upon which we have up until now pretended to rely. It was "as if" we had bet on a certain "as if," this one and not another, the performative rather than another.

The Humanities of tomorrow, in all its departments, will have to study their history, the history of the concepts that, by constructing them, instituted the disciplines and were coextensive with them.

There are many signs that this work has already begun, of course. Like all acts of institution, those that we must analyze will have had a performative force and will have put to work a certain "as if." I just said that one must "study" or "analyze." Is it necessary to make clear that such "studies," such "analyses," for the reasons already indicated, would not be purely "theoretical" and neutral? They would lead toward practical and performative transformations and would not forbid the production of singular *oeuvres*. To these fields I will give therefore six, and then seven thematic and programmatic titles, without excluding, obviously, cross-fertilizations and reciprocal interpellations.

1. These new Humanities would treat the history of man, the idea, the figure, and the notion of "what is proper to man." They will do this on the basis of a nonfinite series of *oppositions* by which man is determined, in particular the traditional opposition of the life form called "human" and of the life form called "animal." I will dare to claim, without being able to demonstrate it here, that none of these traditional concepts of "what is proper to man" and thus of what is *opposed* to it can resist a consistent scientific and deconstructive analysis.

The most urgent guiding thread here would be the problematization (which does not mean the disqualification) of the powerful juridical performatives that have given shape to the modern history of this humanity of man. I am thinking, for example, of the rich history of at least two of these juridical performatives: *on the one hand*, the Declarations of the Rights of Man—*and of woman* (since the question of sexual differences is not secondary or accidental here; we know that these Declarations of the Rights of Man were being constantly transformed and enriched from 1789 to 1948 and beyond: the figure of man, a promising animal, an animal capable of promising, as Nietzsche said, remains still to come)—and, *on the other hand*, the concept of "crime against humanity," which since the end of the Second World War has modified the geopolitical field of international law and will continue to do so more and more, commanding in particular the scene of worldwide confession and of the relation to the historical past in general. The new Humanities will thus treat these performative productions of law or right (rights of man, human rights, the concept of crime against humanity) where they always imply the promise and, with the promise, the conventionality of the "as if."

2. These new Humanities would treat, in the same style, the history of democracy and the idea of sovereignty, that is also to say, of course, the conditions or rather the unconditionality under which the university and within it the Humanities are *supposed* (once again the "as if") to live. The

deconstruction of this concept of sovereignty would touch not only on international law, the limits of the nation-state, and the limits of its supposed sovereignty, but also on the use made of them in juridico-political discourses concerning the *subject* or the *citizen* in general—always presumed to be "sovereign" as such (free, deciding, responsible, etc.)—and thus concerning as well the relations between what is called "man" and "woman." This concept of indivisible sovereignty has been recently at the center of very poorly thought-out and poorly conducted debates, in my country, on the subject of man-woman "parity" in access to political offices.

3. These new Humanities would treat, in the same style, the history of "professing," of the "profession," and of the professoriat, a history articulated with that of the premises or presuppositions (notably Abrahamic, biblical, and above all Christian) of work and of the worldwide-ized confession, where it goes beyond the sovereignty of the head of state, of the nation-state, or even of the "people" in a democracy.

An immense problem: How can one dissociate democracy from citizenship, from the nation-state, and from the theological idea of sovereignty, even from the sovereignty of the people? How can one dissociate sovereignty and unconditionality, the power of an indivisible sovereignty, the powerlessness of unconditionality? Here again, whether it is a question of profession or confession, the performative structure of the "as if" would be at the center of the work.

4. These new Humanities would treat, in the same style, the history of literature. Not only what is commonly called history of literatures or literature themselves, with the great question of its canons (traditional and indisputable objects of the classical Humanities), but the history of the *concept* of literature, of the modern institution named "literature," of its links with fiction and the performative force of the "as if," of its concept of *oeuvre*, author, signature, national language, of its link with the right to say everything (or not to say everything), which founds both democracy and the idea of the unconditional sovereignty claimed by the university and within it by what is called, inside and outside departments, the Humanities.

5. These new Humanities would treat, in the same style, the history of profession, the profession of faith, professionalization, and the professoriat. The guiding thread could be, today, what is happening when the profession of faith, the profession of faith of the professor, gives rise not

only to the competent exercise of some knowledge in which one has faith, not only to the classical alliance of the constative and the performative, but to singular *oeuvres*, to other strategies of the "as if," which are events and which affect the very limits of the academic field or of the Humanities. We are indeed witnessing the end of a certain figure of the professor and of his or her supposed authority, but I believe, as should now be obvious, in a certain necessity of the professoriat.

6. These new Humanities, finally, would thus treat, in the same style, but in the course of a formidable reflexive reversal, both critical and deconstructive, the history of the "as if" and especially the history of this precious distinction between performative acts and constative acts, which seems to have been indispensable for us up until now. It will surely be necessary, even if things have already begun here or there, to study the history and the limits of such a decisive distinction, to which I have made reference today as if I believed in it without reservation up until now, as if I held it to be absolutely "reliable." This deconstructive work would not concern only the original and brilliant *oeuvre* of Austin but also his rich and fascinating inheritance, over the last half-century, in particular in the Humanities.

7. To the seventh point, which is not the seventh day, I finally now arrive. Or rather: I *let perhaps* arrive at the end, now, the very thing that, by *arriving*, as an *arrivant* or arriving one [*en arrivant*], by taking place or having place, revolutionizes, overturns, and puts to rout the very authority that is attached, in the university, in the Humanities,

(a) to knowledge (or at least to its model of constative language),

(b) to the profession or to the profession of faith (or at least to its model of performative language),

(c) to the *mise en oeuvre*, the putting to work, at least to the performative putting to work of the "as if."

That which happens, takes place, comes about in general, that which is called event, what is it? Can one ask with regard to it: "What is it?" It must not only surprise the constative and propositional mode of the language of knowledge (S is P), but also no longer let itself be commanded by the performative speech act of a subject. As long as I can produce and determine an event by a performative act guaranteed, like any performative, by conventions, legitimate fictions, and a certain "as if," then, to be sure, I will not say that nothing happens or comes about, but I will say that what takes place, arrives, happens, or happens *to me* remains still controllable and programmable within a horizon of anticipation or precomprehension, within a *horizon*, period. It is of the order of the masterable possible, it is the unfolding of what is already possible. It is of the order of power, of the "I can," "I may," or "I am empowered to . . ." No surprise, thus no event in the strong sense.

Which is as much as to say that, to this extent at least, it does not happen, it does not come about, or, as I would say in French: *cela n'arrive pas*, it does not arrive. If there is any, if there is such a thing, the pure singular eventness of *what* arrives or of *who* arrives and arrives *to me* (which is what I call the *arrivant*), it would suppose an *irruption* that punctures the horizon, *interrupting* any performative organization, any convention, or any context that can be dominated by a conventionality. Which is to say that this event takes place only where it does not allow itself to be domesticated by any "as if," or at least by any "as if" that can already be read, decoded, or articulated *as such*. So that this small word, the "as" of the "as if" as well as the "as" of the "as such"—whose authority founds and justifies every ontology as well as every phenomenology, every philosophy as science or knowledge—this small word, "as," might well be the name of the true problem, not to say the target, of deconstruction.

It is too often said that the performative produces the event of which it speaks. To be sure. One must also realize that, inversely, where there is the performative, an event worthy of the name cannot arrive. If what arrives belongs to the horizon of the possible, or even of a possible performative, it does not arrive, it does not happen, in the full sense of the word.

As I have often tried to demonstrate, only the impossible *can* arrive.

In frequently pointing out about deconstruction that it is impossible or the impossible, and that it is not a method, a doctrine, a speculative metaphilosophy, but *what arrives, what comes about*, I was relying on the same thought.

The examples with which I have attempted to accede to this thought (invention, the gift, forgiveness, hospitality, justice, friendship, and so forth)[23] all confirmed this thinking of the impossible possible, of the possible *as* impossible, of an impossible-possible that can no longer be determined by the metaphysical interpretation of possibility or virtuality.

I will not say that this thought of the impossible possible, this other thinking of the possible is a thinking of necessity but rather, as I have also tried to demonstrate elsewhere, a thinking of the "perhaps," of the dangerous modality of the "perhaps" that Nietzsche speaks of and that philosophy has always tried to subjugate. There is no future and no relation to the coming of the event without experience of the "perhaps." What takes place does not have to announce itself as possible or necessary; if it did, its irruption as event would in advance be neutralized. The event belongs to a *perhaps* that is in keeping not with the possible but with the impossible. And its force is therefore irreducible to the force or the power of a performative, even if it gives to the performative itself, to what is called the *force* of the performative, its chance and its effectiveness.

The force of the event is always stronger than the force of a performative. In the face of what arrives to me, what happens to me, even in what I decide (which, as I tried to show in *Politics of Friendship*, must involve a certain passivity, my decision being always the decision of the other), in the face of the other who arrives and arrives to me, all performative force is overrun, exceeded, exposed.

This force in keeping with an experience of the perhaps retains, no doubt, an affinity or a complicity with the "if" of the "as if." And thus with a certain grammar of the conditional: What *if* this arrived? This, which is altogether other, *could well* arrive, this *would* happen. To think *perhaps* is to think "if," "what if?" But you see quite clearly that this "if," this "what if," this "as if" is no longer reducible to all the "as if's" that we have been talking about up until now.[24] And if it is declined according to the verbal mode of the conditional, this is also to announce the unconditional, the eventual, or the possible event of the impossible unconditional, the altogether other—which we should from now on (and this is something else I have not yet said or done today) dissociate from the theological idea of sovereignty. Basically, this would perhaps be my hypothesis (it is extremely difficult, and almost im-probable, inaccessible to proof): It would be necessary to dissociate a certain *unconditional* independence of thought, of deconstruction, of justice, of the Humanities, of the university, and so forth from any phantasm of *indivisible sovereignty* and of sovereign mastery.

Well, it is once again in the Humanities that one would have to make arrive, make happen the thinking of this other mode of the "if," this more than difficult, im-possible thing, the exceeding of the performative and of the constative/performative opposition. By thinking, *in* the Humanities, this limit of mastery and of performative conventionality, this limit of performative authority, what is one doing? One is acceding to the place where the always necessary context of the performative operation (a context that is, like every convention, an institutional context) can no longer be saturated, delimited, fully determined.

The brilliant invention of the constative/performative distinction would basically still have sought, in the university, to reassure the university about the sovereign mastery of its interior, about its proper power, a power of its own. One thus touches the very limit *between the inside and the outside*, notably the border of the university itself and, within it, of the Humanities. One thinks *in* the Humanities the irreducibility of their outside and of their future. One thinks *in* the Humanities that one cannot and must not let oneself be enclosed *within the inside* of the Humanities. But for this thinking to be strong and consistent requires the Humanities. To think this is not an academic, speculative, or theoretical operation. Nor a neutral utopia. No more than saying it is a simple enunciation. It is at this always divisible limit that what arrives arrives. It is this limit that is affected by the arriving and that changes. It is this limit that, because it is divisible, has a history. This limit of the impossible, the "perhaps," and the "if," this is the place where the divided university is exposed to reality, to the forces from without (be they cultural, ideological, political, economic, or other). It is there that the university is in the world that it is attempting to think. On this border, it must therefore negotiate and organize its resistance. And take its responsibilities. Not in order to enclose itself and reconstitute the abstract phantasm of sovereignty, whose theological or humanist heritage it will perhaps have begun to deconstruct, if at least it has begun to do so. But in order to resist effectively, by allying itself with extra-academic forces, in order to organize an inventive resistance, through its *oeuvres*, its works, to all attempts at reappropriation (political, juridical, economic, and so forth), to all the other figures of sovereignty.

This is another way of calling upon another topology: The university without conditions is not situated necessarily or exclusively within the walls of what is today called the university. It is not necessarily, exclusively, exemplarily represented in the figure of the professor. It takes place, it seeks its place wherever this unconditionality can take shape. Everywhere that it, perhaps, gives one (itself) to think. Sometimes even beyond, no doubt, a logic or a lexicon of the "condition."

How could one justify such a profession of faith? Could it be done in principle, even if I had the time?

I do not know if what I am saying here is intelligible, if it makes sense.

It is in fact a matter of the sense of sense. I especially do not know the status, genre, or legitimacy of the discourse that I have just addressed to you. Is it academic? Is it a discourse of knowledge in the Humanities or on the subject of the Humanities? Is it knowledge only? Only a performative profession of faith? Does it belong to the inside of the university? Is it philosophy, or literature, or theater? Is it a work, *une oeuvre*, or a course, or a kind of seminar?

I have numerous hypotheses on this subject, but finally it will be up to you now, it will also be up to others to decide this. The signatories are also the addressees. We don't know them, neither you nor I. If the impossible that I'm talking about were perhaps to arrive one day, I leave you to imagine the consequences.

Take your time but be quick about it, because you do not know what awaits you.

§ 5

Psychoanalysis Searches the States of Its Soul:
The Impossible Beyond of a Sovereign Cruelty

(Address to the States General of Psychoanalysis)

First digression, in confidence. If I say right now, speaking in your direction but without identifiable addressee: "Yes, I am suffering cruelly," or again, "You are being *made* or *allowed* to suffer cruelly," or yet again, "You are making *her* or you are letting *him* suffer cruelly," or even, "I am *making* myself or *letting* myself suffer cruelly," well, these grammatical or semantic variations, these differences between *making* suffer, *letting* suffer, *letting . . . make* [*laisser . . . faire*], etc., these changes of person—there could be still others, in the singular or the plural, masculine or feminine, "one," "we, us," "you," "he" or "she," "they" masculine or feminine—these passages into more reflective forms ("I make *myself* or I let *myself* suffer cruelly," you make *yourself* or you let *yourself* suffer cruelly, and so forth), all these possible modifications leave an adverb intact, an invariant that seems, once and for all, to qualify a state of suffering, namely, cruelty, "cruelly."

In the course of these sentences, directed to all these addresses, impassive, "cruelly" does not change. *As if* we knew the meaning of this word. Putting our faith in this "as if," we act *as if* we understood *ourselves* and agreed with *one another* as to what "cruel" means. Whether the word *cruelty* is assigned to its Latin inheritance, that is, to a very necessary history of spilled blood (*cruor, crudus, crudelitas*), of some crime of blood, the ties of blood, or whether it is affiliated to other languages and other semantics (*Grausamkeit*, for example, is Freud's word) unrelated to the flow of blood, this time in order to name the desire to make or to make oneself suffer *just to* suffer; even to torture or kill; to kill oneself or torture oneself to torture or kill, *just to* take a psychic pleasure in evil for evil's sake, or even *just to* find bliss in radical evil, in all these cases cruelty would be difficult to *determine* or *delimit*. Nietzsche, for example, sees there the cunning essence of life: cruelty would be without limit and without opposable term, thus endless and without contrary. But for Freud, who is nevertheless so close to Nietzsche, as always, cruelty might perhaps be without limit but not without opposable term, that is, endless but not without contrary—this will be one of our questions. One can staunch bloody cruelty (*cruor, crudus, crudelitas*), one can put an end to murder by blade, by the guillotine, in the classical or modern theaters of bloody war, but, according to Nietzsche or Freud, a psychic cruelty will always take its place by inventing new resources. A psychic cruelty would still, of course, be a cruelty of the *psyche*, a state of the soul, thus still of the living, but a nonbloody cruelty.

Would such cruelty, if there is any and if it is properly psychical, be one of the horizons most proper to psychoanalysis? Would this horizon even be reserved to psychoanalysis, like the bottomless depth of what it alone would be given *to treat*, the ultimate ground on which one day its figure took shape? I will not exploit this reflection on psychical cruelty, that is, bloodless or not necessarily bloody cruelty, on the acute pleasure derived from the soul in pain, to recall a Jewish joke: the psychoanalyst who declared he chose this therapeutic discipline because he could not stand the sight of blood. I will not do this so as not to reopen the now canonical debate concerning a link between the potential universality of psychoanalysis and the history of Judeity or Judaism. Let us merely ask ourselves whether, yes or no, what is called "psychoanalysis" does not open up the only way that could allow us, if not to know, if not to think even, at least to interrogate what might be meant by this strange and familiar word "cruelty," the worst cruelty, suffering *just to* suffer; the making-suffer, the making- or letting-oneself suffer *just for*, if one can still say that, the pleasure of suffering. Even if, as I am inclined to believe, psychoanalysis alone did not yet give us to know it, think it, treat it, at least one could no longer anticipate doing so without psychoanalysis. Hypothesis on a hypothesis: if there is something irreducible in the life of the living being, in the soul, in the psyche (for I do not limit my remarks to that living being called man, and thus I leave suspended the immense and formidable question, an open question in my view, of animality in general, and of whether psychoanalysis is or is not, through and through, an anthropology), and if this irreducible thing in the life of the animate being is indeed the possibility of cruelty (the drive, if you will, of evil for evil, of a suffering that would play at enjoying the suffering of a making-suffer or a making-oneself-suffer *for the pleasure of it*), then no other discourse—be it theological, metaphysical, genetic, physicalist, cognitivist, and so forth—could open itself up to this hypothesis. They would all be designed to reduce it, exclude it, deprive it of sense. The only discourse that can today claim the thing of psychical suffering as its own affair would indeed be what has been called, for about a century, psychoanalysis. Psychoanalysis would perhaps not be the only possible language or even the only possible treatment regarding this cruelty that has no contrary term and no end. But "psychoanalysis" would be the name of that which, without theological or other alibi, would be turned toward what is most *proper* to psychical cruelty. Psychoanalysis, for me, if I may be permitted yet another confidential remark, would be another name for the "without alibi." The confession of a "without alibi." If that were possible. In any case, it would be that without which one can no longer seriously envision something like psychical cruelty, thus a psychical specificity, and something like the mere self-relation of this cruelty, before any knowledge, before any theory and any practice, even before any therapeutic. Wherever a question of suffering *just to* suffer, of doing or letting one do evil *for* evil, wherever, in short, the question of radical evil or of an evil worse than radical evil would no longer be abandoned to religion or to metaphysics, no other discourse of knowledge stands ready to take an interest in something like cruelty—except what is called psychoanalysis, whose name, associated now with evil, would become in turn more indecipherable than ever, all the more so in that only a psychoanalytic revolution would be, in its very project, up to the task of taking account of the grammatical syntax, conjugations, reflexivities, and persons that I unfolded in order to begin: to enjoy making or letting suffer, making oneself or letting oneself suffer, oneself, the other as other, the other and others in oneself, me, you, he, she, you plural, we, they, and so forth. With your permission, I will spare us any example of this cruelty, even if it be, in these times of ours, the most unprecedented and most inventive, the unbearable and the unforgivable.

After this pensive digression, I will leave still suspended the last word of an ultimate question.

This question will not be: Is there some death drive (*Todestrieb*) that is, and Freud regularly associates them, a *cruel* drive of destruction or annihilation? Or again: Is there also a cruelty inherent in the drive for power or for sovereign mastery (*Bemächtigungstrieb*) beyond or on this side of the principles—for example, the pleasure or reality principles? My question will be, rather and later: Is there, for thought, for psychoanalytic thought to come, another beyond, if I can say that, a beyond that would stand beyond these *possibles* that are still *both* the pleasure and reality principles *and* the death or sovereign mastery drives, which seem to be at work wherever cruelty is on the horizon? In other words, altogether other words, can one think this apparently impossible, but otherwise impossible thing, namely, a beyond the death drive or the drive for sovereign mastery, thus the beyond of a cruelty, a beyond that would have nothing to do with either drives or principles? And thus nothing to do either with all the rest of the Freudian discourse that orders itself around them, with its economy, its topography, its metapsychology, and especially with what Freud, as we will hear, also calls its "mythology" of the drives? He speaks, moreover, of his "mythology" of the drives while evoking right away the hypothesis of an equally "mythological" nature of the hardest, most positive scientific knowledge—Einsteinian theoretical physics, for example. As to this beyond of the beyond, is a decidable answer possible? What I will call the soul-searching states [*les états d'âme*] of psychoanalysis today, this is what perhaps bears witness in this regard, finally, to some experience of the undecidable. To an ordeal of the undecidable.

It is by naming the beyond of the beyond the pleasure principle, the beyond the death drive, the beyond the drive for sovereign mastery, thus the otherwise impossible, the other impossible or the impossible other, that I would like to salute the States General of Psychoanalysis.

For whoever might wish to salute with dignity some States General of Psychoanalysis, what kind of salvation can we be talking about? Is there a salvation for psychoanalysis?

Why give thanks to some States General of Psychoanalysis? And how to thank the psychoanalyst friends who, judging by all appearances, took this historic initiative?

I will try, later, to argue my salvation with reasons. But before I begin, assuming that I ever begin, I must, when all is said and done and in view of the business of the impossible that I just suspended, settle my choice on two common nouns. They have just struck a knock at the door, or struck period; we will answer them without yet being able to answer for them; they are the nouns "cruelty" and "sovereignty."

In the time I've been so graciously given, I would like to privilege two forms, which are major forms in my view, of what *resists*. Still today and for a long time. Cruelty resists; sovereignty resists. The one and the other, the one *like* the other, pose a resistance *to* psychoanalysis, no doubt, but *just as* psychoanalysis also resists them, in the most equivocal sense of this word. Sovereignty and cruelty, very obscure things, resist differently, but they resist, one *like* the other, both without and within psychoanalysis proper. Between the inside and the outside of what is thus defined (in French, it takes the definite article: "*la* psychanalyse"), the border will bear all the weight, in particular, the historical, ethical, juridical, or political weight—and thus the very bearing of our questions.

Cruelty, sovereignty, resistance: I am not at all sure that I know, or even that it is known in general, what these words mean, despite their after all rather common use, in Freud and in psychoanalysis in general. Basically, in a nonequivocal manner, what do *cruelty, sovereignty, resistance* mean? What are they made to mean? And, especially, in what way can the thing defined as psychoanalysis give or even change the sense of this prior question? This is, in short, the concern that, as a sign of gratitude, I would like to share with you.

I will not have the time and the means to elaborate as one should here the hypotheses of the work that I would like to submit to you. Please accept, then, that, contrary to my custom, I outline at the outset, without detour or complication, without too many contortions, their somewhat spectral silhouette. I will not be content to rely on a concept of *resistance* that I worked out elsewhere, while formalizing in particular the heterogeneous uses that Freud proposes of it and attempting thereby to put them to work analyzing two forms of resistance in force, *both* resistance to psychoanalysis in the world *and* resistance to the world within psychoanalysis that also resists itself, that folds back on itself to resist itself, if I can say that, to inhibit itself, in a quasi-autoimmune fashion. By attempting to take another step, I will be asking whether, *today*, here and now, the word and the concept of *resistance* remain still appropriate. Do they represent the most strategic, most economical lever for thinking what is going wrong, what is not going well in the world on the subject and in the vicinity of psychoanalysis, between it and it, if I can say that? What is going wrong? What is not going well? What is suffering and complaining? Who is suffering from what? What is the grievance of psychoanalysis? What registers of mourners has it opened? To be signed by whom? What is not marching along at a steady pace in the prevalent styles of its discourse, its practice, its hypothetical or virtual community, its institutional inscriptions, its relations with what used to be called civil society and the state, in the upheaval of its sociology, and in a differentiated way in each country, in the mutation that affects the figure of patients and practitioners, in the transformation of the demand, of the scene, and what just yesterday was still called the "analytic situation"— whose precariousness and historical artificiality I remember having pointed out decades ago?

What is someone doing who says "it's going wrong" and especially "it's not going well," "it's suffering," "it's suffering" on the side of those who make of suffering, the cruelest suffering, their affair? The one who says "it's not going well" already announces a repairing, therapeutic, restorative, or redemptive concern. It is necessary to save, it is necessary to assure the salvation: that psychoanalysis be saved, let live or live on psychoanalysis. This salutary, sanitary, or immunitary concern triggers simultaneously a gesture of war: the militant would like to cure or save by routing, precisely, a resistance. I am not sure that this rescue project, this salvation or health plan, this profession of public safety is not also, in part, or even in secret, that of your States General, which is already pregnant, virtually, in the dark, with some shadow Committee of Public Safety.[1] As a result, I am not sure, at this point, that I am altogether one of you even if, in part, I remain proud to claim to be by sharing your worry.

I have already expressed some doubts about the homogeneous structure of this multiple concept of *resistance* (*Widerstand*) in Freud. I will do so differently today. No doubt the world, the process of worldwide-ization[2] of the world, as it goes along, with all its consequences—political, social, economic, juridical, techno-scientific, and so forth—resists psychoanalysis today. It does so in new ways that you are doubtless in the process of interrogating. It resists in an unequal fashion that is difficult to analyze. It opposes psychoanalysis not only with a model of positive science, or even positivistic, cognitivistic, physicalistic, psycho-pharmacological, genetistic science, but notably also sometimes the academicism of a spiritualist, religious, or flat-out philosophical hermeneutic, or even (because none of these are mutually exclusive) archaic institutions, concepts, and practices of the ethical, the juridical, and the political that seem to be still dominated by a certain logic, that is, by a certain onto-theological metaphysics of *sovereignty* (autonomy and omnipotence of the subject—individual or state—freedom, egological will, conscious intentionality, or if you will, the ego, the ego ideal, and the superego, etc.). The first gesture of psychoanalysis will have been to explain this sovereignty, to give an account of its ineluctability while aiming to deconstruct its genealogy—which passes also by way of cruel murder. As for the physical, neuronal, or genetic sciences, Freud was the first not to reject, but to expect a lot from them—provided that one knows how to wait expectantly, precisely, and to articulate without confusing, without precipitously homogenizing, without crushing the different agencies, structures, and laws, while respecting the relays, the delays, and, do I dare say, the deferred of differance. In fact, both in the world and in the analytic communities, these positivist or spiritualist models, these metaphysical axioms of ethics, law, and politics, have not even had their surfaces scratched, much less been "deconstructed" by the psychoanalytic revolution. They will resist it for a long time yet; in truth, they are made to resist it. And one may, in fact, call this a fundamental "resistance." When faced with this resistance, psychoanalysis, no doubt, in the statutory forms of its community, in the greatest authority of its discourse, in its most visible institutions, resists *doubly* what remains archaic in this worldwide-ization. It doesn't like what it sees, but it doesn't tackle it, doesn't analyze it. And this resistance is also a self-resistance. There is something wrong, in any case an autoimmune function in psychoanalysis as everywhere else, a rejection of self, a resistance to self, to its own principality, its own principle of protection.

As I see it, psychoanalysis has not yet undertaken and thus still less succeeded in thinking, penetrating, and changing the axioms of the ethical, the juridical, and the political, notably in those seismic places where the theological phantasm of sovereignty quakes and where the most traumatic, let us say in a still confused manner the most cruel events of our day are being produced. This quaking of the human earth gives rise to a new scene, which since the Second World War has been structured by unprecedented juridical performatives (and all the "mythologies" that Freud speaks of, in particular the psychoanalytic mythology of the drives, are tied to conventional fictions, that is, to the authorized authority of performative acts), such as the new Declaration of Human Rights—the rights not just of man, as we say in French, but of woman as well—the condemnation of genocide, the concept of crime against humanity (imprescriptible in France), the creation under way of new international penal authorities, not to mention the growing struggle against the vestiges of forms of punishment called "cruel," which remain the best emblem of the sovereign power of the state over the life and death of the citizen, namely, besides war, the death penalty, which is massively enforced in China, in the United States, and in a number of Arab Muslim countries. It is especially here that the concept of cruelty, this obscure and enigmatic concept, this site of obscurantism both within and without psychoanalysis, calls for indispensable analyses, to which we will have to return.

These are all things about which, if I am not mistaken, psychoanalysis as such, in its statutory and authorized discourse, or even in the quasi totality of its productions, has so far said next to nothing, has had next to nothing original to say. In the very place where one expects the most specific response from psychoanalysis—in truth, the only appropriate response. I mean once again: *without alibi.* All this produces a mutation that I venture to call revolutionary, in particular, a mutation on the subject of the subject and of the citizen subject, that is, the relations among democracy, citizenship, and noncitizenship, in other words, the state and the beyond of the state. If psychoanalysis does not take this mutation into account, if it does not engage with it, if it does not transform itself at this rhythm, it will itself be, as it already is in large measure, deported, overwhelmed, left on the side of the road, exposed to all the drifts of the currents, to all appropriations, to all abductions, or else, inversely, it will remain rooted in the conditions of a period that saw its birth, still aphasic in the Central European cradle of its birth: a certain equivocal aftermath of a French Revolution, whose event, it seems to me, psychoanalysis has not yet thought through. In particular as regards that which, in the said French Revolution and its legacy, will have concerned the obscure concepts of sovereignty and cruelty.

That it is not alone, far from it, in not having thought through this Revolution and its aftermaths, is paltry consolation, especially for those who, like myself, believe that psychoanalysis, having announced as much at its birth, should have something indispensable and essential not just to *say* but also to *do* on this subject. Without alibi. The decisive thing that there would be to say and to do on this subject should register the shock wave of one or more psychoanalytic revolutions. Notably on the subject of what is called, therefore, sovereignty and cruelty. But if the *mondialisation* (worldwide-ization) of the world that we are told is under way resists psychoanalysis in multiple ways, not authorizing it to touch that world's fundamental axioms of ethics, law, and politics, if, inversely, psychoanalysis resists in multiple ways and in an autoimmune fashion, thus failing to think through and to change these axioms, is not then this concept of *resistance*, even where it is as stratified and complicated as I tried to show, just as problematic as those of sovereignty and cruelty? Even in its enigmatic multiplicity (I counted 5 + or - 1 concepts or places of "resistance," according to Freud), does not this concept of resistance still imply border lines, front lines, or theaters of war whose model is precisely what is becoming outdated today? If there is still war, and for a long time yet, or in any case war's cruelty, warlike, torturing, massively or subtlety cruel aggression, it is no longer certain that the figure of war, and especially the difference between individual wars, civil wars, and national wars, still corresponds to concepts whose rigor is assured. A new discourse on war is necessary. We await today new "Thoughts for the Times on War and Death" (I am citing some titles of Freud: "Zeitgemässes über Krieg und Tod," 1915) and a new "Why War?" ("Warum Krieg?" 1932), or at least new readings of texts of this sort. Thus, it is not certain that the concept of front, the figure of a front line or of an indivisible trench, of a beachhead, of a capital front indissociable from that of war, it is not certain that all this can furnish a model of something like a resistance—either internal or external. As much as the concepts of sovereignty or cruelty, it is perhaps the concept of resistance that awaits another revolution, its own, after the French Revolution of two hundred years ago and the political revolutions that followed, likewise after the psychoanalytic revolution and those that perhaps followed it. For there is always more than one revolution possible in the revolution. And what one might also call the technical or techno-scientific revolution (whether it touches on microelectronics, tele-virtualization, or genetics) is never simply external to the others. For example, there is a dimension of tele-technical virtuality, of the tele-technical revolution of the *possible* that psychoanalysis, in its dominant axis, has failed—still fails, no doubt, and this is another resistance—to take rigorously into account, and that, moreover, will have played an essential role in the principle of convocation as in the implementation, the preparation, and the type of exchange of these very States General, in their space, their spacing, their becoming-time of worldwide space, in their horizontal networking, thus in their potential though limited dehierarchization over the networks of the World Wide Web. In a word, what is the revolutionary? And the postrevolutionary? And what is world war and postwar for psychoanalysis today? These are perhaps other forms of the same question.

I was tempted at first, then for lack of time I had to resist the temptation to pursue very far the comparative analysis of the States General of 1789 and the States General of Psychoanalysis. Whence comes the Call? Who convokes whom? What is the supposed or dissimulated hierarchy here? Who has power and who is getting ready to take it? Who will be able to renounce it? How will what was then called the "verification of powers" have occurred, that is, the high-stake decision that triggered the revolutionary process? Although one must not allow oneself to push the analogy too far, which would put us adrift in historical delirium, there is some reason to imagine in the nation and in the psychoanalytic international today, and right here, the equivalent of a third estate (no doubt it is the majority and itself heterogeneous)—assuming it was able to pay the entrance fee—a clergy, a fraction of which allied itself with the third estate, whereas the majority of priests and psychoanalytic interpreters tend to vote with a nobility that counts among its ranks some dissidents, some prerevolutionary subjects, or even some Lafayette determined to do something for the new United States. I leave you to answer these questions: Who here would represent the nobility? And the clergy? And the lower ecclesiastical orders? And the fraction of the clergy or of the prerevolutionary nobility allied with the third estate? Who here represents the third estate of worldwide psychoanalysis, that is, in truth, of an essentially European psychoanalysis—if not in its territory and at its margins, at least in the roots of its culture, in particular its religious, juridical, and political culture?

Why would these questions be outdated? If I had not resisted the temptation, I would have privileged the moment of the register of grievances (*cahiers de doléance*) that preceded the States General. I would have pretended to divide the unity of this motif in two: *death* and *technics*.

If psychoanalysis is not dead, and no one can doubt that, it is mortal and it knows it, like the civilizations that Valéry spoke of. In any case, it seems to be in mourning although it doesn't know whether or not the mourning is its own. What is the grievance, in other words, the pain and sorrow, the suffering and grief, of which psychoanalysis, after a century of existence, finds cause to complain? What is the complaint of psychoanalysis today? What are you complaining about? Who are you complaining about? To whom? What or whom do psychoanalysts throughout the whole world accept or refuse to mourn, to confess their work of mourning, their *grief* but also their *grievance*, their claim, their complaint, their demand? If, in a psychoanalysis that is a century old or young, a promise remains undelivered or, as we say in French, *en souffrance*, what is it in psychoanalysis that exudes death or the threat of death? A regicide in progress? A regicide that is merely imminent, a regicide to come? And what if the promise was a threat, which would be an intolerable ambiguity for speech act theory? One also wonders who would be the Father here, who the King. One's hand is caught in a hive of prior questions, which are like so many wasps that leave you no peace. No one knows any longer who is complaining to whom. There are only alibis. For the States General of political history, up until 1789, a constituted power was the entitled addressee of the grievance. Among you, on the contrary, this power is being sought, the addressee remains to be identified, and no one knows whether the protocols for its identification (the preliminary of the preliminary) ought already to be psychoanalytic or not. And if they are psychoanalytic, by which psychoanalytic filiation, by which "school," if you prefer, are they authorized to authorize themselves? The grievance may concern the presumed *inside* of psychoanalysis: the nonexistence or the dysfunction of a national or international community of psychoanalysts, the always problematic character of an institutionalization of this thing called psychoanalysis, the spectacular and undeniable dispersion of its places of knowledge and teaching, as well as its theoretical discourse, in their very axioms, their rhetoric, their language, their modes of exposition and legitimation, the radical absence of consensus on the subject of practical rules, of protocols of didactic training, and so forth, the radical absence of an ethical, juridical, political discourse, and in any case of a constitutional consensus on this subject, and so forth. One could extend this list; these are only indicative examples, and perhaps later I will privilege one or two of them. The grievance may also concern the presumed *outside* of psychoanalysis: relations with society or with the state, with the classical medical profession, nonrecognition or threatening appropriation by state authorities, apparent recession or unintelligible transformation of both the demand for psychoanalysis and the sociology of analysts, competition from pharmaco-psychiatric discourses that could delegitimize, even discredit or corrupt in public opinion the specificity of the psychoanalytic, development of a political ideology whose hegemony creates unfavorable conditions for psychoanalytic culture; inability of an out-of-breath psychoanalysis, by reason first of all of its native culture—European, Graeco-Abrahamic, liberal-bourgeois, etc.—to measure up to all the processes of worldwide-ization under way. In both of these cases, grievances on the subject of a presumed inside or grievances on the subject of a presumed outside of psychoanalysis, whether it is a matter of foreign or domestic affairs, one has to wonder first of all (1) if this limit exists, and of what value it is, between the inside and the outside, what is proper and not proper to psychoanalysis, and then (2) who addresses the grievance to whom.

The vertiginous originality of your States General is that they have as a radical task, and in a quasi-autoanalytic manner, to institute their own addressee, or to institute themselves as first or ultimate addressees of their register of grievances. They have to invent the destination or address and the addressee of a grievance that is still a little mad. "Mad" would be the trajectory of a movement that, having as yet no *telos* or target, must produce its own destination. If one attempts to translate this question into an already psychoanalytic language, which seems to me the very least one should do, one will say that the movement of transference or countertransference under way here has not yet taken place. It is seeking its place and its subjects. This great amphitheater is *already* but is *not yet* an analytic site.[3] The threat of death I spoke of, whose mourning and grievance would be borne in advance, if I may say that, is perhaps in the process of invading the place left vacant for the transferential destination. It is perhaps a piece of good luck, this threat, the moment at which one begins to think, the Stranger would say, I mean the one who, in addressing you, basically does not belong to a presumed inside of the analytic community. Death and technics, I said. Is there a link between them? And does thinking death suppose that first one think technics? If I had the time, I would link, as I did in the past, this question of death to that of technics, in particular to a nonderivable, nonsecondary technics, of which the unprecedented tele-technical apparatus of these States General would have served as my example, in a history that would go back further than the magic writing pad. But I leave off following this path as well, for lack of time.

Beyond formal and statutory appearances, it is difficult to know who calls whom to the States General and who, at bottom, ever convokes them. I am speaking of all States General in general, well before these here, concerning which I would like to ask myself, along with you, in what way perhaps, over the course of this tradition to which they claim to go back, they are nevertheless inaugural. It does not escape those who have the apparent power to launch this appeal that already they *are responding*, already they have heard a call, whose source and sense, whose *what* and *who*, the States General themselves would have to determine. If what is called psychoanalysis, what is called *to* psychoanalysis, has taught us at least one thing, that is to beware alleged spontaneity—beware autonomy and supposed freedom.

Still before beginning, I will start off again, now on another foot. To illuminate with a still feeble and partial light some of the places toward which I would like to go so as to cross the lexicons of cruelty, sovereignty, and resistance, I will read a few sentences exchanged between Einstein and Freud (in "Warum Krieg?"—whose first title, which Freud refused, was "Recht und Gewalt," right and violence, right and authority, right and force of law). This exchange took place, as you know, in 1931–32—which is not just any date—when the Permanent Committee for Literature and the Arts of the League of Nations asked them to publish a correspondence on burning subjects of the period. We now know to analyze (and René Major had something to do with this) what Freud thought of the more or less legitimate father of the League of Nations, Woodrow Wilson. Freud doesn't hold out much hope, as we know, for this proposal of a correspondence with Einstein; he laughs at it a little and confides to Ferenczi: "He [Einstein] knows as much about psychology as I do about physics, so we had a pleasant conversation." A disillusioned remark, and a very unjust one as it turns out, as attested by the letter from Einstein, which anticipates almost everything Freud will say in response to him. Freud will even admit it himself. Freud's skeptical allusion concerning the respective incompetence of the two great scientists says a lot to us, here, about the front and frontier of forms of knowledge between *phusis* and *psyche*, between the natural sciences and the science of the soul or of man, between, *on the one hand*, a theory of physics, a cosmic time and space, physical, physico-biological, physico-chemical, or pharmacological sciences, and, *on the other hand*, a psychoanalytic science. I will select from these two letters merely what we need to knot together, at least provisionally and for indicative reasons, the questions of sovereignty, cruelty, and resistance.

It is a matter, of course, of war and peace among nations. There is already the difficulty of defining the concept of war, notably the difference between a civil war and an international war. Einstein defines a final goal, and I believe one would not have to change a single word of it today. Here is the fragment of an exchange that first took place in German and was simultaneously published in English:

As one immune from nationalist bias, I personally see a simple way of dealing with the superficial (i.e. administrative) aspect of the problem: the setting up, by international consent, of a legislative and judicial body to settle every conflict arising between nationals. Each nation would undertake to abide by the orders issued by this legislative body, to invoke its decision in every dispute, to accept its judgments unreservedly and to carry out every measure the tribunal deems necessary for the execution of its decrees.[4]

Einstein deduces from this what he calls his first *Feststellung*, his first "axiom," as the Standard Edition translates, namely, that international security implies "unconditional surrender by every nation [*bedingungslosen Verzicht der Staaten*], in a certain measure, of its liberty of action [*ihrer Handlungsfreiheit*], that is to say, its sovereignty [*Souveränität*]" (200). Here again, in a remark that loses nothing of its pertinence today, Einstein notes that an international tribunal does not have at its command the necessary force to enforce its decisions and thus depends on "extrajudicial pressure [*ausserrechtlichen Einflüssen*]." He sets out from what he calls a "fact [*Tatsache*]" that must be taken into account, namely, that force and right (*Macht und Recht*) go hand in hand. Juridical decisions approach the ideal of justice demanded by the human community only to the extent that this community has at its disposal a force of constraint able to command respect for its ideal. Kant had already said this better than anyone: no right without coercion. But alas, another fact, adds Einstein, is that today—and this is still true in the year 2000—we are far from having at our disposal a supranational organization that is competent to render verdicts whose authority is at once indisputable and enforceable. By recommending explicitly and without detour that every nation abandon unconditionally at least a part of its sovereignty, Einstein recognizes the finitude of human institutions and the "strong psychological factors [*mächtige psychologische Kräfte*]" that paralyze efforts toward this international justice. One might say a drive for power (*Machtbedürfnis*)—translated into English as "craving for power" and into French as "besoin de puissance politique"—characterizes the governing class of every nation. This class is spontaneously sovereignist; it opposes a restriction on the sovereign rights of the State. This drive for political power yields to the activities and demands of another group whose aspirations are purely, Einstein charges, mercenary and economic. Despite the ingenuousness that Freud attributes to him as regards things of the psyche, Einstein advances at this point a hypothesis that anticipates the direction of what will be Freud's reply, namely, that of a cruelty drive (that is, basically a death drive), which, without being reduced to it, is coupled with the drive for power (*Bemächtigungstrieb*) that has such an original place in *Beyond the Pleasure Principle*. What could one do with an irreducible death drive and an invincible drive for power in a politics and a law that would be *progressive*, that is to say, confident, as during the Enlightenment, in some perfectibility? With great lucidity, Einstein notes further that the minority in power, in the nation-states, has control over education, the press, and the Church and that if populations respond with enthusiasm to this minority of men in power, at the point of sacrificing their lives for them, it is because, I quote, "man has within him a lust for hatred and destruction" (201). He even speaks several times of a "psychosis" of hatred and annihilation that would not be the sole prerogative of the uneducated masses but would even affect the intelligentsia. Intellectuals satisfy this drive or this desire in writing and on the "printed page." In concluding by asking Freud for his opinion, Einstein takes still further, and in a still more interesting manner, his evocation of an aggression drive. This is not at work only in international conflicts but even in civil wars and in the persecution of racial minorities. Einstein uses at this point a word that will be translated into English as "cruel," a word that will return in force in Freud's response: "But my insistence on what is the most typical, most cruel and extravagant form of conflict between man and man was deliberate, for here we have the best occasion of discovering ways and means to render all armed conflicts impossible."[5]

If the drive for power or the cruelty drive is irreducible, older, more ancient than the principles (the pleasure principle or the reality principle, which are basically the same, the same in differance, I would like to say), then no politics will be able to eradicate it. Politics can only domesticate it, differ and defer it, learn to negotiate, compromise *indirectly* but without illusion with it, and it is this *indirection*, this differing/deferring detour, this system of differantial relays and delays that will dictate Freud's at once optimistic and pessimistic politics, which are courageously disabused, resolutely sobered up. And this at the very moment when the father of psychoanalysis declares nevertheless that he ought not to indulge

[margin handwritten note: Einstein on politics + cruelty — addressed to Freud]

in an ethical evaluation of the drives. We will hear his answer in a moment, and will see the discreet but essential role played there on two occasions by the word "indirect."

Interrupting myself at this point, having hardly begun, I would like, I said, to salute the States General of Psychoanalysis.

Why give thanks to some States General of Psychoanalysis? And how to thank the psychoanalyst friends who, to judge by all appearances, took this historic initiative? How should one address a sign of gratitude to all those who right away heard and understood them, throughout the world, and resolved to make the best of such an event, however unpredictable it still remains and however enigmatic its scene? It is at once an unusual and familiar scene, but *unheimlich*, uncanny far beyond its *mise en scène*. Familiarly unusual, intimately strange because, *on the one hand*, nothing is more familiar to psychoanalysis, apparently, than a scene conforming to the usual imagery of States General: enfranchisement of a regained spontaneity, liberated language, the right to speech finally restored, prohibition lifted, resistance overcome, etc. One would venture to say that what should take place in a certain way at every analytic session is a sort of micro-revolution, preceded by some music from the States General chamber group, lending their voices to all the agencies and all the states of the social body or the psychic body. This should start up again each time that a patient lies down on the couch or, as happens more and more today, undertakes a face-to-face analysis. The analysand would then be initiating a revolution, perhaps the first revolution that matters; he would be opening virtually *his* States General and giving the right to speech within him to all the states, all the voices, all the agencies of the psychic body as multiple social body. Without alibi. After registering all the grievances, griefs, and complaints. In this sense, and by right, a psychoanalysis should be, through and through, a revolutionary process, the first revolution, perhaps, preceded by some States General.

However, without even recalling Freud's lack of sympathy for French revolutions,[6] we may say that nothing, *on the other hand*, has been more foreign to psychoanalysis, up until now, more disturbing for it, than the public space of these States General here, than this decor, these protocols, the duration and the technical apparatus that, for almost three years, have been setting the conditions for your meeting. Another, still invisible scene, therefore, continues to escape you. The signs you've received from this hidden scene remain indecipherable behind a whole staging [*mise en*

scène] organized in view of deliberations in common, authorized by decisions and performative declarations of the organizers or even the participants. Now what happens, comes about, comes to pass, or, as we say in
French, *ce qui arrive*, the event of the other as *arrivant* (the one who or
which arrives), is the impossible that exceeds and puts to rout, sometimes
cruelly, that which the economy of a performative act is supposed to produce in a sovereign manner, when an already legitimated speech takes advantage of some convention. If things happen [*arrivent*], if there are those
of us and those others who arrive, the others especially, the *arrivants*, it is
always as the impossible beyond of all the instituting utterances, beyond
all convention, beyond mastery, beyond the "I can," "I may," beyond the
economy of appropriation of a "that is in my power," an "it is possible for
me," the "this power belongs to me," the "this possible is conferred on
me," all of which presumptions are always implied by performative acts.
If at least others arrive, from close by or far away, from the family or from
the most distant strangeness, they do it, like everything that happens, like
every event worthy of the name, like everything that is coming, in the
form of the impossible, beyond all convention and all scenic control, all
pleasure or reality principle, beyond all drive for power and perhaps all
death drive. It is a hospitality of visitation and not of invitation, when
what arrives from the other exceeds the rules of hospitality and remains
unpredictable for the hosts. I do not know whether, behind their statutory authorities and behind the official signatories of the Call and the
convocation, behind the masters of ceremony, the historical States
General up until 1789 ever had a veritable and sovereign stage director.
What is certain is that no stage director has ever been able to foresee and
program anything whatsoever beyond the first act opening the proceedings. And even that is doubtful.

This should not prevent us, on the contrary, from seeking to identify,
through their representatives or their official bearers, the true forces that
are at work in the organization of these States General. Is it necessary to
recall that in principle these States General, the States General *of Psychoanalysis*, should have as constitutive mission, dare I say as an originary
duty in some way, to carry out as far as possible the self-analysis of their
staging but also the analysis of the forces, drives, desires that are secretly
at work in them, beyond any staging, or even beyond any seeing, any visibility, any phenomenality?

We are well aware of the long-standing connection between psychoanalysis and the stage, between psychoanalysis and the theater. Will it always be the same theatrical structure? Will it still be tomorrow, in the next millennium, the same model, the same apparatus, the same theatrical family? Will it be the theater of the same family, an always more or less royal family, rather patriarchal and heterosexual, installed in sexual difference as binary opposition? Will it be, from now on, a single-parent or tri-parent family, for example? Will the theatrical reference of psychoanalysis still tomorrow be Greek, Shakespearean, Elizabethan theater, that is to say simply, and assuming there has ever been another, European theater, in sum? What still links psychoanalysis to the history of Greek, Jewish, Christian Europe is not very well known. And if I add—or if I don't add—*Muslim* to fill out the list of Abrahamic monotheisms, I am already opening the gulf of an immense interrogation. Its dimensions are not merely demographic. Why does psychoanalysis never get a foothold in the vast territory of the Arabo-Islamic culture? Not to mention East Asia. More broadly, you are wondering why psychoanalysis remains, without advancing into it and without the Mosaic illusion of a promised land, on the external edge of the immense and growing majority of men and women who people the surface of an earth undergoing "globalization" or the becoming worldwide of the world. I will not name the Mosaic illusion of the promised land, even if only to say it is hopeless, without recalling briefly both the insistence of the specter of Moses right away in the opening acts of psychoanalysis and especially, decades before *Moses and Monotheism* appeared right before the Second World War, what Freud said one day to Jung in a letter from 1909. That was the very year Freud fainted before him, the year of the first trip to America, from which he brought back the "American colitis" that, still today, would call for an inexhaustible follow-up and an interminable treatment.[7] It was also soon after Jung had organized the First International Congress of Psychoanalysis (forty-two participants, a "historic event," as good old Jones puts it).[8] Those years were, as you know, the years of an internationalization—altogether relative and very Europocentric—of psychoanalysis. This internationalization has not yet become, as we know too well, a worldwide-ization. Freud names in this connection the promised land of psychiatry—yes, of psychiatry, and psychiatry, psychiatrization, is basically what allies itself with pharmaco-psychiatry and all the new therapies, either chemical or genetic, that today claim, in the world and especially in America, either to have freed themselves from Freudian psychoanalysis by rejecting it, by condemning it to death, or else to have come to

Freud to Jung

terms with it through unusual and always problematic transactions. Naming psychiatry and the future of relations between psychoanalysis and psychiatry, Freud then launches at Jung the well-known apostrophe: "If I am Moses, then you are Joshua and will take possession of the promised land of psychiatry, which I shall only be able to glimpse from afar."[9]

From afar. What distance, what distant places can be in question in Freud's mind? What are we to think of this today?

We know what follows in the case of Joshua Jung. As for what holds itself in reserve on the psychiatric side, as for the cruel destiny of a proper name, as for the name of a Moses of psychoanalysis, history remains open, and I am convinced that these revenants must haunt our debates.

There is no States General without theater. There has not been up until now any States General without that to which, in psychoanalysis, the private theater of the family is linked in an essential fashion, namely, the theater properly speaking, the one that requires a public space. In the insistent vision that I have had to acknowledge, these States General of Psychoanalysis would nevertheless resemble an unprecedented scene, even a first theater of the cruelty that resists, in an autoimmune fashion, its own spectacle, its specular and spectacular temptation. What is titled, what is called, what has called itself States General of Psychoanalysis is that which would put a certain cruelty back on stage, so as to submit it to the hypothesis of a mutation. Which cruelty? The one that is exercised in the name of a sovereignty or the one that must suffer a sovereignty?

So I advance onto the stage of this new theater of cruelty, concerning which I will explain myself in my own rhythm, and it will be, I must ask your pardon, very slow. I would like to avoid alibis. (If ever I had a preference about the analytic session, well, you will find out what it is today at your expense, for you are going to suffer from it: it's that I would be resolutely, incorrigibly in favor of long sessions, very long. And despite the patience required, this is not the preference of a patient [man], quite the contrary.)

Without knowing—as regards the essential—without knowing anything, I advance. I have nothing simple or simply possible to tell you, and basically I know nothing. I don't even know how to admit that, to admit that not only do I know nothing, but I don't even know where to put myself, me and my nonknowledge, any more than I know what to do with my questions about knowledge and power, about the possible and the beyond of the possible. I don't know, to begin with, what, which title, or who authorizes me—certainly not myself—to salute, as I have just done, while thanking them, something like the States General of Psychoanalysis. And yet, you understand me very well, I have been authorized to address you, for the moment. And if I managed, directly or indirectly, to respond *without alibi* to the question "why have I been authorized? by what and by whom, at bottom?" I would perhaps have made a few steps in the direction of the self-analysis that I was evoking a moment ago. My own, perhaps, which does not interest many people, barely myself, for example around the questions that made me choose to speak to you today about the death drive, as I have done too often, but especially about cruel suffering, and that cruelty that is found at the center of a seminar, the last one, that I thought I had to devote elsewhere, and this is not fortuitous, to the death penalty. But well beyond my own, which is not worthy of your attention, it is in the direction of the self-analysis of the States General of Psychoanalysis that I will take my chances more surely.

Imperative will always be the question of principle, the question of the principles, and the question of *the* principle—of the principial, of the sovereign prince, and of princedom. Freudian psychoanalysis—psychoanalysis as science, psychoanalysis that never abandons its aim to be a science, although a science apart from others—will have reckoned a lot with principles, as is well known. Like the distinction between primary and secondary processes, these principles have been treated scientifically, but as indispensable theoretical fictions, just as Freud speaks, in his answer to Einstein, of our "mythological theory of the drives," as if the "as if" were itself still supposed to resist the critique that Freud proposes of it in *The Future of an Illusion*, around Vaihinger's *Die Philosophie des Als Ob*. Freud often named and nicknamed these principles, for example, the pleasure principle or the reality principle, just as he nicknamed "mythologically" what sends them into crisis, beyond or on this side of the principles, namely, a certain death drive that, at the origin of all cruelty, can take the destructive form of sadism, of a ferocity that the narcissistic libido would have detached from the ego so as to train it on the object—unless it is that of a primary masochism, a hypothesis that Freud also retains.

What new forms of cruelty would a psychoanalyst of the year 2000 have to interpret at renewed expense, outside or within the institution? With regard to the political, the geo-political, the juridical, the ethical, are there consequences, or at least lessons to be drawn from the hypothesis of an irreducible death drive that seems inseparable from what is so obscurely called cruelty, in either its archaic or its modern forms? Would there also be, a few steps further beyond the principles, a beyond of the beyond, a beyond of the death drive and thus of the cruelty drive? One would have to note the occurrences of the word "cruelty" in certain political texts of Freud and decipher their scope. At the more distant horizon of these questions would loom the necessity to situate, along with the psychoanalytic theme of sovereignty or mastery (*Herrschaft, Bemächtigung*), which is so present in *Beyond the Pleasure Principle*, at least in the form of a political metaphor, the theme of a *Bemächtigungstrieb*, a drive for ascendancy, for power, or for possession. I tried to show elsewhere, in a long *Post Card*, how the word and concept of *Bemächtigung*, however discreet they are and however underanalyzed by Freud's readers, are present beginning in the *Three Essays* and play in *Beyond* a decisive role, beyond or on this side of the principles, precisely, as principial drive, if I can say that, notably in love/hate ambivalence and the unleashing of cruelty that calls up the hypothesis of originary sadism. Indissociable from that of *Bewältigung* (exercise of power, ascendancy, or possession, movement of appropriation, etc.), there would thus be the concept of a drive for power—that is to say, of the capacitation, of the "I can" or "I may," and in particular of the performative power that organizes, via some sworn faith, the whole order of what Lacan called the symbolic. This drive for power no doubt indicates, before and beyond any principle, before and beyond any power even (the principle being the power, the sovereignty of the power), one of the places where the Freudian psychoanalytic discourse is articulated with juridical and political questions in general, with all that concerns the new givens, today, of this double problematic of sovereignty and cruelty. As for present or future relations between psychoanalytic institutions or practices, on the one hand, and the state, on the other hand (be it a question of status, of visibility and transparency, of fiscality, of articulation with the apparatuses of social security, of secrecy, etc.), one must take into account not only a profound transformation of the social field for the supply and demand of psychoanalysis, but as well mutations that concern, especially in Europe, the sovereignty of states, the abandonment of sovereignty, the harmonization of different systems of legislation, etc. By reason of their very exceptionality, the relations of psychoanalysis with the public space of civil society and the state have always been critical. The profound metamorphosis of these two dimensions of the public space creates a new situation. It calls for new analyses, new axioms, and strategic inventions. If I may confide in you the feeling of a foreign observer, it seems to me that everything remains to be done and there is not, there never will be the least consensus in view in any of these places, neither among psychoanalysts throughout the world, nor among their social, political, juridical interlocutors. But I do not exclude the possibility that this is how things must be and that this dissensus must remain a fortunate fate.

Here then, in another form, is the question of the principle and thus of the beginning, namely, the inaugural act that is supposed to produce the event, the performative power of the appeal or the convocation that always carries with it the "as if" of a convention on the basis of which, whether authorized or authorizing itself, an act of authority holds the power to say "I can," "I may." Everything happens, everything has already happened *as if* someone, or more than one, among you, according to the *as if* of convention, had *had* the right, had *taken* or had been recognized to have the right to call or convoke a meeting of the States General, to open a first session, to give a speech or issue inaugural invitations while addressing a general assembly, a national or international assembly. Before even knowing who opens the first session, one will wonder who calls, who calls himself, who "convokes," and *who* convokes *whom* to a meeting of the States General in general, while rightly counting on an already forthcoming response. Who, since the death of a certain king of France, who alone had the capacity to do it from the fourteenth century up until the Revolution, including in 1788–89? It is still, in principle and by right, a king of France, as you know, who in 1788 convoked by decree those last States General of which we are all thinking and during which a first mutation occurred, a series of transgressions affecting the number of deputies from the Third Estate, inflecting that decisive thing called the "verification of powers," imposing a per capita vote, a vote by "voice" and not by order, that is, by individual subject, by "I-me," all egos being equal, leading finally to the transformation of the States General into a National Constituent Assembly after a certain tennis court oath had contracted that heterogeneous thing identified under the name of the French Revolution—and which, even before the Terror, passed by way of a patri-regicide, which from now on I will call a paregicide. Never, one will never be able to respond without alibi to the agonizing question of whether or not the States General, convoked by a king, were the fatal prelude to the paregicide, the first gesture of the cruel execution of the king, the father of the nation, or, on the contrary, or whether they were the ultimate attempt, the last desperate gathering of all the forces that were striving, but in vain, to prevent, along with the threatened paregicide, a cruel Terror. Were they going to decapitate the king or save his neck? Were they going to erect him by decapitating him or re-erect him, resuscitate him, beyond the year 2000? For who will seriously claim that our republic is not monarchical, and that modern democracy, in the form we know it, does without a monarchical principle and a founding reference to a prince, as to a principle of sovereignty? Were they going to re-erect the patriarcho-monarchical function in as interminable and infinite a way as that analysis said to be finite-infinite?

We will never know. By definition, we will never know whether the States General, at the moment of their first convocation, were destined to condemn or save the king's head, and it matters little, no doubt, because in any case the two gestures, condemning and saving, remain indissociable. They inscribe in the concepts of sovereignty and cruelty an ambiguity that is as unrelievable as autoimmunity itself. It is too late, even for the question. That is perhaps the ultimate signification of any paregicide, of any Oedipus, any totem-and-taboo, any republican or democratic installation of the equality of brothers after some paregicide: it is too late, no more alibi, the paregicide has taken place without taking place, whether it took place or not, before any question, before any question about it, about what preceded it and what might have turned out otherwise. Too late, which means that the Revolution put an end to the very possibility of this question. More precisely, this is what is called a revolution, and it is the sign by which one recognizes that the revolution has taken place. No doubt one could say the same thing about the event in general, about *what* comes or *who* comes, about the arriving [*arrivance*] of the *arrivant* who or which is always a revolution. The latter, the event, the *who* and the *what* of what arrives, makes outdated in advance the question about it that always comes too late. It is too late, ineradicably too late for the question. I would say the same thing, mutatis mutandis, for the psychoanalytic revolution, which has already taken place and remains ineradicable. I will say the same thing for *all* figures and names of fathers that have presided over it while risking their head, losing *and* saving it at the same time, dying and surviving at the same stroke, like so many inexhaustible specters, occupying in turn or simultaneously not only 2 but 2 + n bodies of the king. Psychoanalysis is ineradicable, its revolution is irreversible—and yet it is, as a civilization, mortal.

No one, therefore, will ever be able to say whether the proper moment of the States General was in itself, in its original instance, *destined* to condemn or save the king's head. And whether even the king, by convoking these last States General, by turning the cruelty against himself, did not sign his death warrant with his own hand. Perhaps, like Freud when deciding that he would not take the presidency of the International Psyschoanalytic Association, and thereby erecting himself (this was only a first example in the history of psychoanalysis) into an absolute master, all-powerful and powerless, powerless in his sovereign omnipotence, in advance decapitated and resuscitated. More than two centuries later, is a meeting of the States General of Psychoanalysis destined to save or condemn a King or a Father of the nation? Which king, which father, and of which nation? Is it already too late for this question? Are these States General destined, without knowing it, to consecrate the death of the Father or to save the head of the Father—or yet a third hypothesis, to begin to *think* what is at stake there? Or yet again, more confusedly, but this would be the price to pay for their originality: all three at once? And then, inevitable transposition, who would here be the menaced king or the suicidal king? What would be a paregicide, without even mentioning the Terror, in psychoanalysis?

There are a few of us here who have insisted on the fact that psychoanalysis, as science and if it would *also* be a theoretical science, a scientific institution and community, is the only one that involves in an intrinsic fashion the proper name of its founder, in a logic of transferential filiation that it claims to be able to analyze and whose concept it has produced. Will we say here that the name of Freud, the name of a still *Freudian* psychoanalysis, is, in this literal form or in more subtle metonymic forms, what is at stake in the autoimmune paregicide to be provoked, avoided, or thought? This question is not limited to this or that death of Freud. Survival, like some cruelty toward oneself, always consists in enduring more than one death, and already during one's lifetime, even if one of these deaths seems more significant than another, for example the one that Elisabeth Roudinesco calls the death of Freud in America. "Freud is dead in America," she says in her latest book.

I allude to America so as to indicate virtually what should be a more insistent return to what this country's name designates for us here, today, whether it is a matter of the so-called globalization or worldwide-ization under way, in which American hegemony is at once obvious and more and more critical, I mean vulnerable, whether it is a matter of the Anglo-American language about to become, irresistibly, the only effectively universal language, whether it is a matter of the market in general, of teletechnics, of the principle of nation-state sovereignty, which the United States protects in an inflexible manner when it's a question of their own and limits when it's a question of others, of less powerful countries (see Arendt), whether it is a matter of the fate of Freudian psychoanalysis, more and more ostracized in the U.S., or again (and I take this to be one of the most significant signs), whether it is a matter of the convulsive crisis that this country is undergoing with regard to the death penalty. Here there would be too much to say about the past, recent, and present history of this problem, notably in the United States. Even while asserting too quickly that, so long as a coherent psychoanalytic discourse will not have treated (and to my knowledge it has not yet done so)[10] the problem of the death penalty and of sovereignty in general, of the sovereign power of the state over the life and death of citizens, this will make manifest a double resistance, *both* that of the world to psychoanalysis *and* that of psychoanalysis *to itself as to the world*, of psychoanalysis to psychoanalysis as being-in-the-world.

Of this immense and urgent problem of the death penalty, in its new phase, I can retain here only one signal. I choose it for reasons of the double motif of sovereignty and cruelty that I have decided to privilege. It is because the death penalty was deemed cruel, a "cruel and unusual punishment," that the U.S. Supreme Court judged it to be incompatible with two amendments to the American Constitution and its application was suspended in 1972. (One of these amendments forbids "cruel and unusual punishment.") Executions recommenced five years later, at the monstrous rhythm that everybody knows, when certain U.S. states determined, with the approval of the Supreme Court, that lethal injection is not "cruel," despite all the international conventions on human rights that likewise, in a great number of equivocal versions and without daring to violate the sovereignty of states, denounced but did not proscribe the death penalty as "cruel" torture. Throughout all this history that I have just evoked, from the American Constitution to modern international declarations, as in the discourse of common *doxa* for centuries, before and after Sade, it is the obscure word *cruelty* that concentrates all the equivocations. What does "cruel" mean? Do we have, did Freud have a rigorous concept of the cruelty that, like Nietzsche, he spoke of so much (as regards the death drive, the aggression drive, or sadism, etc.)? Where does cruelty begin and end? Can an ethics, a legal code, a politics put an end to it? What would psychoanalysis have to tell us on this subject? I draw your attention in passing to the trait of an apparent coincidence, in truth to a fact that I believe is not fortuitous but would deserve long and patient analyses. Although as of this date there has never been a psychoanalytic discourse as such, a majority or statutory psychoanalytic discourse, and no discourse by Freud criticizing expressly both the death penalty and nation-state sovereignty, it so happens that, with the notable exception of the U.S.—the only Western-style democracy, with a dominant Christian culture, to maintain the death penalty and to remain inflexible about its own sovereignty—all the states of old Europe, birthplace of psychoanalysis, have *at the same time* abolished the death penalty and begun an ambiguous process that, without putting an end to nation-state sovereignty, exposes it in any case to an unprecedented crisis or puts it back in question.

Before interrogating Freud's response to Einstein, I wanted to refer to Elisabeth Roudinesco's last book and to what she says about America, even if she does not take up these themes (cruelty, sovereignty, death penalty, etc.). It is important not to dissimulate what these States General owe, as to their premises, to the work and trajectories of Elisabeth Roudinesco and René Major, which could not be more different but are here not fortuitously allied. Along with all those who, in an admirable show of collegiality without hierarchy, gave direction to the committees of the States General, each one with his or her history, trajectory, his or her own work, I do not name them out of friendship, expected politeness, the gratitude of one who is in their debt, or to obey, out of conventional complacency, some rite of hospitality. We here owe it not only to responsible honesty but also to analytic and political lucidity to analyze, to exhibit even, in so much different but intersecting work, in its location within and at the border of the worldwide analytic field, in the interpretations, engagements, political and theoretical alliances contracted long ago, what made it possible and necessary to hold this meeting of the States General. One would not understand the genesis of this unheard-of meeting, not even the name "States General," if, through a fiction, out of modesty or ignorance, one were to avoid taking into account, if only to contest it, everything that for a long time has been driving the research, publications, commitments of Major, of Roudinesco, and all the members of the two preparatory committees, the French one and the international one. I am referring to what can be read *in* their books, *through* their books, in the ethico-politico-institutional positions they have taken, and the affinities and conflicts that determine them, within and without the psychoanalytic communities, in France and outside France. Many things could distinguish or separate the positions and the works of all those who took the initiative of these States General. But what should be analyzed as one of the symptoms, the secrets, the public secrets of the event I am talking about is their association here, their agreement, the network of national and international solidarities in which their work has come to inscribe itself and which supports this common cause. Not to give the necessary attention to this situation and these motivations on the pretext that, by rights, these States General would have spontaneously given themselves their own law, in an *auto-nomous* fashion, on the pretext that they would be autoconvoked and not hetero-convoked, would be, in my opinion, a political failing, a disavowal or even an analytic abdication. How an authentic *auto-nomy* (egalitarian and democratic) institutes itself, and *must* do so, on the basis of a *hetero-nomy* that still survives what survives it, on the basis of a law of the other, as coming of the sur-viving other, this is one of the forms of the question "What is to be done?" that I would like to take, without alibi, beyond all possible sovereignty and all possible cruelty. This question is not foreign to that of the paregicide.

I just said "public secret." The tennis court oath was public. It committed those who took the oath not to leave the assembly until they had adopted a constitution. You are wondering then for which constitution, for which new charter you now bear the responsibility before you leave, for which new institutions, for which forms of transition and transmission, in which language, for which state or trans-state power.

Oh, oaths! The performative force of oaths and promises! Oh, sworn faith! Oh, perjuries and perjurers! Oh, the fatal cruelty of perjurers! To seal the first institutional community of psychoanalysis, in a secret manner and independently of the public founding of the International Psychoanalytic Association, a short time after this founding, there was also some oath, some sworn faith and rings, more than two, seven, finally, with which to commit the Committee. Seven rings, each time a single time for all, each time a Greek intaglio—neither Egyptian nor Jewish— that came from Freud's collection: a head of Jupiter! To save time, I gave up the idea of making this conference lecture turn in the circumference around the turn of this ring. Of *these* rings, rather, and of what became of them, whether they were lost, bequeathed in legacy, or returned to their case. One must take seriously, in psychoanalysis and elsewhere, this question of secrecy, in its ethical and political implications, there where it *delimits* the very authority, power, and legitimacy of the political—not only of the political in general, of its right of inspection over the life and the death, the conscience, the exchanges (economic or not) of citizen subjects, but even of the political inside the analytic institution. The professional secrecy of psychoanalysis must not be, at least it claims not to be, like any other professional secrecy. I need not spell out, for you are better aware of them than I, the socio-economico-political consequences of this vocation to secrecy—whether or not it is respected. It is a matter once again of the relations between the state (*polis, politeia*, police and politics) and you. And us. I insist on this episode of the Committee, which might appear anecdotal or inessential, because at the moment of the seven rings, Freud recognizes, to be sure, that there is "a boyish and perhaps a romantic element too in this conception," but he demands that "the existence and action of this Committee" remain "*strictly secret.*"[11] One could say that in countless ways this secret was in itself constitutive and allegorically representative of that which, in psychoanalysis, remains and perhaps must remain at odds with the *res publica* of the political, or even of the democratic, I mean, in any event, of a democracy that is still founded, for some time yet, in a statist, nation-statist, sovereignist concept, and thus citizen of the political; but at odds also with the publicity of its own institutionalization, since the secret Committee remained external and inaccessible to the International Association. One may wonder what Freud would have thought of the worldwide States General of Psychoanalysis. In 1913, before the first worldwide war, all Freud's principal disciples were Europeans. Along with that of the secret Committee, the scene of the IPA is essentially incompatible with an idea of the States General. This incompatibility can also be described as an allergy to its very other.

Behind the scene of the institution and the statutes, other powers, secret or not, are always at work. To return for a moment to the States General of 1789, beneath the statutory capacitation, that is, the official power of the king, beneath the two bodies of a king who was himself authorized by God the Father of Christ, one may always wonder who in truth convoked the States General. Just as one can wonder the same thing here today. Is it a matter of a hetero-convocation of some by the other? Or of a spontaneous auto-convocation of forces that as yet have no name? Or of a hetero-convocation by the force of an as yet unnamable other, of un-expected visitors and unforeseen or unidentifiable *arrivants*? What about hierarchy and heteronomy in this affair? And what does the network of the Web de-hierarchize, affecting both the analytic scene and the scene of transference and counter-transference? This question would call for a se-ries of others, the same and so many others: Who convokes whom to States General that are worldwide, this time, but still in France, and in Paris, in a postrevolutionary France? Who convokes them all the same be-yond the nation-state? And States General *of Psychoanalysis*, more than two centuries later, but one century after the birth of psychoanalysis and the *Traumdeutung*, at a moment when one has the right to wonder if what is called psychoanalysis supposes in some way, inscribed at the heart of its own possibility, the memory, the conscious or unconscious archive of the French Revolution and a few other revolutions, all European, that fol-lowed it in February and then in June 1848, then during the Commune, then in 1917. An enormous, bottomless memory where the worst cruelty, the cruelty of a paregicide that still remains to be thought, the cruelty of the Terror, the cruelty of the death penalty on a massive scale, the cruelty of all the tortures and executions in the aftermath of the 1917 revolution, the still open list of the most relentless cruelties, *Shoah*, genocides, mass deportations, and so forth, go side by side indissociably, as if the two processes were inseparable, with the invention of human rights, the foundation of the grounds of modern international law undergoing transformation, from which derives the condemnation of crimes against humanity (imprescriptible in France since 1964), the condemnation of genocide, as well as the promise, beginning on 4 Brumaire of year IV,[12] made by the Convention, to abolish the death penalty in the French Republic, "effective on the day of the general peace proclamation." This day of the abolition of the death penalty did not arrive in France until al-most two centuries later, in 1981, which gives one a lot to think about the historical scale and what can be meant by "the general peace proclama-tion," in Europe, in the European Union, the birthplace of psychoanaly-sis (where the death penalty is abolished) rather than in the United States, the last Western country of European and Christian filiation that main-tains and massively applies, with a cruelty that is more and more obscene, unjust, and barbaric, a now nonbloody cruelty, "lethal injection."

I am purposely piling up allusions to the United States, where the des-tiny of psychoanalysis is waging its most critical and perhaps, on more than one front, its most decisive battle. In the thorny, thick, dense un-derbrush of the dangerous liaisons between psychoanalysis and North America, I select a rarely cited passage from *The Future of an Illusion*. Freud is comparing the American people to the chosen people, to the one that believes it has been chosen by God the only father, out of the "pa-ternal nucleus" that Freud recalls is "hidden behind every divine figure as its nucleus." Every people returns to "the historical beginnings of the idea of God" when it claims to represent ideal justice, the justice that rewards good, punishes evil, at least after death (which facilitates and legitimizes the death penalty), adjoins the invisible part of the specter to the visible, and so forth. Freud then adds:

Now that God was a single person, man's relations to him could recover the in-timacy and intensity of the child's relation to his father. But if one had done so much for one's father, one wanted to have a reward, or at least to be his only beloved child, his Chosen People. Very much later, pious America laid claim to being "God's own Country"; and, as regards one of the shapes in which men wor-ship the deity, the claim is undoubtedly valid.[13]

One could find here, from one chosen people to another, from one Father to the other, the matrix of an effective deciphering of "globaliza-tion," worldwide-ization, or what I call elsewhere the *mondialatinisation*[14] of religion under way, of that which, actually or potentially, constitutes and threatens hegemonies there. I also refer too briefly and for all the rea-sons I've mentioned to at least two of the works by René Major that are essential in this regard: *De l'élection* (already in 1986) and *Au commence-ment—la vie la mort* (1999). I underscore in particular his analysis in the first chapter of *De l'élection*, "De la fondation," of the madness of cho-senness and of what, he says, "psychoanalysis does to politics." In his chapter "Le recommencement," Major comments at least twice on texts of 1914–15 in which Freud uses, and I emphasize, the word *cruelty*; he does this under conditions whose essential and organizing ambiguity, I believe, should be stressed. On the one hand, these conditions imply an ethics and a politics that correspond to a condemnation and thus tend toward the elimination of this cruelty, to be sure, but at the same time and on the other hand, given the originary and ineradicable origin of the death or ag-gressivity drive, as well as the drive for power and thus sovereignty, one can have no illusions about the eradication of evil. Whence a figure—and I would say a lesson—that is *at once* progressivist *and* pessimist, still faith-

ful *and* already unfaithful to a certain spirit of Enlightenment. Here are
the passages that Major interrogates. I will later cite others that are analogous in the answer to Einstein and in the wake of *Beyond the Pleasure
Principle*, which is the direct inspiration for the letter to Einstein. First
quotation:

> In a letter addressed to Frederik van Eeden a few months after the war began,
> Freud points out to his correspondent that "*cruelties* [my emphasis] and injustices
> which the most civilized nations commit, the different ways in which they judge
> their own lies and misdeeds in comparison with those of their enemies" show the
> degree to which psychoanalysis is right to infer from its observations that man's
> most primitive impulses will never be abolished in each of us and that we are al-
> ways ready to conduct ourselves in an underhanded or stupid manner at their
> least resurgence.[15]

It is next a matter, more precisely, of the indissociable tie between cruelty and state sovereignty, state violence, the state that, far from combating violence, monopolizes it. A few years later, this will be Benjamin's
theme in *Critique of Violence*, around which I elaborated a few propositions on law (or right) and justice in "Force of Law." This monopoly on
violence is of a piece with the motif of sovereignty. It is also what will always have grounded the death penalty, the right of the state, the right of
the sovereign to punish by death. Following closely Freud's "Thoughts for
the Times on War and Death," Major writes, and this will be my second
quotation:

> Two motives of disillusionment, prompted by the war of 1914, will be put for-
> ward. One is the lack of morality of states that, elsewhere, do not fail to hold
> themselves up as guarantors of moral values. Which leads one to think that in
> peacetime, the state does not prohibit violence in order to abolish it but in order
> to monopolize it and that in wartime, it shamelessly withdraws from treaties and
> conventions that tie it to other states while asking its citizens for their approval
> in the name of patriotism. The other motive is a consequence of the first. Where
> the community no longer poses any objection to the conduct of the state, sub-
> jects indulge in acts of *cruelty* [my emphasis] and perfidy, of betrayal and bar-
> barity that are so incompatible with their degree of civilization that one would
> have thought them impossible.[16]

Why speak of the most *critical* and most decisive battle, which is being
waged here today, on more than one front, for psychoanalysis, notably in

the United States? If there is one feature common to all the States General of history, it would be this one, which historians never fail to point out: the States General are always convoked at critical moments, when a political *crisis* calls for deliberation, first of all, a liberation of speech in view of an exceptional decision that should involve the future. One cannot therefore avoid the question: What is the crisis of worldwide psychoanalysis today? Or again, or rather, what is the crisis of worldwide-ization for psychoanalysis? What is its specific crisis? Is it merely, which I don't believe, a *crisis*, a passing and surmountable crisis, a *Krisis* of psychoanalytic reason as reason, as European science or as European humanity (to do more than just parody Husserl's title)? Is it thus a decidable difficulty calling for a decision, a *krinein* that would pass once again by way of a reactivation of the origins? One cannot entertain these questions unless one supposes knowledge of what is or what would be, today, specifically, in its irreducible singularity, psychoanalysis or psychoanalytic reason, the humanity of psychoanalytic man, or even the human right to psychoanalysis. On what criteria of recognition does it rely? And as for crisis, this knowledge would be the knowledge of what puts psychoanalysis in crisis, to be sure, but just as well of *what* the psychoanalytic revolution itself puts in crisis. The two things seem, moreover, as indissociable as two forces of resistance: resistance to psychoanalysis, autoimmune resistance *of* psychoanalysis to its outside and to itself. It is through its power to put in crisis that psychoanalysis is threatened and thus enters its own crisis. When he asks what is wrong with the *mondialisation* that began at least after the First World War and with certain projects of international law, with certain appeals to abandon sovereignty, to constitute the League of Nations, which was then a prefiguration of the United Nations in its very impotence to put an end to war and to the most cruel exterminations, well, it is still around the word "cruelty" and the sense of *cruelty* that Freud's argumentation in "Why War?" becomes at once more political and, in its logic, more rigorously psychoanalytic. Not that the sense of the word "cruelty" (*Grausamkeit*) is clear, but it plays an indispensable operative role, and that is why I make it bear all the weight of the question. Having recourse more than once to this word, Freud reinscribes it in a psychoanalytic logic of destructive drives indissociable from the death drive. He alludes more than once to the "lust for aggression and destruction" (*Die Lust an der Aggression und Destruktion*), to the "countless cruelties in history" (*ungezählte Grausamkeiten der Geschichte*), to the "atrocities of the past" (*Greueltaten der Geschichte*), to the "cruelties of the Inquisition" (*Grausamkeiten der hl. Inquisition*) (210). Making use once again, as in *Beyond* . . . , of the word "speculation," here associated with the word "mythology," he specifies that this death drive, which is always at work returning life to nonliving matter through disintegration, becomes a drive of destruction when it is turned, with the help of particular organs (and weapons can be prostheses), toward the outside, toward "objects."

Can this logic induce, if not found (and if so, how?), an ethics, a code of law, and a politics capable of measuring up, on the one hand, to this century's psychoanalytic revolution, and, on the other hand, to the events that constitute a cruel mutation of cruelty, a technical, scientific, juridical, economic, ethical and political, ethical and military, and terrorist and policing mutation of our age? What remains to be thought *more psychoanalytico* would thus be a mutation of cruelty itself—or at least new historical figures of an ageless cruelty, as old and no doubt older than man. The psychoanalytic revolution, if that's what it was, is just a century old. A very short time, a very long time. It would have been necessary to analyze closely Freud's response to Einstein and the motifs that articulate it with other of Freud's texts. Unable to do that here, I isolate the scheme of a singular strategy in the Freudian articulation. Notice I say *articulation*, which supposes link and dissociation: articulation between psychoanalysis on the one hand, ethics, law, economy, and politics on the other. It would be a matter of sketching the limits or the horizon (the horizon is a limit) as the background against which this originality stands out. These limits, it seems to me, have not yet been thought by and on the basis of what is called psychoanalysis.

Treating first of all the relation between right and power (*Recht und Macht*), Freud proposes deriving the one from the other on the basis of a genealogy that goes back to the small human horde, to the murder of the enemy that satisfies an inclination of the drive. The passage from violence to law happens through banding together in common, "l'union qui fait la force," as Freud puts it in French. Right becomes the power or the violence of the community that, by monopolizing force, protects itself against individual violence. Force against force, deferred economy of force: this is what makes right. In the course of analyzing this process, Freud comes around to remarking something that is still true today, namely that the League of Nations did not obtain the force belonging to a new union because the separate states were not ready to renounce the sovereignty of their own power. There is thus as yet no true international law. Freud's remarks in passing about the history of panhellenism, the Christian states, or communism are very interesting, but I can retain only that which in the second part of his response, in what he calls his gloss on Einstein's remarks, signals, to be sure, a pacifist and progressive hope, the responsibility that must be taken in this direction but also the radical absence of illusion: Freud believes in the ineradicable existence of drives of hatred and destruction. Making very frequent use of the words "cruelty," "aggression drive," "hatred drive," and "death drive," he denounces an illusion: that of an eradication of the cruelty drives and the drives for power and sovereignty. What *it is necessary* to cultivate (for it is necessary that an "it is necessary," and thus the tie of an ethical, juridical, political obligation, take shape) is a differential transaction, an economy of detour and difference, the strategy, one can even say the method (for it is a question here of path, path breaking, and road), of *indirect* progress: an indirect, always indirect way of combating the cruelty drive. The word "indirect" is articulated like the pivot of this progressivism without illusion. Freud thinks, like the Nietzsche of *Genealogy of Morals*, that cruelty has no contrary, that it is tied to the essence of life and the will to power. When I speak yet again, in the double wake of Nietzsche and Freud, of a cruelty that would have no contrary or that in any case would be irreducible, with the result that any contrary would have to compromise with it, I mean this: there are only differences in cruelty, differences in modality, quality, intensity, activity, or reactivity within a *same* cruelty. Freud writes for example (but one could proliferate the examples): "There is no use in trying to get rid of men's aggressive inclinations. . . . The Russian Communists, too, hope to be able to cause human aggressiveness to disappear by guaranteeing the satisfaction of all material needs and by establishing equality in other respects among all the members of the community. That, in my opinion, is an illusion [*Ich halte das für eine Illusion*]" (211–12).

After having explained why hatred does not disappear and why it cannot be a question of eradicating the drives of cruel aggression, Freud recommends a method, in fact a politics, of *indirect* diversion: one should see to it that the cruel drives are diverted, deferred, and do not find expression in war. He adds: "Our mythological theory of instincts makes it easy for us to find a formula for *indirect* methods of combating war [*indirekte*

Wege zu Bekämpfung des Krieges; the word *indirect* is italicized in the English version, which appeared simultaneously]."

Indirection, the ruse of the detour (*Umweg*), consists, to put it too succinctly (but this is not the essential thing that concerns me here), in bringing into play the antagonistic force of Eros, love and the love of life, against the death drive. There is thus a contrary to the cruelty drive, even if the latter knows no end. There is an opposable term, even if there is not a term that puts an end to the opposition. This *indirect* stratagem of the antagonism between Thanatos and Eros operates in two ways, that is, by cultivating two sorts of ties, which are emotional ties. First, those that tie us to the loved one, the love object, even when there is no sexual aim. Psychoanalysis, Freud adds, has no cause to be embarrassed in speaking here of love, as religion does, with the same words—which he quotes, forgetting to mention that these are not the words of just any religion ("Love thy neighbor as thyself"). A thing that is easier to require than to carry out, he underscores with a smile. But this "as thyself" defines the second tie, the second type of ligature or obligation that comes to limit the outbreak and the breakdown of ties. Using once again the word "indirect" (*Die anderen Wege einer indirekten Verhinderung des Krieges*, "another suggestion for the indirect combating of the propensity to war," 212), Freud proposes to take into account the ineradicable and innate inequality of men, which divides them into the two classes of chiefs, guides, leaders (*Führer*) and, far more numerous, the dependent masses who follow the leaders (*Abhängige*). It would thus be necessary to educate the upper layer of men with independent minds, who are capable of resisting intimidation and concerned about truth so that they give direction to the dependent masses. Of course, the state and the church tend to limit the production of such minds. The ideal, Freud then says, and he even speaks at this point of utopia, would be a community in which freedom consisted in submitting the life of the drives to a "dictatorship of reason" (*Diktatur der Vernunft*) (213). Freudian philosophy of culture, civilization, or history, in this rather perfunctory letter and elsewhere, always comes back to this motif: teleology of a progress by *indirect* displacement and restriction of the forces of the drives, thus of a cruelty that, indestructible in any event, produces war or murder and may lead, the word is Freud's, to the "extermination" of the enemy. What are the most significant and problematic structuring features of this sobered-up progressivism and rationalism, of this new Enlightenment for our age?

1. First of all, this difficult concept of *indirection*, of a certain irrecti-

tude, of an oblique, angular, or mediating nonstraightness. This concept, to which I think I must devote much attention without abusing Freud's text, does not signify only detour, strategic ruse, *continuous* transaction with an inflexible force, for example, with the cruelty or sovereign-power drive. Even though Freud does not say it, certainly not in this way, this concept of the *indirect* seems to me to take into account, in the mediation of the detour, a radical discontinuity, a heterogeneity, a leap into the ethical (thus also into the juridical and political) that no psychoanalytic knowledge as such could propel or authorize. On the subject of the polarity love/hatred (which out of politeness toward Einstein he compares to the polarity attraction/repulsion), Freud says clearly in fact that, like the polarity preservation/cruel destruction, it must not be hastily submitted to ethical judgments evaluating "good and evil" (209). It is not for the psychoanalyst *as such* to evaluate or devaluate, to discredit cruelty or sovereignty from an ethical point of view. First of all, because he knows that there is no life without the competition between the forces of two antagonistic drives. Whether one is talking about the cruelty or the sovereignty drive, psychoanalytic knowledge as such has neither the means nor the right to condemn it. In this regard, it is and must remain, as knowledge, within the neutrality of the undecidable. Whence what I call the "états d'âme," that is, the hesitation, the confused mental state, or the soul-searching of psychoanalysis. To cross the line of decision, a leap that expels one outside psychoanalytic knowledge *as such* is necessary. In this hiatus, I would say, the chance or risk of responsible decision is opened up, beyond all knowledge concerning the possible. Is that to say that there is no relation between psychoanalysis and ethics, law, or politics? No, there is, there must be an *indirect* and *discontinuous* consequence: to be sure, psychoanalysis as such does not produce or procure any ethics, any law, any politics, but it belongs to responsibility, in these three domains, to take account of psychoanalytic knowledge. The task, which is immense and remains entirely to be done, both for psychoanalysts and for whomever, citizen, citizen of the world, or mega-citizen, concerned with responsibility (in ethics, law, politics), is to organize this taking account of psychoanalytic reason without reducing the heterogeneity, the leap into the undecidable, the beyond of the possible, which is the object of psychoanalytic knowledge and economy, in particular, of its mythological discourse on the death drive and beyond the principles. It is in this place that is difficult to delimit, the space of undecidability and thus of decision opened up by the discontinuity of the indirect, that the transformation to come of ethics, law, and politics should *take into account* psychoanalytic knowledge (*which does not mean seeking a program there*) and that, recip-rocally, the analytic community should take into account history, notably the history of law, whose recent or ongoing performative mutations have not, with only few exceptions, interested it or called upon its contribu-tions. Everything here, it seems to me, remains to be done, on both sides.

2. At the very point at which he recalls that there is no ethical evaluation in the description of the polarities of the drives and no sense in wanting to rid oneself of the destructive drives, without which life itself would cease, Freud continues, and clearly this is important to him, to find in life, in or-ganic life, in the self-protective economy of organic life, and thus in one of the poles of the polarity, the roots of the whole ethico-political rationality in whose name he proposes to subjugate or restrict the forces of the drives. It is thus by life, by organic life, that he justifies the right to life (therefore implicitly the condemnation not only of war, but of the death penalty—and you know that, by adding the "right to life" to human rights, many in-ternational conventions over the last half century have risen up against the cruelty of the death penalty, but in an implicit fashion, without con-demning it and above all without putting constraints on sovereign states in this regard). As for the right to life, the fact that "everyone has a right to his own life" (*jeder Mensch ein Recht auf sein eigenes Leben hat*; 213), Freud recognizes explicitly, in his letter to Einstein, that one may say this. But he puts this argument forward with caution. In his view, the question remains open as to whether the "community ought not to have a right to dispose of individual lives" (214), for, he specifies, "every war is not open to con-demnation to an equal degree." He thus retreats to a position that he does not try to justify by right or by an appeal to the ethics of a pure practical reason or a categorical imperative. He retreats without further ado to the factual givens of personal taste or a biological, even idiosyncratic nature, to, in sum, each one's constitution, in short, to what each is capable of doing, in the economy of what is possible for him or her. "We are pacifists," says Freud, and this "we" assembles all those who have raised the "dictatorship of reason" above cruel drives, "because we obliged to be for organic reasons [*aus organischen Gründen*]." Our rejection of war and cru-elty, he adds, is not only intellectual and emotional. "This is not merely an intellectual and emotional repudiation; we pacifists have a *constitutional* intolerance of war, an idiosyncrasy magnified, as it were, to the highest de-

gree. It seems, indeed, as though the lowering of aesthetic standards in war plays a scarcely smaller part in our rebellion than do its cruelties" (215).

"I trust you will forgive me if what I have said has disappointed you" (*Ich grüsse Sie herzlich und bitte Sie um Verziehung, wenn mein Ausführungen Sie enttäuscht haben*). These are the last words from Freud to Einstein, as he signs off with a cordial salutation.

Asking your forgiveness in turn for having disappointed you and tried your patience, I hasten to my conclusion in a dryly programmatic—telegraphic—fashion. And algebraic—that is, hyperformalized. I do not even know if what I am preparing to expedite in this way defines a task or a horizon for psychoanalysis, at the end of its States General. It is for me a question, rather, of what remains to be thought, done, lived, suffered, with or without bliss, but *without alibi*, beyond even what could be called a horizon and a task, thus beyond what remains not only necessary but possible. For what I am going to name at top speed punctures the horizon of a task, that is, exceeds the anticipation of what *must* come about as possible. As possible *duty*. Beyond any theoretical knowledge, and thus any constative, but also beyond any power, in particular the power of any performative institution. What I am going to name defies the *economy* of the possible and of power, of the "I can," "I may." It is in fact a matter of economy in all senses of the term, that of the law of the proper (*oikonomia*) and of familial domesticity, that of the sovereign state, of the right of property, of the market, capital, modes of appropriation in general, and, more broadly, of all that Freud calls "psychic economy." Here I am calling on a beyond of economy, thus of the appropriable and the possible. One may well believe that economy is already defied by the so-called mythological speculation on the death drive and the drive for power, thus on cruelty as well as sovereignty. One may well recognize in the death drive, namely, the beyond of the pleasure and reality principles, an aneconomic appearance. And what is more aneconomic, you may say, than destruction? And cruelty?

In truth, Freud works constantly to reintegrate this aneconomy, thus to take it into account, to bring reason to bear on it, in a calculable fashion, in an economy of the possible. And one cannot blame him for that. He always reduces both knowledge and ethics, even law and politics, to this economy of the possible. Even if one reckons with the detour through the indirect, and even if the indirect supposes a hiatus, according to the most visible tendency of Freud's interpretation of Freud, it is a question of a

strategy of the possible and thus of economic conditionality: appropriation, the possible as power of the "I can," "I may," the mastery of the performative that still dominates and thus neutralizes (symbolically, in the
order of the "symbolic," precisely) the event it produces, the alterity of the
event, the very arriving of the *arrivant*.

Well, I will affirm that there is, it is indeed necessary that there be reference to some unconditional, an unconditional without sovereignty, and
thus without cruelty, which is no doubt a very difficult thing to think. It
is necessary for this economic and symbolic conditionality to constitute itself. The affirmation I am advancing advances itself, in advance, already,
without me, without alibi, as the originary affirmation *from which*, and
thus *beyond which* the death drive and the power, cruelty, and sovereignty
drives determine themselves as "beyond" the principles. The originary
affirmation, which advances itself in advance, lends rather than gives itself.
It is not a principle, a princedom, a sovereignty. It comes then from a beyond the beyond, and thus from beyond the economy of the possible. It is
attached to a life, certainly, but to a life other than that of the economy of
the possible, an im-possible life no doubt, a sur-vival, not symbolizable,
but the only one that *is worthy* of being lived, without alibi, once and for
all, the only one from which to depart (notice I say from which *to depart*)
for a possible thinking of life. Of a life that is still worthy of being lived,
once and for all. One cannot justify a pacifism, for example, and the *right*
to life, in a radical fashion, by setting out from an *economy of life*, or from
what Freud alleges, as we saw, under the names of a biological constitution
or an idiosyncrasy. This can only be done on the basis of a *sur-vival* that
owes nothing to the alibi of some mytho-theological beyond.

This originary affirmation of beyond the beyond offers itself on the
basis of numerous figures of the impossible. I have studied a few of these
elsewhere: hospitality, gift, forgiveness—and above all the unpredictabil-
ity, the "perhaps," the "what if" of the event, the coming, and the coming of the other in general, his or her or its arriving. Their possibility is always announced as the experience of a non-negative im-possible.

The hospitable exposure to the event, to the coming, to the visitation
of the unpredictable *arrivant* cannot be made into the horizon of a task,
not even for psychoanalysis, although it claims some privilege in the experience of the unpredictable coming of the other, at the arrival of the *arrivant*. But what may, *perhaps*, become a task, tomorrow, for psychoanalysis, for a new psychoanalytic reason, for a new psychoanalytic

Enlightenment, is a revolution that, like all revolutions, will come to terms with the impossible, negotiate with the non-negotiable that has remained non-negotiable, calculate with the unconditional as such, with the inflexible unconditionality of the unconditional.

For this revolution of psychoanalytic reason, I believe I can recognize at the moment the heterogeneous order of *three instances*, I dare not say of three *orders* or three *states*. Orders to be called, assembled, then articulated even along a line of disarticulation—or on the external border of an inarticulation. For the sake of convenience at least, and to put some order in these orders, I will make use of those categories of speech acts to which I have already had recourse more than once up till now, for the sake of convenience: on the one hand, the *constative* (namely, the order of theoretical knowledge or of science as such, the order of neutral description, the taking account of *what is in fact*, as such); on the other hand, the *performative*, which covers, along with the power or the possibility of the "I can," "I may," or the obligation of the "I must" (do what I can), along with the order of the promise, of sworn faith, and thus of the law, the symbolic, all institutionality in general, ethical, juridical, political, and more singularly, here, psychoanalytic responsibility.

Three instances, then, or three states.

1. In the order of the *constative*, that is, of theoretical or descriptive knowledge, which is habitually opposed to the performative, psychoanalysis could in the future, as Freud himself prescribed, take seriously into account the totality of knowledge, in order to keep a rigorous account of it, and in particular of all scientific knowledge that stands on the border of a supposedly pure psychical realm (the organic, the biological, the genetic with their theoretical and therapeutic powers—for let us not forget that our theme will have been evil, suffering, torment, torture), but also the techno-scientific mutations that are inseparable from them, and all that which, in the order of performative prescription, gives rise to a knowledge (for example, the history of law, morality, and politics: as history of what is happening, for example, in our time).

2. In the order of the *performative*, where it is not a matter of knowing and describing, not even prescription, psychoanalysis must take its responsibilities, invent or reinvent its law, its institutions, statutes, norms, etc. I am assuming that this is why you are here. It must do this while keeping in mind its own knowledge, its own most specific and inflexible knowledge (for example, on the subject of cruelty, of the desire to cause or allow

suffering—just for the pleasure of it) but also of what is happening in our time (for example, the transformations of the economic field, of the market, and of what also depends there on techno-science, the social field, the field of the political and the juridical—I am thinking especially of problems of sovereignty, thus of cruelty, of juridical performatives concerning a humanity of man that remains to be rethought, and human rights, and crimes against humanity, and the crime of genocide, and the becoming international of law, and the war of languages, and thus the concept of language itself, whether national or not, etc.). But allow me to insist once again that between the order of *constative* knowledge and *performative* institution, the articulation, however *indirect* it may remain, cannot avoid or economize an absolute hiatus, the hiatus of a heterogeneity that must remain forever open, precisely, like a hiatus, that of a mouth that speaks or a wound that bleeds. The indirection of this indirect thus passes by way of the other, by the indirect other, by an infinite alterity in the indirection, by heteronomy: it marks here an absolute cut. Another concept or another structure of indirection. This discontinuity calls for a leap, this interruption gives a chance, a threatened and threatening chance, wounded or wounding, to responsibility, to what classical humanist philosophers called freedom, or, in a more problematic fashion, the freedom of the subject. This free responsibility will never be deduced from a simple act of knowledge.

3. Here, beyond the most difficult, the im-possible itself. Even where they register or produce some event, the orders of the constative or performative remain orders of power and the possible. They thus belong to the economy of the reappropriable. But an event, the coming of an event worthy of this name, its unpredictable alterity, the arrivance of the arrivant, all of this is what exceeds even any power, any performative, any "I can," I may," and even any "I must," any duty and any debt in a determinable context. Wherever there is law and performative, even if they are heteronomous, there can certainly be event and some other, but they are right away neutralized, in the main, and reappropriated by the performative force or the symbolic order. The unconditional coming of the other, its event without possible anticipation and without horizon, its death or death itself are irruptions that can and must put to rout the two orders of the constative and performative, of knowledge and the symbolic. Perhaps beyond any cruelty.

Along with a few others, you psychoanalysts know this. You could or you should know it better than anyone. The proof is that it was not enough for you to suppose you know; you knew how to make the leap toward the im-possible, by exposing yourself, with the gracious gift of an almost unconditional hospitality, to the visit of a stranger come to salute you as a sign of gratitude, to be sure, but without assurance of salvation, at your own risk and peril.

The stranger speaks badly of evil; he no longer believes in the sovereign, neither in sovereign good nor sovereign evil.

He only suffers from it, but know that he always hopes to make it known.

Without cruelty, with humble gratitude toward those who will have lent him an ear—and without alibi.

One rarely speaks of alibis, moreover, without some presumption of a crime. Nor of crime without a suspicion of cruelty.

Postscript

Without alibi? No "crime without a suspicion of cruelty," really?

Again the question of "Thou shalt not kill." But just who, exactly? Freud seemed to admit, as we heard, the necessity of just wars.

I am wondering today if the last words of this address, namely, a "crime," which would always bring with it a "suspicion of cruelty," can still be in keeping with the first words of an initial hypothesis: that psychoanalysis would be, I said at the outset, the only possible approach, and *without alibi*, to all the virtual translations between the cruelties of a *suffering* "for the pleasure of it," of the *making-suffer* or the *letting-suffer* in this way, of the *making-oneself* or *letting-oneself suffer*, oneself, one another, the ones and the others, and so forth, according to all the grammatical persons and all the implicit verbal modes—active, passive, middle voice, transitive, intransitive, and so on. Wrongly, in contradiction with these premises, the conclusion one has just read might then seem to accredit at least one difference between two crimes, between two transgressions of the "Thou shalt not kill": between, on the one hand, the murder that consists in killing the other, *in him- or herself or in oneself,* and, on the other hand, what is commonly called suicide, or the crime against oneself. This difference can never be erased, to be sure, without ruining the seriousness of a certain principle of responsibility. But I would be tempted to say, too quickly, that this difference is at once infinite and null. One will have to accommodate this as one can, but this would be *perhaps* the origin as well as the aporetic sense of this cruelty, concerning which we were asking ourselves at the beginning, without, you will have noticed, ever answering the question: What is this, cruelty? Where does it begin? Where does it end? And what if there were, sometimes, cruelty in *not* putting to death? And what if there were love in *wanting* to give death by twos, one to the other, one for the other, simultaneously or not? And what if there were some "it is suffering cruelly in me, in some me" without it being possible to suspect anyone of *exercising* cruelty? Or of *wanting* it? There would then be cruelty without anyone having been cruel. No crime, no possible incrimination or recrimination, no judgment, no right. Cruelty there is. Cruelty there will have been, before any personal figure, before "cruel" will have become an attribute, still less anyone's fault.

One could draw from this a nasty or mean consequence, among many others, one that touches on meanness [*méchanceté*] itself, on the insignificant bad luck [*méchance*] of evil, on the aleatory nature of the encounter, in love or in hatred: if a forgiveness can be asked, according to good common sense, for the *evil* inflicted, for the wrong, the crime, the offense of which the other is, by my doing, the victim, can I not also have to be forgiven the evil I am suffering from? "Forgive me for the hurt I feel, my heart, there where no one wants to hurt me, for hence comes the hurt I do to you, without wanting to, without faith or law, *sans foi ni loi. . . .*"

Avoir mal, faire mal, vouloir du mal, en vouloir à quelqu'un (to feel hurt, to cause hurt, to wish evil, to begrudge someone): I already imagine the sufferings of the translator who would like to respect each of these three words: *d'avoir* à *faire mal* à quelqu'un (to have to hurt someone), not to mention *vouloir du mal* à quelqu'un (to wish hurt or evil on someone). An apparently impossible translation. The French language seems to me the only one that deals out such a fate or such a welcome to the unheard-of and absolutely singular configuration of these words, these very large words: *avoir, faire, vouloir,* and *mal.*

—Am I somehow to blame for this impossibility of translation? For the impossibility of translating word for word?

—No, of course not, it's in the language. You inherit it.

—Yes I am, on the contrary; look what I'm doing with this inheritance. I'm betraying its truth.

—Is the alibi still avoidable? Is it not already too late?

JULY 16, 2000

Notes

Provocation

1. *Provocatio* ("provocation," "challenge," etc.) had a juridical and political sense in Imperial Roman law. It was the *appeal*, the right to *make an appeal*, to *call upon*; "ad populum provocatio esto," Cicero wrote, in *De legibus* (3, 6): "that there be the right to appeal to the people." For reasons that will become clear as we proceed, I am insisting right away on what links the *provocatio* to the law (*lex*, between *legere* et *ligare*), thus what also links it, precisely, to what links, to the link and the ligament as well as to reading (*lecture*), legacy, legation, and allegation—thus to the alibi, which is always an allegation before the law.

2. For reasons that, likewise, will continue to be confirmed, we must recall at least two semantic matrices, which are at once well known and often confused: (1) *Lego, avi, atum, legare* means to send, delegate, bequeath (for example, in a will), to charge the other with a mission or responsibility, or unburden oneself of these onto the other, in sum. Legation or delegation can thereby always become an allegation and an alibi. (2) *Lego, legi, lectum, legere* means to pick up, gather, thus collect, bring together, privilege, select, choose, elect, and thus read. See the Greek *legein* (to pick out, gather, choose, speak), which Heidegger associates with the German words *Legen, Lesen, Lese, Erlesen, Auslese*: "Legen ist Lesen"; "*Ho logos, to legein*, ist die lesende Lege" ("Logos," in *Vorträge und Aufsätze* [Pfullingen: Neske, 1951], pp. 201, 220). As for the controversial origin of the word "religion," which puts in play *another* verb (opinion is divided between *legere* or *ligare*), cf. Emile Benveniste, *Indo-European Language and Society*, trans. E. Palmer (London: Faber and Faber, 1973), pp. 516 ff., and J. Derrida, "Faith and Knowledge," trans. S. Weber, in Derrida and G. Vattimo, eds. *Religion* (Stanford: Stanford University Press, 1998), pp. 36–78.

3. At the moment I am writing this, the United States (since it's so often a

question of the U.S. in this book) has just been refused the right to sit on the United Nations Commission on Human Rights. This happened only in part because the U.S. maintains the death penalty, both in principle and often in practice, even if there are many signs of increased worry concerning the conditions of its application.

4. As one might suspect, my use of the word "supple" carries no negative connotation. On the one hand, it signals toward Kripke's problematic concerning more or less rigid designations, but on the other hand and above all, toward the remarkable and rigorously regulated function Kamuf assigns to it in relation to certain privileged concepts, those of *work, enigma*, as well as the concepts of some correlative instruments of deconstruction: "Because the reduction of *oeuvre* can take different forms (e.g., appropriation to the domain of knowledge or exclusion from it), instruments for its analysis and deconstruction have to be *supple*. I think we have been saying, in effect, that this "enigmatic concept of *oeuvre*" is extraordinarily *supple*. It can in principle take account of many forms of resistance, that *unclosed* category, without essence or essential trait, around which this *supple* concept or enigma unfurls" (p. 20). I have emphasized "supple" and "unclosed." Just as resistance can be praised or denounced, praised as the good fight against dogmatic forces, denounced as reactive or frightened disavowal, likewise the suppleness of a concept can be interpreted in two ways. On the one hand, in the comprehension or extension of the concept, it points to some heuristic, plastic, integrative (thus, formalizing) resources. But, on the other hand, the same suppleness can be a sign of indetermination, fuzziness, vagueness, the lack of rigor, a conceptualization that is not yet sufficiently refined. It is difficult, within the dominant philosophical tradition (to be deconstructed) to separate rigor from rigidity. I will come back later to this ambivalence, which allows the rhetoric of defense to turn very quickly, regardless of one's wishes, into the rhetoric of accusation.

5. By insisting on the idea that what responds in the response supposes some resistance, precisely where it "responds, *as this one and no other*," by underscoring "*as this one and no other*," Kamuf suggests, if I understand her correctly, that a response, and thus a responsibility worthy of the name, involve *without alibi*: here I am, it is I who assumes my irreplaceable place, I find myself here responding and not elsewhere, unique and without possible substitute. Agreeing with her (since I would respond as she does to the question being posed here implicitly), I always wonder, nevertheless, how a universalizing substitution still can and must be lodged, without contradicting it—be it only by making itself intelligible through language—in this unicity that absolutely resists any substitution. The old and inexhaustible question of the "I": the most universal in the most singular of *alibis without alibi*. But to respond and correspond to what Kamuf is saying here, I wanted also to evoke another turn that resistance imposes on the

response, another aporia in which I found myself some time ago, in a situation in which, precisely, I had to respond and attempt to respond *justly*: "In any case, if one responded without failing the other; if one responded precisely, fully, adequately; if one adjusted the response perfectly to fit the question, the demand or the expectation, would one still be responding? Would something happen? Would an event occur? Or just the accomplishment of a program, a calculable operation? To be worthy of this name, must a response not surprise by some disruptive novelty? And thus by an anachronic disadjustment? Mustn't it respond 'beside the point [*à côté de la question*]' in sum? *Precisely* and just beside the point [*justement et juste à côté de la question*]? Not just anywhere, or anyhow, or anything, but *precisely and just* beside the point—but at the very moment that the question is doing everything to address itself to the other, truly, to the expectation of the other, in consensually defined conditions (contract, rules, norms, concepts, language, code, and so on) and with *directness* [droiture] itself? These two conditions of the question appear incompatible, but each is as incontestable, it seems to me, as the other. Here, perhaps, is the impasse in which I find myself paralyzed. Here is the aporia where I've put myself. I find myself put here, in truth, even before establishing myself here" (Jacques Derrida, "As if it were possible, 'within such limits,'" in *Questioning Derrida*, ed. Michel Meyer [Ashgate: Athenaeum Press, 2001], pp. 98–99; translation slightly modified).

6. Allow me to note here that I subscribe to all of Kamuf's remarks on the comparison between French and American universities. Whether in programs of "creative writing" or in departments of all sorts of arts, in particular "performance art," U.S. professors have for a long time been able to produce and sign works. All the same, I wonder if they can do this *while teaching*, in the very act of their teaching. Would not some refined analysis bring out here a complex play of internal and external limits? These would concern not only the teaching and the *oeuvre* of an artist-writer-*professor* but also of *students* and of *whoever* remains outside the *instituted* university. The university without condition that I speak of in the essay by that title is not always to be found within what is today called, legally, statutorily, the university. "Outside," it can be more faithful to the founding principle of what is found "inside." And then, does not a work worthy of the name always open up, within itself, a sort of virtual university? As if it appealed, by provocation, to the foundation of a new universal knowledge on its own scale, capable of "reading" it, countersigning it, assuring its tradition?

Introduction: Event of Resistance

1. On continents, see *The Other Heading: Reflections on Today's Europe*, trans. Pascale-Anne Brault and Michael B. Naas (Bloomington: Indiana University Press, 1992).

2. For more on the word *oeuvre*, see below, n. 14; on *travail*, see "The University Without Condition," in this volume.

3. As cited in "Typewriter Ribbon," p. 102.

4. Jacques Derrida, "Structure, Sign, and Play in the Discourse of the Human Sciences," in *Writing and Difference*, trans. Alan Bass (Chicago: University of Chicago Press, 1978), p. 278.

5. "The event I called a rupture, the disruption I alluded to at the beginning of this paper, presumably would have come about when the structurality of this structure had to begin to be thought, that is to say, repeated, and this is why I said that this disruption was repetition in every sense of the word. Henceforth, it became necessary to think both the law which somehow governed the desire for a center in the constitution of structure and the process of signification which orders the displacements and substitutions for this law of central presence—but a central presence which has never been itself, has always already been exiled from itself into its own substitute. The substitute does not substitute itself for anything which has somehow existed before it. Henceforth, it was necessary to begin thinking that there was no center, that the center could not be thought in the form of a present-being, that the center had no natural site, that it was not a fixed locus but a function, a sort of nonlocus in which an infinite number of sign-substitutions came into play. This was the moment when language invaded the universal problematic, the moment when, in the absence of a center or origin, everything became discourse—provided we can agree on this word—that is to say, a system in which the central signified, the original or transcendental signified, is never absolutely present outside a system of differences. The absence of the transcendental signified extends the domain and the play of signification infinitely" ("Structure, Sign, and Play," p. 280).

6. I am not in fact venturing very far from Derrida's own description here: "Even while recognizing the power, the legitimacy, and the necessity of the distinction between constative and performative, I have often had occasion, after a certain point, not to put it back in question but to analyze its presuppositions and to complicate them. I will do so once again today, but this time from another point of view and after having made this pair of concepts count for a lot, I will end up designating a place where it fails and must fail. This place will be precisely *what happens*, comes to pass, that at which one arrives or that which happens to us, arrives to us, the event, the place of the taking-place—and which cares as little about the performative—the performative power—as it does about the constative" ("The University Without Condition," p. 209).

7. This is not to say, of course, that speech act theory has resonated only in an English-speaking academy. In Germany, Karl-Otto Apel's analysis of communicative action draws, although rather loosely, on Austin's distinction, and Jürgen Habermas has followed Apel in this regard. For a critical assessment of the

charge of "performative contradiction" that both level against other contemporary discourses, including deconstruction, see Barbara Herrnstein Smith, *Belief and Resistance: Dynamics of Contemporary Cultural Controversy* (Cambridge: Harvard University Press, 1997), pp. 88–104; a less probing but still useful assessment of the same critical phenomenon is found in Martin Jay's *Force Fields: Between Intellectual History and Cultural Critique* (New York: Routledge, 1993), pp. 25–37. Derrida has responded (and forcefully) to this charge of "performative contradiction" from Habermas in "Afterword: Toward an Ethic of Discussion," in *Limited Inc*, trans. Samuel Weber (Evanston: Northwestern University Press, 1988).

8. This word was also strongly marked, of course, by Sartrian existentialism. In a 1996 text for the fiftieth anniversary edition of *Les Temps Modernes*, Derrida reflected on what has been saved or should be saved of Sartre's work and epoch. About the word *engagement*, he writes: "Imperative necessity to keep the word 'engagement,' a fine and still altogether new word (*gage, gageure*, and language, 'situation,' infinite responsibility, critical freedom in relation to all apparatuses, etc.) while drawing it perhaps in another direction: turned toward where we find ourselves looking to find ourselves, 'us' today. To keep or reactivate the forms of this 'engagement' by changing its content and strategies" ("Il courait mort: salut, salut, Notes pour un courrier aux *Temps Modernes*," *Les Temps Modernes*, no. 587 [March–May 1996], p. 40; my translation).

9. *The Structuralist Controversy: The Languages of Criticism and the Sciences of Man*, ed. Richard Macksey and Eugenio Donato (Baltimore: Johns Hopkins University Press, 1970), p. 269.

10. Ibid., p. 271.

11. See "The University Without Condition," p. 221.

12. See in particular, *Specters of Marx*, trans. Peggy Kamuf (New York: Routledge, 1994).

13. Derrida remarks on this for him nostalgia-charged word, but then warns that the secret of this nostalgia will resist analysis in all he will be saying about its general and nonidiosyncratic meanings in psychoanalysis: "This word, which resonated in my desire and my imagination as the most beautiful word in the politics and history of this country, this word loaded with all the pathos of my nostalgia, as if, at any cost, I would like not to have missed blowing up trains, tanks, and headquarters between 1940 and 1945—why and how did it come to attract, like a magnet, so many other meanings, virtues, semantic or disseminal chances? I am going to tell you which ones even if I cannot discern the secret of my inconsolable nostalgia—which thus remains to be analyzed or which resists analysis" ("Resistances," in *Resistances of Psychoanalysis*, trans. Peggy Kamuf [Stanford: Stanford University Press, 1998], p. 2).

14. It would seem that the literary value of *oeuvrer* is conveyed especially by

the diphthong. There was a more popular spelling, *ouvrer* (the citation in the *Petit Robert* is, "Il est défendu d'ouvrer les fêtes et les dimanches"), which confirms the affinity between work and opening, *oeuvre* and *ouvre*.

15. Of course, all could be described as sites of some resistance in de Man's reading. One has to do with the sexual dynamic in play in the scene of Rousseau's lie, a dynamic that de Man dismisses with what Derrida reads as a pretty flimsy excuse. Toward the end of the essay, he remarks that, for him, de Man's text is "insufficiently 'psychoanalytic' " (p. 157).

16. Derrida has himself taken Augustine's *Confessions* as guide to this "genre." See his "Circonfession," in Geoffrey Bennington and Jacques Derrida, *Jacques Derrida*, trans. Geoffrey Bennington (Chicago: University of Chicago Press, 1991).

17. The figure of the Marrano is elaborated most fully in Derrida, *Aporias*, trans. Thomas Dutoit (Stanford: Stanford University Press, 1993).

18. Capital punishment was the subject of Derrida's seminar in 1999–2001. However, his writings on the death penalty, specifically as applied in the U.S., date back to a brief, unpublished text on Caryl Chessman. He has also given vocal and public support for the organized resistance to the conviction of Mumia Abu-Jamal (whose book, *Live From Death Row*, was translated in France with a preface by Derrida). His numerous public seminars in the U.S. on capital punishment have been conducted at the invitation of legal scholars as well as philosophers.

19. As I write, the U.S. president is encountering vigorous demonstrations in Göteberg, Sweden, protesting many of his administration's policies, including the continued legality of capital punishment. No doubt many American citizens, especially citizen-intellectuals, were given cause to wonder at the relative silence on this question in the U.S., especially on university campuses.

20. For example: "A question is then posed, and it is not merely economic, juridical, ethical, or political: Can the university (and if so, how?) affirm an unconditional independence, can it claim a sort of *sovereignty* without ever risking the worst, namely, by reason of the impossible abstraction of this sovereign independence, being forced to give up and capitulate without condition, to let itself be taken over and bought at any price? What is needed then is not only a principle of resistance, but a force of resistance—and of dissidence" ("The University Without Condition," pp. 206–7).

21. This report is published as an appendix in Derrida, *Du droit à la philosophie* (Paris: Galilée, 1990). See especially pp. 566–68, 610–11. Derrida also points out there that, by contrast with French and European universities, in U.S. universities the organized integration of practicing, creative artists is routine. [This appendix is forthcoming in English in *The Eyes of the University* (see n. 22).— Trans.]

22. Many of Derrida's writings on the university, the teaching of philosophy, and education in general are collected in *Du droit à la philosophie*, translated by Jan Plug as *Who's Afraid of Philosophy?: Right to Philosophy 1* (Stanford: Stanford University Press, 2002) and *The Eyes of the University: Right to Philosophy 2* (Stanford: Stanford University Press, forthcoming).

23. Since Frank Lentricchia's *After the New Criticism* (Chicago: University of Chicago Press, 1980), there have been several other studies: Mark Jancovich, *The Cultural Politics of the New Criticism* (New York: Cambridge University Press, 1983); Art Berman, *From the New Criticism to Deconstruction: The Reception of Structuralism and Post-Structuralism* (Urbana: University of Illinois Press, 1988); William J. Spurlin and Michael Fischer, eds., *The New Criticism and Contemporary Literary Theory: Connections and Continuities* (New York: Garland, 1995).

24. Derrida has been very direct in predicating deconstruction as justice: "It is this deconstructible structure of law (*droit*), or if you prefer of justice as *droit*, that also insures the possibility of deconstruction. Justice in itself, if such a thing exists, outside or beyond law, is not deconstructible. No more than deconstruction itself, if such a thing exists. Deconstruction is justice" ("Force of Law: The 'Mystical Foundation of Authority,'" trans. Mary Quaintance in *Cardozo Law Review* 11, nos. 5–6 [July–August, 1990]: 945).

25. That the idea of justice requires such a responsibility to past and future is affirmed by Derrida in the prefatory pages of *Specters of Marx*: "No justice—let us not say no law and once again we are not speaking here of laws—seems possible or thinkable without the principle of some *responsibility*, beyond all living present, within that which disjoins the living present, before the ghosts of those who are not yet born or who are already dead" (*Specters of Marx*, p. xix).

26. At least, in principle, everyone in the post-Enlightenment scientific university, which has tried to set knowledge apart from faith. That it can never separate them altogether is Derrida's point in insisting on the irreducible *profession of faith* in the "truth" of what one calls knowledge. The essential link between faith and knowledge would be no less true in the sciences, of course.

27. For the relation between fiction, or literature, and democracy, see Derek Attridge, ed., *Jacques Derrida: Acts of Literature* (New York: Routledge, 1992), both the editor's introduction, "Derrida and the Questioning of Literature," and his interview with Derrida, "This Strange Institution Called Literature"; see also Derrida, *On the Name*, ed. Thomas Dutoit, trans. David Wood et al. (Stanford: Stanford University Press, 1993).

28. "Now, such a concept remains confused, in the 'psychology' it implies. It is also logically incompatible with the rigor of any classical concept of the lie. . . . To lie will always mean to deceive the other *intentionally* and *consciously* and while *knowing* what it is that one is *deliberately* hiding, therefore while not lying to oneself. . . . The *self*, if this word has a sense, excludes the self-lie. Any other

experience, therefore, calls for another name and no doubt arises from another zone or another structure, let us go quickly, from intersubjectivity or the relation to the other, to the other in oneself, in an ipseity more originary than the *ego* (whether individual or collective), an enclaved ipseity, a divisible ipseity. . . . Not that psychoanalysis or the analytic of *Dasein* (these two discourses that are no longer ordered principially around a theory of the ego or the self) are alone capable of taking the measure of the phenomena that Arendt calls lying to oneself or self-suggestion. . . . But both Arendt and Koyré, at the point at which both of them speak of lying to oneself in politics, apparently do everything to avoid the least allusion to Freud and to Heidegger on these problems" ("History of the Lie," p. 67).

Despite the incoherence that plagues this concept, it remains a tool of choice among "experts" when they are called upon to explain lies that are difficult to account for otherwise. A case in point is that of Professor Joseph J. Ellis, the eminent historian at Mount Holyoke College who invented a past for himself as Vietnam veteran, war protestor, and civil rights activist. A story in the *Los Angeles Times*, "Top Historian Becomes Entangled in Fictions" (June 20, 2001), cites one such expert: "Perhaps, speculated Sissela Bok, author of a book called *Lying: Moral Choice in Public and Private Life*, this was a case of 'self-deception,' where someone says something that is not true—but says it so often that to the person saying it, it becomes true. 'To some extent we all try to make sense of our lives. I can well understand a certain drifting when it comes to the facts,' said Bok."

29. The irreducible indirection of address is argued particularly in the essay's last pages. But the essay also calls frequent attention to the staging and thus indirection of its own direct address to the States General of Psychoanalysis.

30. This may be to suggest that Derrida has been tending to the "care of the language" that John McCumber would see as an essential task of the philosopher. Although this is not the place to discuss it, I want to signal the interest for all we have been saying here of McCumber's exceptionally fine book, *Time in the Ditch: American Philosophy and the McCarthy Era* (Evanston: Northwestern University Press, 2001). It mounts a very strong argument about the "forgetting" that has shaped, or rather crippled, the discipline and the institution of philosophy in the U.S. university over the last fifty years, ever since they came under attack during the McCarthy era. He analyzes in particular the withdrawal of philosophical inquiry, in its massively dominant formation since those events, from every idea of truth but the truth of propositions. McCumber's analysis seeks less to open old wounds than to rehabilitate a crippled discipline by opening up again some of the doors that got closed when it retreated in the face of the assault and then "forgot" to lift the bans when the danger subsided. McCumber clearly writes in the faith that American philosophy can recover from this aberration by rediscovering and reactivating all those traditional tasks of the philosopher that have for so long

been abandoned or left to others in the university, notably to literary studies. Without questioning in the least the necessity of McCumber's argument or the care with which it is unfolded, one may still wonder about this rehabilitated philosophical discourse insofar as it would remain, in McCumber's description, no less able to dispense with consideration of neighboring literary theoretical discourses (but also, of course, with psychoanalysis) than the dominant "analytical" formation has done, for which McCumber roundly criticizes it.

History of the Lie

1. "The first problem, then, centers upon the question as to what constitutes a lie, for the person who utters a falsehood does not lie if he believes or, at least, is of the opinion that what he says is true [*si credit opinatur verum esse quod dicit*]. There is a distinction between belief and opinion. Sometimes, he who believes realizes that he does not understand that which he believes, although if he believes it very firmly he does not doubt at all about the matter which he realizes he does not understand. On the other hand, he who holds an opinion thinks that he knows what he does not know. Whoever gives expression to that which he holds either through belief or opinion does not lie even though the statement itself be false [*etiamsi falsum sit*]" (Saint Augustine, "On Lying," in *Treatises on Various Subjects*, chap. 3, *The Fathers of the Church*, vol. 16, ed. Roy J. Deferrari [Washington: The Catholic University of America Press, 1952], pp. 54–55).

2. "To lie for our own advantage is deceit; to lie for the advantage of another is fraud; to lie in order to harm is slander and is the worst kind of lie. To lie without profit or prejudice to ourselves or another is not to lie: it is not a lie, it is a fiction" (Jean-Jacques Rousseau, *The Reveries of the Solitary Walker*, trans. Charles E. Butterworth [Indianapolis: Hackett, 1979], p. 48).

3. Ibid., p. 58.

4. Rousseau's confession indicates clearly that this thinking about the lie cannot be separated from a thinking of sacrifice: "But what makes me more inexcusable is the motto I had chosen. This motto obligated me more than any other man to a strict commitment to the truth, and it was not enough for me to *sacrifice* my interest and my inclinations to it in all things; I should also have *sacrificed* my weakness and my timid natural temperament to it. I should have had the courage and the strength to be truthful always, on every occasion, and never to let fictions or fables come out of a mouth and a pen which had been specifically *consecrated* to the truth" (ibid.).

5. Saint Augustine, "On Lying," p. 60.

6. Ibid., p. 57. In another manner, Plato's *Hippias Minor* also takes into account the possibility of saying the truth while intending to lie or of not lying while saying what is false (367 a).

7. Michel de Montaigne, "On Liars," *The Essays of Michel de Montaigne*, trans. M. A. Screech (New York: Penguin, 1991), p. 36.

8. Rousseau, *The Reveries of the Solitary Walker*, pp. 47, 51.

9. Hannah Arendt, "Truth and Politics," in *Between Past and Future: Eight Exercises in Political Thought* (New York: Viking, 1961), p. 227; henceforth references to this essay will be abbreviated TP.

10. Hannah Arendt, "Lying in Politics: Reflections on the Pentagon Papers," in her *Crises of the Republic* (New York: Harcourt, Brace, Jovanovich, 1972), pp. 3–4; henceforth references to this essay will be abbreviated LP.

11. Reiner Schürmann, *Heidegger on Being and Acting: From Principles to Anarchy* (Bloomington: Indiana University Press, 1990), p. 351 n. 194.

12. Immanuel Kant, "On a Supposed Right to Lie Because of Philanthropic Concerns," in *Grounding for the Metaphysics of Morals*, trans. James Ellington (Indianapolis: Hackett, 1993), p. 64, trans. modified.

13. See Montaigne, "On Liars": "Lying is an accursed vice. It is only our words which bind us together and make us human." Elsewhere, in "On Giving the Lie" ("Du démentir"), he writes: "Our understanding is conducted solely by means of the word; anyone who falsifies it betrays public society. It is the only tool by which we communicate our wishes and our thoughts; it is our soul's interpreter. If we lack that, we can no longer hold together; we can no longer hold together; we can no longer know each other. When words deceive us, it breaks all our intercourse and loosens the bonds of our polity" (*The Essays of Michel de Montaigne*, pp. 35, 757).

14. "The moral principle stating it is a duty to tell the truth would make any society impossible if that truth were taken singly and unconditionally. We have proof of this in the very direct consequences which a German philosopher has drawn from this principle. The philosopher goes as far as to assert that it would be a crime to tell a lie to a murderer who asked whether your friend who is being pursued by the murderer had taken refuge in your house" (Benjamin Constant, as cited in Kant, "On a Supposed Right to Lie," p. 63).

15. "The shortest way, however, and an unerring one, to discover the answer to this question, whether a lying promise is consistent with duty, is to ask myself, Should I be content that my maxim (to extricate myself from difficulty by a false promise) should hold good as universal law, for myself as well as for others? and should I be able to say to myself, 'Every one may make a deceitful promise when he finds himself in a difficulty from which he cannot otherwise extricate himself'? Then I presently become aware that while I can will the lie, I can by no means will that lying should be a universal law. For with such a law there would be no promises at all, since it would be in vain to allege my intention in regard to my future actions to those who would not believe this allegation, or if they overhastily did so, would pay me back in my own coin. Hence my maxim, as

soon as it should be made a universal law, would necessarily destroy itself" (Immanuel Kant, *Fundamental Principles of the Metaphysics of Morals*, trans. T. K. Abbott [Buffalo, N.Y.: Prometheus Books, 1987], p. 28).

16. Kant, "On the Supposed Right to Lie," p. 65.

17. Jean-Pierre Chevènement, "Vichy, laver or noyer la honte?" *Libération*, August 7, 1995.

18. This series of questions ("Did he lie?" "Who lied?") might resemble (I say merely resemble), by recalling it, another historical question where, perhaps not fortuitously, it was already a matter of knowledge regarding the Jews. It is the question "Did Paul lie?" on the subject of circumcision when, professing that it in no way prepared one for salvation, he nevertheless said: "I have been all things to all men"; I do "everything in order to win them all over," including circumcise Timothy, son of a gentile. This "Did Paul lie?" is recalled by Michèle Sinapi in "Le Mensonge officieux dans la correspondance Jérôme-Augustin" (*Rue Descartes* 8/9 [1993]).

19. *New York Times*, July 23, 1995. Can one ask a newspaper to be consistent with its own archives? The counter-truth put forward by Tony Judt had been dismissed in advance in a three-year-old article signed by the *New York Times*'s special correspondent in Paris, Alan Riding, on June 22, 1992. Under the title "Paris Asked to Admit Vichy's Crimes Against Jews," the article reported on a petition that had been sent to President Mitterrand: "The signers of the appeal to Mr. Mitterrand, however, are asking the President to make a statement about the nature of the Vichy Government—saying it committed crimes against Jews 'for the sole and only reason that they were Jews. . . . The signers—who included the composer Pierre Boulez, the philosopher Jacques Derrida, the actor Michel Piccoli, and the writer Régis Debray—do not ask Mr. Mitterrand to apologize in the name of France, but rather to proclaim officially that 'the French state of Vichy' carried out these crimes. 'This symbolic act is demanded by the memory of the victims and their descendants,' the appeal said. 'It is also demanded by the French collective memory, which is disturbed by this denial.'"

20. Alexandre Koyré, "La Fonction politique du mensonge moderne," *Rue Descartes* 8/9 (November 1993), republished with its original title, *Réflexions sur le mensonge* (Paris: Editions Allia, 1996).

21. Alexandre Koyré, "The Political Function of the Modern Lie," *The Contemporary Jewish Record* 8, no. 3 (June 1945): 290–91.

22. Ibid., p. 291.

23. J. L. Austin, *How to Do Things with Words*, 2d ed. (Cambridge: Harvard University Press, 1962), p. 150. If it were possible to refine things here a little, one would have to analyze closely Austin's distinctions between, for example, a promise made in bad faith, without the intention to fulfill it, and a lie. A bad faith promise remains an effective promise "but it is not a lie or a misstatement" (p. 11).

24. Koyré, "The Political Function of the Modern Lie," emphasis in the orig-

inal. [This note and many others were omitted in the English translation. It appears on p. 25 of the reissued *Réflexions sur le mensonge.*—Trans.]

25. See Francine Muel Dreyfus, *Vichy et l'éternel féminin* (Paris: Seuil, 1996), p. 27.

26. Ibid., p. 291, trans. modified.

27. "The story of the conflict between truth and politics is an old and complicated one, and nothing would be gained by simplification and moral denunciation" (TP, p. 229).

28. The image is the key word or major concept of all the analyses devoted to the political lie in our time ("lying image," "image-makers," "propaganda image," "image" versus "event," etc.; TP, p. 255 ff.). The word and concept of image lend themselves here to some confusion. The analysis of this transformation of the icon is merely sketched by Arendt, it seems to me. What is at stake— and she does not say this—is a mutation that affects the substitutive status of a substitute that there is a tendency to represent and accredit (for example, in the allegation of "live" broadcasts) no longer as, precisely, a representative, as a substitute-replacement-representative-referring, but as the "thing-itself" come to replace, in perception itself, the "thing-itself," which, assuming that it ever existed as such, then disappears forever without anyone ever dreaming of "demanding" it or requiring its difference. Not to mention framing, selection, interpretation and all the kinds of intervention that are now technically possible in a fraction of a second between recording and its reproduction-broadcast.

29. Derrida is referring to a contrived "interview" with Castro conducted by French news anchorman Patrick Poivre d'Arvor.—Trans.

30. TP, p. 246; "To look upon politics from the perspective of truth, as I have done here, means to take one's stand outside the political realm" (TP, p. 259); "The standpoint outside the political realm—outside the community to which we belong and the company of our peers—is clearly characterized as one of the various modes of being alone. Outstanding among the existential modes of truth-telling are the solitude of the philosopher, the isolation of the scientist and the artist, the impartiality of the historian and the judge, and the independence of the fact-finder, the witness, and the reporter. (This impartiality . . . is not acquired inside the political realm but is inherent in the position of the outsider required for such occupations)" (TP, p. 259–60); "It is quite natural that we become aware of the non-political and, potentially, even anti-political nature of truth—*Fiat veritas, et pereat mundus*—only in the event of conflict, and I have stressed up to now this side of the matter" (TP, p. 260).

31. This motif is very present from the first pages of "Lying in Politics": for example, "A characteristic of human action is that it always begins something new, and this does not mean that it is ever permitted to start *ab ovo*, to create *ex nihilo*. In order to make room for one's own action, something that was there be-

fore must be removed or destroyed, and things as they were before are changed. Such change would be impossible if we could not mentally remove ourselves from where we physically are located and *imagine* that things might as well be different from what they actually are. In other words, the deliberate denial of factual truth—the ability to lie—and the capacity to change facts—the ability to act—are interconnected; they owe their existence to the same source: imagination" (LP, p. 5). One should, of course, relate this organizing concept of *imagination* to the discourse on the "image" that we referred to above.

32. For example, "The images, on the contrary, can always be explained and made plausible—this gives them their momentary advantage over factual truth—but they can never compete in stability with that which simply is because it happens to be thus and not otherwise"(TP, pp. 257–58), or this even more optimistic statement: "Power, by its very nature, can never produce a substitute for the secure stability of factual reality, which, because it is past, has grown into a dimension beyond our reach. Facts assert themselves by being stubborn, and their fragility is oddly combined with great resiliency—the same irreversibility that is the hallmark of all human action" (TP, pp. 258–59). In "Lying in Politics," Arendt writes with a valiant optimism: "No matter how large the tissue of falsehood that an experienced liar has to offer, it will never be large enough, even if he enlists the help of computers, to cover the immensity of factuality" (LP, p. 7). But assuming, *concesso non dato*, that one subscribes to these statements when they concern facts of the type "in August 1914 Germany invaded Belgium," an example of which Arendt is very fond, how can one still subscribe to them when the "facts" in question are already phenomena of performativo-mediatic discourses, structured by the simulacrum and the virtual, and incorporating their own interpretive moment? In truth, the question remains how to determine the structure of the substitute, here, the image in information and in narration today. The substitute-image still referred to the very thing it replaces, even to the "truth" of its revelation. As we pointed out above (in note 28), in the "modern" simulacrum ("live television," for example) the substitute takes the place of what it replaces and destroys even reference to the alterity of what it replaces, by means of its selective and interpretive performativity, and by means of the absolute and indubitable "truth effect" that it produces. Here, then, is doubtless the space of an absolute lie that *can always* survive indefinitely without anyone ever knowing anything about it or without anyone being there any longer to know it or remember it. It *can always do so, perhaps*, but we must maintain this regime of the *perhaps* and this clause of possibility if we want to avoid effacing once again the history of the lie into a history of the truth, into a theoretical knowledge that comes under the authority of determinant judgments.

33. On this question of *to bebaion* as the value of stability and fiability founded on stability, of *fiastability*, see my *Politiques de l'amitié* (Paris: Galilée,

1994), passim; *The Politics of Friendship*, trans. George Collins (London: Verso, 1997).

34. In a note to "Truth and Politics" (TP 298, n. 5), Hannah Arendt does in fact allude to a "crucial passage" of the *Republic* (414c). She recalls correctly that in Greek *pseudos* can signify "fiction," "error," or "lie" "according to the context." But other than the fact that she never mentions, to my knowledge, Plato's explicit treatise on the lie, the *Hippias Minor*, it is not certain that a context is ever decidable enough to become decisive, ever determinable enough to carry out the determination of meaning.

35. As cited in Michèle Sinapi's fine article, "Le Mensonge officieux dans la correspondance Jérôme-Augustin," to which I hope to return elsewhere. Through this correspondence, Sinapi, who also finds inspiration in the work of Pierre Legendre, analyzes the crossing of two heterogeneous traditions, that of a "conception of speech supported by an image ontology" and that of "Roman law," of "trial science," and a "new elaboration of notions of proof and cause" (p. 65).

Typewriter Ribbon

The initial version of this translation, which corresponded to the lecture Derrida gave at the University of California, Davis, Humanities Center in 1998, is included in *Material Events: Paul de Man and the Afterlife of Theory*, ed. Barbara Cohen et al. (Minneapolis: University of Minnesota Press, 2000), as noted in the Acknowledgments, above. Derrida considerably revised the essay for publication. Our revised translation has retained some marks of the initial occasion, although it follows in every other way the version of the essay that now appears in Derrida, *Papier Machine* (Paris: Galilée, 2001).—Trans.

1. Jean-Jacques Rousseau, *The Confessions*, trans. J. M. Cohen (New York: Penguin Books, 1953), p. 88; the translation, as here, will often be modified to remain closer to the literality of Rousseau's text. When dual pages are cited, the second page number refers to Rousseau, *Oeuvres complètes*, vol. 1, ed. Bernard Gagnebin et al. (Paris: Gallimard, 1959).

2. J. L. Austin, "A Plea for Excuses," in *Philosophical Papers*, 3d ed. (Oxford: Oxford University Press, 1979), p. 175. Since delivering this lecture, I have published a text entitled "Comme si c'était possible—'within such limits,'" in *Revue Internationale de Philosophie*, 3 (1998).

3. The brief allusions he makes (pp. 10, 68, 101, 102) in Paul de Man, *The Rhetoric of Romanticism* (New York: Columbia University Press, 1984), do not touch on this history.

4. Saint Augustine, *The Confessions of St. Augustine*, trans. John K. Ryan (New York: Doubleday, 1960), book 2, chap. 4, p. 70.

5. Paul de Man, *Allegories of Reading: Figural Language in Rousseau, Nietzsche, Rilke, and Proust* (New Haven: Yale University Press, 1979), p. 287.

6. Jean-Jacques Rousseau, *The Reveries of the Solitary Walker*, trans. Charles E. Butterworth (Indianapolis: Hackett, 1992), p. 20. When the French text is cited, page references are from Rousseau, *Oeuvres complètes*, vol. 1.

7. Jean-Jacques Rousseau, *The Creed of a Priest of Savoy*, trans. Arthur H. Beattie (New York: Frederick Ungar, 1956), p. 80.

8. Augustine, *Confessions*, book 1, chap. 2, p 20. "For I am not ashamed of the Gospel of Christ: for it is the power of God unto salvation to every one that believeth; to the Jew first, and also to the Greek. . . . Because that which may be known of God is manifest in them; for God hath shewed it unto them. . . . so that they are without excuse [*ita ut sint inexcusabiles, eis to einai autous anapologētous*]" (Romans, 1:16–20).

9. *The Confessions of Saint Augustine*, book 5, chap. 10, p. 126.

10. Austin, "A Plea for Excuses," p. 185.

11. Paul de Man, "Kant and Schiller," in *Aesthetic Ideology*, ed. Andrzej Warminski (Minneapolis: University of Minnesota Press, 1996), p. 133.

12. See Derrida, *Mal d'archive: Une impression freudienne*, trans. Eric Prenowitz (Chicago: University of Chicago Press, 1996).

13. De Man, *Allegories of Reading*, p. 286.

14. Derrida is exploiting here, as he has often done, the opposite meanings of the homonymic expressions *plus de*, no more, and *plus de*, more.—Trans.

15. De Man, *Allegories of Reading*, p. 286.

16. It would be necessary, of course, to mobilize other readings de Man undertook around the motifs of the materiality of inscription and effacement (cf. "Shelley Disfigured," where it is a question of the materiality of inscription, and "Autobiography as De-facement," both in *The Rhetoric of Romanticism*).

17. De Man, *Allegories of Reading*, p. 294; my emphasis.

18. On arbitrariness and gratuitousness, see *Allegories of Reading*, p. 357.

19. De Man, *Aesthetic Ideology*, p. 89; "Aesthetic Formalization: Kleist's 'Uber das Marionettentheater,'" in *The Rhetoric of Romanticism*.

20. Austin, "Three Ways of Spilling Ink," *Philosophical Papers*, p. 274.

21. See Derrida, *Adieu à Emmanuel Levinas* (Paris: Galilée, 1997); *Adieu to Emmanuel Levinas*, trans. Pascale-Anne Brault and Michael Naas (Stanford: Stanford University Press, 1999).

22. See, among other texts, Paul de Man, "The Concept of Irony," in *Aesthetic Ideology*, pp. 163 ff.

23. Austin, *Philosophical Papers*, p. 233.

24. When this lecture was first delivered, I did not know, I confess, that Or-

twin de Graef had already pointed out what he calls in quotation marks "the 'mistake' in de Man's translation," or again "de Man's erratic anacoluthonic translation" ("Silence to Be Observed: A Trial for Paul de Man's Inexcusable Confessions," in *Yale Journal of Criticism* 3, no. 2 [1990]: 214–15. The article was also published in *Postmodern Studies* 2 (1989) and was reviewed by Robert J. Ellrich in "De Man's Purloined Meaning" *MLN* 106 (1991): 1048–51. I thank Erin Ferris for having brought these publications to my attention.

25. Lacan analyzed this ruse more than once, in particular in "Subversion of the Subject and Dialectic of Desire" (in *Ecrits: A Selection*, trans. Alan Sheridan [New York: Norton, 1977], p. 298): "I think, for example, that I recognized the subject of the enunciation in the signifier 'ne,' which grammarians call the expletive, a term that already prefigures the incredible opinion of those, and they are to be found among the best, who regard its form as being a matter of mere chance." Still more exactly, Lacan elsewhere deploys the same argument around the *je crains* (*qu'il vienne ou qu'il ne vienne*). (See "Das Ding (II)," in *The Seminar, Book VII: The Ethics of Psychoanalysis*, trans. Dennis Porter [New York: Norton, 1986]). "The negative particle *ne* only emerges at the moment when I really speak, and not at the moment when I am spoken, if I am on the level of the unconscious. This is no doubt what Freud means. And I think it is a good idea to interpret Freud in a similar way when he says that there is no negation at the level of the unconscious" (ibid., p. 64). In French, one may notice the strange grammar and the unstable status of this *ne* in italics: "La particule négative *ne* vient au jour qu'à partir du moment. . . ."

26. "The mutilation seems to be incurable and the prothesis [*sic*] only serves to mark this fact more strongly" (de Man, *Allegories of Reading*, pp. 295–96).

27. This paragraph from the Geneva Manuscript is omitted in Cohen's translation of the *Confessions.*—Trans.

28. See, in particular, the first part of this work, "Rousseau and the Modern Signature." In the analyses she devotes in particular to the figure of the "dépositaire," Kamuf specifies the logic of this archival tragedy, the legacy of a single copy: "We can approach the way the *dépositaire* articulates this death in the work by remarking first that the *dépositaire* is not necessarily the *destinataire* of the *Dialogues*. This other figure, nevertheless, hovers ghostlike over the concluding pages of the epilogue, where Rousseau makes a final calculation of the best strategy for passing on his text: 'To multiply copies incessantly in order to place them here and there in the hands of people who approach me would be to tax my strength to no avail. It is not reasonable to hope that of all the copies thus dispersed, a single one of them will arrive intact at its destination [une seule parvint entière à sa destination]. I am thus going to limit myself to one copy, which I will pass among those acquaintances whom I believe to be the least unjust'" (Peggy Kamuf, *Signature Pieces: On the Institution of Authorship* [Ithaca: Cornell University Press, 1988], p. 110). Question: Which then is the *just* addressee, reader,

and, first of all, *dépositaire*? Everything is turned over to what one must call—however enigmatic the word remains and however difficult the thing is to think—justice, the justice of the inheritance, the justice of reading, the justice of the responsible counter-signature. Let us specify in order to be just with the letter of Rousseau's text: not justice itself but the least injustice.

29. In Geoffrey Bennington, *Legislations: The Politics of Deconstruction* (London: Verso, 1994). Question once again of justice and of correctness. At the end of a powerful and subtle reading of de Man's Pascal, notably around the "wager" and the famous fragment "Justice, force" ("It is just that what is just should be followed; it is necessary that what has the most power should be followed"), Bennington concludes: "'Death is a displaced name for a linguistic predicament,' wrote Paul de Man (*Rhetoric of Romanticism*, p. 81). 'Paul de Man,' we might add, has become a displaced name for a set of machines and aberrations that are now as alive as ever. A signature, a tombstone, a text, a reading, a machine" (*Legislations*, p. 150).

30. Rousseau, *Oeuvres complètes* I: 1230.

31. These two common expressions, which use the same construction as *je m'excusai sur*, mean "I took my revenge on," "I took it out on the first thing that presented itself."—Trans.

32. Derrida, *Mémoires for Paul de Man*, trans. Cecile Lindsay, Jonathan Culler, and Eduardo Cadava (New York: Columbia University Press, 1986), p. 143.

33. De Man, *Aesthetic Ideology*, p. 128.

34. "We must, in other words, disarticulate, mutilate the body in a way which is closer to Kleist than to Winckelmann . . . material disarticulation not only of nature but of the body. . . . To this dismemberment of the body corresponds a dismemberment of language, as meaning-producing tropes that are replaced by the fragmentation of sentences and propositions into discrete words, or the fragmentation of words into syllables or finally letters. In Kleist's text, one would isolate the dissemination of the word *Fall*" (de Man, *Aesthetic Ideology*, pp. 88–89).

35. In Derrida, "Avances," preface to Serge Margel, *Le Tombeau du dieu artisan* (Paris: Minuit, 1995).

36. "An Interview with Paul de Man," in de Man, *The Resistance to Theory* (Minneapolis: University of Minnesota Press, 1986), p. 118.

"Le Parjure," Perhaps

1. Henri Thomas, *Le Parjure* (Paris: Gallimard, 1964), p. 134. Page references for all other citations from this book will appear in parentheses in the text.

2. J. Hillis Miller, "The Anacoluthonic Lie," in *Reading Narrative* (Norman, Oklahoma: University of Oklahoma Press, 1998), p. 149.

3. J. Hillis Miller, *The Ethics of Reading* (New York: Columbia University Press, 1987), p. 43. This passage is extracted from chap. 3, entitled "Reading Unreadability: de Man." Among other reasons, I choose it because I would like what I will write here to say, very indirectly to be sure, but let no one be in a hurry to interpret or conclude, something of the friendship of thinking, of the friendship, period, that binds us: Paul de Man, Hillis Miller, and me. As a response, but an impossible response, to the impossible injunction that I cite here: "You will write it, won't you?"

4. To go directly, without delay, toward the facts of the perjury, that is, the "false oath" that is at the center of this exchange and of the novel, let's quote a few more lines. They represent only one stage in the narration. The narrator says: "Thus I learned that Chalier had taken a false oath before the American magistrate, before marrying Judith Samson. He had declared under oath that he had not been previously married or divorced. The letter from the Committee briefly mentioned the fact, but gave the date of the marriage along with a numerical reference proving that an inquiry had taken place—and above all it mentioned additional information concerning his marriage in Europe and the two children who had been born from it" (p. 112).

5. The most recent and no doubt most ample and rich of these essays has just appeared at the moment I am finishing this text. I refer to "Fractal Proust," in *Black Holes / J. Hillis Miller; or, Boustrophedonic Reading*, the section signed by Miller in the book published with Manuel Asensi (Stanford: Stanford University Press, 1999), pp. 313–483, odd pages. Allusions to de Man's text "Reading (Proust)" are numerous here, and the question of what Proust calls "lying fictions" is central (see, e.g., p. 473).

6. J. Hillis Miller, "The Anacoluthonic Lie," p. 149.

7. Ibid.; my emphasis on "probably."

8. Ibid.; my emphasis on "may be," of course, but it would also have been necessary to emphasize the insistence on the necessity (which is, however, aleatory) of paying attention to what always risks escaping attention. Ethics of reading: "To anyone who *notices* it . . . ," "The difficulty is in *noticing*."

9. Ibid., p. 154. My emphasis on "perhaps," of course, but it would also have been necessary to emphasize, once more, the "we can *notice*."

10. Cited by Miller, *Ethics of Reading*, p. 41.

11. See esp. my "Like the Sound of the Sea Deep Within a Shell: Paul de Man's War," trans. Peggy Kamuf, in *Mémoires for Paul de Man*, rev. ed. (New York: Columbia University Press, 1989), and "Biodegradables: Seven Diary Fragments," trans. Peggy Kamuf, *Critical Inquiry* 15, no. 4 (Summer 1989): 812–73.

12. Without mixing fiction and reality (we will continue to grant this rigorous distinction), may I be permitted to cite a passage from the novel that seems to describe, beneath the features of Stéphane Chalier, what Henri Thomas, like so many of his other friends, like "all those who knew him," thought of Paul de

Man: "If it had not been found to be justified in one way or another, then his existence, since he had met Judith, would have been nothing more than an abject drifting, and all those who knew him during those years agree with the assertion that there was no moral sloppiness on his part, no debasing of the heart and the mind. He did not seek to be true; he was. When the people who knew him learned about the unbelievable difficulties in which he found himself finally caught, no one would have wanted to be in his place, and yet they did not speak of him with commiseration. In a sense, they were pitiless: He had wanted it, this existence. He was even, let us speak frankly, *guilty*. No one pitied him because everyone continued to find him very strong, always up to the ordeal, without wondering too much where he found his strength: the little laugh, the blue eyes whose look quickly became more resolved, with the cold assurance that was needed, no doubt put a stop to all curiosity" (pp. 69–70).

13. Miller, *The Ethics of Reading*, p. 43.

14. They met, no doubt (but this remains to be verified and specified), when Henri Thomas was professor of French at Brandeis University, between 1958 and 1960.

15. I underscore "He was not thinking about this." Once again, what is it we call "not thinking"?

16. May I be permitted to refer here to *Mémoires for Paul de Man* and, more precisely, to a text that I devote to the de Manian reading of the "purloined ribbon": "Typewriter Ribbon: Limited Ink (2)," in this volume.

17. The idiom *fausser compagnie à quelqu'un* has, alas, not even an approximate equivalent in English that would combine the key word "company" with another formed on "false." We will continue to note the French expression in brackets.—Trans.

18. Pierre Fontanier, *Les Figures du discours* (Paris: Flammarion, 1968), p. 315.

19. The title of Conrad's novella is translated in French as *Le Compagnon secret*, the secret companion—or acolyte.

20. "Who is the liar here, Albertine as the example of the eternal feminine, evasive and unpossessable, in this case, perhaps betraying Marcel in covert lesbian liaisons? Or is the prime liar Marcel Proust himself, who has displaced into a misogynist fiction his own experience of betrayal in a 'real life' homosexual liaison?" (Miller, "The Anacoluthonic Lie," p. 151).

21. The premises of this episode were made apparent earlier. For example:

Those who considered Stéphane Chalier guilty had no personal existence; they represented the law, they were far away, in Washington (where I went to see them a little later); in sum, I would say that the Justice system was perfectly incapable of judging such a man.

But at the moment I'm talking about (the operation), I did not know that the Immigration Police had discovered what they called Stéphane Chalier's false testimony: a single line on the form filled out by Stéphane at the marriage bureau in Tucson, Arizona. He declared that he had never been married before marrying Judith Samson on the same day. (pp. 71–72)

I will not expatiate on the choice of these biblical names, Judith Samson, for the second (legitimate illegitimate) wife of Stéphane with the "long hair, falling onto his shoulders" who had just "grabbed the wrist of the hand that was stirring in his hair" (pp. 41–43).

22. Elsewhere I have tried to show, from another point of view and in another context, the fatal necessity of this originary perjury; cf. *Adieu to Emmanuel Levinas*, trans. Pascale-Anne Brault and Michael Naas (Stanford: Stanford University Press, 1999), pp. 33–34.

23. Is it useful to underscore here what these last lines of the quotation say and to underscore, precisely on the subject of what the narrator underscores while quoting and on the subject of what he "made say" the one he claims to be quoting ("I made him say that, a moment ago, and there I've underscored the word. Now I believe he said this word once")? The movement he is analyzing, honestly, and following closely, his own movement, is it not the very one that I, doing this, am following here?

24. The canonical question of the death of God as death of God the Father is elsewhere treated explicitly by the narrator, speaking like the professor that he is and Chalier's colleague, colleague in effect of both Chaliers, father and son, just as Thomas was also Paul de Man's colleague. In the voice of the narrator and the author, we hear a professor speaking (who was also a great novelist, a great poet, a great translator—of Shakespeare, Melville, and Jünger, among others): "The famous *God is dead*—for that's what we're talking about—is familiar to all students beyond a certain not very advanced level, who know where the formula comes from. But it is far less frequent to hear discussion of the idea that the God who is dead was above all, if not uniquely, the Father, and that the death of the Father is that of all paternity as spiritual reality. The father only ever had any being, only ever had any authority because there was the Father. Rupture of a tie that ceases to be sacred . . . the seed of all romantic distress is planted there" (p. 98).

25. Søren Kierkegaard, *Stages on Life's Way*, trans. Walter Lowrie (Princeton: Princeton University Press, 1940), pp. 279–80.

26. *Søren Kierkegaard's Journals and Papers*, ed. and trans. Howard V. Hong and Edna H. Hong (Bloomington: Indiana University Press, 1978), vol. 6, p. 88.

The University Without Condition

1. The original title of the lecture was: "The Future of the Profession; or, The University Without Condition (Thanks to the 'Humanities,' What *Could Take Place* Tomorrow)."

2. I have taken up elsewhere, in several places, first of all in *Of Spirit: Heidegger and the Question* (trans. Geoffrey Bennington and Rachel Bowlby [Chicago: University of Chicago Press, 1989], pp. 129–36), this "question" of the authority of the question, this reference to a preoriginary acquiescence that, without being either credulous, positive, or dogmatic, remains presupposed by any interrogation, however necessary and unconditional it may be—first of all, at the very origin of philosophy.

3. I am provisionally associating affirmation with performativity. The "yes" of the *affirmation* is not reducible to the positivity of a *position*. But it does, in fact, *resemble* a performative speech act. It neither describes nor states anything; it engages by responding. Later, at the end of our trajectory, I will try to situate the point at which performativity is itself exceeded by the experience of the *event*, by the unconditional exposure to what or who is coming. Performativity is still found, like the power of language in general, on the side of the sovereignty that I would like, however difficult this may seem, to distinguish from a certain unconditionality in general, an unconditionality without power.

4. Jacques Le Goff, *Un autre Moyen Age* (Paris: Gallimard, 1999), p. 172.

5. Since I cannot justify or make more explicit this remark about justice, which is not law or right, I refer here to what I have written elsewhere, in *Specters of Marx: The State of the Debt, the Work of Mourning, and the New International*, trans. Peggy Kamuf (New York: Routledge, 1994), and "Force of Law: The 'Mystical Foundation of Authority,'" trans. Mary Quaintance, *Cardozo Law Review* 11, no. 5–6 (July–August 1990): 919–1045.

6. See in particular "Signature Event Context," in *Margins of Philosophy*, trans. Alan Bass (Chicago: University of Chicago Press, 1982).

7. See the chapter "CyberDemocracy: The Internet and the Public Sphere," in Mark Poster, *What's the Matter with the Internet?* (Minneapolis: University of Minnesota Press, 2001).

8. Immanuel Kant, *Kritik der Urtheilskraft*, Introduction, IV and V, in *Kants Werke* (Berlin: B. Cassirer, 1912–23) V, p. 181 (XXVII) and p. 184 (XXXIV); *Critique of Judgement*, trans. J. H. Bernard (New York: Macmillan, 1951), pp. 17 and 20.

9. Ibid., § 60

10. Samuel Weber, *Institution and Interpretation* (Minneapolis: University of Minnesota Press, 1987), p. 143; expanded edition (Stanford: Stanford University Press, 2001).

11. Samuel Weber, "The Future of the Humanities," in *Unisa as Distinctive University for our Time*, ed. C. S. de Beer (Pretoria: Interdisciplinary Discussion Forum, University of South Africa, 1998), pp. 127–54; *Institution and Interpretation*, expanded edition, pp. 236–52.

12. Peggy Kamuf, *The Division of Literature, or the University in Deconstruction* (Chicago: University of Chicago Press, 1997), p. 15.

13. Jacques Derrida, "Economimesis," in Sylviane Agacinski et al., *Mimésis (des articulations)* (Paris: Aubier Flammarion, 1975); trans. Richard Klein, in *Diacritics* 11, no. 2 (1981): 3–25; "Mochlos ou le conflit des facultés," in *Philosophie* 2 (1984); "Mochlos; or, The Conflict of the Faculties," trans. Richard Rand and Amy Wygant, in Richard Rand, ed., *Logomachia: The Conflict of the Faculties* (Lincoln: University of Nebraska Press, 1992), pp. 1–34.

14. "An einem Producte der schönen Kunst muss man sich bewusst werden, dass es Kunst sei, und nicht Natur; aber doch muss die Zweckmässigkeit in der Form desselben von allem Zwange willkürlicher Regeln so frei scheinen, *als ob* es ein Product der Blossen Natur sei" (*Kritik der Urtheilskraft*, § 45, p. 306; emphasis added).

15. Ibid., § 43; cf. as well Jacques Derrida, "Economimesis," p. 59.

16. See Kant, *Religion Within the Limits of Reason Alone*, trans. Theodore M. Greene and Hoyt H. Hudson (New York: Harper Torchbooks, 1960), pp. 67–68 n.

17. Jeremy Rifkin, *The End of Work: The Decline of the Global Labor Force and the Dawn of the Post-Market Era* (New York: G. P. Putnam's Sons, 1995).

18. V. I. Lenin, *L'Etat et la révolution* (Paris: Editions sociales, 1984), p. 175.

19. Rifkin, *The End of Work*, p. xvii.

20. Le Goff, *Un autre Moyen Age*, pp. 69–70.

21. "*Time is a gift of God and thus cannot be sold.* The taboo on time that the Middle Ages opposed to the merchant was lifted at the dawn of the Renaissance. The time that belonged only to God is from now on the property of man. . . . From now on what counts is the hour—the new measure of life . . . *never lose an hour of time.* The cardinal virtue is temperance, to which the new iconography, beginning in the fourteenth century, assigns as attribute the clock—from now on the measure of all things" (ibid., p. 78).

22. See ibid., pp. 889–90, for the hierarchy of crafts. "This unity, however, of the world of work, as over against the world of prayer and the world of war, if it ever existed, did not last very long" (ibid., p. 102).

23. These motifs have been at the center of my publications and seminars for the last fifteen years.

24. This "as if," as we see, is no longer simply philosophical. It is thus, for all these reasons, not that of *The Philosophy of the As If* (*Die Philosophie des Als ob*) by Vaihinger. Nor is it the one to which Freud alludes, when he makes reference to Vaihinger's work, at the end of the third chapter of *The Future of an Illusion*. (The reference is to Hans Vaihinger, *Die Philosophie des Als Ob : System der theoretischen, praktischen und religiösen Fiktionen der Menschheit auf Grund eines idealistischen Positivismus* [Berlin: Reuther & Reichard, 1913].—Trans.)

Psychoanalysis Searches

1. The *Comité de Salut Public*, formed in April 1793, was the main instrument of the Terror, authorizing summary arrests, trials, and executions of "enemies of the state." The *salut* in its title also translates as "salvation."—Trans.

2. Derrida has frequently drawn attention to the connotative differences between the English term "globalization" and the French term *mondialisation*. In particular, the latter's reference to the world (*monde*) rather than to the globe retains ties to the originally European vision of one world under one God, and above all the Christian God. Hence his neologizing of *mondialisation* into *mondialatinisation*, for example here, p. 267. See also, in this volume, "The University Without Condition" and elsewhere, "Faith and Knowledge: The Two Sources of 'Religion' at the Limits of Reason Alone," in *Religion*, edited by Jacques Derrida and Gianni Vatimo (Stanford: Stanford University Press, 1996), 1–78.—Trans.

3. A reference to the historic main amphitheater of the Sorbonne, where the sessions of the States General of Psychoanalysis took place.—Trans.

4. Albert Einstein and Sigmund Freud, "Why War," in *The Standard Edition of the Complete Psychological Works of Sigmund Freud*, vol. 22 (London: Hogarth Press, 1964), pp. 199–200. Page references for all other citations from this work will appear in parentheses in the text.

5. Derrida points out that the term here translated as "cruel," *unheilvollste*, is rendered in French by *funeste*: harmful, disastrous, baneful.—Trans.

6. See Elisabeth Roudinesco, "Freud et le régicide: Eléments d'une réflexion," in *Revue Germanique Internationale* 14 (2000).

7. Derrida seems to be referring to a passage in Jones's biography that endeavors to explain Freud's aversion to the United States after his trip there. "Freud himself attributed his dislike of America to a lasting intestinal trouble brought on, so he very unconvincingly asserted, by American cooking, so different from what he was accustomed to" (Ernest Jones, *The Life and Work of Sigmund Freud* [New York: Basic Books, 1955], vol. 2, pp. 59–60).—Trans.

8. Ibid., p. 40.

9. *The Freud/Jung Letters: The Correspondence between Sigmund Freud and C. G. Jung*, ed. William McGuire (Princeton: Princeton University Press, 1974), letter dated 17 January 1909, pp. 196–97.

10. With the exception of a few words that Freud authorized Theodor Reik to sign in his name, in 1926, and in response to a questionnaire on punishment and the death penalty. At the end of these very ambiguous three pages, which ought to be carefully interrogated as to their logic, signature, and status (I will try to do that elsewhere), Reik concludes, in Freud's name, as follows: "I profess to be an opponent of murder, whether committed by the individual as a crime or by the state in its retaliation" ("Postscript: Freud's View on Capital Punishment,"

in Theodor Reik, *The Compulsion to Confess: On the Psychoanalysis of Crime and Punishment* [New York: Farrar, Strauss and Cudahy, 1959], p. 474).

11. Jones, *Freud,* vol. 2, p. 153.

12. A date from the French Revolutionary calendar, which was inaugurated in 1792 (year I) and abandoned under Napoleon in 1806.—Trans.

13. Sigmund Freud, *The Future of an Illusion,* in *The Standard Edition of the Complete Psychological Works of Sigmund Freud,* vol. 21, p. 19.

14. On this term, see above, note 2.—Trans.

15. René Major, *De l'élection* (Paris: Aubier, 1986), pp. 88–89; Freud's letter is dated December 28, 1914.

16. Major, pp. 90–91.

Crossing Aesthetics

Jacques Derrida, *Without Alibi*, edited by Peggy Kamuf

Cornelius Castoriadis, *On Plato's 'Statesman'*

Jacques Derrida, *Who's Afraid of Philosophy? Right to Philosophy 1*

Peter Szondi, *An Essay on the Tragic*

Peter Fenves, *Arresting Language: From Leibniz to Benjamin*

Jill Robbins, ed., *Is It Righteous to Be?: Interviews with Emmanuel Levinas*

Louis Marin, *Of Representation*

Daniel Payot, *The Architect and the Philosopher*

J. Hillis Miller, *Speech Acts in Literature*

Maurice Blanchot, *Faux Pas*

Jean-Luc Nancy, *Being Singular Plural*

Maurice Blanchot / Jacques Derrida, *The Instant of My Death / Demeure: Fiction and Testimony*

Niklas Luhmann, *Art as a Social System*

Emmanual Levinas, *God, Death, and Time*

Ernst Bloch, *The Spirit of Utopia*

Giorgio Agamben, *Potentialities: Collected Essays in Philosophy*

Ellen S. Burt, *Poetry's Appeal: French Nineteenth-Century Lyric and the Political Space*

Jacques Derrida, *Adieu to Emmanuel Levinas*

Werner Hamacher, *Premises: Essays on Philosophy and Literature from Kant to Celan*

Aris Fioretos, *The Gray Book*

Deborah Esch, *In the Event: Reading Journalism, Reading Theory*

Winfried Menninghaus, *In Praise of Nonsense: Kant and Bluebeard*

Giorgio Agamben, *The Man Without Content*

Giorgio Agamben, *The End of the Poem: Studies in Poetics*

Theodor W. Adorno, *Sound Figures*

Louis Marin, *Sublime Poussin*

Philippe Lacoue-Labarthe, *Poetry as Experience*

Ernst Bloch, *Literary Essays*

Jacques Derrida, *Resistances of Psychoanalysis*

Marc Froment-Meurice, *That Is to Say: Heidegger's Poetics*

Francis Ponge, *Soap*

Philippe Lacoue-Labarthe, *Typography: Mimesis, Philosophy, Politics*

Giorgio Agamben, *Homo Sacer: Sovereign Power and Bare Life*

Emmanuel Levinas, *Of God Who Comes To Mind*

Bernard Stiegler, *Technics and Time, 1: The Fault of Epimetheus*

Werner Hamacher, *pleroma—Reading in Hegel*

Serge Leclaire, *Psychoanalyzing: On the Order of the Unconscious and the Practice of the Letter*

Serge Leclaire, *A Child Is Being Killed: On Primary Narcissism and the Death Drive*

Sigmund Freud, *Writings on Art and Literature*

Cornelius Castoriadis, *World in Fragments: Writings on Politics, Society, Psychoanalysis, and the Imagination*

Thomas Keenan, *Fables of Responsibility: Aberrations and Predicaments in Ethics and Politics*

Emmanuel Levinas, *Proper Names*

Alexander García Düttmann, *At Odds with AIDS: Thinking and Talking About a Virus*

Maurice Blanchot, *Friendship*

Jean-Luc Nancy, *The Muses*

Massimo Cacciari, *Posthumous People: Vienna at the Turning Point*

David E. Wellbery, *The Specular Moment: Goethe's Early Lyric and the Beginnings of Romanticism*

Edmond Jabès, *The Little Book of Unsuspected Subversion*

Hans-Jost Frey, *Studies in Poetic Discourse: Mallarmé, Baudelaire, Rimbaud, Hölderlin*

Pierre Bourdieu, *The Rules of Art: Genesis and Structure of the Literary Field*

Nicolas Abraham, *Rhythms: On the Work, Translation, and Psychoanalysis*

Jacques Derrida, *On the Name*

David Wills, *Prosthesis*

Maurice Blanchot, *The Work of Fire*

Jacques Derrida, *Points . . . : Interviews, 1974-1994*

J. Hillis Miller, *Topographies*

Philippe Lacoue-Labarthe, *Musica Ficta (Figures of Wagner)*

Jacques Derrida, *Aporias*

Emmanuel Levinas, *Outside the Subject*

Jean-François Lyotard, *Lessons on the Analytic of the Sublime*

Peter Fenves, *"Chatter": Language and History in Kierkegaard*

Jean-Luc Nancy, *The Experience of Freedom*

Jean-Joseph Goux, *Oedipus, Philosopher*

Haun Saussy, *The Problem of a Chinese Aesthetic*

Jean-Luc Nancy, *The Birth to Presence*